GRADE 5

TOTAL READING

AMERICAN EDUCATION PUBLISHING™
Columbus, Ohio

School Specialty Publishing

Send all inquiries to:
School Specialty Publishing
8720 Orion Place
Columbus, OH 43240-2111

ISBN 0-7696-3885-6

2 3 4 5 6 7 8 9 WAL 09 08 07 06 05

Table of Contents

Name ______________________________

Root and Base Words

A **root**, or **base word**, is the word that is left after you **take off a prefix or suffix**.

Directions: Divide the following words into parts so the root is separate.

auto	self
autobiography	the story of a person's life written by that person
autograph	a person's signature or handwriting
automatic	having a self-acting or self-regulating mechanism; done without thought or conscious effort
automobile	a passenger vehicle with its own engine
autonomous	self-governing

1. automobile

   ______________ ________________

2. autobiography

   ______________ ________________

3. automatic

   ______________ ________________

4. autograph

   ______________ ________________

5. autonomous

   ______________ ________________

Directions: Complete each sentence using a word from the word box.

1. The writer finished the ______________________ about her life.
2. Sally got an ______________________ camera for her birthday.
3. José was excited when he got the celebrity's ______________________.
4. The people who lived on the island did not wish to be governed by a mother country any longer. They wanted to be ______________________.
5. Jack checked under the hood of his ______________________.

Name ______________________________

Root and Base Words

multi	many
multicolored	having many colors
multimedia	combining more than two artistic techniques or means of communication or expression, such as acting, lighting effects, and music
multimillionaire	a person who has at least two million dollars
multiple	having many parts or elements
multitude	a large number of persons or things

Directions: Unscramble the word and write the definition.

Example: limptule multiple having many parts or elements

1. rollutimedoc ______________ ______________________
2. lemonlimitailiur ______________ ______________________
3. demiltutu ______________ ______________________
4. immediatul ______________ ______________________

Directions: Complete each sentence using a word from the word box.

1. The unhappy result of John's skiing accident was a ________________ fracture of the arm.
2. A kaleidoscope is constructed with ________________ glass.
3. The rock concert with television screens and a light show was a ________________ event.
4. A ________________ donated money for the starving children.
5. The ________________ of people followed the celebrity into the theater.

Name ______________________________

Root and Base Words

pre	before
preamble	a statement that introduces a formal document, explaining its purpose
precede	to come or go before in rank, time, or order
prehistoric	of the period before written history
preoccupied	wholly occupied or absorbed in one's thoughts; absentminded
preschool	school before kindergarten; nursery school
prevent	to take action before an event to stop the event from happening

Directions: Write a short definition for each word.

Example: prehistoric   of the period before written history.

1. precede ______________________________
2. precedent ______________________________
3. preoccupation ______________________________
4. prevention ______________________________
5. preventable ______________________________

Directions: Complete each sentence using a word from the word box.

1. The four-year-old child will attend a ____________ class.
2. The dinosaurs lived during ____________ times.
3. The teacher said we had to memorize the ____________ to the United States Constitution.
4. Roger couldn't enjoy the movie because he was ____________ about the test the next day.
5. Seventh grade ____________(s) eighth grade.

Name ______________________________

Root and Base Words

bi, di	two
biceps	any muscle having two points of origin
bilingual	able to use two languages equally well
biped	a two-footed animal
bisect	divide into two (usually equal) parts
dichromatic	having two colors
dilemma	a situation requiring a choice between two equal alternatives
diploma	a certificate awarded when a student has successfully completed a particular course of study
dipterous	having two wings

Directions: Complete each sentence using a word from the word box.

1. A fly is a ______________________ insect.
2. Lorenzo was taking a course in weight training, and would proudly flex his ______________________ when anyone asked how he was progressing.
3. Charlotte faced the ______________________ of whether to go to the movie with her friends or take the babysitting job.
4. Silvia is ______________________ because she speaks Spanish at home and English at school.
5. The geometry teacher told the students to ______________________ the circle.

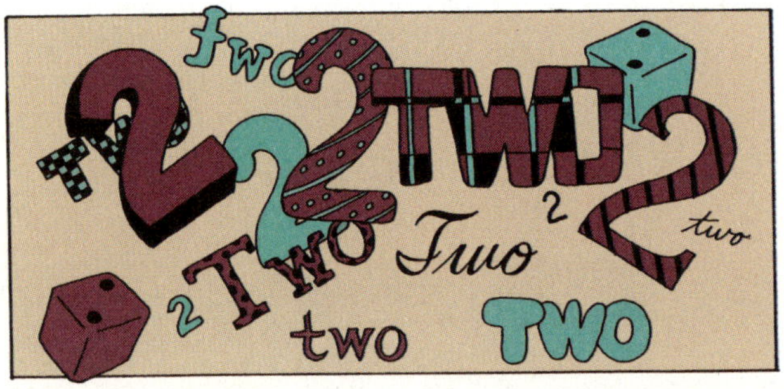

Directions: Write a word with the prefix **bi** to complete each phrase.

1. *Annual* means once a year. ______________________ means twice a year.
2. A *biennium* is a two-year period. ______________________ means once every two years.
3. *Centum* is the Latin word for one hundred. ______________________ means once every two hundred years.
4. A ______________________ event happens twice a month.
5. A ______________________ event happens twice a week.

Name ______________________________

Root and Base Words

ben, bene	good, well
benediction	a blessing
benefactor	a person who gives help or support, especially financial aid
beneficial	having a good or helpful effect
beneficiary	a person who receives a benefit or advantage, such as an inheritance
benevolent	doing good things; being good-hearted, kind
benign	gentle and kind; not threatening life

Directions: Fill in each blank with a word from the word box.

1. The musician needed a ____________________ to support him financially.
2. The priest said the ____________________ after the mass.
3. It is ____________________ to study vocabulary before taking a standardized test.
4. The ____________________ of his life insurance policy would receive $25,000.
5. My grandmother was very relieved when the tests showed that the tumor was ____________________.

Directions: Circle each word below in which **ben** or **bene** is used as a prefix meaning *good, well.*

beneath	Benelux
Benedict	benighted
benefactor	benignant
benefit	benumb

Directions: List five things that are beneficial to your health.

1. ____________________
2. ____________________
3. ____________________
4. ____________________
5. ____________________

Name ______________________________

Root and Base Words

cred	to believe
accredit	to give credit for; to authorize or recognize officially
credence	acceptance or belief
credential	letter or document that proves or affirms a person's identity or right to hold a certain position
credo	a set of beliefs or opinions
credulous	inclined to believe anything, often without sufficient proof
discredit	to reject as untrue; to cast doubt on; to disgrace
incredible	unbelievable

Directions: Fill in each blank with a word from the word box.

1. His explanation for not having his homework was truly ________________.
2. The golden rule is an important part of my ________________.
3. Five years of college study are usually required to obtain a teaching ________________.
4. Because they knew that enrollment had been dropping, they gave ________________ to the rumor that the school would soon close.
5. Little Mikey was still ________________; he would believe anything his big brothers told him.
6. The candidate's staff was trying hard to find ways to ________________ the opponent.

Directions: Look up the following words and phrases in a dictionary and write a brief definition for each.

1. on credit ______________________________
2. to one's credit ______________________________
3. creditor ______________________________
4. incredulous ______________________________
5. credibility ______________________________

Name ______________________________

Prefixes

A **prefix** is a part **added to the beginning** of a word to change its meaning. The prefix **un** means *not* and the prefix **re** means *again*.

Directions: Add the correct prefix to each word in the word box. Write the new words in the correct column.

draw	lucky	new	clear
wise	fill	happy	safe
main	spell	fair	search

Prefixes

Directions: Read each definition. Complete each sentence using a word with the prefix **un** or **re**.

1. I ____________________ my sled.
painted again

2. Did you ____________________ your answer?
consider again

3. Mei-Ling will ____________________ her poster.
draw again

4. The treasure chest was ____________________.
not locked

5. David's skates are ____________________.
not laced

6. Grandfather likes to ____________________ that story.
tell again

7. The writing was ____________________ and hard to read.
not clear

8. Watch the ____________________ to see the touchdown.
play again

9. How did she ____________________ the book report?
do again

10. It is best to avoid ____________________ words.
not kind

11. Jan will ____________________ the bookcase.
finish again

12. The ____________________ stairway was marked with a sign.
not safe

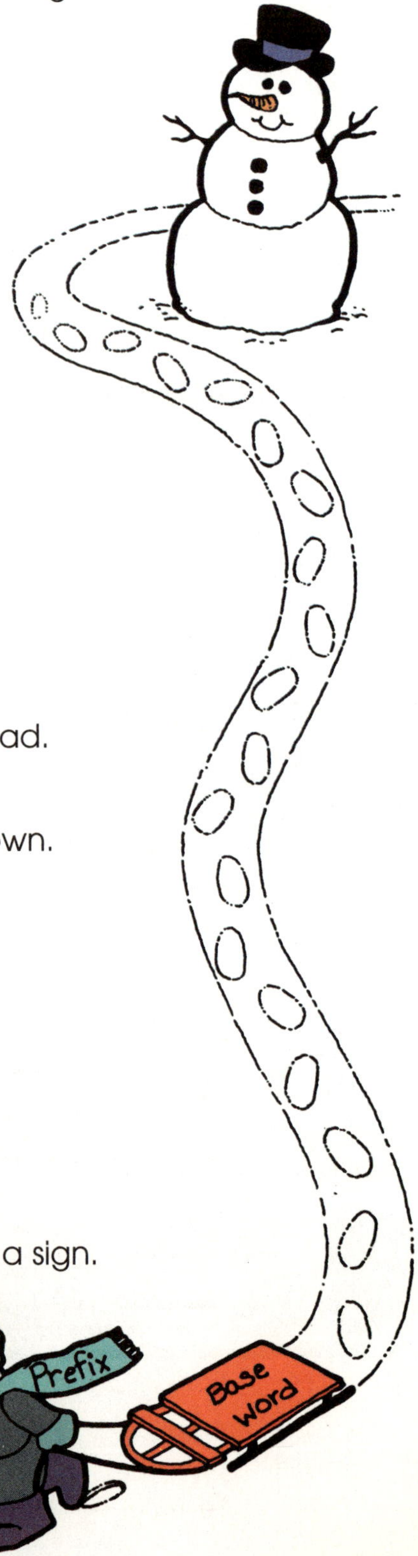

Name ______________________________

Prefixes

The prefix **mis** means *wrongly* and the prefix **non** means *not*.

Directions: Add the correct prefix to each word in the word box. Write the new words in the correct column.

stop	take	skid	fire	count
spell	fat	place	sense	human

Name ______________________

Prefixes

The prefix **mis** means *wrongly* and the prefix **pre** means *before*.

Directions: Add the prefix to each word. Write the new word and then write its meaning.

Base Word	Prefix	New Word	Meaning
1. cook	pre	________	________
2. spell	mis	________	________
3. view	pre	________	________
4. school	pre	________	________
5. pay	pre	________	________
6. place	mis	________	________
7. use	mis	________	________
8. treat	mis	________	________

Name ______________________________

Suffixes

A **suffix** is a word part added to the **end of a word** to change its meaning.

-ist
A noun-forming suffix, -ist means a person who makes, does, or practices.

-less
An adjective-forming suffix, -less means without or lacking.

-ness
A noun-forming suffix, -ness means state or quality of being.

-ly
An adverb- or adjective-forming suffix, -ly means when, how, like, or in the manner of.

-fy
A verb-forming suffix, -fy means to make or cause to be or become.

-ize
A verb-forming suffix, -ize means to cause to be or to become.

Directions: From the following list, select the correct word to complete each sentence. Write the word on the line.

vaporize **naturalist** **harshly** **purify** **pitiless** **correctness**

1. Before drinking river water you should ____________________ it because it may be polluted.
2. A person who practices the study of nature is a ____________________.
3. The ____________________ football coach made the team run an extra mile.
4. Check your spelling for ____________________ when using new words.
5. The angry man spoke ____________________ to the telephone operator.
6. High temperatures will make water ____________________.

Directions: Use the suffixes in the word box to make new words that answer each phrase. Write the word on the line.

1. An adjective meaning without power. ____________________
2. An adverb that tells how a brave person acts. ____________________
3. A verb meaning to make simple. ____________________
4. A noun meaning a person who makes works of art. ____________________
5. A verb meaning to form crystals. ____________________
6. A noun meaning the state of being dark. ____________________

Name ______________________________

Suffixes

Directions: Use the word box to fill in the blanks with words containing suffixes. Put each boxed letter in the matching numbered blank below to find out the state you might visit to get something necessary for school.

invitation	penniless	wonderful	hopeless
careful	noisy	collection	peaceful
addition	followed	winning	

1. h ___ □ ___ ___ ___ ___ s
2. □ ___ d ___ t ___ ___ ___
3. ___ ___ □ ___ ___ w ___ d
4. w ___ ___ ___ □ ___ ___
5. w ___ □ d ___ ___ ___ ___ ___
6. ___ □ r ___ f ___ ___
7. i ___ □ ___ t ___ ___ ___ ___ ___
8. c ___ ___ ___ e □ ___ ___ ___ ___
9. □ ___ i ___ y
10. ___ ___ a ___ □ ___ ___ l
11. ___ ___ n n □ ___ ___ ___ ___

___ ___ ___ ___ ___ ___ - ___ ___ ___ ___ ___
1 10 5 8 11 3 7 2 9 4 6

Name ____________________

Suffixes

The suffix **able** means *capable of*. For example, a wire that is **bendable** can bend.

Directions: Add **able** to the words below. (If a word ends in a silent *e*, you may need to drop the *e* before adding a suffix beginning with a vowel.)

break__________ notice__________ reason__________

The suffixes **en** and **ize** mean to *make* or *cause to be*. Add **en** to the words below.

bright__________ hard__________ sharp__________

Add **ize** to the words below.

modern__________ tender__________ sterile__________

The suffix **ist** means *one who does something*. Add **ist** to the words below.

type__________ violin__________ perfection__________

The suffix **ous** means *having the quality of*. Add **ous** to the words below.

marvel__________ nerve__________ courage__________

Directions: Use the words you wrote above to complete the sentences below.

1. Pat's answer was so ______________, everyone agreed she must be right.
2. The soldier received a medal for his ______________ act in battle.
3. We went to the concert to listen to my favorite ______________.
4. In a hospital, someone must ______________ instruments that are used in operations.
5. My friends who read that novel said that it was ______________!
6. Mrs. Grant wants to ______________ her kitchen by replacing the old cupboard doors.
7. Painting this room white will help to ______________ its appearance.
8. Mr. Burns is such a ______________ that he will redo his work many times over.
9. Before a test, try to stay calm and not get ______________.
10. If you display the bulletin on this wall, it will be more ______________.
11. Clay will ______________ and be difficult to mold if you leave it out.
12. Try not to drop the vase because it is ______________.

Name ____________________

Suffixes

Read the passage carefully.

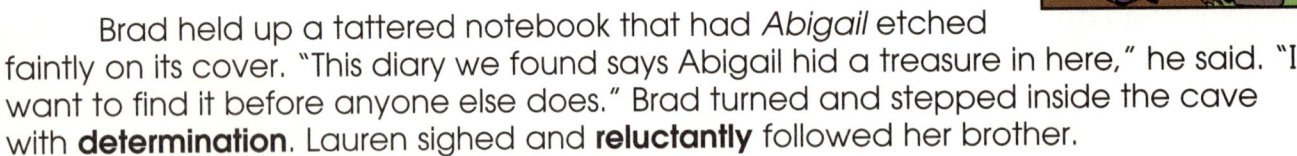

"The treasure must be in here!" yelled Brad. He and his sister Lauren stood outside the **entrance** of a cave. As Brad took a step towards the **darkness**, Lauren touched his arm.

"Let's rest a bit," said Lauren, still **breathless** from running. "Besides, it might be **dangerous** in there."

Brad held up a tattered notebook that had *Abigail* etched faintly on its cover. "This diary we found says Abigail hid a treasure in here," he said. "I want to find it before anyone else does." Brad turned and stepped inside the cave with **determination**. Lauren sighed and **reluctantly** followed her brother.

Brad waved his flashlight impatiently around the cave. Moments later, he cried, "I see something!" Brad stooped down and started digging in the earth with a rock. Lauren came to help. Soon the two uncovered a small **wooden** box. Brad's hands shook with **excitement**. He took the box outside and opened it. Brad and Lauren gasped and looked at the contents in **astonishment**. Inside were letters addressed to Abigail.

"Nothing but letters!" moaned Brad with **disappointment**. "There's no treasure here at all." He sank to the ground feeling tired and a bit **foolish**.

Lauren stood with a **thoughtful** look on her face. "If it's any **consolation**," she said slowly, "we did find Abigail's treasure." Lauren fingered the letters **gently** and continued, "These letters were written by someone whose **friendship** Abigail felt very strongly about. She probably put the letters in the cave for safekeeping."

Directions: Write the **boldfaced** words beside their meanings below. Circle the suffix in each word.

1. place of entry ____________________
2. out of breath ____________________
3. state of being excited ____________
4. having little or no light ____________
5. great surprise ____________________
6. unwise ________________________
7. deep in thought ______________
8. state of being friends ____________
9. with unwillingness ______________
10. act of being comforted ____________
11. feeling let down ______________
12. quality of being firm ____________
13. in a gentle manner ______________
14. made of wood ________________
15. involving something that can cause harm ________________

Name ______________________________

Synonyms

Synonyms are words that mean the **same** thing.
Cute and *adorable* are synonyms.

Directions: Circle the synonyms for the first word in each row.

1. fast — quick — hard — swift — speedy — small
2. bright — dazzling — dull — glittering — sparkling
3. friend — stranger — companion — chum — pal — buddy
4. scary — scream — frightening — rough — terrifying
5. throw — fling — carry — hurl — toss — catch

Directions: Look at the pictures below. Using the words you circled, write a list of synonyms to describe each picture.

1. fast

____
____
____

2. bright

____
____
____

3. friend

____
____
____
____

4. scary

____
____

5. throw

____
____
____

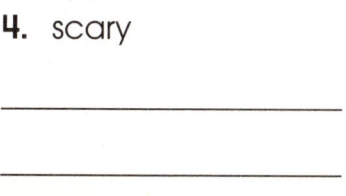

Name ______________________________

Synonyms

Directions: Choose the word from the word box that could replace the **boldfaced** word in each sentence. Write the word on the line.

fortunate	discovered	grimy	ancient
sizzling	entire	select	chuckle

1. The dinosaur bones were **old**.

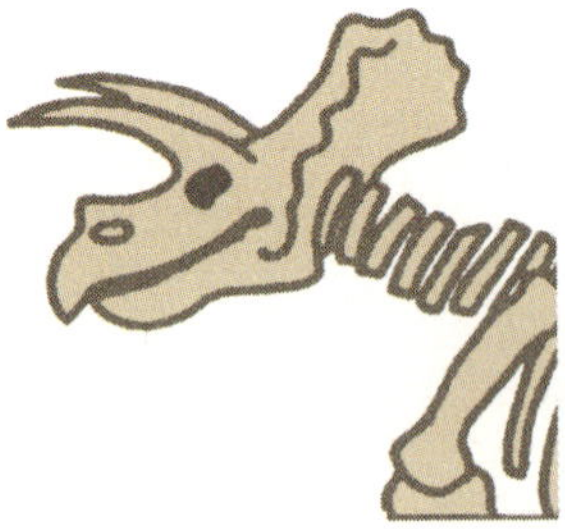

____

2. We were **lucky** that it didn't rain.

____

3. After playing football, my clothes were **dirty**.

____

4. That joke made me **laugh**.

____

5. I rode my bike the **whole** way home.

____

6. I had to **choose** a book for my report.

____

7. It was a **hot** day in the desert.

____

8. I **found** the missing puzzle piece on the floor.

____

Name ______________________________

Synonyms

Directions: Use the words from the word box to write a synonym for each underlined word.

enjoyable
receive
also
scorching
most
friend
tease
like
happy
watching

Dear Pen Pal,

I was glad ________________

to get ________________

your letter. Soccer is my

favorite sport too ______________.

And I have three brothers who

always bother ________________

me, too! Seattle sounds like a great ________________ place to live, but I wouldn't enjoy ________________ all the rain. It's always sunny and hot ________________ in Houston. My friends and I like viewing ________________ movies and going out for ice cream afterwards. I like chocolate best ________________.

Your pal ________________,

____

Name ______________________________

Synonyms

Directions: Circle the two words in each row that are synonyms.

1.	mistake	error	repair
2.	rich	money	wealthy
3.	frighten	startle	secret
4.	song	noisy	loud
5.	imitate	copy	return
6.	hasty	funny	speedy
7.	cheap	expensive	inexpensive
8.	break	repair	fix
9.	travel	vacation	work
10.	gift	present	watch
11.	friend	enemy	pal
12.	watch	see	mean

Name ____________________

Synonyms

Directions: Answer the clues using words from the word box to complete the puzzle.

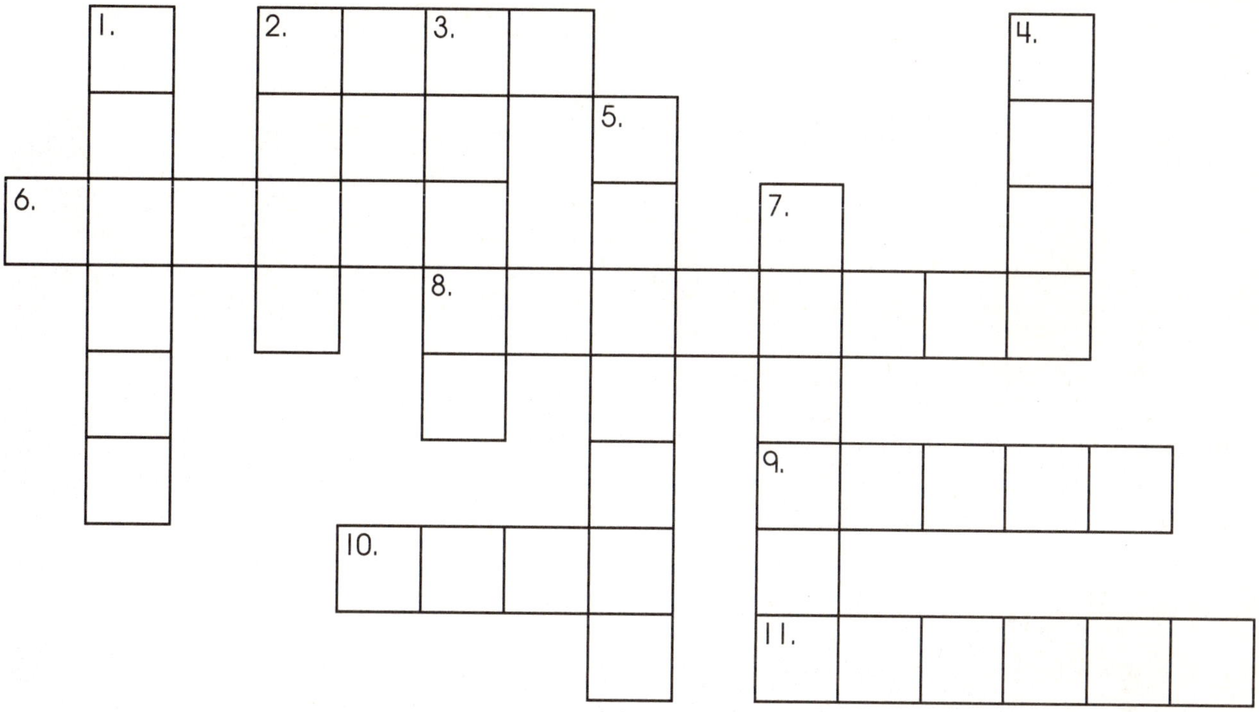

chuckle	elect	full	arrive
cautious	burrow	dread	hinder
repair	exit	less	even

Across

2. synonym for *same*
6. synonym for *come*
8. synonym for *careful*
9. synonym for *fear*
10. synonym for *crowded*
11. synonym for *fix*

Down

1. synonym for *dig*
2. synonym for *leave*
3. synonym for *choose*
4. synonym for *fewer*
5. synonym for *laugh*
7. synonym for *obstruct*

Name ______________________________

Locating Synonyms

Directions: Read each sentence. Find a word in each sentence that is a synonym for the word in the parentheses. Write the synonym on the line.

1. Leslie and Mike enjoy soccer. (like) ______________
2. Today, they will begin practicing for the upcoming season. (start) ______________
3. They bought new shin guards and cleats and were ready for practice. (purchased) ______________
4. Leslie and Mike are strong competitors. (tough) ______________
5. While they are cautious about avoiding injury, they show no fear. (careful) ______________
6. As Mike dribbles the ball down the field, he manages it with remarkable control. (fantastic) ______________
7. Leslie heads the ball into the goal. Her aim is exact. (accurate) ______________
8. Leslie and Mike are clever players who can execute the complex strategies needed to win games. (complicated) ______________
9. The fans are appreciative for an exciting season. (grateful) ______________
10. The number of wins this year has surpassed all other years. (exceeded) ______________

Name ______________________________

Antonyms

An **antonym** is a word that means the **opposite**.

Directions: Answer the clues using words from the word box to complete the puzzle.

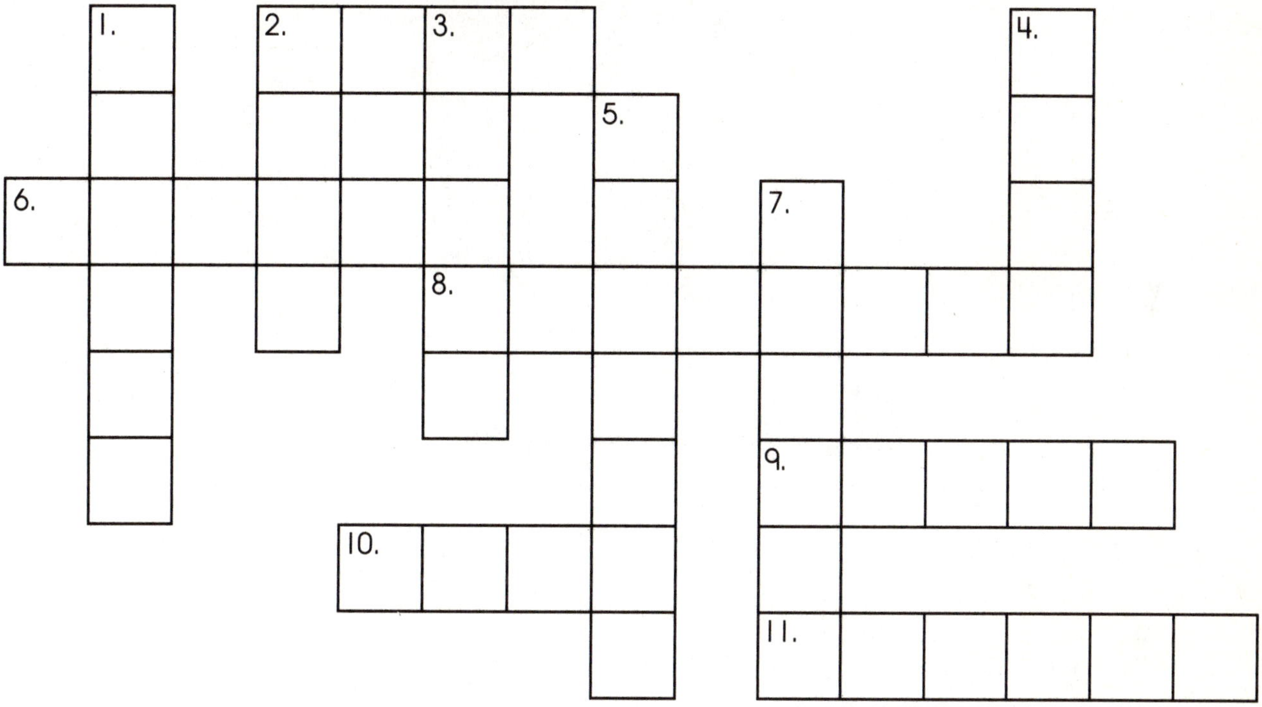

chuckle	elect	full	arrive
cautious	borrow	dress	hinder
repair	exit	less	even

Across

2. antonym for *odd*
6. antonym for *depart*
8. antonym for *careless*
9. antonym for *undress*
10. antonym for *empty*
11. antonym for *break*

Down

1. antonym for *lend*
2. antonym for *enter*
3. antonym for *impeach*
4. antonym for *more*
5. antonym for *cry*
7. antonym for *help*

Antonyms

Directions: Write an antonym on the line to complete each sentence.

old	select
big	cute
play	wild
female	hard
tell	loves
baby	friend
found	long

Dear Pen Pal,

I have something exciting to ______ (ask) you! Yesterday we went to the animal shelter. I ______ (lost) three kittens that were ______ (ugly). It was ______ (easy) to decide which one to ______ (refuse). I chose a ______ (male) kitten. She is six weeks ______ (young). She has ______ (short) white fur with a ______ (small) black spot on her face. She ______ (hates) to ______ (work) with a tissue on a string. She acts like a ______ (tame) tiger. We made a cozy bed for her in a box. My ______ (adult) sister gave her a warm blanket for her box. I'll send you a picture of my cat soon. Do you have any pets?

Your ______ (enemy),

______

Antonyms

Directions: Circle the two words in each row that have opposite meanings.

1.	return	break	fix
2.	rich	poor	wealthy
3.	light	sun	dark
4.	loud	nosy	quiet
5.	borrow	lend	reduce
6.	haste	slow	speedy
7.	cheap	expensive	silly
8.	watch	break	repair
9.	travel	play	work
10.	lost	found	cook
11.	write	buy	sell
12.	kind	friendly	mean

Name ______________________

Antonyms

Directions: Write an antonym for each word.

1. son ______________
2. lost ______________
3. chilly ______________
4. whole ______________
5. speak ______________
6. sent ______________
7. bare ______________
8. won ______________
9. male ______________
10. high ______________
11. sell ______________
12. girl ______________
13. dark ______________
14. empty ______________
15. inside ______________

Name ______________________________

Antonyms

Directions: Each sentence below was meant to say the opposite. Circle the incorrect word in each sentence. Choose a word from the word box to replace it. Rewrite each sentence using the new word.

sad	after	hard	odd	apart	borrow

1. I chipped a tooth on the soft candy.

____

2. Three and five are even numbers.

____

3. My puzzle pieces fell together.

____

4. June comes before May.

____

5. I was happy when my friend moved.

____

6. May I lend your eraser?

____

Name ______________________________

Can You Match This?

Directions: Can you identify the antonyms below? Draw a line to match each pair. Then, write the antonym pair that best completes each sentence.

dishonest	prevent
start	problem
calm	different
change	preceding
alike	apart
allow	discourteous
together	finish
solution	remain
polite	truthful
following	violent

1. They will not ________________ us to board the plane because the severe weather conditions ________________ a safe take-off.
2. My twin sisters may look exactly ________________, but you will soon discover how ________________ they are.
3. It took weeks to put this jigsaw puzzle ________________ and just minutes to take it ________________.
4. If you are ________________ instead of ________________, you will lose the respect of your friends.
5. Seas that were ________________ grew ________________ as an unexpected storm hit full force.
6. We used all the clues to find the ________________ to the ________________.
7. You can ________________ seats with me or ________________ where you are.
8. If we ________________ on time, we will ________________ this project in three hours.
9. If this is June, then the ________________ month is July and the ________________ month was May.
10. An operator must always be patient and ________________, even though callers are sometimes rude and ________________.

Name ______________________________

Homophones

Homophones are words that sound alike but have different spellings and meanings.

Directions: Write the correct homophone in each blank.

Examples: rein, rain ewe, you to, two, too

1. We couldn't decide ________________ to visit Boston or St. Louis. (weather, whether)
2. We chose to visit Boston, the ________________ of Massachusetts. (capital, capitol)
3. We drove ______________ the city in ______________ days. (to, too, two)
4. Our ______________ was over interstate highways. (route, root)
5. We ______________ many signs along the way. (read, red)
6. My brothers couldn't hide ______________ excitement. (their, there)
7. We found that ______________ an exciting city. (its, it's)
8. It was interesting to ______________ the accent of the people. (hear, here)
9. Many people related interesting ______________ to us about the city's history. (tales, tails)
10. We appreciated the ______________ and quiet of the parks. (peace, piece)
11. We walked up and down __________ of houses in the historic district. (rows, rose)
12. I wore a ___________ in one of my shoes from ____________ much walking. (whole, hole) (so, sew)
13. Luckily, this caused me ___________ ___________. (know, no) (pain, pane)
14. I had to have the ______________ of the shoe repaired. (soul, sole)
15. My family did little sightseeing at ______________. (night, knight)

Name ______________________________

Definitely Daffy Definitions

Directions: Write a pair of homophones to complete each definition. The homophones are spelled phonetically in the box.

plane	horss	strayt	dihr
fair	payl	sent	reel
mye-nur	flou-ur	beet	stay-shuh-ner-ee
wale	hayl	foul	bair

1. A very tired reddish-purple vegetable is a ________ ________
2. The forest animal with antlers that everyone likes is a ________ ________
3. A large animal that's missing its thick, coarse fur is a ________ ________
4. A nasty farm bird is a ________ ________
5. A four-legged animal with hoofs that has a sore throat is a ________ ________
6. A young coal digger is a ________ ________
7. A water channel that is not crooked is a ________ ________
8. The cry of the world's largest sea mammal is a ________ ________
9. A very simple, no-frills flying machine is a ________ ________
10. An old, faded bucket is a ________ ________
11. A mailed bottle of perfume is a ________ ________
12. A genuine spool for holding fish line is a ________ ________
13. Writing paper that has been weighted down is ________ ________
14. The reasonable cost for riding a bus or cab is a ________ ________
15. Dried and finely ground blossoms used for baking make ________ ________
16. Hardy pellets of ice falling from the clouds are ________ ________

Name ______________________________

What's the Meaning of This?

Directions: Underline the pair of homophones in each sentence. Then, write each word next to its meaning.

1. Will you help me haul this trunk down the hall to my room?

    ____________ passageway ____________ carry

2. No one guessed the identity of the mystery guest until he removed his mask.

    ____________ company ____________ surmised

3. We do not think it is fair that the bus has doubled the fare.

    ____________ just ____________ cost of a ride

4. My brother accidentally threw a baseball through our neighbor's window.

    ____________ in one side and out the other ____________ past tense of "to throw"

5. Luxury cruise ships require large crews of men and women to meet the needs of the passengers.

    ____________ groups of workers ____________ sail

6. If you heed the lesson in this chapter, you will lessen your risk of injury.

    ____________ reduce; make less ____________ something taught

7. You should have seen the final scene of the play!

    ____________ viewed ____________ part of an act

8. A principal must be a person of very high principle to set a good example for students.

    ____________ rule of behavior ____________ head of a school

9. Do you know whether tomorrow's weather will be clear and mild?

    ____________ climate ____________ if

10. We are going to see the newly built capitol at our state's capital.

    ____________ city ____________ building where state legislature meets

Name ______________________________

What's the Difference?

Directions: Write the correct homophone from the box next to each definition. Then, write the boxed letters in order to discover the answer to the riddle below.

threw/through
peace/piece
base/bass
colonel/ kernel
scents/cents
brood/brewed
caret/carrot
herd/heard
threw/through
creek/creak
right/rite
vise/vice
hanger/hangar
berry/bury
slay/sleigh
stationery/stationary
wade/weighed
suite/sweet
heir/air
missed/mist

1. military rank ____
2. odors ____
3. tossed ____
4. flock ____
5. grating noise ____
6. sled ____
7. writing paper ____
8. walk in water ____
9. sugary ____
10. successor ____
11. an orange, edible root ____
12. group of animals ____
13. put underground ____
14. tranquility ____
15. grain of corn ____
16. fog ____
17. used for hanging things ____
18. clamp ____
19. correct ____
20. deep voice ____

What's the difference between someone who parks a car and someone who is smashing dishes?

____ ____ ____ ____ ____

____ ____ ____ ____ ____

Name ______________________________

Watch for Grandpa's Watch

Directions: Each "watch" in the title of this activity sheet has a different meaning. One means "to look for," and the other means "timepiece." Write two meanings for each of the words below.

	Meaning 1	Meaning 2
1. spring	______________	______________
2. run	______________	______________
3. ruler	______________	______________
4. duck	______________	______________
5. suit	______________	______________
6. cold	______________	______________
7. fall	______________	______________
8. tire	______________	______________
9. rose	______________	______________
10. face	______________	______________
11. train	______________	______________
12. play	______________	______________
13. foot	______________	______________
14. pen	______________	______________
15. box	______________	______________
16. dice	______________	______________
17. fly	______________	______________
18. seal	______________	______________
19. bowl	______________	______________
20. ride	______________	______________

Choose some of the above words and illustrate both meanings on another sheet of paper.

Name ______________________________

Which Is It?

Some words with more than one meaning are spelled the same but pronounced differently. Phonetic spellings can help you figure out how to pronounce the words.

Directions: Two words written with phonetic spellings appear above each pair of sentences. Write the regular spelling for the two words in the sentences. Then, write the letter that tells the correct phonetic spelling of the word in each sentence.

1. (a) kon´•tent (b) kuhn•tent´

Does this cereal have a high sugar ____________________? ______

We are ____________________ to stay inside and read. ______

2. (a) dez´•urt (b) di•zurt´

Why did the soldier ____________________ his platoon? ______

It took weeks to cross the ____________________. ______

3. (a) meye•noot´ (b) min´•it

We will be there in just one ____________________. ______

There is a ____________________ speck of dust on the telescope lens. ______

4. (a) ri•fyooz´ (b) ref´•yoos

Volunteers picked up ____________________ the along the road. ______

The children ____________________ to do what they were asked. ______

5. (a) prez´•uhnt (b) pri•zent´

Everyone was ____________________ in class today. ______

The mayor will ____________________ us with a special award. ______

6. (a) bays (b) bas

I caught one ____________________ the last time we went fishing. ______

My older brother sings ____________________ in the choir. ______

7. (a) leed (b) led

Are these pipes made of copper or ____________________? ______

Our coach will ____________________ our team to victory this year. ______

Name ______________________________

Look Alikes

Some words have more than one meaning.

Example: ear and ear

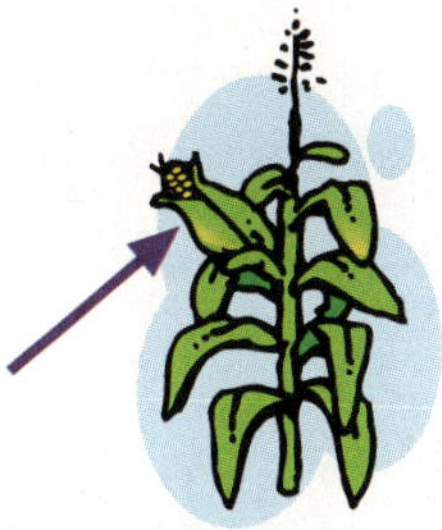

Directions: Find each word in the puzzle that correctly completes two sentences below. Circle the word in the puzzle. Then, write it correctly in the sentences.

G	F	R	E	S	H	T
S	R	B	I	L	L	I
M	T	O	C	H	O	P
A	B	E	U	R	N	U
T	E	A	R	N	G	P
C	A	N	N	N	D	I
H	H	U	S	K	Y	L

1. We have a new ________________ in our class.
2. The ________________ is soggy after two days of rain.
3. We need a ________________ to light the grill.
4. That child is so ________________ she has few friends.
5. Megan opened a savings account at the ________________.
6. The electric ________________ was higher than usual last month.
7. Your sweater, shirt, and socks ________________ perfectly.
8. Light enters your eye through the ________________.
9. We dried the corn and ________________ it into meal.
10. We bought ________________ vegetables at the farmers' market.
11. A cardinal's ________________ is perfect for cracking open seeds.
12. We fished from the ________________ instead of renting a boat.

Name ____________________

What's the Word?

Directions: Each rebus below makes a word with more than one meaning. Follow the clues and write the word.

1.  + 10 - n +r
= ____________________

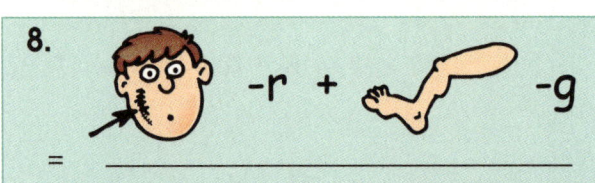

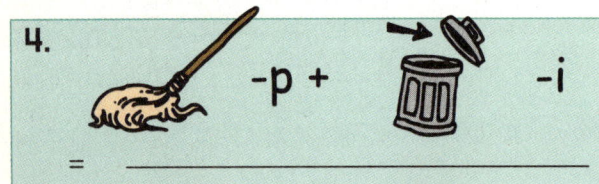

2.  -x + 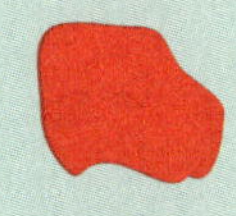 -d
= ____________________

3. 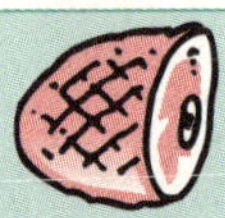 + 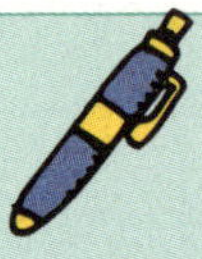 -n +r
= ____________________

4.  -p +  -i
= ____________________

5.  +  -ry
= ____________________

6.  -t +  -s +d
= ____________________

7.  -t +  -n
= ____________________

8.  -r + 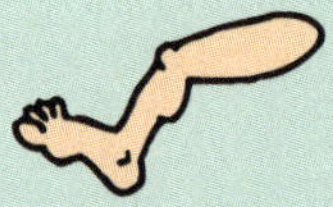 -g
= ____________________

9.  -a +  -b  -c
= ____________________

10.  -rn +  -o
= ____________________

Directions: Read the meanings below. Then, write the number of the rebus next to the matching definition.

_____ **a.** flour, egg, and milk mixture; player who hits the ball

_____ **b.** fungus; a form or shape

_____ **c.** 36 inches; enclosed space around a house

_____ **d.** make a hole; make weary

_____ **e.** player who throws the ball; container for pouring liquid

_____ **f.** noise; a tennis paddle

_____ **g.** balance; series of notes

_____ **h.** large basket; hold back

_____ **i.** unit of weight; hit hard repeatedly

_____ **j.** kind of bird; gulp

Name ______________________________

Compound Words

A **compound word** is made up of **two words** that can stand alone.

Directions: Match two words from the word box to make a compound word. Write the words on the lines.

 light	 basket	 lip	 dog
 house	 candle	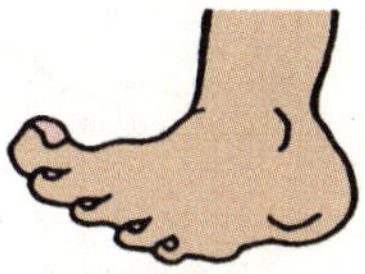 foot	 boat
 broom	 moon	 stick	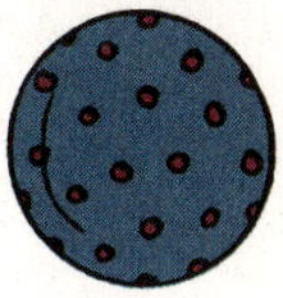 ball

1. ______________________
2. ______________________
3. ______________________
4. ______________________
5. ______________________
6. ______________________
7. ______________________
8. ______________________
9. ______________________
10. ______________________
11. ______________________
12. ______________________

Name ______________________________

Compound Words

Directions: Match two words from the word box to make compound words. Write six sentences using the compound words you made.

 fire	 gold	 rain	 star
 coat	 man	 bird	 bath
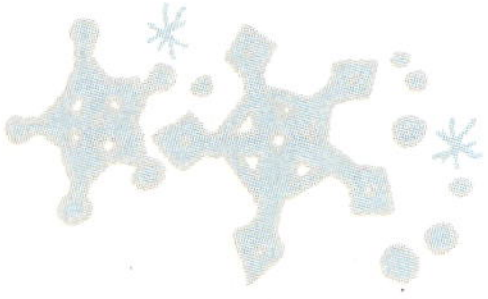 snow	 bed	 fish	 room

1. ______________________________

2. ______________________________

3. ______________________________

4. ______________________________

5. ______________________________

6. ______________________________

Name ______________________________

Compound Words

Directions: Match two words from the word box to make compound words. Write definitions for six of the compound words you made.

 night	 down	 bed	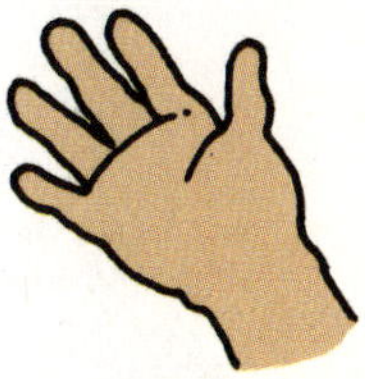 hand
 town	 hill	 boy	 up
 back	 stairs	 time	 paper

1. ______________________________

2. ______________________________

3. ______________________________

4. ______________________________

5. ______________________________

6. ______________________________

Name ______________________________

Compound Words

Directions: Write a sentence using each compound word from the word box.

classmate	tiptoe
starfish	somebody
woodland	airport
popcorn	hardware

1. ______________________________

2. ______________________________

3. ______________________________

4. ______________________________

5. ______________________________

6. ______________________________

7. ______________________________

8. ______________________________

Name ______________________________

Conquering Compounds

There are three types of compound words:

(1) **closed compound**—two separate words joined together, that create a new meaning and are written as one word

(2) **open compound**—two separate words that create a new meaning, but the two words are not joined together

(3) **hyphenated compound**—two or more words, written separately but connected by a hyphen, that create a new meaning

barnyard
blastoff
brand-new
chairperson
cupboard
hide-and-seek
homesick
ice skate
jack-o'-lantern
peanut butter
polar bear
post office
seagull
snowstorm
topsy-turvy
town crier
yardstick
zip code

Directions: Add a word or words to each word below to form a compound word from the spelling list.

1. cup ______________________
2. snow ______________________
3. home ______________________
4. barn ______________________
5. chair ______________________
6. yard ______________________
7. sea ______________________
8. hide- ______________________
9. brand- ______________________
10. polar ______________________
11. ice ______________________
12. peanut ______________________
13. blast ______________________
14. post ______________________
15. topsy- ______________________
16. town ______________________
17. zip ______________________
18. jack- ______________________

Name ______________________________

Puzzling Compounds

baseball	basketball	breakfast	classroom	driftwood	firefly
flagpole	harmless	knickknack	lifetime	motorcycle	paperback
playhouse	railway	switchboard	taxicab	textbook	tiptoe

Directions: Write a spelling word that matches each clue. Then, read down the boxed letters to solve the riddle.

1. a place to learn ☐ ___ ___ ___ ___ ___ ___ ___ ___
2. the morning meal ___ ☐ ___ ___ ___ ___ ___ ___ ___
3. not capable of hurting ___ ☐ ___ ___ ___ ___ ___ ___
4. game played with a bat and a ball ☐ ___ ___ ___ ___ ___ ___ ___
5. to walk softly ☐ ___ ___ ___ ___ ___
6. sometimes called a lightning bug ___ ___ ☐ ___ ___ ___ ___
7. one's entire period of existence ___ ___ ___ ☐ ___ ___ ___ ___
8. it supports Old Glory ___ ___ ___ ___ ___ ___ ___ ☐

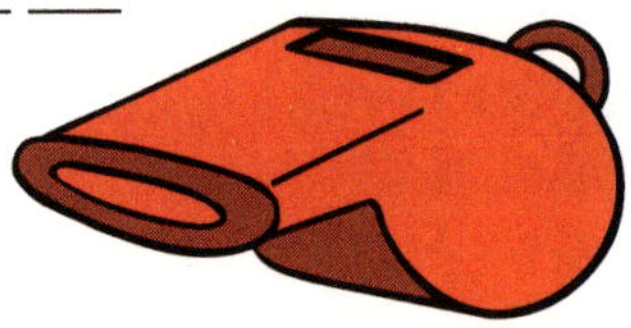

Riddle: *Which tree is the most difficult to get along with?*

Answer: ______________________________

Directions: Write a compound word that belongs in each group.

1. hoop, whistle, ____________________
2. tracks, railroad, ____________________
3. school, subjects, ____________________
4. toys, games, ____________________
5. wood, ashore, ____________________
6. circuit, panel, ____________________
7. read, novel, ____________________
8. 2-wheeled, helmet, ____________________
9. fare, driver, ____________________
10. trinket, decoration ____________________

Name ________________________________

Following Directions

Directions: Read and follow the directions.

1. Draw a vertical line from the top midpoint of the square to the bottom midpoint of the square.
2. Draw a diagonal line from top left to bottom right of the square.
3. In each of the two triangles, draw a heart.
4. Draw a picture of a cat's face below the square.
5. Draw a horizontal line from the left midpoint to the right midpoint of the square.
6. Draw two intersecting lines in each of the two smaller squares so they are equally divided into four quadrants.
7. Draw a triangle-shaped roof on the square.
8. Draw a circle next to each heart.
9. Write your name in the roof section of your drawing.

GRADE 5

Name ____________________

Following Directions: Continents

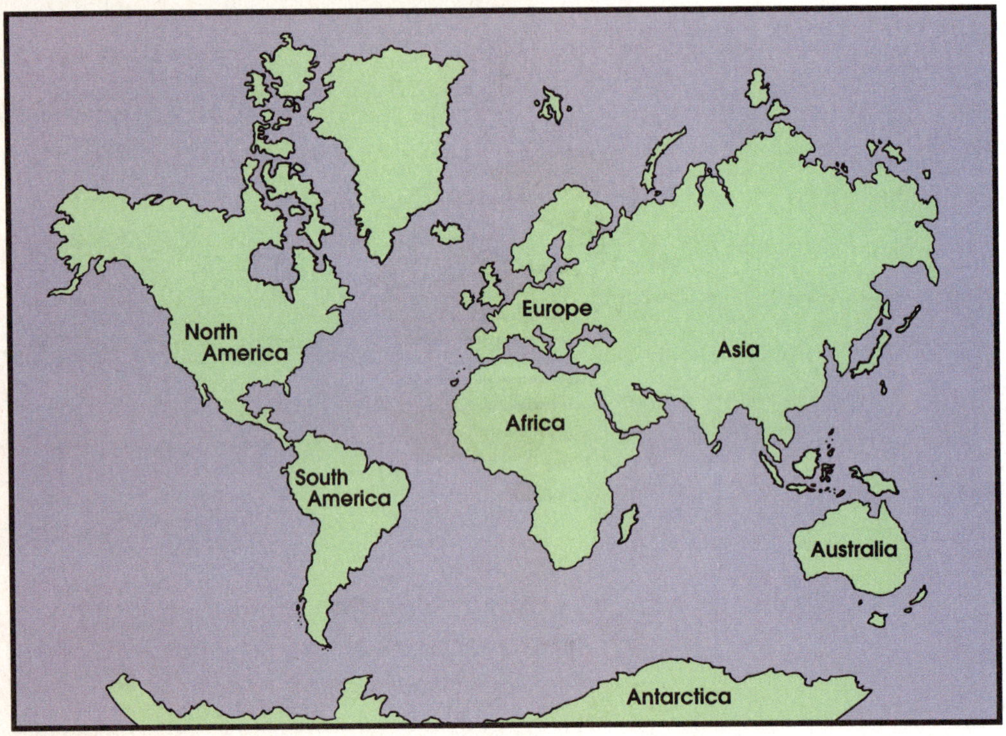

Directions: Read the facts about the seven continents and follow the directions.

1. Asia is the largest continent. It has the largest land mass and the largest population. Draw a star on Asia.
2. Africa is the second largest continent. Write a **2** on Africa.
3. Australia is the smallest continent in area: 3 million square miles, compared to 17 million square miles for Asia. Write **3,000,000** on Australia.
4. Australia is not a very crowded continent, but it does not rank lowest in population. That honor goes to Antarctica, which has no permanent population at all! This ice-covered continent is too cold for life. Write **zero** on Antarctica.
5. Australia and Antarctica are the only continents entirely separated by water. Draw circles around Australia and Antarctica.
6. North America and South America are joined together by a narrow strip of land. It is called Central America. Write an **N** on North America, an **S** on South America and a **C** on Central America.
7. Asia and Europe are joined together over such a great distance that they are sometimes called one continent. The name given to it is Eurasia. Draw lines under the names of the two continents in Eurasia.

Name ______________________________

Direction Pictures

Directions: In each set of directions there is a missing step. Look at the pictures and decide which one shows the correct missing step. Write a direction that tells how to do each step on the line.

1. Push the power button. Place the CD in the drawer. Push the close button. Push the play button.

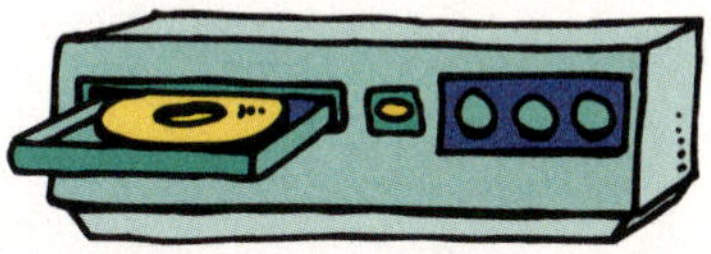

Missing step: ______________________________

2. Make a T with the sticks. Attach the sticks to the kite paper. Tie one end of the string to the center of the T. Hold the string and run.

Missing step: ______________________________

3. Lay all the pieces out on the table. Use the picture on the top of the box as a reference. Fill in the center pieces.

Missing step: ______________________________

4. Put the clothes in. Turn the water level knob to high. Turn the knob to regular wash. Pull the knob out.

Missing step: ______________________________

Name ____________________

Mapping the Way

Tamika's Aunt Keisha and Uncle Terence are visiting. They need to go to the library, video store, supermarket, and post office. Tamika wrote out directions, but her aunt and uncle are confused.

Directions: Rewrite Tamika's directions using landmarks and street names from the map.

Go two blocks and turn left.

Walk one block.

Then, cross the street and walk one block.

Then, cross the street again and go to the corner.

Take a left at the next corner and go two blocks.

Turn right and go one block.

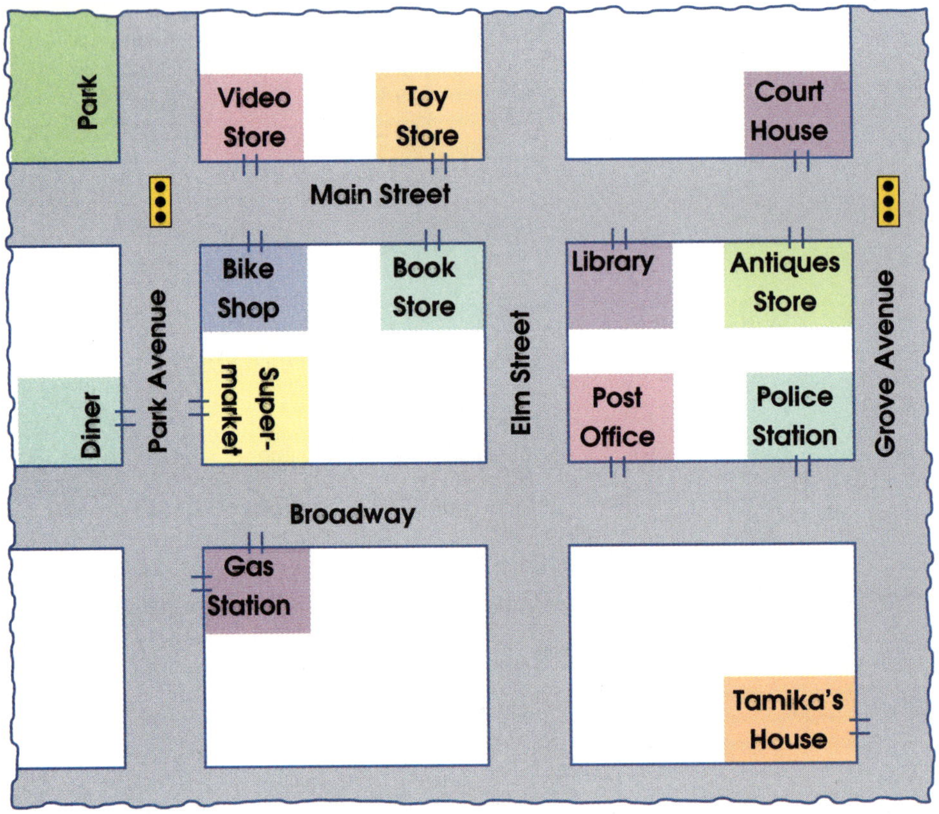

____

____

____

____

____

____

____

Name ______________________________

Following Directions: Chunky Tomato and Green Onion Sauce

Following directions means to do what the directions say to do, step by step, in the correct order.

Directions: Read the recipe for chunky tomato and green onion sauce. Answer the questions below.

Ingredients:

- 2 tablespoons corn oil
- 2 cloves of garlic, finely chopped
- $1\frac{1}{2}$ pounds plum tomatoes, cored, peeled, seeded, then coarsely chopped
- 3 green onions, cut in half lengthwise, then thinly sliced
- salt
- freshly ground pepper

Heat oil in a heavy skillet over medium heat. Add garlic and cook until yellow, about 1 minute. Stir in tomatoes. Season with salt and pepper. Cook until thickened, about 10 minutes. Stir in green onions and serve.

1. What is the last thing the cook does to prepare the tomatoes before cooking them?

____

2. What kind of oil does the cook heat in the heavy skillet? ______________________

3. How long should the garlic be cooked? ______________________________

4. What does the cook do to the tomatoes right before removing the seeds?

____

5. Is the sauce served hot or cold? ______________________________

Name ______________________________

Follow the Clues

When you write a story, be sure to describe the events in sequence, that is, in the order in which they happen. Use time-order words such as *first, next, then,* and *finally* to help the reader figure out the sequence.

Directions: Read the paragraph. Fill in the missing time-order words.

Go, Sting Rays!

We were getting ready for the Regional Soccer Tournament. Unfortunately, things did not look promising. ____________ practice was delayed because of rain. ____________ once it stopped raining and practice actually began, two forwards ran after the same ball, collided, and needed to recover from their collision. As if all this wasn't enough, the ____________ thing that happened really got the coach upset. We forgot one of the new plays he taught us. He went over the play again, and ____________ we remembered it. Things were looking up!

Directions: Think about the steps you take to clean your room. Write them in order. Be sure to use time-order words.

____

____

____

____

____

____

____

Name ______________________________

When Things Happened

A **time line** is a chart that shows important dates and events in the order they happened.

Directions: The time line shows events in the history of Santa Fe. Use the time line to answer the questions. Write your answers on the lines.

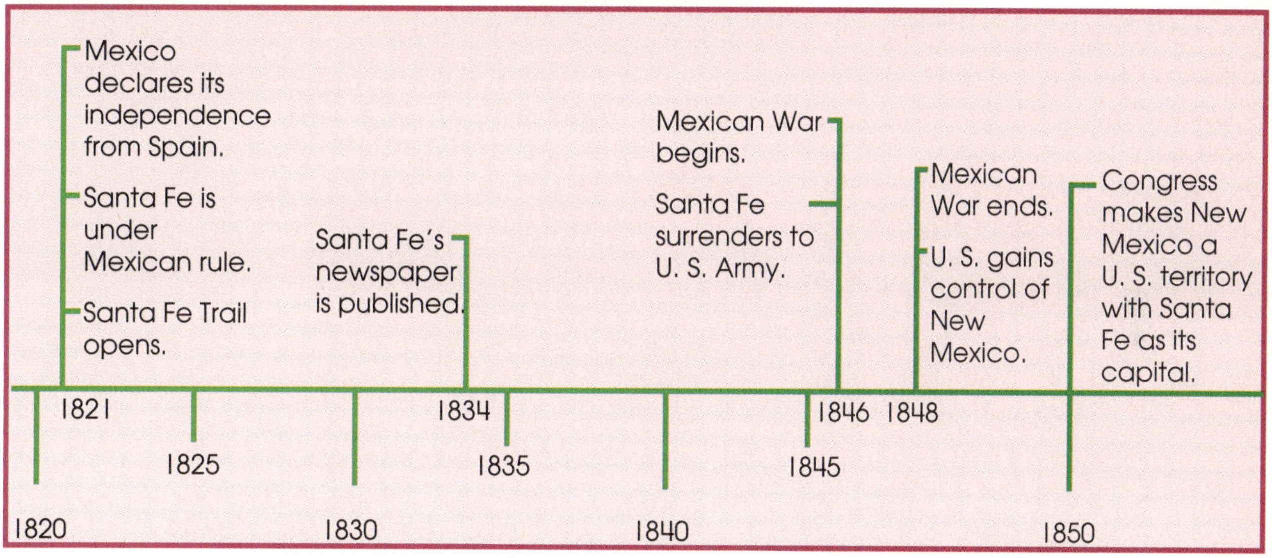

1. What year does the time line begin? __________ What year does it end? __________

2. When did Mexico declare its independence from Spain? ______________________

3. How many years after the Mexican War began did New Mexico become a U. S. territory? ______________________

4. How many years passed between Mexico's declaration of independence from Spain and the end of the Mexican War? ______________

5. Which happened first, Santa Fe surrendered to the U. S. Army or the opening of the Santa Fe Trail?

____

6. During which decade did the most events occur? ______________________

State Flag of New Mexico

Name ________________________________

Sequencing: Chocolate Chunk Cookies

These chocolate chunk cookies require only five ingredients. Before you combine them, preheat the oven to 350 degrees. Preheating the oven to the correct temperature is always step number one in baking.

Now, into a large mixing bowl, empty an $18\frac{1}{4}$-ounce package of chocolate fudge cake mix (any brand). Add a 10-ounce package of semi-sweet chocolate, broken into small pieces, two $5\frac{1}{8}$-ounce packages of chocolate fudge pudding mix (any brand), and $1\frac{1}{2}$ cups chopped walnuts.

Use a large wooden spoon to combine the ingredients. When they are well-mixed, add $1\frac{1}{2}$ cups mayonnaise and stir thoroughly. Shape the dough into small balls and place the balls 2 inches apart on an ungreased cookie sheet. Bake 12 minutes. Cool and eat!

Directions: Number in correct order the steps for making chocolate chunk cookies.

________ Place $1\frac{1}{2}$ cups of mayonnaise in the bowl.

________ Shape dough into small balls and place them on a cookie sheet.

________ Empty the package of chocolate fudge cake mix into the bowl.

________ Bake the dough for 12 minutes.

________ Place two $5\frac{1}{8}$-ounce packages of chocolate fudge pudding in the bowl.

________ Put $1\frac{1}{2}$ cups chopped walnuts in the bowl.

________ Preheat the oven to 350 degrees.

________ Place the 10-ounce package of semi-sweet chocolate pieces in the bowl.

________ Stir everything thoroughly.

GRADE 5

Name ______________________________

Delivery Dilemma

Dilly's Deliveries is under new management, and the new boss just instructed his top driver to follow a most peculiar route. The driver is to deliver packages to each of the eight businesses shown below, but she is not necessarily meant to visit them in a logical order.

Green Grocer ____ ____ Troy's Toys ____ ____ Tourist Travel ____ ____ Myer's Tires ____ ____

Melody's Music ____ ____ Hank's Bank ____ ____ Peter's Pets ____ ____ Reta's Restaurant ____ ____

Directions: Help the confused driver plan her route. Number the businesses above in the order in which they should be visited in the first blank. Write the number of packages to be delivered in the second blank.

1. The second delivery is directly north of the first delivery and has one fewer package than the first.
2. Melody's Music needs all five packages delivered before 11:00 A.M.
3. By the time the paperwork is completed, the packages are verified and greetings are exchanged between the driver and the recipient, each delivery takes fifteen minutes.
4. The bank is never the last delivery. It always receives four packages.
5. Troy's Toys has the most packages of all. His delivery will contain as many packages as all the others combined.
6. Pete's deliveries are live animals, which need to be unloaded first when the store opens at 9:30 A.M.
7. The fourth delivery is directly east of the first delivery and contains twice the number of packages.
8. The travel agency and the pet store combined are to receive the same number of packages as the music store.
9. The fifth delivery contains three boxes.
10. The third delivery is two stores west of the second.
11. The tire store, the grocery store, and the pet store will all receive the same number of packages. They are the only ones to receive this exact amount.

Name ______________________________

Sequencing: Maps

Directions: Read the information about planning a map.

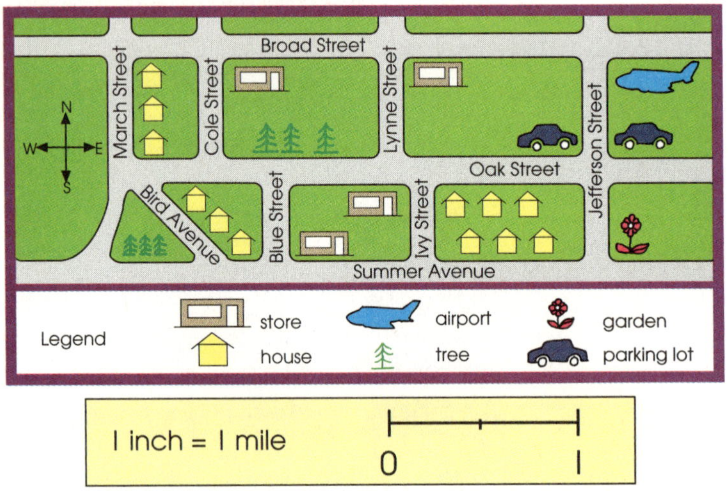

Maps have certain features that help you to read them. A **compass rose** points out directions. Color is often used so you can easily see where one area (such as a county, state, or country) stops and the next starts.

To be accurate, a map must be drawn to scale. The **scale** of a map shows how much area is represented by a given measurement. The scale can be small: one inch = one mile; or large: one inch = 1,000 miles.

Symbols are another map tool. An airplane may represent an airport. Sometimes a symbol does not look like what it represents. Cities are often represented by dots. A map **legend** tells what each symbol means.

One of the best ways to learn about maps is to make one of your own. You may be surprised at how much you learn about your neighborhood, too. You will need a large piece of paper, a ruler, a pencil, and colored pencils.

You will need to choose the area you want to map out. It is important to decide on the scale for your map. It could be small: one inch = three feet, if you are mapping out your own backyard. Be sure to include symbols, like a picnic table to represent a park or a flag to represent a school. Don't forget to include the symbols and other important information in your legend.

Directions: Number in order the steps to making your own map.

______ Figure out the scale that will work best for your map.

______ Obtain a large piece of paper, ruler, pencil, and colored pencils.

______ Make a legend explaining the symbols you used.

______ Draw your map!

______ Draw symbols to represent features of the area you are mapping.

______ Decide on the area you want to map out.

Name ______________________________

Main Idea

The **main idea** is the most important idea, or main point, in a sentence, paragraph, or story.

Directions: Read the paragraphs below. For each paragraph, underline the sentence that tells the main idea.

Sometimes people think they have to choose between exercise and fun. For many people, it is more fun to watch television than to run 5 miles. Yet, if you don't exercise, your body gets soft and out of shape. You move more slowly. You may even think more slowly. But why do something that isn't fun? Well, there are many ways to exercise and have fun.

One family solved the exercise problem by using their TV. They hooked up the television to an electric generator. The generator was operated by an exercise bike. Anyone who wanted to watch TV had to ride the bike. The room with their television in it must have been quite a sight!

Think of the times when you are just "hanging out" with your friends. You go outside and jump rope, play ball, run races, and so on. Soon you are all laughing and having a good time. Many group activities can provide you with exercise and be fun, too.

Maybe there aren't enough kids around after school for group games. Perhaps you are by yourself. Then what? You can get plenty of exercise just by walking, biking, or even dancing. In the morning, walk the long way to the bus. Ride your bike to and from school. Practice the newest dance by yourself. Before you know it, you will be the fittest dancer of all your friends!

Directions: Write other ideas you have for combining fun and exercise below.

____

____

____

____

____

____

____

Name ______________________________

Topics and Main Ideas

To find the **topic** of a paragraph, ask yourself what the paragraph is about. To find the **main idea**, look for the sentence that best tells about the topic.

Directions: Read each paragraph. Then, identify the topic and the main idea of each of the paragraphs.

"Be a Bazillionaire" is a popular television game show. In the game, contestants answer questions on different topics. As they answer correctly, contestants reach different money levels and can use one of three lifelines to get help in answering questions. The chance to win a bazillion dollars and Reggie Binphil, the engaging host, have made the show popular.

1. What is the topic of this paragraph? ______________________________

2. Which sentence states the most important idea about the topic? ______________________________

____

____

Everyone has seen "Celestial Wars," a classic movie loved by many generations. There are tons of exciting special effects used to create realistic space battles between the forces of good and evil. The story, about a father and son who battle against each other, is also memorable. "Celestial Wars" is one of the greatest and most well-known movies of all time.

1. What is the topic of this paragraph? ______________________________

2. Which sentence states the most important idea about the topic? ______________________________

____

____

Name ______________________________

Main Idea Multiple Choice

Directions: Read each science report. Circle the sentence that states the main idea of each report.

Isaac Newton lived during the 1600s. He was known for his scientific accomplishments. Among these accomplishments are a new form of math, the invention of the reflecting telescope, the discovery of the range of colors in visible light, the formulation of the laws of motion, and most importantly, the discovery of the laws of gravity. Isaac Newton is one of the greatest scientists of all time.

1. Which of the following is the main idea sentence?

A. Isaac Newton lived during the 1600s.

B. Isaac Newton was known for his scientific accomplishments.

C. Isaac Newton is one of the greatest scientists of all time.

Clouds can be used to predict weather. This is because different types of clouds bring different kinds of weather. Cirrus clouds, which are made of ice crystals, usually appear before a storm. Stratus clouds, which are low, dark clouds, may indicate snow or rain. Cumulus clouds are white and may appear during good weather or during heavy rain showers. So, watch the clouds to figure out tomorrow's weather!

2. Which of the following is the main idea sentence?

A. Clouds can be used to predict weather.

B. So, watch the clouds to figure out tomorrow's weather!

C. This is because different types of clouds bring different kinds of weather.

Water can appear in three forms: solid, liquid, or gas. These are all in the Earth's atmosphere. Solid and liquid water are seen in clouds, snowflakes, and raindrops. But water as a gas is invisible. It is found in the atmosphere in the form of water vapor.

3. Which of the following is the main idea sentence?

A. These are all in the Earth's atmosphere.

B. Solids and liquids are found in clouds, snowflakes, and raindrops.

C. Water can appear in three forms: solid, liquid, or gas.

Name ______________________________

Main Idea Match

Directions: Look at the illustrations for six different social studies topics. Circle the sentence that best tells the main idea of the illustration.

1. Women worked to get the right to vote.

   Women liked to protest.

   It is important to vote.

2. The Capitol is a large, white building.

   Washington D.C. has many important monuments.

   Congress is the branch of government that makes new laws.

3. Flags are pretty.

   The American flag is a symbol of the United States.

   Every country has a flag.

4. People traveled to California during the Gold Rush.

   In 1849, people known as Forty-niners panned for gold.

   Gold is an important metal.

5. There are lots of things to see in space.

   Becoming an astronaut takes a lot of time and effort.

   The United States was the first nation to land a person on the moon.

6. Thomas Edison invented the electric light bulb.

   Thomas Edison made many important discoveries.

   Thomas Edison lived in New Jersey.

Name ___________________________

Main Idea: Where Did Songs Come From?

Historians say the earliest music was probably connected to religion. Long ago, people believed the world was controlled by a variety of gods. Singing was among the first things humans did to show respect to the gods.

Singing is still an important part of most religions. Buddhists (bood-ists), Christians, and Jews all use chants and/or songs in their religious ceremonies. If you have ever sung a song—religious or otherwise—you know that singing is fun. The feeling of joy that comes from singing must also have made ancient people feel happy.

Another time people sang was when they worked. Egyptian slaves sang as they carried the heavy stones to build the pyramids. Soldiers sang as they marched into battle. Farmers sang one song as they planted and another when they harvested. Singing made the work less burdensome. People used the tunes to pace themselves. Sometimes they followed instructions through songs. For example, "Yo-oh, heave ho!/Yo-oh, heave ho!" was sung when sailors pulled on a ship's ropes to lift the sails. *Heave* means "to lift," and that is what they did as they sang the song. The song helped sailors work together and pull at the same time. This made the task easier.

Directions: Answer these questions about music.

1. Circle the main idea:

Singing is fun, and that is why early people liked it so much.

Singing began as a way to show respect to the gods and is still an important part of most religious ceremonies.

Traditionally, singing has been important as a part of religious ceremonies and as inspiration to workers.

2. Besides religious ceremonies, what other activity fostered singing? ______________

____

3. When did farmers sing two different songs? ______________________

4. How did singing "Yo-oh, heave ho!" help sailors work? ______________

____

Name ____________________

Main Idea: Penguins

Directions: Read the information about penguins.

People are amused by the funny, duck-like waddle of penguins and by their appearance because they seem to be wearing little tuxedos. Penguins are among the best-liked animals on Earth, but are also a most misunderstood animal. People may have more wrong ideas about penguins than any other animal.

For example, many people are surprised to learn that penguins are really birds, not mammals. Penguins do not fly, but they do have feathers, and only birds have feathers. Also, like other birds, penguins build nests and their young hatch from eggs. Because of their unusual looks, though, you would never confuse them with any other bird!

Penguins are also thought of as symbols of the polar regions, but penguins do not live north of the equator, so you would not find a penguin on the North Pole. Penguins don't live at the South Pole, either. Only two of the seventeen *species* of penguins spend all of their lives on the frozen continent of Antarctica. You would be just as likely to see a penguin living on an island in a warm climate as in a cold area.

Directions: Draw an **X** on the blank for the correct answer.

1. The main idea is:

____ Penguins are among the best-liked animals on Earth.

____ The penguin is a much misunderstood animal.

2. Penguins live

____ only at the North Pole.

____ only at the South Pole.

____ only south of the equator.

3. Based on the other words in the sentence, what is the correct definition of the word *species*?

____ number

____ bird

____ a distinct kind

Directions: List three ways penguins are like other birds.

____

Name ______________________________

Recognizing Details: The Coldest Continent

Directions: Read the information about Antarctica. Then, answer the questions.

Antarctica lies at the South Pole and is the coldest continent. It is without sunlight for months at a time. Even when the sun does shine, its angle is so slanted that the land receives little warmth. Temperatures often drop to 100 degrees below zero, and a fierce wind blows almost endlessly. Most of the land is covered by snow heaped thousands of feet deep. The snow is so heavy and tightly packed that it forms a great ice cap covering more than 95 percent of the continent.

Considering the conditions, it is no wonder there are no towns or cities in Antarctica. There is no permanent population at all, only small scientific research stations. Many teams of explorers and scientists have braved the freezing cold since Antarctica was sighted in 1820. Some have died in their effort, but a great deal of information has been learned about the continent.

From fossils, pieces of coal, and bone samples, we know that Antarctica was not always an ice-covered land. Scientists believe that 200 million years ago it was connected to southern Africa, South America, Australia, and India. Forests grew in warm swamps, and insects and reptiles thrived there. Today, there are animals that live in and around the waters that border the continent. In fact, the waters surrounding Antarctica contain more life than oceans in warmer areas of the world.

1. Where is Antarctica? ______________________________

2. How much of the continent is covered by an ice cap? ______________________________

3. When was Antarctica first sighted by explorers? ______________________________

4. What clues indicate that Antarctica was not always an ice-covered land?

____

5. Is Antarctica another name for the North Pole? Yes No

Name ______________________________

Recognizing Details: The Frozen Continent

Directions: Read the information about explorers. Then, answer the questions.

By the mid-1800s, most of the seals of Antarctica had been killed. The seal hunters no longer sailed the icy waters. The next group of explorers who took an interest in Antarctica were scientists. Of these, the man who took the most daring chances and made the most amazing discoveries was British Captain James Clark Ross.

Ross first made a name for himself sailing to the north. In 1831, he discovered the North Magnetic Pole—one of two places on Earth toward which a compass needle points. In 1840, Ross set out to find the South Magnetic Pole. He made many marvelous discoveries, including the Ross Sea, a great open sea beyond the ice packs that stopped other explorers, and the Ross Ice Shelf, a great floating sheet of ice bigger than all of France!

The next man to make his mark exploring Antarctica was British explorer Robert Falcon Scott. Scott set out in 1902 to find the South Pole. He and his team suffered greatly, but they were able to make it a third of the way to the pole. Back in England, Scott was a great hero. In 1910, he again attempted to become the first man to reach the South Pole. But this time he had competition: an explorer from Norway, Roald Amundsen, was also leading a team to the South Pole.

It was a brutal race. Both teams faced many hardships, but they pressed on. Finally, on December 14, 1911, Amundsen became the first man to reach the South Pole. Scott arrived on January 17, 1912. He was bitterly disappointed at not being first. The trip back was even more horrible. None of the five men in the Scott expedition survived.

1. After the seal hunters, who were the next group of explorers interested in Antarctica?

____

2. What great discovery did James Ross make before ever sailing to Antarctica?

____

3. What were two other great discoveries made by James Ross?

______________________ ______________________

4. How close did Scott and his team come to the South Pole in 1902?

____

5. Who was the first person to reach the South Pole? ______________________

Name ______________________________

Recognizing Details: The Cactus Family

Directions: Read the information about cacti. Pay close attention to details. Answer the questions.

Although cacti are the best-known desert plants, they don't live only in hot, dry places. While cacti are most likely to be found in the desert areas of Mexico and the southwestern United States, they can be seen as far north as Nova Scotia, Canada. Certain types of cacti can live even in the snow!

Desert cacti are particularly good at surviving very long dry spells. Most cacti have a very long root system so they can absorb as much water as possible. Every available drop of water is taken into the cactus and held in its fleshy stem. A cactus stem can hold enough water to last for 2 years or longer.

A cactus may be best known for its spines. Although a few kinds of cacti don't have spines, the stems of most types are covered with these sharp needles. The spines have many uses for a cactus. They keep animals from eating the cactus. They collect raindrops and dew. The spines also help keep the plant cool by forming shadows in the sun and by trapping a layer of air close to the plant. They break up the desert winds that dry out the cactus.

Cacti come in all sizes and shapes. The biggest type in North America is the saguaro. It can weigh 12,000 to 14,000 pounds and grow to be 50 feet tall! A saguaro can last several years without water, but it will grow only after summer rains. In May and June, white blossoms appear. Many kinds of birds nest in these enormous cacti: white-winged doves, woodpeckers, small owls, thrashers, and wrens all build nests in the saguaro.

1. Where are you most likely to find a cactus growing?

   ____

2. How long can most cacti survive without water?

   ____

3. What are two ways the spines help a cactus?

   ____

4. What is the biggest cactus in North America?

   ____

5. What animals live in a saguaro cactus?

   ____

Name ______________________________

Sort 'Em Out

Vertebrates are animals with backbones. Animals without backbones are called **invertebrates**. At the bottom of the page are pictures of both kinds of animals. Write the name of each animal under the correct heading below.

Vertebrates	Invertebrates
1. ____________________	1. ____________________
2. ____________________	2. ____________________
3. ____________________	3. ____________________
4. ____________________	4. ____________________
5. ____________________	5. ____________________

Name ___________________________

Sorting Word Pairs

Directions: Look at the pairs of words in the box. Classify the pairs as **synonyms** or **antonyms**. Remember, synonyms are words with almost the same meaning and antonyms are words with the opposite meaning.

smooth, rough
terrific, great
started, began
relieved, worried
ran, jogged
forget, remember
simple, complex
delicate, frail

Synonym Pairs

____
____
____
____

Antonym Pairs

____
____
____
____

Directions: Classify each word from the box as an action, a feeling, or a characteristic. Write the words correctly on the lines.

Action

____
____
____
____
____
____

Feeling

____
____
____
____

Characteristic

____
____
____
____
____
____

GRADE 5

Name ______________________________

Categories Galore

Directions: In the box below are names of sports. Write the names of the sports that best fit in each category.

baseball	tennis	surfing	volleyball	fishing
soccer	football	golf	basketball	swimming

Team Sport

____

____

____

____

____

Individual Sport

____

____

____

____

____

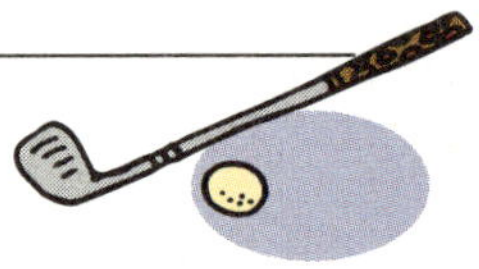

Directions: In the box below are names of musical instruments. Classify them into four groups.

violin	trumpet	xylophone	tuba
string bass	cymbals	trombone	snare drum
bassoon	cello	viola	clarinet
flute	triangle	French horn	oboe

Strings

____

____

____

____

Brass

____

____

____

____

Woodwinds

____

____

____

____

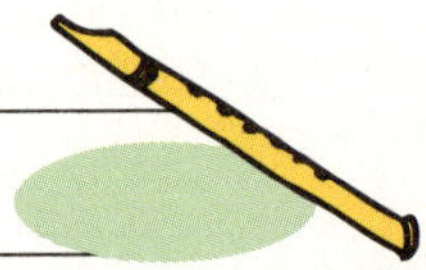

Percussion

____

____

____

____

Name ______________________________

Classifying

Classifying means putting items into categories based on similar characteristics.

Example: Apple pie, cookies, and ice cream could be classified as desserts.

Directions: Cross out the word in each group that does not belong. Then, add a word of your own that does belong. The first one has been done for you.

1.	wren	robin	~~feather~~
	sparrow	eagle	bluebird
2.	sofa	stool	chair
	carpet	bench	______________
3.	lettuce	salad	corn
	broccoli	spinach	______________
4.	pencil	chalk	crayon
	pen	drawing	______________
5.	perch	shark	penguin
	bass	tuna	______________
6.	rapid	quick	unhurried
	swift	speedy	______________
7.	lemon	daisy	melon
	lime	grapefruit	______________

Directions: Write a category name above each group of words. Then, write a word of your own that belongs in each group.

______________	______________
blizzard hurricane thunder	ankle shin thigh
______________	______________
______________	______________
antenna speaker battery	hockey ice skating bobsledding
______________	______________

Name ______________________________

Classifying

Directions: Write three objects which could belong in each category.

1. whales ____________ ____________ ____________
2. songs ____________ ____________ ____________
3. sports stars ____________ ____________ ____________
4. fruit ____________ ____________ ____________
5. schools ____________ ____________ ____________
6. teachers ____________ ____________ ____________
7. tools ____________ ____________ ____________
8. friends ____________ ____________ ____________
9. books ____________ ____________ ____________
10. mammals ____________ ____________ ____________
11. fish ____________ ____________ ____________
12. desserts ____________ ____________ ____________
13. cars ____________ ____________ ____________
14. hobbies ____________ ____________ ____________
15. vegetables ____________ ____________ ____________
16. insects ____________ ____________ ____________

Name ______________________________

Classifying: Regional Forecast

Directions: Read the forecast. Then, write words in the correct categories..

The very warm, early spring weather will continue to spread along the East Coast today. With some sunshine, afternoon temperatures will climb to 90 degrees in many places. Columbia, South Carolina, and neighboring areas could reach 100 degrees. Showers are expected from Washington, D.C., to New York City. Severe thunderstorms are likely in Virginia and North Carolina. Central South Carolina will be under a tornado watch during the afternoon.

Cities

____

____

____

States

____

____

____

Weather Conditions

____

____

____

____

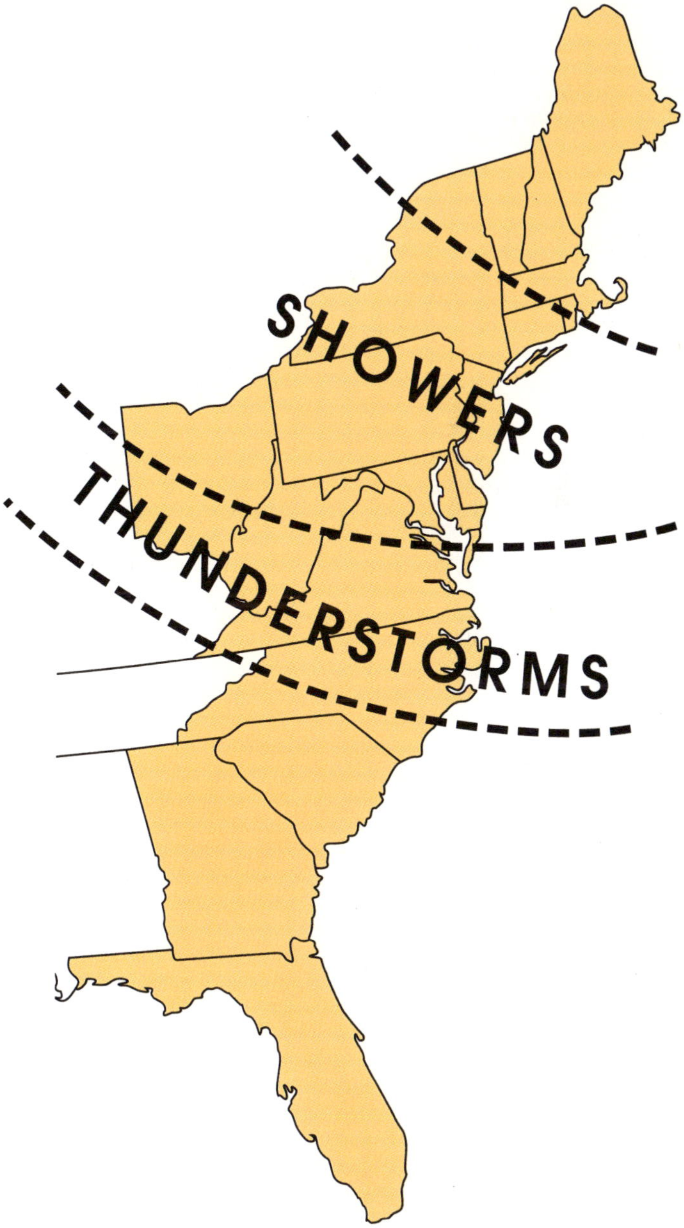

Name ____________________

Clue Search

When you come to a word you do not know, you can look at its **context**, or the words and phrases around it, to try to figure out its meaning. Context clues within a sentence can include synonyms, antonyms, and explanations.

Directions: As you read each of the following sentences, look for context clues to help determine the meaning of each underlined word. Circle the clues. Write what you think each word means. You can use a dictionary to see if you are correct.

1. Two flood victims clung tenaciously to a branch, refusing to let go or give up hope.

   ____

2. The man will be incarcerated for breaking the law and will not be paroled until 2015.

   ____

3. The doctor waited until the hysterical child had calmed down enough to be examined.

   ____

4. So many wild animals live in our backyard that it is like a menagerie, only without the cages.

   ____

5. After exploring cartography as a possible career, I've decided that map making would be quite interesting.

   ____

6. The man was so frugal in his spending for meals that they were barely enough to satisfy his hunger.

   ____

7. As a philatelist, I subscribe to *Stamp Collectors' Digest.* ____________________

8. Thomas Edison and Alexander Graham Bell were not only contemporaries but were even born in the same year of 1847.

   ____

9. Try to make your definitions concise by using as few words as possible.

   ____

10. John is a conscientious student whose work shows great care and concern for detail.

    ____

Name ______________________________

A Fitting Choice

Directions: Read each sentence. Look at the three word choices. Use context clues to help you choose the correct word to complete the sentence. Write it on the line.

1. The chef prepared a s________________s meal that absolutely everyone enjoyed.

scrumptious   scrunches   sponges

2. The text was extremely difficult to read and beyond my c________________n.

communication   complain   comprehension

3. High-wire performers have a rather p________________s job when you consider what could happen if they should fall.

previous   princess   precarious

4. It was with great r________________e that John agreed to take on such a dangerous job.

responsible   reluctance   receive

5. The v________________y of light is approximately 186,000 miles per second.

velocity   velvety   victory

6. The judge issued a w________________t allowing the police to search the building.

wrist   wallet   warrant

7. It is an a________________d idea and obviously untrue.

absurd   award   aboard

8. Maria's tale of her journey through South America made an interesting n________________e for her readers.

native   nature   narrative

9. The wolves attacked their prey with such f________________y that it was difficult for some of us to observe.

family   ferocity   fiery

10. Unearthing fossil remains of dinosaurs is l________________s work requiring time, skill, and patience.

laborious   laboratories   labors

Name ____________________________

Comprehension and Context

Comprehension is understanding what is seen, heard, or read.

Context is the rest of the words in a sentence or the sentences before or after a word. Context can help with comprehension.

Context clues help you figure out the meaning of a word by relating it to other words in the sentence.

Directions: Use the context clues in the sentences to find the meanings of the bold words.

1. Jane was a **wizard** at games. She mastered them in no time and seldom lost.

☐ evil magician ☐ gifted person ☐ average player

2. The holiday was so special that she was sure she'd never forget it. The memory would be **imprinted** forever on her mind.

☐ found ☐ weighed ☐ fixed

3. "John will believe anything anyone tells him," his teacher said. "He's a very **impressionable** young man."

☐ easily influenced ☐ unhappy ☐ unintelligent

4. "Do you really think it's **prudent** to spend all your money on clothes?" his mother asked crossly.

☐ foolish ☐ wise ☐ funny

5. "Your plan has **merit**," Elizabeth's father said. "Let me give it some thought."

☐ value ☐ awards ☐ kindness

6. John was very **gregarious** and loved being around people.

☐ shy ☐ outgoing ☐ unfriendly

Name ______________________________

Context Clues: Remember Who You Are

Directions: Read each paragraph. Then, use context clues to figure out the meanings of the bold words.

During the 1940s, Esther Hautzig lived in the town of Vilna, which was then part of Poland. Shortly after the **outbreak** of World War II, she and her family were **deported** to Siberia by Russian communists, who hated Jews. She told what happened to her and other Polish Jews in a book. The book is called *Remember Who You Are: Stories About Being Jewish*.

1. Choose the correct definition of **deported**.

☐ sent away ☐ asked to go ☐ invited to visit

2. Choose the correct definition of **outbreak**.

☐ a sudden occurrence ☐ to leave suddenly

Remember Who You Are: Stories About Being Jewish is a nonfiction book that tells true stories. An interesting **fiction** book is *Leave the Cooking to Me* by Judie Angell. It tells the story of a girl named Shirley, who learns about cooking from her best friend's mother. Shirley gets very good at making fancy food. Most young people have a hard time finding jobs that pay well, but Shirley's cooking skills help her land a **lucrative** summer job.

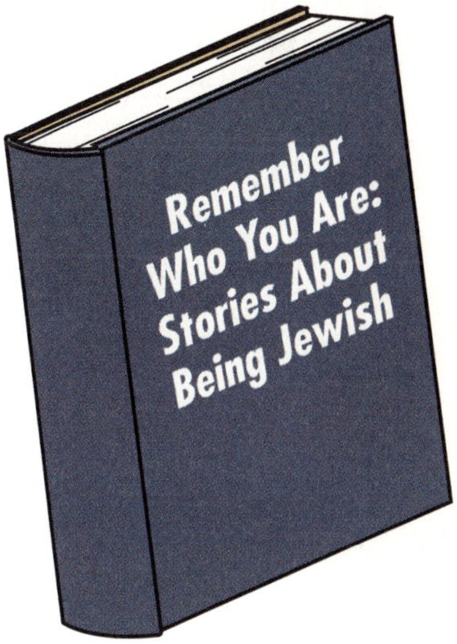

3. Choose the correct definition of **fiction**.

☐ stories that are true ☐ stories that are not true

4. Choose the correct definition of **lucrative**.

☐ interesting ☐ profitable ☐ nearby

Name ______________________________

Context Clues: Kids' Books Are Big Business

Between 1978 and 1988, the number of children's books published in the United States doubled. The publishing **industry**, which prints, promotes, and sells books, does not usually move this fast. Why? Because if publishers print too many books that don't sell, they lose money. They like to wait, if they can, to see what the "public demand" is for certain types of books. Then, they accept manuscripts from writers who have written the types of books the public seems to want. More than 4,600 children's books were published in 1988, because publishers thought they could sell that many titles. Many copies of each title were printed and sold to bookstores and libraries. The publishers made good profits and, since then, the number of children's books published each year has continued to grow.

The title of a recent new book for children is *The Wild Horses of Sweetbriar* by Natalie Kinsey-Warnock. It is the story of a girl and a band of wild horses that lived on an island off the coast of Massachusetts in 1903. The story sounds very exciting! Wild horses can be quite dangerous. The plot of *The Wild Horses of Sweetbriar* is probably filled with danger and suspense.

Directions: Answer these questions about how interest in writing, reading, and selling children's books has grown.

1. Use context clues to choose the correct definition of **industry**.

☐ booksellers ☐ writers ☐ entire business

2. If 4,600 books were sold in 1988, how many books were sold in 1978? ______________

3. The number of children's books published in the United States doubled between 1978 and 1988. Fact Opinion

4. *The Wild Horses of Sweetbriar* is the story of a girl and a band of wild horses that lived on an island in 1903. Fact Opinion

5. The story sounds very exciting! Fact Opinion

6. The plot of *The Wild Horses of Sweetbriar* is probably filled with danger and suspense. Fact Opinion

Name ______________________________

Context Clues: Leonardo da Vinci

Directions: Read the sentences below. Use context clues to figure out the meaning of the bold words.

1. Some people are **perplexed** when they look at *The Last Supper*, but others understand it immediately.

☐ unhappy ☐ happy ☐ puzzled

2. Because his model felt **melancholy** about the death of her child, da Vinci had music played to lift her spirits as he painted the *Mona Lisa*.

☐ sad ☐ unfriendly ☐ hostile

3. Because da Vinci's work is so famous, many people **erroneously** assume that he left behind many paintings. In fact, he left only 20.

☐ rightly ☐ correctly ☐ wrongly

4. Leonardo da Vinci was not like most other people. He didn't care what others thought of him—he led an interesting and **unconventional** life.

☐ dull ☐ not ordinary ☐ ordinary

5. The **composition** of *The Last Supper* is superb. All the parts of the painting seem to fit together beautifully.

☐ the picture frame ☐ parts of the picture

6. Leonardo's **genius** set him apart from people with ordinary minds. He never married, he had few friends, and he spent much of his time alone.

☐ great mental abilities ☐ great physical abilities

☐ improper way to do things ☐ proper way to do things

7. Because he was a loner, da Vinci worried no one would come to his funeral when he died. In his will, he set aside 70 cents each to hire 60 **mourners** to accompany his body to his grave.

☐ friends ☐ people who grieve ☐ people who smile

Name ______________________________

Facts and Opinions

A **fact** is information that can be proved.

Example: Hawaii is a state.

An **opinion** is a belief. It tells what someone thinks. It cannot be proved.

Example: Hawaii is the prettiest state.

Directions: Write **F** (fact) or **O** (opinion) on the line by each sentence. The first one has been done for you.

__F__ 1. Hawaii is the only island state.

______ 2. The best fishing is in Michigan.

______ 3. It is easy to find a job in Wyoming.

______ 4. Trenton is the capital of New Jersey.

______ 5. Kentucky is nicknamed the Bluegrass State.

______ 6. The friendliest people in the United States live in Georgia.

______ 7. The cleanest beaches are in California.

______ 8. Summers are most beautiful in Arizona.

______ 9. Only one percent of North Dakota is forest or woodland.

______ 10. New Mexico produces almost half of the nation's uranium.

______ 11. The first shots of the Civil War were fired in South Carolina on April 12, 1861.

______ 12. The varied geographical features of Washington include mountains, deserts, a rainforest, and a volcano.

______ 13. In 1959, Alaska and Hawaii became the 49th and 50th states admitted to the Union.

______ 14. Wyandotte Cave, one of the largest caves in the United States, is in Indiana.

Directions: Write one fact and one opinion about your own state.

Fact: ______________________________

____

Opinion: ______________________________

____

Name ______________________________

More Facts and Opinions

Directions: Write **F** if the statement is a fact. Write **O** if the statement is an opinion.

1. _____ The Grand Canyon is the most scenic site in the United States.

2. _____ Dinosaurs roamed Earth millions of years ago.

3. _____ Scientists have discovered how to clone sheep.

4. _____ All people should attend this fair.

5. _____ Purebreds are the best dogs to own because they are intelligent.

6. _____ Nobody likes being bald.

7. _____ Students should be required to get straight A's to participate in extracurricular activities.

8. _____ Reading is an important skill that is vital in many careers.

9. _____ Snakes do not make good pets.

10. _____ Many books have been written about animals.

11. _____ Thomas Edison invented the lightbulb.

12. _____ Most people like to read science fiction.

13. _____ Insects have three body parts.

Name ______________________________

Wolfways

Wolves are often pictured in fairy tales as ferocious animals, always ready to attack and kill anything they can catch. The Three Little Pigs flee from the "big, bad wolf." Little Red Riding Hood must beware of the wolf that dresses up like Grandma and wants to eat her. But are wolves really that vicious?

Wolves are social animals and live together in packs of anywhere from two or three to twenty wolves. Each pack has a male and a female leader called the *alpha wolves*. The leaders are usually the strongest and healthiest animals. Usually, only the alpha female has cubs. The members of a pack generally cooperate and get along with one another.

Wolves are often pictured howling at the moon. Scientists have discovered that the howl is actually a way of locating other wolves, assembling the pack, sounding an alarm, or announcing a kill. Besides their howl, wolves use body language to communicate. The position of their back, neck, ears, and tail send distinct messages that other wolves understand. A wolf with its ears and tail up is high-ranking. A wolf with its tail down is showing submission.

Because they are hunters, wolves have a strong sense of smell, much greater than a human's sense of smell. That means they can smell their prey while it's still far away, and they also know where their enemies are. Wolves use smell to mark the edges of their territory. This tells other wolves to stay away.

Wolves usually feed on large animals such as deer and elk, with the pack working together to bring down their prey. They kill only when they are hungry and need to eat.

Who are the worst enemies of wolves? Humans! Wolves are more likely to run from a person than to attack, but because of their ferocious reputation, they have been hunted and killed for years. Wolves were once common across much of North America, but they are now rare and can be found only in remote wooded regions.

Name ______________________________

Wolfways

Directions: The following sentences are either facts stating that something is true or opinions stating how someone may feel about something. Write **F** beside a statement if it is a fact, and **O** if it is an opinion.

1. ______ Wolves are big, bad, and ferocious.
2. ______ Wolves live in packs.
3. ______ I'd like to find a wolf in my yard.
4. ______ A wolf pack is very large.
5. ______ Members of wolf packs usually cooperate with one another.
6. ______ Wolves like to howl at the moon.
7. ______ A wolf's howl communicates a message to other wolves.
8. ______ Wolves have a strong sense of smell.
9. ______ Wolves hunt large animals.
10. ______ Elk tastes better to a wolf than other animals.
11. ______ When a wolf has its tail down, it is communicating a message to other wolves.
12. ______ Wolves are scary animals.

Directions: What is your opinion about the following statement: Wolves are ferocious animals that should be hunted and killed. Defend your opinion with facts from the article.

____

____

____

____

Name ______________________________

Scrambled Sentences

Directions: Unscramble each sentence below. Write it correctly on the lines. Then, if the sentence is a fact, write **F**. If it is an opinion, write **O**.

1. ____ U.S. Presidents Virginia eight in were born ____________________

____

2. ____ Mount Rushmore everyone should to see South Dakota to go ____________________

____

3. ____ can get sandwiches cheese steak great only you in Philadelphia ____________________

____

4. ____ vacation winter your best the Colorado place is to spend ____________________

____

5. ____ Mt. McKinley is the Alaska's United States point highest in the ____________________

____

6. ____ parks enjoy Utah's awesome all visitors really ____________________

____

7. ____ is state area in Rhode Island the smallest ____________________

____

8. ____ thinks is everyone that spectacular Yellowstone Park ____________________

____

9. ____ North America is only state on the Hawaii not the mainland of ____________________

____

10. ____ Union the first join to state the Delaware was ____________________

____

11. ____ beaches nicest the states coastal of all the has Florida ____________________

____

Name ______________________________

Then and Now

You **compare** to show how things are alike. You **contrast** to show how they are different. You can compare and contrast things, ideas, facts, people, or stories. Here are some clue words you can use to show readers that you are comparing or contrasting things.

similarly	in the same way	however	opposite
likewise	and	in contrast	different from
too	also	but	on the other hand
in addition	or	rather	

Directions: Read the following passage. Then, write three sentences that compare and three sentences that contrast the one-room school of the 1800s and your school today. Use clue words from the box.

Imagine that you live in a rural American town during the 1800s. Chances are you attend a one-room school with your brothers, sisters, and friends. There is only one teacher and she teaches all the grades. Your teacher doesn't stand for any nonsense either; she is a very strict disciplinarian. She has to be with 60 children in one room. Reading, writing, and arithmetic are the main subjects. You spend a lot of time memorizing because that is the method of learning. Everyone learns to read using William H. McGuffey's *Eclectic Reader*. These readers emphasize patriotism. Your teacher also stresses that to be a good American, you must work hard and be honest, thrifty, and courageous.

Compare ______________________________

____

____

____

____

Contrast ______________________________

____

____

____

____

Name ______________________________

Compare! Contrast! Choose!

Directions: Kobe wants to buy a bike and has saved $125. He found some information about one bike from a company online. He also cut out an ad from the newspaper for a similar bike. Help Kobe compare and contrast the two bikes. Complete the chart.

Rally Boy's Mountain Master

When it comes to bicycles for active, hard-playing boys, ages 10-14, sturdiness and safety are essential. This yellow and black 24"-wheel Mountain Master offers both and is sure to please both parents and kids. It features a unique oversized frame that makes getting on and off a snap, a large derailleur guard, alloy hubs and rims, and many other dependable components. A 21-speed drive train makes riding effortless. The twist shifters come equipped with an easy-to-read gear display to let you know what gear you're in. Top-notch linear pull brakes allow young riders to stop when they need to. The 1.95-inch all-terrain tires perform well on any surface. Your cost is only $229.99.*

*Price does not include shipping. Delivery 4-5 working days. Assembly required.

FOR SALE

Used boy's 24" blue Rally Mountain King bike 21-speed, easy-to-read gear shift display, pull brakes, large derailleur guard, and an extra set of 1.95 all-terrain tires. Just a year old, still like new. Perfect for a 10- to 14-year-old boy. Come and check it out. Take it for a spin around the block. Asking only $100. Call 555-1234 for more details.

Compare

Contrast

If you were Kobe, which bike would you buy? Why?

Name ______________________________

Mandy Muffet's Maze

Directions: Sometimes one cause can have many effects and lead to a series of events. Complete the maze to find out everything that happened to Mandy Muffet. Start at BEGIN and read the sentence in the first square. Then, read the sentence in a square that's above, below, or next to the one you're on. Decide which one has the correct effect and draw a line to connect the boxes. Continue to identify each effect in sequential order until you get to the end of the maze.

END (above the top right square)

Mandy Muffet screamed and tossed the bowl into the air.	The bowl fell to the floor.	The bowl broke into pieces.	Curds and whey spilled everywhere.	A doctor put Mrs. Muffet's leg in a cast.	Mandy Muffet said she'd never ever go to bed without supper.
The yucky arachnid scared the daylights out of Mandy Muffet.	A spider that had been hanging around saw the strange mixture and came down to get a better look.	She prepared an extra large bowl of curds and whey and sat down to eat on her tuffet.	Mrs. Muffet came running and slipped across the wet floor.	Mrs. Muffet went to the emergency room.	An ambulance arrived at the Muffet home.
Mandy Muffet wasn't hungry last night.	Mandy Muffet went to bed without supper.	Mandy Muffet was famished in the morning.	Mrs. Muffet fell over Missy Muffet's tuffet.	Poor Mrs. Muffet broke her ankle.	Mandy Muffet dialed 911.

BEGIN (below the bottom left square)

Name ______________________________

Niagara Falls

Niagara Falls is one of the most spectacular natural wonders of the world. Part of the Falls is in Ontario, Canada, and part is in New York State.

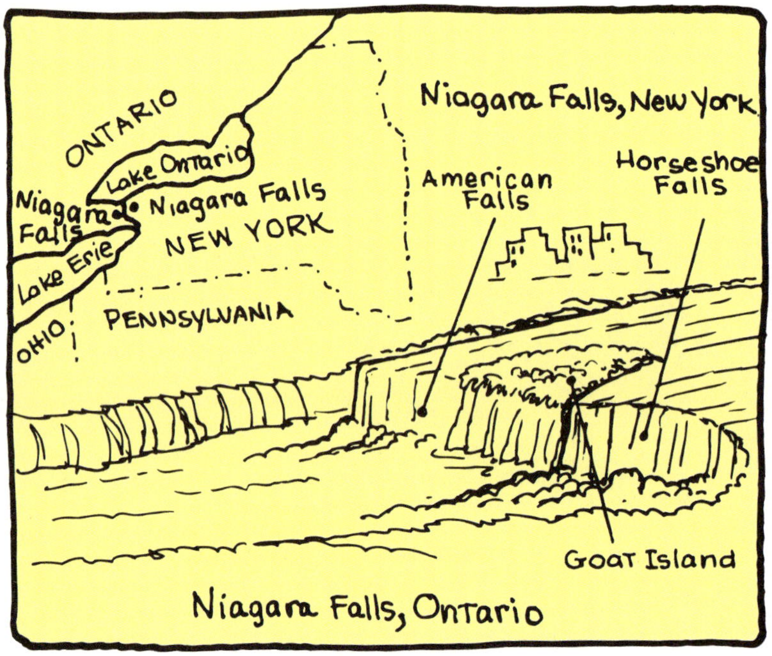

The Falls are supplied by the Niagara River, which connects Lake Ontario and Lake Erie. The Niagara Falls are located midway in the river. They pour 500,000 tons of water a minute into a deep gorge.

Scientists believe that Niagara Falls was formed after the last ice sheet from the Ice Age withdrew from the area. The surface of the land was changed by the ice. This caused waterways and streams to develop new paths. The result was an overflow of Lake Erie, which produced Niagara Falls. Scientists believe that the Falls are approximately 20,000 years old.

The Falls are formed over an outer layer of hard dolomitic limestone. This covers a softer layer of shale. The shale is more easily worn away, which causes the harder limestone to form an overhanging edge. This allows the Falls to drop straight down at a sharp angle, which produces a spectacular sight.

Over the years, the outer layer has broken off at times. This is causing the Falls to gradually move back up the river. This erosion is happening to the American Falls at the rate of three to seven inches a year. But the edge of the Horseshoe Falls is being worn back at the rate of approximately three feet a year.

Over the years, Niagara Falls has been a spectacular attraction for sightseers. Observation towers and a special area, Cave of the Winds, behind the Falls, have allowed remarkable views. At night, the Falls are flooded with lights. A steamer, called the Maid of the Mist, takes visitors for a ride around the base of the Falls.

Niagara Falls has also irresistibly drawn daredevils who have wanted to test their courage. One such man, Charles Blondin, crossed the Falls on a tightrope in 1859. Four days later, he crossed again, only this time with a blindfold. A month later, he crossed for the third time carrying a man on his shoulders. And as if that weren't daring enough, he returned to cross the Falls once again—on stilts!

Name ______________________

Niagara Falls

Directions: Answer the following questions about Niagara Falls.

1. What was the effect of the Ice Age on the region of Niagara Falls?

____

____

2. How have the attractions at Niagara Falls been changed to make them even more attractive for tourists?

____

____

3. The Falls are formed over a layer of dolomitic limestone and shale. What effect has the Falls had on these two surfaces?

____

____

____

4. What might be the effect of so many daredevils trying to cross over the Falls?

____

____

____

Directions: The **cause** is the reason for the action or **why** something happened. The **effect** is the result of the action or **what** actually happened. Match each effect to its correct cause.

Effect	Cause
1. remarkable views of the Falls from above	erosion
2. Niagara Falls was created	limestone overhanging edge
3. Niagara Falls drops down at a sharp angle	Maid of the Mist
4. waterways and streams developed new paths	overflow of Lake Erie
5. Horseshoe Falls is worn back three feet a year	ice sheets changed the land
6. visitors ride near base of the Falls	observation towers

Name ______________________________

Cause and Effect

A **cause** is an event or reason which has an effect on something else.

Example:

The heavy rains produced flooding in Chicago.
Heavy rains were the **cause** of the flooding in Chicago.

An **effect** is an event that results from a cause.

Example:

Flooding in Chicago was due to the heavy rains.
Flooding was the **effect** caused by the heavy rains.

Directions: Read the paragraphs. Complete the charts by writing the missing cause (reason) or effect (result).

Club-footed toads are small toads that live in the rainforests of Central and South America. Because they give off a poisonous substance on their skins, other animals cannot eat them.

Cause:	Effect:
They give off a poisonous substance.	______________________________

Civets (siv its) are weasel-like animals. The best known of the civets is the mongoose, which eats rats and snakes. For this reason, it is welcome around homes in its native India.

Cause:	Effect:
______________________________	It is welcome around homes in its native India.

Bluebirds can be found in most areas of the United States. Like other members of the thrush family of birds, young bluebirds have speckled breasts. This makes them difficult to see and helps them hide from their enemies. The Pilgrims called them "blue robins" because they are much like the English robin. They are the same size and have the same red breast and friendly song as the English robin.

Cause:	Effect:
Young bluebirds have speckled breasts.	______________________________
______________________________	The Pilgrims called them "blue robins."

The New Outfit

When you **predict**, you tell what you think will happen next. Predictions are based on things that have already happened.

Directions: Read each paragraph. Answer each set of questions. Then, write your own ending to the story.

Millie and her mother are shopping for a new outfit for a party at her father's office. Her father's boss will be there so it's important that Millie look nice. At the first store, Millie's mom chooses a dress with big flowers all over it and a frilly white collar. The dress Millie picks is simple, black, and very short. Her mom looks at the black dress and raises her eyebrow.

1. What will happen next? ______________________________

____

2. What makes you think so? ______________________________

____

Millie and her mom disagree. Millie says she will not wear the flowered dress. Millie's mom says she can't wear the black dress. Then Millie's mom has a suggestion.

3. What will the suggestion be? ______________________________

____

4. What makes you think so? ______________________________

____

Millie's mom suggests that they go to another store and try to find an outfit they can agree on. At the next store, Millie looks for a dress that isn't so short. Millie's mom looks for a dress that doesn't have a frilly white collar. When they meet at the dressing room, they are both holding the same dress!

5. What will happen next? ______________________________

____

Name ______________________________

To Your Health!

Directions: Read the following passage about the food pyramid. Then, answer the questions at the bottom of the page.

Have you ever skipped a meal and regretted it later? Have you ever felt tired or sluggish after eating junk food? Most of us can say "yes" to at least one of these questions. That's why it's so important that we use the food pyramid to help us eat properly.

The group at the bottom of the food pyramid is called the Bread, Cereal, Rice, and Pasta Group. Foods in this group contain **carbohydrates**, which give us energy. Foods high in carbohydrates and low in sugar, such as rice, wheat bread, pasta, and low-sugar cereals, provide lasting energy for school, play, and other activities.

The Vegetable Group is also important; vegetables contain **vitamins** and **minerals** to keep your body running smoothly and **fiber** to help digest your food properly. If you don't get the correct amount of vitamins, minerals, and fiber, it's hard for your body to process the other foods you eat. You might even get sick.

The Fruit Group provides more vitamins, as well as natural **sugar** (different from the sugar found in sweets). Natural sugar gives you concentrated bursts of energy—perfect for running in a short race, getting through that extra-long homework assignment, or keeping you from being hungry until dinnertime.

The Meat, Beans, Eggs, and Nuts Group is important because foods from this group give you the vitamins and minerals you need, as well as **protein**. Proteins are called the "building blocks" of life; they help build strong muscles and organs, as well as keep your body strong to fight off diseases. Even if you ate lots of carbohydrates and natural sugars, you would still get tired quickly if you weren't getting enough protein.

The Milk, Yogurt, and Cheese Group provides proteins and **calcium** for strong bones and teeth. Your bones and teeth have to last your entire life, so you need to get enough calcium to keep them healthy into your old age.

The Fats, Oils, and Sweets Group is at the top of the pyramid; that's because it contains foods with refined (not natural) sugar, **fats**, and artificial ingredients. You need some fat and sugar in your diet. However, you can get all the fats and sugar you need from foods in the other five food groups. So try not to eat too much from the Fats, Oils, and Sweets Group.

1. Predict what might happen to someone who ate lots of fruit and sugary foods but not enough foods from the Bread, Cereal, Rice, and Pasta Group.

____

____

2. Predict what might happen to someone who ate foods from the Fats, Oils, and Sweets Group; the Milk, Yogurt, and Cheese Group; and the Meat, Beans, Eggs, and Nuts Group—but not enough from the other groups.

____

____

Name ______________________________

In Conclusion . . .

A **conclusion** is a sensible decision you make from the information you have been given.

Directions: Read the following paragraphs and circle the sentences that are the best possible conclusions to each paragraph. Underline the information in each paragraph that helped you draw your conclusions.

1. Dale and his friends want to make a music video. They each want to play an instrument. No one wants to sing except Dale, but he doesn't have a good singing voice. Dale sings the song anyway.
   - Dale is a good piano player.
   - The song does not sound as good as it could.
   - Dale's friends are no good at playing their instruments.
   - They should get someone else to sing the song.

2. Carlos's class wants to act out a scene from the Civil War. All the actors must bring props and costumes to go with their characters. On Thursday, Carlos brings a suit, a fake beard, and a tall black top hat.
   - Carlos will be acting in the play.
   - Carlos will be a soldier in the play.
   - Carlos will be George Washington in the play.
   - Carlos will be Abraham Lincoln in the play.

3. Janice's friends stop by unexpectedly. They have been playing basketball all afternoon. They are very thirsty. Janice looks around her kitchen for something to drink, but there's no soda or juice. All she can find is sugar, bread, cereal, and some lemons. Then, she has an idea.
   - Janice eats some cereal.
   - Janice makes some lemonade.
   - Janice tells her friends not to stop by unexpectedly anymore.
   - Janice gives her friends some soda.

4. Michelle hasn't been to school all week. Her mother sent the teacher a note at the beginning of the week explaining that Michelle had a fever. The next day, Michelle's brother told the whole class that she was covered with itchy spots and that the doctor didn't want her around other children.
   - Michelle might have chicken pox.
   - Michelle is having a tooth removed.
   - Michelle can have her brother bring home her assignments.
   - Michelle can't come to school because she might make other children sick.

Name ______________________________

The Lady With the Lamp

Directions: Read the article below. Then, answer the questions.

Do you recognize the famous lady shown here? She is the Statue of Liberty, one of the most famous statues in the world. She has been an important symbol for immigrants to the United States for over 100 years.

France gave the statue to the United States as a gift in the late 19th century. It was designed by French artist Frederic Auguste Bartholdi and was constructed from tons of copper and iron. The statue was erected in New York Harbor in 1886, and, with its pedestal, it stands over 306 feet tall—making it also one of the largest statues in the world.

Millions of immigrants have passed the Statue of Liberty on their way to new lives in the United States. More than 12 million people were greeted by "The Lady With the Lamp" between the years of 1892 and 1924 alone!

Many of these people stopped at Ellis Island, a large immigration center near the statue. Important information was recorded there such as the names, occupations, and original nationalities of the immigrants. The immigration center was closed in 1954, but now there is a museum there. And people from all over the world are still greeted by the Statue of Liberty when they enter New York Harbor.

In 1903, Emma Lazarus wrote a poem to describe the Statue of Liberty and what it meant to the people who had passed it on their way to America. In the poem, the statue says, "with silent lips":

Give me your tired, your poor,
Your huddled masses yearning to breathe free,
The wretched refuse of your teeming shore.
Send these, the homeless, the tempest-tossed, to me;
I lift my lamp beside the golden door.

—from "The New Colossus"

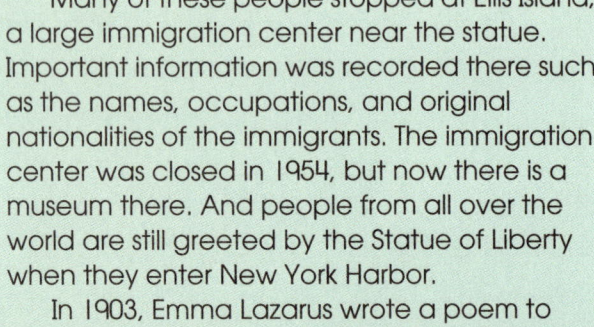

1. What do you think the Statue of Liberty is a symbol of? Use examples from the article to support your argument.

____

____

____

____

2. In the last line of the poem, what do the words "golden door" mean? Why do you think the author chose these words?

____

____

____

____

Bestseller Summaries

When you **summarize** something, you restate the important ideas from a piece of writing. A summary gives the most important information from a selection. It includes the topic, main idea, and details about the plot or information provided such as "who" or "what" the selection is about.

Directions: Read the short summaries below. Make a check mark next to each one that includes the topic, main idea, and important supporting details. If you think a summary is not complete, explain why on the lines below it.

☐ ***Cowboys of the Wild West***
by Russell Freedman

This book contains everything you ever wanted to know about the cowboy way of life: the equipment cowboys used, the clothing they wore, and the work they did. It also contains many exciting photographs to illustrate this adventurous and sometimes difficult profession.

____

____

____

☐ ***Little House on the Prairie***
by Laura Ingalls Wilder

In the 1800s, many families moved to the American West hoping to build better lives for themselves. The trip was not easy, and life on the frontier was sometimes tough, too.

____

____

____

☐ ***Galileo***
by Leonard Everett Fisher

This book is a biography of Galileo, one of the most famous astronomers of all time. It includes information about Galileo's life, scientific studies, and theories. It also explains why many people disagreed with his ideas.

____

____

____

☐ ***The Impressionists***
by Yolanda Baillet

This book is about Impressionism. Edgar Degas, Eduard Manet, Claude Monet, and Berthe Morisot were all important Impressionist painters.

____

____

____

☐ ***Treasure Island***
by Robert Louis Stevenson

This exciting book includes tales of pirates and treasure. It has many chapters, but you will enjoy reading it if you like adventure.

____

____

____

Name ______________________________

Get Organized

When writing summaries, it is sometimes helpful to make a graphic organizer, such as a story web, to help organize your ideas.

Directions: Read the article below. Then, fill in the story web, putting the main point in the middle and important details in the outer circles. Use the web to write a summary of the article on a separate sheet of paper.

When it comes to the best athletes in the world, animals have us beat. The strongest human weightlifter can lift about four times his or her own weight. An ant can pick up and carry 50 times its own weight.

When it comes to swimming, people definitely don't come in first. Olympic swimmers can reach speeds around 5 miles per hour. A tiny shrimp swims at around 2 miles per hour. But the fastest swimmer is the sailfish. It has been recorded going as fast as 68 miles per hour!

The fastest runner is the cheetah. It can run at speeds of up to 70 miles per hour. The fastest a person can run is about 27 miles an hour.

Compared to other animals, people do the best in the long jump. A person can jump about 30 feet. The kangaroo still wins, though. A kangaroo can jump about 43 feet!

Name ______________________________

One Wild Ride

You can use details from your reading to make **judgments**, or educated opinions, about what you have read.

Directions: Callie and Ryan are having an argument about amusement park rides. Use details from the argument to make your own judgment about which ride is better.

Callie and Ryan went to the park together. They agreed to go on the best ride first. But they had a decision to make. They could go to the Ultimate Scream Machine roller coaster or to the Wild Rapids water slide.

"Oh, let's go on the roller coaster first," said Callie.

"No way. Let's go on the best ride here, the water slide," said Ryan.

"How can you possibly think the water slide is the best ride? The roller coaster not only goes higher than the trees, but you also flip upside down twice," Callie said.

"The water slide is just as cool. It takes almost three minutes to climb the stairs up to the very top. The best part is there's no turning around once you get up there," Ryan explained.

"Well, once you think the roller coaster has stopped, you have to do the entire ride backwards. Besides, while you wait in line, you get to listen to everyone screaming while they are on the ride," Callie said.

"I've never done anything more exciting than jumping down a slide and flying through a huge tube into a pool," Ryan said.

1. What details does Callie give to make her argument? ______________________________

____

____

2. What details does Ryan give? ______________________________

____

____

3. Whose argument is stronger? What makes you think so? ______________________________

____

____

4. What is your own favorite ride? Why? ______________________________

____

____

Name ______________________________

A New Movie Theater

Because each person has different experiences, feelings, and opinions, everyone has his or her own **perspective**. In writing, perspective is the point of view from which something is written.

Directions: Residents of Oakdale are concerned about a new movie theater that is being built. Match each letter with the correct author. Use details from the letter to guess the perspective of each one.

Theodore T. Theobus, Mayor

Mrs. Lillian Tataki, a concerned mother

Walter Little, President of the Oakdale Historical Society

Angela Ardsley, a resident of Park Street

Dear Editor,

The children of this town don't need to spend more time inside watching movies and eating junk food. What they need is a new park where they can breathe fresh air and get exercise! I propose that, instead of building a movie theater at 199 Park Street, we turn the lot into a park for the families of Oakdale.

Signed,

____

____

Dear Editor,

I am opposed to building the movie theater on Park Street. Park Street is the town's oldest street and has many beautiful buildings dating back over 100 years. It was the site of the first house built in Oakdale and the original town hall. The new movie theater will be an eyesore and an insult to our town's heritage!

Yours truly,

____

____

Dear Editor,

We do not need a movie theater. If a movie theater is built on Park Street, traffic will get out of control and it will be dangerous to cross the street. It will also produce litter and noise which is totally unfair to people who live in the neighborhood!

Thank you,

____

____

Dear Editor,

The majority of the people in Oakdale have told me they want the movie theater. It will provide jobs and entertainment for the people of this town, and I want to provide them with what they want.

Sincerely,

____

____

Name ______________________________

Judging a Book by Its Cover

The **setting** of a story is the time and location in which it takes place.

Directions: The following is a collection of books for Mrs. Smith's class to read over the summer. But these books are missing their titles! First, look at each cover and identify the book's setting. Write the setting on the line underneath. Then, use this information to choose the correct book title from the choices in the box. Write the number in the small box.

1. Dr. Wizmo's Strange Experiment
2. Our Fantastic Journey
3. Big City Budget Tours
4. Exercising to Stay Healthy
5. Rover's Trip
6. Steve's Stupendous Shopping Spree
7. Growing Vegetables the Easy Way
8. Cooking With Grandpa

____

____

____

____

____

____

____

____

Name ____________________________

Story Theme Match-Up

The main idea or subject of a piece of writing is called its **theme**. You can usually figure out the theme of a work by reading it closely.

Directions: Below are examples of some common story themes. Read the six story excerpts and choose the theme that goes with each one. Write your choice on the line beneath each one. Each theme is used twice.

sportsmanship
perseverance
practice makes perfect

The events at field day were almost over and the students in Mr. Amato's class were feeling discouraged. Their class had won First Place only once. But they had received Second and Third places several times. When the scores were added up, they couldn't believe it—theirs was the winning class! All the students congratulated each other.

____

Andy felt tired. He didn't think he would be able to finish the run. People were clapping on the sidelines, but still he wanted to give up. He looked ahead and saw a stop sign at an intersection. He kept his eyes on the sign. In his mind, he said to himself over and over "Just get to the stop sign! Just get to the stop sign!" But right after he passed it, people started cheering wildly. The stop sign marked the end of the course, and he had finished!

____

Ginny followed the directions exactly. She measured all the ingredients as it said in the book. But the pie just didn't taste right. She knew it had something to do with either how she handled the dough or how she mixed the ingredients. To practice, she made pie every day for a week. Finally, on Friday, she made a perfect pie.

____

If Jessica's mom nagged her one more time about practicing the piano, she was going to scream. It was tedious and boring. Saturday finally arrived and she played her song for the director of the music school. While Jessica was waiting in the hallway, her mom came to tell her that she had played so well she had qualified for a scholarship to a performing arts camp.

____

The mathletes of Maywood School were on stage smiling, hooting, and accepting a huge trophy. Sitting in the audience with his team from Wayside, Justin knew that Maywood's team deserved the award. While his own team had also known the answers, Maywood's team had been quicker to respond to every question. Justin stood up and clapped for them.

____

RJ knew he needed to find a summer job. Each day, he looked in the classifieds and called every listing for restaurant help. On his eighth interview, he finally got a job at Rick's Raft House. He'd have to start as a dishwasher, but he would show them he could also be a great waiter.

____

Name ______________________________

Plot Out the Action

The **plot** is the main storyline in any work of fiction. The most important parts of a plot are:

background: the introduction; what the reader needs to know about the characters and the general situation	**conflict:** the problem that the main character/ characters must solve or the goal that he/she/they want to achieve	**rising action:** what the characters do to overcome the conflict; this may include encountering more problems	**climax:** usually the most exciting part of the story, often when character(s) must resolve the conflict	**falling action:** events that occur after the conflict has been resolved

Directions: Read this story about Luis. Then, answer the questions at the bottom of the page. Make sure to use complete sentences.

Luis's mom needed his help. She was planning a backyard party for his grandmother. She was so busy getting the house ready, she needed someone to help her do the shopping. She gave Luis her shopping list and $40.

Luis had been to the store many times before but never by himself. He got a cart and walked up the first aisle. As he put each item in the cart, he crossed it off the list.

While he was in the snacks aisle, he decided to add some things to the cart. His mom had written only pretzels on the list, but he put potato chips and popcorn in the cart, too. In the drink section, Luis added orange drinks and root beer.

When he got to the checkout, the cashier told him that the total was $47.25. But Luis had only $40. He couldn't believe his mother hadn't given him enough money! Then, he remembered that he had put extra things in the cart. He asked the cashier if he could put some of his items back. When she told him yes, he gave back the extra snacks and drinks. By doing this, he brought the total down to $38.

When Luis arrived home with the groceries, he unpacked them and told his mom what had happened. She thanked him and told him that next time he went to the grocery store, she would give him some extra money. That way he could choose something special to buy as a reward for helping her out!

1. Give the background for this story. ______________________________

____

2. What is the main conflict in this story? ______________________________

____

3. Describe the rising action of the story. ______________________________

____

Name ____________________

Doing Your Chores

Directions: Read the story. Then, fill in the story web with what you know about setting, plot, theme, and story elements.

Ellie and Allen were in the backyard playing basketball when Ellie's mother came out and reminded her to give her dog, Marley, a bath. Ellie hated this job because Marley hated his bath. Allen told Ellie he would help her. They came inside, picked up Marley, and took him down to the basement.

"I'll get the tub and fill it with water while you get the towels and shampoo," said Ellie.

"No problem," said Allen. When he put Marley down, the dog ran back up the stairs. So when Ellie and Allen had everything ready for the bath, they couldn't find Marley.

"He must have gone back upstairs," said Allen.

"Let's go find him," said Ellie.

They looked everywhere but couldn't find the dog. Ellie finally found him under the bed in her bedroom. But he wouldn't come out. He knew what was going to happen. Neither Ellie nor Allen could reach the dog because he was too far under the bed.

"I know!" said Ellie. She ran into the kitchen and put peanut butter on a small dog biscuit and brought it up to the bedroom.

She held it under the bed for Marley to smell. The lure of peanuts was too great for the dog. He came out from under the bed, and, as he took the cracker from Ellie, Allen grabbed him. They took him downstairs and finally gave him a bath.

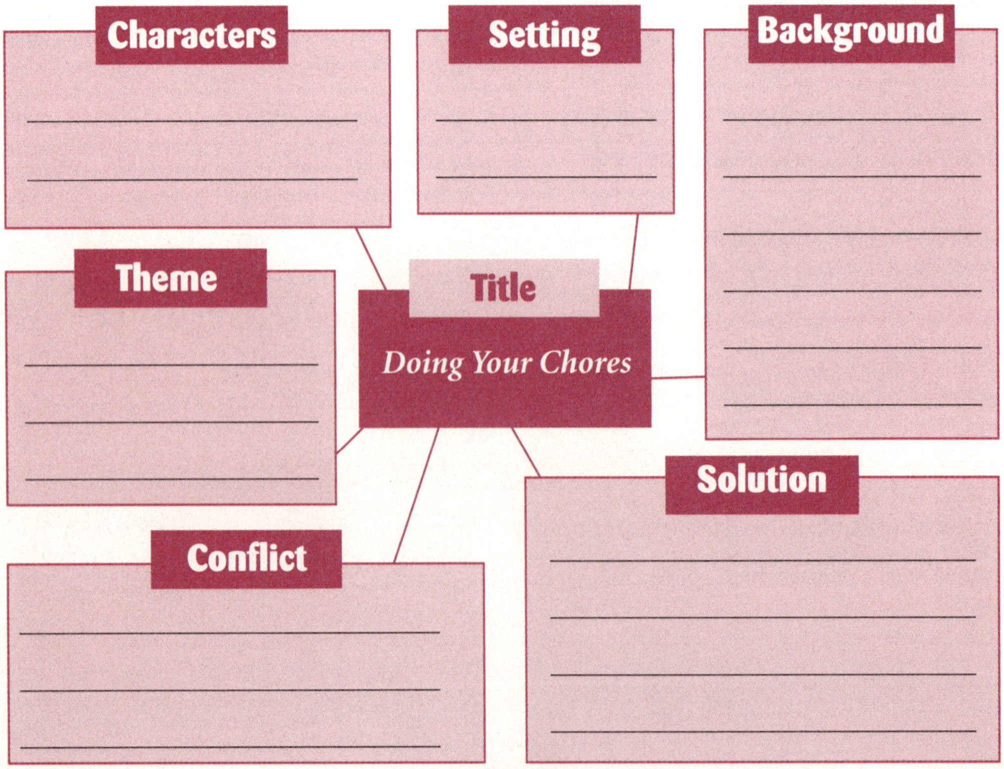

Name ______________________________

Half Empty?

Directions: Read what happens while Tim and Tom are in the park. Then, answer the questions at the bottom of the page. Use complete sentences.

On the way to the park, Tim stopped to see if Tom wanted to hang out at the park.

"It's such a sunny day, we should go to the park and see who is around," said Tim.

"It's too hot to be out in the sun," said Tom.

Riding to the park was easy since the road to the entrance was blocked off. There were no cars allowed on the street. The bike path started at the entrance to the park. They rode past the tennis courts, the picnic area, and the duck pond. Tim was smiling and cracking jokes the whole time. But Tom never smiled once. All of a sudden, it started to rain.

"This is great," said Tim. "The rain will cool things down."

"This isn't great," said Tom. "I'm going to get soaked. Let's just hurry up and get out of here."

As they curved around a bank of trees, there was a police barricade blocking off the bike path.

"I knew this wasn't going to be easy. Why did you talk me into this?" asked Tom.

Tim said, "Tom, my grandfather once put a glass of water on the table and asked me how much water was in it. I told him it was half full. He liked my answer. He said there are two kinds of people: the 'half-full' people and the 'half-empty' people. Tom, I think you should try to be a 'half-full' person."

"Yeah, well, why don't you just go and fill the glass with all the rain that's falling on us right now!" Tom said angrily.

1. Who are the characters in this story? ______________________________

2. On these lines, list the traits of each character in the story. ______________________________

____

____

____

____

3. What does Tim mean by the phrase "half-full"? Do you agree that Tom should try to be a "half-full" type of person? Why? ______________________________

____

____

____

Name ______________________________

The Amusement Park

Directions: Arrowhead Camp is spending a day at Six Banners Amusement Park. Read the story. Then, answer the questions at the bottom of the page. Circle your answers.

When the kids arrived at the park, Joe—the head counselor—gave them permssion to go explore the park on their own. They would all meet back at the big water fountain at 4:00. Cindy and Katie started looking at their map. Roberto and Bucky took off running down the path towards the roller coaster.

"See you later," Roberto yelled to the rest of the group as he sped off. He and Bucky didn't want to waste one second standing around talking! They planned to go on as many rides as possible in their short time at the park.

Cindy and Katie started walking and saw a hot dog stand.

"I'm a little hungry," Cindy said.

"I could go for something to eat, too," said Katie.

"I think I'll sit here in the shade while I eat," Cindy said after she got her lunch and drink.

"I'm going into the arcade to play some games," said Katie.

"Don't forget to be back in time for the dolphin show! It starts in twenty minutes," Cindy said.

By the time Cindy and Katie arrived at the dolphin show, Bucky and Roberto were already on their fourth ride. They had ridden the Scream Machine twice, the Dare Devil twice, and were waiting for their turn on the Big Splash.

"I can't wait to get soaked," said Bucky.

"How wet do you think we'll get?" asked Roberto.

"We'll have to wait and see," said Bucky.

When they got off the Big Splash, both boys were drenched. Six rides later, their clothes were still wet!

At quarter to four, Cindy and Katie got on the Ferris wheel. They knew they had plenty of time to ride the Ferris wheel before they had to be at the water fountain. But Bucky and Roberto were still waiting in line at the bumper cars. When they finally got into the ride, they were so excited they lost track of time. They didn't get back to the fountain until twenty after four!

"I'm glad I asked you to meet back here at 4:00. The bus isn't supposed to leave for another half an hour," said Joe as they arrived. "We'll still be on time getting home—even though Bucky and Roberto were late to meet the group!"

1. What is the best adjective to describe Joe?
   a. older
   b. counselor
   c. in charge
   d. practical

2. What is the reason that Bucky and Roberto were late to meet the group?
   a. They decided to ride the bumper cars.
   b. They wanted to go on as many rides as possible.
   c. They were already running toward the roller coaster when Joe told them to meet at 4:00.
   d. They lost track of time.

3. What is a good adjective to describe Bucky and Roberto?
   a. adventurous
   b. helpful
   c. friends
   d. fast

4. What is the reason Cindy and Katie were on time to meet the group?
   a. They were sure to leave enough time to ride the Ferris wheel before they had to meet the group at the water fountain.
   b. They read their map before entering the park.

Name ______________________

What a Character!

Directions: Who is your favorite TV character? List words to describe the character on the left side of the Venn diagram. Do the same for your favorite character from a book, listing his or her traits on the right. Make sure that any traits the two share are listed in the middle. Then, answer the questions at the bottom of the page.

Favorite TV Character ______________ Favorite Book Character ______________

Show: ______________ Book Title: ______________

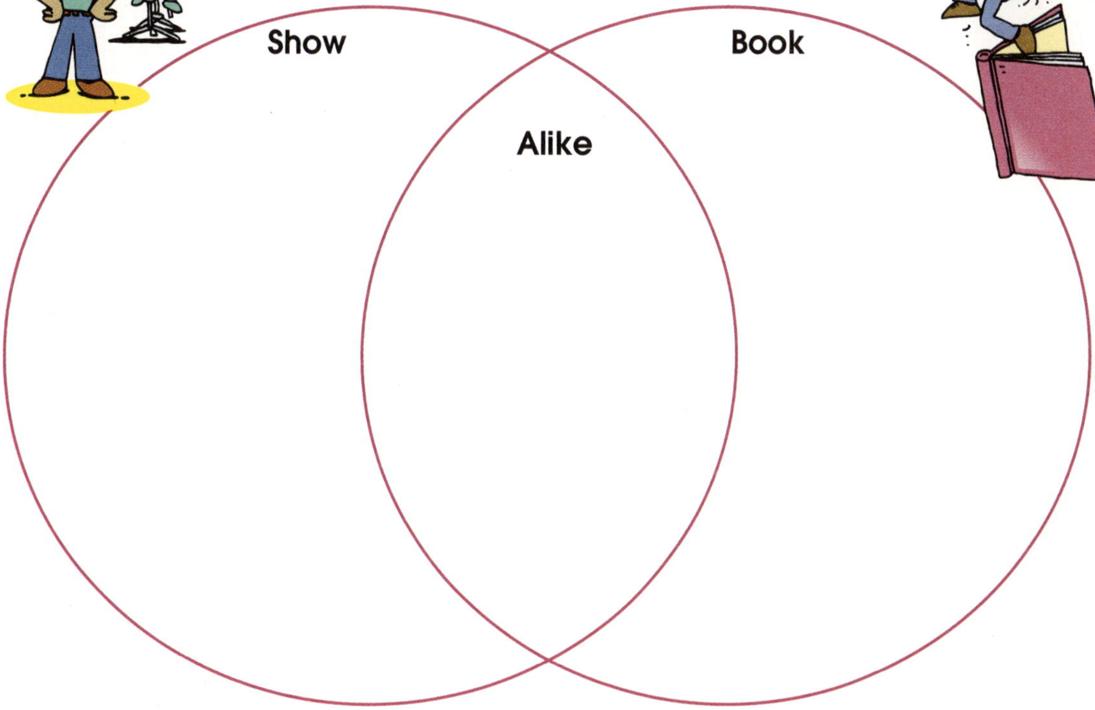

1. What is your favorite TV character's most unusual trait? ______________

____

____

2. What is your favorite book character's most unusual trait? ______________

____

____

Name ______________________________

Have It Your Way!

Directions: Here's your chance to create some crazy characters for a short story of your own! But there's a catch—each character must have certain traits, as shown on the chart below. Complete the chart with more ideas for each character. Then, use the chart to write a short story, at least four paragraphs long, on a separate sheet of paper.

	Physical Traits	Personality Traits	Other
Character #1	5 years old; brown hair and brown eyes		lives in the same house as character #3
Character #2 Louis		loves to play baseball	
Character #3	11 years old; boy; very tall; glasses		wants to go to the movies; fights a lot with little sister
Character #4	11 years old; girl	friendly; has known Louis for a long time	

Name ______________________________

Comprehension: Jaguars

The jaguar is a large cat, standing up to 2 feet tall at the shoulder. Its body can reach 73 inches long, and the tail can be another 30 inches long. The jaguar is characterized by its yellowish-red coat covered with black spots. The spots themselves are made up of a central spot surrounded by a circle of spots.

Jaguars are not known to attack humans, but some ranchers claim that jaguars attack their cattle. This claim has given jaguars a bad **reputation**.

The jaguar can be found in southern North America, but is most **populous** in Central and South America. Jaguars are capable climbers and swimmers, and they eat a wide range of animals.

Female jaguars have between one and four cubs after a **gestation** of 93 to 105 days. Cubs stay with the mother for 2 years. Jaguars are known to have a life expectancy of at least 22 years.

Directions: Use context clues for these definitions.

1. populous: ______________________________

2. reputation: ______________________________

3. gestation: ______________________________

Directions: Answer these questions about jaguars.

1. Describe the spots on a jaguar's coat.

____

____

2. Why would it be to a jaguar's advantage to have spots on its coat?

____

____

Name ____________________________________

Comprehension: Leopards

The leopard is a talented **nocturnal** hunter and can see very well in the dark. Because of its excellent climbing **ability**, the leopard is able to stalk and kill monkeys and baboons. Leopards are also known to **consume** mice, porcupines, and fruit.

Although the true leopard is characterized by a light beige coat with black spots, some leopards can be entirely black. These leopards are called *black panthers*. Many people refer to other cat species as leopards. Cheetahs are sometimes referred to as *hunting leopards*. The clouded leopard lives in southeastern Asia and has a grayish spotted coat. The snow leopard, which has a white coat, lives in Central Asia. A leopard's spots help to camouflage (cam-o-floj) it as it hunts.

True leopards can grow to over 6 feet long, not including their 3-foot-long tail. Leopards can be found in Africa and Asia.

Directions: Use context clues for these definitions.

1. consume: ____________________________________

2. ability: ____________________________________

3. nocturnal: ____________________________________

Directions: Answer these questions about leopards.

1. List three differences between the leopard and the jaguar.

____

____

____

____

____

____

2. What makes a leopard able to hunt monkeys and baboons?

____

Name ______________________________

Comprehension: Lynxes

Lynxes are strange-looking cats with very long legs and large paws. Their bodies are a mere 51 inches in length, and they have short tails. Most lynxes have a clump of hair that extends past the tip of their ears.

Lynxes not only are known to chase down their **prey**, but also to leap on them from a **perch** above the ground. They eat small mammals and birds, as well as an occasional deer.

There are four types of lynxes. Bobcats can be found in all areas of the United States except the Midwest. The Spanish lynx is an endangered species. The Eurasian lynx, also known as the northern lynx, and the Canadian lynx are two other kinds of lynxes.

Directions: Use context clues for these definitions.

1. prey: ______________________________

2. perch: ______________________________

Directions: Answer these questions about lynxes.

1. What are the four types of lynxes? ______________________________

____

2. Use the following words in a sentence of your own.

mammal ______________________________

endangered ______________________________

3. Do you believe it is important to classify animals as "endangered" to protect a species that is low in population? Explain your answer.

____

____

____

Name ______________________________

Comprehension: Pumas

The puma is a cat most recognized by the more popular names of "cougar" or "mountain lion." Just like other large cats, the puma is a carnivore. It feeds on deer, elk, and other mammals. It can be found in both North and South America.

Pumas have small heads with a single black spot above each eye. The coat color ranges from bluish-gray (North America) to reddish-brown (South America). The underside of the body, as well as the throat and muzzle, are white. The puma's body can be almost 6 feet long, not including the tail.

Female pumas give birth to two to four young. When first born, pumas have brown spots on their backs, and their tails are lined with dark brown rings.

As with the jaguar, pumas are blamed for killing cattle. Because of this, pumas are either nonexistent in some areas or are endangered.

Directions: Answer these questions about pumas.

1. What is a muzzle? ______________________________

2. As the population increases in North America, predict what might happen to pumas.

____

____

____

3. What are two other popular names for the puma? ______________________________

4. What other cat besides the puma is blamed for killing cattle? ______________________________

5. Reviewing the sizes of cats discussed so far, write their names in order, from smallest to largest.

1) ______________________________ 2) ______________________________

3) ______________________________ 4) ______________________________

Name ______________________________

Comprehension: Tigers

Tigers live on the continent of Asia. The tiger is the largest cat, often weighing over 500 pounds. Its body can grow to be 9 feet long and the tail up to 36 inches in length.

There are three types of tigers. The Siberian tiger is very **rare** and has a yellow coat with dark stripes. The Bengal tiger can be found in southeastern Asia and central India. Its coat is more orange and its stripes are darker. There is a tiger that lives on the island of Sumatra as well. It is smaller and darker in color than the Bengal tiger.

Tigers lead **solitary** lives. They meet with other tigers only to mate and share food or water. Tigers feed primarily on deer and cattle but are also known to eat fish and frogs. If necessary, tigers will also eat dead animals.

Female tigers bear one to six cubs at a time. The cubs stay with their mother for almost 2 years before going out on their own.

Because tiger parts are in high demand for use in Chinese medicine and recipes, tigers have been hunted almost to **extinction**. All tigers are currently listed as endangered.

Directions: Use context clues for these definitions.

1. rare: ______________________________

2. solitary: ______________________________

3. extinction: ______________________________

Directions: Answer these questions about tigers.

1. Why have tigers been hunted almost to extinction?

____

____

2. Name the three types of tigers.

____

Name ________________________________

Comprehension: Lions

The lion, often referred to as the king of beasts, once commanded a large **territory**. Today, their territory is very limited. Lions are **savanna**-dwelling animals, which has made them easy targets for hunters. The increasing population of humans and their livestock has also contributed to the lion's decreased population.

Lions are heavy cats. Males weigh over 500 pounds and can grow to be over 8 feet in length, with a tail more than 36 inches long. Males are characterized by a long, full mane that covers the neck and most of the head and shoulders. Females do not have a mane and are slightly smaller in size. Both males and females have beige coats, hooked claws, and powerful jaws. Their roars can be heard up to 5 miles away!

Lions tend to hunt in the evening and spend the day sleeping. They prefer hunting zebra or giraffe but will eat almost anything. A lion is **capable** of eating more than 75 pounds of meat at a single kill and then going a week without eating again. Generally, female lions do the hunting, and the males come to share the kill.

Lions live in groups called **prides**. Each pride has between 4 and 37 lions. Females bear one to four cubs approximately every 2 years.

Directions: Answer these questions about lions.

1. What are the differences between male and female lions? ________________________

____

2. Why would living on a savanna make the lion an "easy target"? ________________________

____

Directions: Use context clues for these definitions.

1. pride: ____

2. territory: ____

3. savanna: ____

4. capable: ____

Name ______________________________

Comprehension: All About Sheep

Did you ever wonder what really happened to the tails of Little Bo-Peep's sheep? Here's the real story.

When sheep are born, they are called *lambs*. Lambs are born with long tails. A few days after lambs are born, the shepherd cuts off their tails. Because they get dirty, the lambs' long tails can pick up lots of germs. Cutting them off helps to prevent disease. The procedure is called **docking**. This is probably what happened to Bo-Peep's sheep! Another shepherd must have cut off their tails without telling her.

Little lambs are cute. A lamb grows inside its mother for 150 days before it is born. This is called the *gestation period*. Some types of sheep, such as hill sheep, give birth to one lamb at a time. Other types of sheep, such as lowland sheep, give birth to two or three lambs at a time.

After it is born, it takes a lamb 3 or 4 days to recognize its mother. Once it does, it stays close to her until it is about 3 weeks old. After that, the lamb becomes friendly toward other lambs.

Young lambs then form play groups. They chase each other in circles. They butt into each other. Like children, they pretend to fight. When play gets too rough, the lambs run back to their mothers for protection.

Lambs follow their mothers as they graze on grass. Usually, sheep move in single file behind an older female sheep. Female sheep are called *ewes*. The ewes teach their lambs how to keep themselves clean. This is called *grooming*. Sheep groom only their faces. Here is how they do it: They lick one of their front legs, then they rub their faces against the spot they have licked.

Directions: Follow the instructions below.

1. Define the word **docking**. ______________________________

2. Name a type of sheep that gives birth to one lamb at a time. ____________

3. Name a type of sheep that gives birth to two or three lambs at a time.

____

4. Female sheep are called

☐ grazers. ☐ ewes. ☐ dockers.

5. Lambs begin playing in groups when they are

☐ 2 weeks old. ☐ 3 weeks old. ☐ 4 weeks old.

Name ______________________________

Comprehension: Pigs Are Particular

Have you ever wondered why pigs wallow in the mud? It's not because they are dirty animals. Pigs have no sweat glands. They can't sweat, so they roll in the mud to cool themselves. The next time you hear anyone who's hot say, "I'm sweating like a pig!" be sure to correct him or her. Humans can sweat but pigs cannot.

Actually, pigs are particular about their pens. They are very clean animals. They prefer to sleep in clean, dry places. They move their bowels and empty their bladders in another area. They do not want to get their homes dirty.

Another misconception about pigs is that they are smooth. Only cartoon pigs are pink, smooth, and shiny-looking. The skin of real pigs is covered with bristles—small, stiff hairs. Their bristles protect their tender skin. When pigs are slaughtered, their bristles are sometimes made into hair brushes or clothes brushes.

Female pigs are called *sows*. Sows have babies twice a year and give birth to 10 to 14 piglets at a time. The babies have a gestation period of 16 weeks before they are born.

All the piglets together are called a *litter*. Newborn piglets are on their tiny feet within a few minutes after birth. Can you guess why? They are hungrily looking for their mother's teats so they can get milk. As they nurse, piglets snuggle in close to their mother's belly to keep warm.

Directions: Answer these questions about pigs.

1. Why do pigs wallow in mud? ______________________________

2. How long is the gestation period for pigs? ______________________________

3. What are pig bristles used for? ______________________________

4. Tell two reasons pigs are on their feet soon after they are born.

1) ______________________________ 2) ______________________________

5. A female pig is called a

☐ bristle. ☐ piglet. ☐ sow.

6. Together, the newborn piglets are called a

☐ group. ☐ family. ☐ litter.

Name ____________________

Context Clues: No Kidding About Goats

Goats are independent creatures. Unlike sheep, which move easily in herds, goats cannot be driven along by a **goatherd**. They must be moved one or two at a time. Moving a big herd of goats can take a long time, so goatherds must be patient people.

Both male and female goats can have horns, but some goats don't have them at all. Male goats have beards but females do not. Male goats also have thicker and shaggier coats than females. During breeding season, when goats mate to produce babies, male goats have a very strong smell.

Goats are kept in **paddocks** with high fences. The fences are high because goats are good jumpers. They like to **nibble** on hedges and on the tips of young trees. They can cause a lot of damage this way! That is why many farmers keep their goats in a paddock.

Baby goats are called *kids,* and two or three at a time are born to the mother goat. Farmers usually begin to bottle-feed kids when they are a few days old. They milk the mother goat and keep the milk. Goat's milk is much easier to digest than cow's milk, and many people think it tastes **delicious**.

Directions: Answer these questions about goats.

1. Use context clues to choose the correct definition of **goatherd**.

☐ person who herds goats ☐ goats in a herd ☐ person who has heard of goats

2. Use context clues to choose the correct definition of **paddock**.

☐ pad ☐ fence ☐ pen

3. Use context clues to choose the correct definition of **nibble**.

☐ take small bites ☐ take small drinks ☐ take little sniffs

4. Use context clues to choose the correct definition of **delicious**.

☐ delicate ☐ tasty ☐ terrible

Name ____________________

Comprehension: Cows Are Complicated

If you believe cows have four stomachs, you're right! It sounds incredible, but it's true.

Here are the "hows" and "whys" of a cow's digestive system. First, it's important to know that cows do not have front teeth. They eat grass by wrapping their tongues around it and pulling it from the ground. They do have back teeth, but still they cannot properly chew the grass.

Cows swallow grass without chewing it. When it's swallowed, the grass goes into the cow's first stomach, called a *rumen* (roo-mun). There, it is broken up by the digestive juices and forms into a ball of grass. This ball is called a *cud*. The cow is able to bring the cud back up into its mouth. Then, the cow chews the cud into a pulp with its back teeth and re-swallows it.

After it is swallowed the second time, the cud goes into the cow's second stomach. This second stomach is called the *reticulum* (re-tick-u-lum). The reticulum filters the food to sort out any small stones or other non-food matter. Then it passes the food onto the cow's third stomach. The third stomach is called the *omasum* (oh-mass-um).

From there, any food that is still undigested is sent back to the first stomach so the cow can bring it back up into her mouth and chew it some more. The rest goes into the cow's fourth stomach. The fourth stomach is called the *abomasum* (ab-oh-ma-sum). Digesting food that can be turned into milk is a full-time job for cows!

Directions: Answer these questions about cows.

1. List in order the names of a cow's four stomachs.

1) ____________ 2) ____________ 3) ____________ 4) ____________

2. What is the name of the ball of grass a cow chews on? ____________

3. A cow has no

☐ front teeth. ☐ back teeth. ☐ fourth stomach.

4. Which stomach acts as a filter for digestion?

☐ reticulum ☐ rumen ☐ abomasum

Name ______________________________

Context Clues: Dairy Cows

Some cows are raised for beef. Other cows, called *dairy cows*, are raised for milk. A dairy cow cannot produce any milk until after its first calf is born. Cows are not mature enough to give birth until they are 2 years old. A cow's gestation period is 40 weeks long, and she usually gives birth to one calf. Then she produces a lot of milk to feed it. When the calf is 2 days old, the dairy farmer takes the calf away from its mother. After that, the cow is milked twice a day.

The dairy cow's milk comes from the large, smooth udder beneath her body. The udder has four openings called *teats*. To milk the cow, the farmer **grasps** a teat and squeezes it with his thumb and forefinger. Then he gently but firmly pulls his hand down the teat to squeeze the milk out. Milking machines that are hooked to the cow's teats **duplicate** this action and can milk many cows quickly.

A dairy cow's milk production is not at the same level all the time. When the cow is pregnant, milk production gradually **decreases**. For 2 months before her calf is born, a cow is said to be "dry" and is not milked. This happens because, like humans, much of the cow's food is actually being used to nourish the unborn calf.

Farmers give the cow extra food at this time to make sure the mother and unborn calf are **well-nourished**. Again, like humans, well-nourished mother cows are more likely to produce healthy babies.

Directions: Answer these questions about dairy cows.

1. Use context clues to choose the correct definition of **grasp**.

☐ pull firmly ☐ hold firmly ☐ hold gently

2. Use context clues to choose the correct definition of **duplicate**.

☐ correct ☐ make ☐ copy

3. Use context clues to choose the correct definition of **decrease**.

☐ become more ☐ become less ☐ become quicker

4. Use context clues to choose the correct definition of **nourish**.

☐ to be happy ☐ to be friendly ☐ to feed

Name ______________________________

Comprehension: Chickens

Have you ever heard the expression "pecking order"? In the pecking order of a school, the principal is at the top of the order. Next comes the assistant principal, then the teachers and students.

In the pecking order of chickens, the most **aggressive** chicken is the leader. The leader is the hen that uses her beak most often to peck the chickens she bosses. These chickens, in turn, boss other chickens by pecking them, and so on. Chickens can peck all others who are "below" them in the pecking order. They never peck "above" themselves by pecking their bosses.

Directions: Answer these questions about chickens.

1. Put this pecking order of four chickens in order.

_______ This chicken pecks numbers 3 and 4 but never 1.

_______ No one pecks this chicken. She's the top boss.

_______ This chicken can't peck anyone.

_______ This chicken pecks chicken number 4.

2. Use context clues to figure out the definition of **aggressive**. ______________________

____

____

3. Who is at the top of the pecking order in a school? ______________________

____

Name ______________________________

Comprehension: Cooking With Care

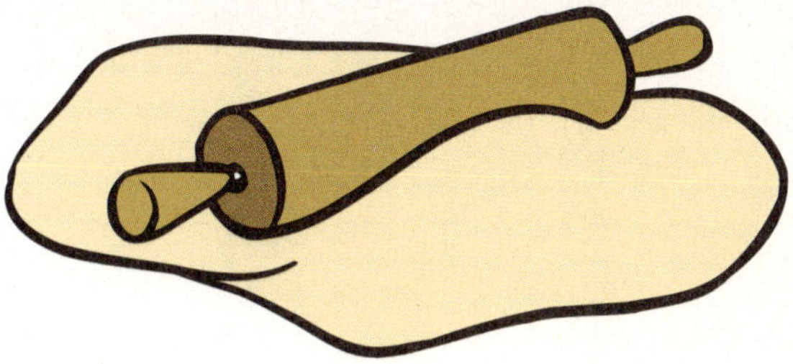

People are so busy these days that many have no time to cook. This creates a problem, because most families love home cooking! The food tastes good and warm, and a family meal brings everyone together. In some families, meals are often the only times everyone sees one another at the same time.

Another reason people enjoy home cooking is that it is often a way of showing love. A parent who bakes a batch of chocolate chip cookies isn't just satisfying a child's sweet tooth. He or she is sending a message. The message says, "I care about you enough to spend an hour making cookies that you will eat up in 15 minutes if I let you!"

There's also something about the smell of good cooking that appeals to people of all ages. It makes most of us feel secure and loved—even if we are the ones doing the cooking! Next time you smell a cake baking, stop for a moment and pay attention to your mood. Chances are, the good smell is making you feel happy.

Real estate agents know that good cooking smells are important. They sometimes advise people whose homes are for sale to bake cookies or bread if prospective buyers are coming to see the house. The good smells make the place "feel like home." These pleasant smells help convince potential buyers that the house would make a good home for their family, too!

Directions: Answer these questions about good cooking.

1. Why do fewer people cook nowadays? ______________________________

2. Why are family meals important? ______________________________

3. What do homemade cookies do besides satisfy a child's sweet tooth?

____

4. Real estate agents often advise home sellers holding open houses to

☐ clean the garage. ☐ bake cookies or bread.

5. The smell of baking at open houses may encourage buyers to

☐ bake cookies. ☐ buy the house. ☐ bake bread.

Name ________________________________

Comprehension: Eating High-Fiber Foods

Have you heard your parents or other adults talk about "high-fiber" diets? Foods that are high in fiber, like oats and other grains, are believed to be very healthy. Here's why: The fiber adds bulk to the food the body digests and helps keep the large intestines working properly. Corn, apples, celery, nuts, and other chewy foods also contain fiber that helps keep the body's systems for digesting and eliminating food working properly.

Researchers at the University of Minnesota have found another good reason to eat high-fiber food, especially at breakfast. Because fiber is bulky, it absorbs a lot of liquid in the stomach. As it absorbs the liquid, it swells. This "fools" the stomach into thinking it's full. As a result, when lunchtime comes, those who have eaten a high-fiber breakfast are not as hungry. They eat less food at lunch. Without much effort on their parts, dieters eating a high-fiber breakfast can lose weight.

The university researchers say a person could lose 10 pounds in a year just by eating a high-fiber breakfast! This is good news to people who are only slightly overweight and want an easy method for losing that extra 10 pounds.

Directions: Answer these questions about eating high-fiber foods.

1. Why is fiber healthy? ________________________________

____

2. How does fiber "fool" the stomach? ________________________________

____

3. How does "fooling" the stomach help people lose weight? ________________________________

____

4. How many pounds could a dieter eating a high-fiber breakfast lose in a year?

☐ 20 pounds ☐ 30 pounds ☐ 10 pounds

5. The university that did the research is in which state?

☐ Michigan ☐ Minnesota ☐ Montana

Name ______________________________

Comprehension: The French Eat Differently

Many people believe that French people are very different from Americans. This is certainly true where eating habits are concerned! According to a report by the World Health Organization, each year the French people eat four times more butter than Americans. The French also eat twice as much cheese! In addition, they eat more vegetables, potatoes, grain, and fish.

Yet, despite the fact that they eat larger amounts of these foods, the French take in about the same number of calories each day as Americans. (French and American men consume about 2,500 calories daily. French and American women take in about 1,600 calories daily.)

How can this be? If the French are eating more of certain types of foods, shouldn't this add up to more calories? And why are so few French people overweight compared to Americans? The answer—Americans consume 18 times more refined sugar than the French and drink twice as much whole milk!

Although many Americans believe the French end each meal with grand and gooey desserts, this just isn't so. Except for special occasions, dessert in a typical French home consists of fresh fruit or cheese. Many American families, on the other hand, like to end their meals with a bowl or two of ice cream or another sweet treat.

It's believed that this difference in the kind of calories consumed—rather than in the total number of calories taken in—is what causes many Americans to be chubby and most French people to be thin.

Directions: Answer these questions about the eating habits of French and American people.

1. How many calories does the average French man eat each day? ____________

2. How much whole milk does the average French person drink compared to the average American? ______________________________

3. How much more refined sugar do Americans eat than the French?

☐ 2 times more ☐ 18 times more ☐ 15 times more

4. What do French families usually eat for dessert?

☐ refined sugar ☐ ice cream ☐ fruit and cheese

Name ______________________________

Comprehension: Chinese Cabbage

Many Americans enjoy Chinese food. In big cities, like New York and Chicago, many Chinese restaurants deliver their food in small boxes to homes. It's just like ordering a pizza! Then, the people who ordered the "take-out" food simply open it, put it on their plates, and eat it while it's hot.

Because it tastes so good, many people are curious about the ingredients in Chinese food. Siu choy and choy sum are two types of Chinese cabbage that many people enjoy eating. Siu choy grows to be 2 to 3 feet! Of course, it is chopped into small pieces before it is cooked and served. Its leaves are light green and soft. It is not crunchy like American cabbage. Siu choy is used in soups and stews. Sometimes it is pickled with vinegar and other ingredients and served as a side dish to other courses.

Choy sum looks and tastes different from siu choy. Choy sum grows to be only 8 to 10 inches. It is a flowering cabbage that grows small yellow flowers. The flowers are "edible," which means they can be eaten. Its leaves are long and bright green. After its leaves are boiled for 4 minutes, choy sum is often served as a salad. Oil and oyster sauce are mixed together and poured over choy sum as a salad dressing.

Directions: Answer these questions about Chinese cabbage.

1. Which Chinese cabbage grows small yellow flowers? ____________________

2. Which Chinese cabbage is served as a salad? ____________________

3. Is siu choy crunchy? ____________________

4. What ingredients are in the salad dressing used on choy sum?

____

5. To what size does siu choy grow? ____________________

6. Name two main dishes in which siu choy is used. ____________________

Name ______________________________

Comprehension: Roman Legends

Long ago, people did not know as much about science and astronomy as they do today. When they did not understand something, they thought the "gods" were responsible. The ancient Romans believed there were many gods and that each god or goddess (a female god) was responsible for certain things.

For example, the Romans believed Ceres (Sir-eez) was the goddess who made flowers, plants, trees, and other things grow. She was a lot like what people today refer to as Mother Nature. Ceres was also responsible for the good weather that made crops grow. You can see why Ceres was such an important goddess to the ancient Romans.

Apollo was the god of the sun. People believed he used his chariot to pull the sun up each day and take it down at night. Apollo was extremely good-looking. His home was a golden palace near the sun surrounded by fluffy white clouds. Apollo had to work every single day, but he lived a wonderful life.

Jupiter was the most important god of all. He was the god who ruled all of the other gods, as well as the people. Jupiter was also called Jove. Maybe you have heard someone use the exclamation, "By Jove!" That person is talking about Jupiter! The word **father** is derived from the word "Jupiter." Although he did not really exist, Jupiter influenced our language.

Directions: Answer these questions about Roman legends.

1. What imaginary figure is Ceres compared to today? ______________________________

2. Where did Apollo live? ______________________________

3. The word **father** is derived from the name of this god:

☐ Ceres ☐ Apollo ☐ Jupiter

4. Which is not true of Apollo?

☐ He had to work every day.

☐ He lived in a mountain cave.

☐ He was very handsome.

Comprehension: Apollo and Phaethon

Apollo, the sun god, had a son named Phaethon (Fay-a-thun). Like most boys, Phaethon was proud of his father. He liked to brag to his friends about Apollo's important job, but no one believed that the great Apollo was his father.

Phaethon thought of a way to prove to his friends that he was telling the truth. He went to Apollo and asked if he could drive the chariot of the sun. If his friends saw him making the sun rise and set, they would be awestruck!

Apollo did not want to let Phaethon drive the chariot. He was afraid Phaethon was not strong enough to control the horses. But Phaethon begged until Apollo gave in. "Stay on the path," Apollo said. "If you dip too low, the sun will catch the earth on fire. If you go too high, people will freeze."

Unfortunately, Apollo's worst fears came true. Phaethon could not control the horses. He let them pull the chariot of the sun too close to the earth. To keep the earth from burning, Jupiter, father of the gods, sent a thunderbolt that hit Phaethon and knocked him from the driver's seat. When Phaethon let go of the reins, the horses pulled the chariot back up onto the proper path. Phaethon was killed as he fell to earth. His body caught fire and became a shooting star.

Directions: Answer these questions about the Roman legend of Apollo and his son.

1. Who did not believe Apollo was Phaethon's father? ______________________________

2. What did Phaethon do to prove Apollo was his father? ______________________________

____

3. Why did Jupiter send a lightning bolt? ______________________________

____

4. Which was not a warning from Apollo to Phaethon?

☐ Don't go too close to the earth. It will burn up.

☐ Don't pet the horses. They will run wild.

☐ Don't go too far from the earth. It will freeze.

Name ______________________________

Context Clues: Mighty Hercules

Some people lift weights to build their strength. But Hercules (Her-cu-lees) had a different idea. He carried a calf on his shoulders every day. As the calf grew, it got heavier, and Hercules got stronger. Eventually, Hercules could carry a full-grown bull!

Hercules used his **enormous** strength to do many kind things. He became famous. Even the king had heard of Hercules! He called for Hercules to kill a lion that had killed many people in his kingdom. Hercules tracked the lion to its **den** and **strangled** it. Then, Hercules made clothes for himself from the lion's skin. This kind of **apparel** was unusual, and soon Hercules was recognized everywhere he went. Hercules was big and his clothes made it easy to pick him out in a crowd!

The king asked Hercules to stay in his kingdom and help protect the people who lived there. Hercules performed many **feats** of strength and bravery. He caught a golden deer for the king. The deer had outrun everyone else. Then Hercules killed a giant, a dragon and other dangerous creatures. Hercules became a hero and was known throughout the kingdom.

Directions: Answer these questions about Hercules.

1. Use context clues to choose the correct definition of **enormous**.

☐ huge ☐ tiny ☐ smart

2. Use context clues to choose the correct definition of **strangle**.

☐ beat ☐ choke ☐ tickle

3. Use context clues to choose the correct definition of **den**.

☐ pond ☐ hutch ☐ home

4. Use context clues to choose the correct definition of **apparel**.

☐ appearance ☐ clothing ☐ personality

5. Use context clues to choose the correct definition of **feat**.

☐ trick ☐ treat ☐ act

Name ______________________________

Comprehension: Ceres and Venus

Remember Ceres? She was like Mother Nature to the ancient Romans.

Ceres made the flowers, plants, and trees grow. She made crops come up and rain fall. Ceres was a very important goddess. The ancient Romans depended on her for many things.

Although the gods and goddesses were important, they had faults like ordinary people. They argued with one another. Sometimes they got mad and lost their tempers. This is what happened to Ceres and another goddess named Venus (Veen-us). Venus, who was the goddess of love and beauty, got mad at Ceres. She decided to hurt Ceres by causing Pluto, gloomy god of the underworld, to fall in love with Ceres' daughter, Proserpine (Pro-sur-pin-ay).

To accomplish this, Venus sent her son Cupid to shoot Pluto with his bow and arrow. Venus told Cupid that the man shot by this arrow would then fall in love with the first woman he saw. Venus instructed Cupid to make sure that woman was Ceres' daughter. Cupid waited with his bow and arrow until Pluto drove by Ceres' garden in his chariot. In the garden was Proserpine. Just as Pluto's chariot got near her, Cupid shot his arrow.

Ping! The arrow hit Pluto. It did not hurt, but it did its job well. Pluto fell instantly in love with poor Proserpine, who was quietly planting flowers. Pluto was not a gentleman. He did not even introduce himself! Pluto swooped down and carried Proserpine off in his chariot before she could call for help.

Directions: Answer these questions about Ceres and Venus.

1. With whom was Venus angry? ______________________________

2. How did Venus decide to get even? ______________________________

____

3. Ceres' daughter's name was

☐ Persperpine. ☐ Prosperline. ☐ Proserpine.

4. Venus' son's name was

☐ Apollo. ☐ Cupid. ☐ Persperpine.

Comprehension: Proserpine and Pluto

Proserpine was terrified in Pluto's palace in the underworld. She missed her mother, Ceres, and would not stop crying.

When Ceres discovered her daughter was missing, she searched the whole earth looking for her. Of course, she did not find her. Ceres was so unhappy about Proserpine's disappearance that she refused to do her job, which was to make things grow. When Ceres did not work, rain could not fall and crops could not grow. Finally, Ceres went to Jupiter for help.

Jupiter was powerful, but so was Pluto. Jupiter told Ceres he could get Proserpine back from Pluto if she had not eaten any of Pluto's food. As it turned out, Proserpine had eaten something. She had swallowed six seeds from a piece of fruit. Because he felt sorry for the people on earth who were suffering, Pluto told Jupiter that Proserpine could return temporarily to Ceres so she would cheer up and make crops grow again. But Pluto later came back for Proserpine and forced her to spend six months each year with him in the underworld—one month for each seed she had eaten. Every time she returned to the underworld, Ceres mourned and refused to do her job. This is how the Romans explained the seasons—when Proserpine is on earth with Ceres, it is spring and summer; when Proserpine goes to the underworld, it is fall and winter.

Directions: Answer these questions about Proserpine and Pluto.

1. What happened to Ceres when Pluto took her daughter? ______________________

____

2. Whom did Ceres ask for help to get her daughter back? ______________________

3. Why did Proserpine have to return to Pluto's underworld? ______________________

____

4. How long did Proserpine have to stay in the underworld each time she returned?

____

Name ____________________

Comprehension: Orpheus Saves the Day

Orpheus (Or-fee-us) was a talented Greek musician. Once, by playing beautiful music on his lyre (ly-er), he caused a ship that was stuck in the sand to move into the water. (A lyre is a stringed instrument that looks like a small harp and fits in the musician's lap.) The song was about how wonderful it was to sail upon the sea. The ship itself must have thought the song was wonderful, too, because it slipped into the water and sailed away!

There was a reason the ship understood Orpheus' song. Inside the ship was a piece of wood that a goddess had given to the captain of the ship. The captain's name was Jason. Once, Jason had helped an old woman across a deep river. He later learned that the old woman was a goddess. To thank him, the goddess gave Jason a piece of wood that could talk. She told him to use the wood when he built a new ship. If he ever got stuck while building the ship and did not know what to do, the goddess told Jason to ask the wood.

Several times, Jason and his crew got instructions from the wood. Finally, the ship was finished. It was beautiful and very large. Because it was so big, Jason and his men were unable to move it into the water. They called on Hercules for help, and even he could not make it budge. That's when Orpheus saved the day with his lyre.

Directions: Answer these questions about Orpheus' amazing talent.

1. Who owned the ship that was stuck? ____________________

2. Where was the ship stuck? ____________________

3. Why did the ship get stuck? ____________________

4. A lyre looks like what other instrument?

☐ harmonica ☐ guitar ☐ harp

5. Who did Jason first ask for help to move the ship?

☐ Orpheus ☐ Hercules ☐ Jupiter

Name ______________________________

Comprehension: The *Constitution*

The *Constitution*, or "Old Ironsides," was built by the United States Navy in 1798. Its success in battle made it one of the most famous vessels in the United States.

The *Constitution's* naval career began with the war with Tripoli from 1803 to 1804. Later, it was also used in the War of 1812. During this war, it was commanded by Isaac Hull. The *Constitution* won a 30-minute battle with the British ship, *Guerriere*, in August of 1812. The *Guerriere* was nearly demolished. Later that same year, the *Constitution* was used to capture a British frigate near Brazil.

The *Constitution* was taken out of service in 1829 and was rebuilt many times over the years. Today, it is on display at the Boston Navy Yard.

Directions: Answer these questions about the *Constitution*.

1. What is the main idea of the selection? ______________________________

____

2. Which ship was almost demolished by the *Constitution*? ______________________________

3. In which two wars was the *Constitution* used? ______________________________

4. Where is the *Constitution* now on display? ______________________________

5. Complete the following time line with dates and events described above.

_________ _________ _________ _________ _________

Name ______________________________

Comprehension: The *Santa Maria, Niña,* and *Pinta*

When Christopher Columbus decided to attempt a voyage across the ocean, the ships he depended upon to take him there were called *caravels.* A caravel is a small sailing ship built by Spain and Portugal in the 15th and 16th centuries. The caravels Columbus used to sail to the New World were named the *Santa Maria, Niña,* and *Pinta.*

The ships were not very large. It is believed the *Santa Maria* was only 75 to 90 feet long, and the *Niña* and *Pinta* were only about 70 feet long. Caravels typically had three to four masts with sails attached. The foremast carried a square sail, while the others were more triangular in shape. These triangular-shaped sails were called *lateen sails.*

These three small ships were quite seaworthy and proved excellent ships for Columbus. They got him where he wanted to go.

Directions: Answer these questions about the *Santa Maria, Niña,* and *Pinta.*

1. What is a lateen sail? ______________________________

2. What is the main idea of the selection? ______________________________

____

____

3. What is a caravel? ______________________________

4. Where did Columbus sail in his caravels? ______________________________

5. Do some research and compare a 15th-century caravel with a ship built in the 20th century.

____

____

____

____

Name ____________________

Comprehension: The *Lusitania*

The *Lusitania* was a British passenger steamship. It became famous when it was torpedoed and sunk by the Germans during World War I. On May 7, 1915, the *Lusitania* was traveling off the coast of Ireland when a German submarine fired on it without warning. The ship stood no chance of surviving the attack and sunk in an astonishing 20 minutes. 1,198 people **perished**, of whom 128 were American citizens. At the time the ship was torpedoed, the United States was not yet involved in the war. Public opinion over the attack put pressure on President Woodrow Wilson to declare war on Germany. The Germans **proclaimed** that the *Lusitania* was carrying weapons for the use of the **allies**.

This claim was later proven to be true. President Wilson demanded that the German government apologize for the sinking and make **amends**. Germany did not accept responsibility but did promise to avoid sinking any more passenger ships without first giving a warning.

Directions: Answer these questions about the *Lusitania*.

1. What does **proclaimed** mean? ____________________

2. What does **perished** mean? ____________________

3. What does **amends** mean? ____________________

4. What does **allies** mean? ____________________

5. If the *Lusitania* was carrying arms, do you think the Germans had a right to sink it? Why or why not?

____

____

____

____

Name ______________________________

Comprehension: The *Titanic*

The British passenger ship, the *Titanic*, debuted in the spring of 1912. It was billed as an unsinkable ship due to its construction. It had 16 watertight compartments that would hold the ship afloat even in the event that four of the compartments were damaged.

But on the evening of April 14, 1912, during the *Titanic's* first voyage, its design proved unworthy. Just before midnight, the *Titanic* struck an iceberg, which punctured 5 of the 16 compartments. The ship sunk in a little under 3 hours. Approximately 1,513 of more than 2,220 people onboard died. Most of these people died because there weren't enough lifeboats to accommodate everyone onboard. These people were left floating in the water. Many died from exposure, since the Atlantic Ocean was near freezing in temperature. It was one of the worst ocean disasters in history.

Because of the investigations that followed the *Titanic* disaster, the passenger ship industry instituted many reforms. It is now required that there is ample lifeboat space for all passengers and crew. An international ice patrol and full-time radio coverage were also instituted to prevent such disasters in the future.

Directions: Answer these questions about the *Titanic*.

1. How did most of the 1,513 people onboard the *Titanic* die? ______________________

2. Why did this "unsinkable" ship sink? ______________________

____

3. What changes have been made in ship safety as a result of the *Titanic* tragedy?

____

____

4. There have been many attempts to rescue artifacts from the *Titanic*. But many families of the dead wish the site to be left alone, as it is the final resting place of their relatives. They feel burial sites should not be disrupted. Do you agree or disagree? Why?

____

____

____

Name ______________________________

Comprehension: The *Monitor* and the *Virginia*

During the Civil War, it became **customary** to cover wooden warships with iron. This increased their **durability** and made them more difficult to sink. Two such ships were built using iron. They were the *Monitor* and the *Virginia*.

Most people are more familiar with the name the *Merrimack*. The *Merrimack* was a U.S. steam frigate that had been burnt and sunk by Union forces when the Confederates were forced to abandon their navy yard. The Confederate Navy raised the hull of the *Merrimack* and rebuilt her as the **ironclad** *Virginia*.

Both the *Monitor* and the *Virginia* engaged in battle on March 9, 1862. After several hours of battle, the bulky *Virginia* had no choice but to withdraw in order to avoid the lowering tides. This battle, called *Hampton Roads*, was considered to be a tie between the two ships.

Although both ships survived the battle, they were later destroyed. Two months later, the *Virginia* was sunk by her crew to avoid capture. The *Monitor* sunk on December 31, 1862, during a storm off the coast of North Carolina.

Directions: Use context clues for these definitions.

1. customary: ______________________________

2. durability: ______________________________

3. ironclad: ______________________________

Directions: Answer these questions about the *Monitor* and the *Virginia*.

1. Who won the battle between the *Virginia* and the *Monitor*? ______________________________

2. Why would lowering tides present danger to a ship? ______________________________

____

3. Describe how each ship was finally destroyed. ______________________________

____

____

____

Name ____________________

Comprehension: Railroads

Directions: Read the information about railroads. Then, answer the questions.

As early as the 1550s, a rough form of railroad was already being used in parts of Europe. Miners in England and other areas of western Europe used horse- or mule-drawn wagons on wooden tracks to pull loads out of mines. With these tracks, the horses could pull twice as much weight as they could without them. No one could have known then that one day this simple idea would change the world.

There were many developments along the way that helped make railroads a practical and valuable form of transportation. Two of the most important were the iron track and the "flanged" wheel, which has a rim around it to hold it onto the track. The most important invention was the steam engine by James Watt in 1765.

The first railroads in the United States were built during the late 1820s and caused a lot of excitement. They were faster than other forms of travel, and they could provide service year-round, unlike boats and stagecoaches. Trains were soon the main means of travel in the U.S.

Railroads played a major part in the Industrial Revolution—the years of change when machines were first used to do work that had been done by hand for many centuries. Trains provided cheaper rates and quicker service for transporting goods. Because manufacturers could ship their goods over long distances, they could sell their products all over the nation instead of only in the surrounding cities and towns. This meant greater profits for the companies. Trains also brought people into the cities to work in factories.

1. What was the source of power for the earliest railroads? ____________________

____

2. What were three important developments that made railroads a practical means of transportation?

____

____

____

3. What is meant by the Industrial Revolution? ____________________

____

4. What were two ways that railroads changed life in America? ____________________

____

Name ______________________________

Main Idea: Locomotives

Directions: Read the information about locomotives. Then, answer the questions.

In the 1800s, the steam locomotive was considered by many to be a symbol of the new Industrial Age. It was, indeed, one of the most important inventions of the time. Over the years, there have been many changes to the locomotive. One of the most important has been its source of power. During its history, the locomotive has gone from steam to electric to diesel power.

The first railroads used horses or mules for power, but the development of the steam locomotive made railroads a practical means of transportation. The first steam locomotive was built in 1804 in Great Britain by Richard Trevithick. It could haul 50,000 pounds, but it was not very successful because it was so heavy it caused the tracks to fall apart. However, it encouraged other engineers to try to build steam locomotives. Two of the most important men to accept the challenge were George Stephenson and his son, Robert. Robert once won a contest to build the best locomotive. *The Rocket*, as he called it, had a top speed of 29 miles per hour.

In America, developments in steam engines were close behind those of the British. In 1830, Peter Cooper's tiny locomotive, called *Tom Thumb*, lost a famous race against a horse-drawn coach. In spite of the loss, it still convinced railroad officials that steam power was more practical than horsepower.

Just before the turn of the century, the electric locomotive was widely used. At its peak in the 1940s, U.S. railroads had 2,400 miles of electric routes.

The diesel locomotive was invented in the 1890s by Rudolf Diesel, a German engineer. The power of this locomotive was supplied by a diesel fuel engine. The diesel locomotive is still used today. It costs about twice as much as a steam locomotive to build, but it is much cheaper to operate.

1. What is the main idea of this selection?
   ___ The steam locomotive was considered a symbol of the Industrial Age.
   ___ Over the years, there have been many changes to the locomotive.

2. Who built the first steam locomotive in 1804?

   ____

3. How fast could *The Rocket* travel?

   ____

4. Who built the locomotive called *Tom Thumb*?

   ____

5. *Tom Thumb* was in a race against a horse-drawn coach. Which won?

   ____

6. What kind of fuel does a diesel engine use?

   ____

Name ______________________________

Comprehension: Railroad Pioneer

Directions: Read the information about railroad pioneers. Then, respond to the statements by circling **True** or **False**.

George Stephenson was born in Wylam, England, in 1781. His family was extremely poor. When he was young, he didn't go to school but worked in the coal mines. In his spare time, he taught himself to read and write. After a series of explosions in the coal pits, Stephenson built a miner's safety lamp. This helped bring him to the attention of the owners of the coal mines. They put him in charge of all the machinery.

In 1812, Stephenson became an engine builder for the mines. The owners were interested in locomotives because the cost of horse feed was so high. They wanted Stephenson to build a locomotive to pull the coal cars from the mines. His first locomotive, The *Blucher*, was put on the rails in 1814.

Stephenson was a good engineer, and he was fortunate to work for a rich employer. Between 1814 and 1826, Stephenson was the only man in Great Britain building locomotives.

When the Stockholm and Darlington Railway, the first public railroad system, was planned, Stephenson was named company engineer. He convinced the owners to use steam power instead of horses. He built the first locomotive on the line. *The Locomotion*, as it was called, was the best locomotive that had been built anywhere in the world up to that time. Over the years, Stephenson was responsible for many other important developments in locomotive design, such as improved cast-iron rails and wheels, and the first steel springs strong enough to carry several tons.

Stephenson was convinced that the future of railroads lay in steam power. His great vision of what the railroad system could become was a driving force in the early years of its development.

1. George Stephenson was an excellent student in school. True False
2. Stephenson's first invention was a miner's safety lamp. True False
3. Between 1814 and 1826, Stephenson was one of many engineers building locomotives in Great Britain. True False
4. The Stockholm and Darlington Railway was the first public railroad system. True False
5. The first locomotive on the Stockholm and Darlington line was *The Locomotion*, built by Stephenson. True False
6. Stephenson's ideas did not influence the development of the railroad system. True False

Name ______________________________

Tall Tales

A **tall tale** is a fictional story with exaggerated details and a "super" hero. The main character in a tall tale is much larger, stronger, smarter or better than a real person. Tall tales may be unbelievable, but they are fun to hear.

America had nearly 200,000 miles of railroad track by 1900. Because of the rapid growth and the excitement over the railroads, many colorful tall tales about railroad heroes and their adventures were told.

Directions: Read the story about John Henry. Then, answer the questions.

A Steel-Driving Man

On the night John Henry was born, forked lightning split the air and the earth shook. He weighed 44 pounds at birth, and the first thing he did was reach for a hammer hanging on the wall. "He's going to be a steel-driving man," his father told his mother.

One night, John Henry dreamed he was working on a railroad. Every time his hammer hit a spike, the sky lit up with the sparks. "I dreamed that the railroad was going to be the end of me, and I'd die with a hammer in my hand," he said. When John Henry grew up, he did work for the railroad. He was the fastest, most powerful steel-driving man in the world.

In about 1870, the steam drill was invented. One day, the company at the far end of a tunnel tried it out. John Henry's company, working at the other end, continued to use men to do the drilling. There was much bragging from both companies as to which was faster. Finally, they decided to have a contest. John Henry was matched against the best man with a steam drill.

John Henry swung a 20-pound hammer in each hand. The sparks flew so fast and hot that they burned his face. At the end of the day, the judges said John Henry had beaten the steam drill by 4 feet!

That night, John Henry said, "I was a steel-driving man." Then, he laid down and closed his eyes forever.

1. How much was John Henry said to have weighed at birth? ______________________
2. Why did his father think he would be a steel-driving man? ______________________
3. What invention was John Henry in a contest against? ______________________
4. Why was the contest held? ______________________
5. What tools did John Henry use in the contest? ______________________
6. Who won the contest? ______________________
7. What happened to John Henry after the contest? ______________________

Name ____________________

Context Clues: Passenger Cars

Directions: Read the information about passenger cars. Use context clues to determine the meaning of words in bold. Check the correct answers.

Early railroad passenger cars were little more than stagecoaches fitted with special wheels to help them stay on the tracks. They didn't hold many passengers, and because they were made out of wood, they were fire **hazards**. They also did not hold up very well if the train came off the track or had a **collision** with another train.

In the United States, it wasn't long before passenger cars were lengthened to hold more people. Late in the 1830s, Americans were riding in **elongated** cars with double seats on either side of a center aisle. By the early 1900s, most cars were made of metal instead of wood.

Sleeping and dining cars were introduced in the United States by the early 1860s. Over the next 25 years other improvements were made, including electric lighting, steam heat, and covered **vestibules** that allowed passengers to walk between cars. All of these **luxuries** helped make railroad travel much more comfortable.

1. Based on the other words in the sentence, what is the correct definition of **hazards**?

____ engines ____ risks ____ stations

2. Based on the other words in the sentence, what is the correct definition of **collision**?

____ crash ____ race ____ track

3. Based on the other words in the sentence, what is the correct definition of **elongated**?

____ wooden ____ new ____ lengthened

4. Based on the other words in the sentence, what is the correct definition of **vestibules**?

____ passageways ____ cars ____ depots

5. Based on the other words in the sentence, what is the correct definition of **luxuries**?

____ additions ____ things offering the greatest comfort ____ inventions

Name ____________________

Reading Skills: Railroads

Directions: Read the information about railroads. Then, answer the questions.

When railroads became the major means of transportation, they replaced earlier forms of travel, like the stagecoach. Railroads remained the unchallenged leader for a hundred years. Beginning in the early 1900s, railroads faced **competition** from newer forms of transportation.

Today, millions of people have their own automobiles. Buses offer inexpensive travel between cities. Large trucks haul goods across the country. Airplanes provide quick transportation over long distances. The result has been a sharp drop in the use of trains.

Today, nearly all railroads face serious problems that threaten to drive them out of business. But railroads still provide low-cost, fuel-saving transportation that will remain important. One gallon of diesel fuel will haul about four times as much by railroad as by truck. In a time when the world is concerned about saving fuel, this is but one area in which the railroads still have much to offer.

1. What is the main idea of this selection?

____ When railroads became the major means of transportation, they replaced earlier forms of travel.

____ Beginning in the early 1900s, railroads have faced competition from newer forms of transportation.

2. Based on the other words in the sentence, what is the correct definition of **competition**?

____ businesses trying to get the same customers

____ problems

____ support

3. What are four newer forms of transportation that have challenged railroads?

____

4. One gallon of diesel fuel will haul about twice as much by railroad as by truck. True False

Name ______________________________

Comprehension: Printing

Directions: Read the information about printing. Then, answer the questions.

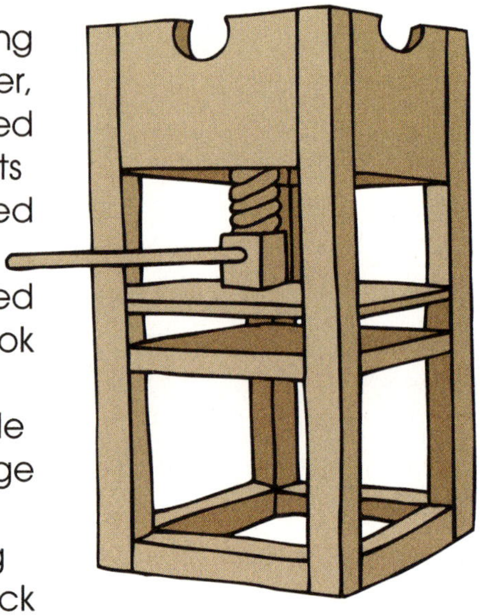

When people talk about printing, they usually mean making exact copies of an original document, such as a newspaper, magazine, or an entire book. The inventions that have allowed us to do this are some of the most important developments in history. Look around you at the many examples of printed materials. Can you imagine life without them?

Until the thirteenth century, all material had to be printed by hand, one copy at a time. To make a copy of a book took much time and effort.

The oldest known example of a printed book was made in China in 848 A.D. by Wang Chieh, who carved each page of a book by hand onto a block of wood. He then put ink on the wood and pressed it on paper. The idea of printing with wood blocks spread to Europe. The letters in these block books were made to look handwritten.

In about 1440, a German goldsmith named Johann Gutenberg developed the idea of movable type. He invented separate letters made of metal for printing. The letters could be joined together to make words and sentences. Ink was applied to the letters to print many copies of the same material. Because they were made of metal, the letters could be used over and over. This wonderful invention made it possible to have more printed material at a lower cost.

Gutenberg had other ideas that were important to printing. He developed a special type of ink that would stick to the new metal letters. Gutenberg's ideas were so successful that the process of printing went almost unchanged for more than 300 years.

1. In what country was the oldest known printed book made?

____

2. Who made the first printed book?

____

3. What is "movable type"?

____

4. Who developed the idea of movable type?

____

5. What was another important invention of Gutenberg?

____

Name ______________________________

Comprehension: Newspapers

Directions: Read the information about newspapers. Then, answer the questions.

Newspapers keep us informed about what is going on in the world. They entertain, educate, and examine the events of the day. For millions of people worldwide, newspapers are an important part of daily life.

Newspapers are published at various intervals, but they usually come out daily or weekly. Of the nearly 60,000 newspapers published around the world, about 2,600 are published in the United States. More than half—about 1800—of them are dailies.

Some newspapers have many subscribers—people who pay to have each edition delivered to them. *The Wall Street Journal* and *USA Today* each have about two million subscribers. There are many, many newspapers with only a few thousand subscribers. These include small-town weeklies and special-interest papers, like those written for people who enjoy the same hobby.

Newspapers provide a service to the community by providing information at little cost. But newspaper publishing is a business, so like other businesses, newspapers need to make money. They can keep the cost to subscribers low and still stay in business by selling space to businesses and individuals who want to advertise products or services. In most newspapers, between one-third and two-thirds of the paper is taken up by advertising.

1. About how many newspapers are published worldwide?

____

2. What services do newspapers provide?

____

3. What are subscribers?

____

4. How often are most newspapers published?

____

5. What do newspapers do to keep the cost to the reader low, but still make money?

____

6. In most newspapers, about how much of the paper is taken up by advertising?

____

Name ____________________

Comprehension: Newspapers

Directions: Read the information about the first newspapers. Then, answer the questions.

Long ago, town criers walked through cities reading important news to the people. The earliest newspapers were probably handwritten notices posted in towns for the public to read.

The first true newspaper was a weekly paper started in Germany in 1609. It was called *The Strassburg Relation*. The Germans were pioneers in newspaper publishing. Johann Gutenberg, the man who developed movable type, was German.

One of the first English-language newspapers, *The London Gazette*, was first printed in England in 1665. *Gazette* is an old English word that means "official publication." Many newspapers today still use the word *gazette* in their names.

In America, several papers began during colonial days. The first successful one, *The Boston News-Letter*, began printing in 1704. It was very small—about the size of a sheet of notebook paper with printing on both sides.

An important date in newspaper publishing was 1833. In that year, *The New York Sun* became the first penny newspaper. The paper actually did cost only a penny. The penny newspapers were similar to today's papers: they printed news while it was still new, they were the first to print advertisements and to sell papers in newsstands, and they were the first to be delivered to homes.

1. How were the earliest newspapers different from today's newspapers?

   ____

2. In what year and where was the first true newspaper printed?

   ____

3. What was the name of the first successful newspaper in America?

   ____

4. Why was 1833 important in newspaper publishing?

   ____

5. List four ways penny newspapers were like the newspapers of today.

   ____

   ____

   ____

   ____

Name ______________________________

Comprehension: Newspaper Jobs

Directions: Read the information about jobs at a newspaper. Then, answer the questions.

It takes an army of people to put out one of the big daily newspapers. Three separate departments are needed to make a newspaper operate smoothly: editorial, mechanical, and business.

The editorial department is the one most people think about first. That is the news-gathering part of the newspaper. The most familiar job in this department is that of the reporter—the person who obtains information for a story and writes it. A photographer takes pictures to go along with the reporter's story.

Editors are the decision-makers. There are many editors at a large newspaper. They assign stories to reporters, read the stories to be certain they are correct, and decide where and if the stories should appear in the paper. The most important stories go on the front page. There are also photo editors who choose which pictures will appear in the paper. Other workers in the editorial department include artists, copy editors, proofreaders, and cartoonists.

The biggest job in the mechanical department is printing the paper. Most large newspapers have their own printing presses. Some small papers send their work to outside printing shops. After an issue, or edition, is printed, it is ready to be sold or "circulated" to the public.

Circulation of the paper is one of the jobs of the business department. This department also sells advertising space. This is very important for newspapers. Many papers make more money selling advertising space than selling newspapers. The business department also takes care of normal business jobs, like paying employees, paying bills, and keeping records.

1. What are the three main departments at a newspaper?

   ____

2. Who gets the information for a story and writes it?

   ____

3. Who are the decision-makers at a newspaper?

   ____

4. What is the biggest job for the mechanical department?

   ____

5. What is the most important job of the business department?

   ____

Name ______________________________

Comprehension: News Stories

Directions: Read the information about news stories. Then, draw an **X** on the line to show the correct meaning of the bold word.

Here is an example of how a story gets into the newspaper:

Let's imagine that a city bus has turned over in a ditch, injuring some of the passengers. An **eyewitness** calls the newspaper. The editor assigns a reporter to go to the scene. The reporter talks to the passengers, driver, and witnesses who saw the accident. She finds out what they saw and how they feel, writing down their comments or tape recording their answers. At the same time, a photographer is busy taking pictures.

If there isn't time for the reporter to go back to the newsroom, she could call and **dictate** the story to a copytaker who types the story into a computer. Many reporters use portable computers which allow them to write the story on the spot and then send it back to the office over the telephone by modem.

Next, an editor reads the story, checking facts, grammar, and spelling. Meanwhile, the photographer's film is developed and a picture is chosen.

The story is set in print. On most newspapers today, this is done with a computer. The computer makes sets of columns of type, which are pasted onto a sheet of paper exactly the same size as a newspaper page. A **proofreader** checks the story for mistakes. The newspaper is now ready for printing. The presses begin to run.

Miles of paper are turned into thousands of printed, cut, and folded newspapers. They are counted, put into bundles, and placed in waiting trucks. Within a few hours, people can read about the bus accident in their daily newspaper.

1. Based on the other words in the sentence, what is the correct definition of **eyewitness**?

   ________ a reporter

   ________ a person who saw what happened

   ________ a lawyer

2. Based on the other words in the sentence, what is the correct definition of **dictate**?

   ________ govern without regard for what people want

   ________ use a dictionary

   ________ read a story word for word for someone else to write

3. Based on the other words in the sentence, what is the correct definition of **proofreader**?

   ________ person who checks for mistakes

   ________ person who shows proof he has read a book

   ________ a teacher

Name ______________________________

Comprehension: News Services

Directions: Read the information about news services. Then, answer the questions.

When people read daily newspapers, they expect to see current news from all over the world. Some newspapers have offices or reporters in Washington, D.C., and other major cities around the world. Most newspapers rely on news services for international news. News services are organizations that gather and sell news to papers, radio, and television stations. They are sometimes referred to as "wire services," because they originally sent stories over telegraph or Teletype lines, or "wires."

The two largest news services are the Associated Press and United Press International. Stories sent by these services have their initials—AP or UPI—at the beginning of the article. All large American newspapers are members of either the AP or UPI service.

At one time, people had to wait for messengers to arrive by foot, horse, or ship to learn the news. By the time it reached a newspaper, news could be months old.

Gathering news from around the world became much faster after the invention of the telegraph, Teletype, telephone, and transatlantic cable. Today, satellites, computer modems, and fax machines can send stories, pictures, and even videos around the world in seconds.

1. What is another name for news service organizations?

____

2. What are the two largest news service organizations?

____

3. What are three inventions that have speeded up worldwide news-gathering?

____

4. Why do newspapers use news services?

____

5. How was news delivered before the invention of modern communication devices?

____

Name ______________________________

Comprehension: Samuel Clemens

Directions: Read the information about Samuel Clemens.

Samuel Langhorne Clemens was born in Florida, Missouri, in 1835. In his lifetime, he gained worldwide fame as a writer, lecturer, and humorist.

Clemens first worked for a printer when he was only 12 years old. Soon after that he worked on his brother's newspaper.

Clemens traveled frequently and worked as a printer in New York, Philadelphia, St. Louis, and Cincinnati. On a trip to New Orleans in 1857, he learned the difficult art of steamboat **piloting**. Clemens loved piloting and later used it as a background for some of his books, including *Life on the Mississippi*.

A few years later, Clemens went to Nevada with his brother and tried gold mining. When this proved unsuccessful, he went back to writing for newspapers. At first he signed his humorous pieces with the name "Josh." In 1863, he began signing them Mark Twain. The words "mark twain" were used by riverboat pilots to mean two fathoms (12 feet) deep, water deep enough for steamboats. From then on, Clemens used this now-famous **pseudonym** for all his writing.

As Mark Twain, he received attention from readers all over the world. His best-known works include *Tom Sawyer* and *The Adventures of Huckleberry Finn*. These two books about boyhood adventures remain popular with readers of all ages.

Directions: Check the correct answer.

1. Based on the other words in the sentence, what is the correct definition of **pseudonym**?
   _____ book title
   _____ a made-up name used by an author
   _____ a humorous article

2. Based on the other words in the sentence, what is the correct definition of **piloting**?
   _____ driving an airplane
   _____ steering a steamboat on a river
   _____ being a train engineer

Directions: Write the answers.

1. Under what name did Samuel Clemens write his books?

   ____

2. What do the words "mark twain" mean?

   ____

3. Besides author, list two other jobs held by Mark Twain.

   ____

4. List two of the best-known books written by Mark Twain.

   ____

Name ______________________________

Comprehension: The Arctic Circle

Directions: Read the article about the Arctic Circle. Then, answer the questions.

On the other side of the globe from Antarctica, at the northernmost part of the earth, is another icy land. This is the Arctic Circle. It includes the North Pole itself and the northern fringes of three continents—Europe, Asia, and North America, including the state of Alaska—as well as Greenland and other islands.

The seasons are opposite at the two ends of the earth. When it is summer in Antarctica, it is winter in the Arctic Circle. In both places, there are very long periods of sunlight in summer and very long nights in the winter. On the poles themselves, there are six full months of sunlight and six full months of darkness each year.

Compared to Antarctica, the summers are surprisingly mild in some areas of the Arctic Circle. Much of the snow cover may melt, and temperatures often reach 50 degrees in July. Antarctica is covered by water—frozen water, of course—so nothing can grow there. Plant growth is limited in the polar regions not only by the cold, but also by wind, lack of water, and the long winter darkness.

In the far north, willow trees grow but only become a few inches high. The annual rings, the circles within the trunk of a tree that show its age and how fast it grows, are so narrow in those trees that you need a microscope to see them!

A permanently frozen layer of soil, called **permafrost**, keeps roots from growing deep enough into the ground to anchor a plant. Even if a plant could survive the cold temperatures, it could not grow roots deep enough or strong enough to allow the plant to get very big.

1. What three continents have land included in the Arctic Circle?

______________________ ______________________ ______________________

2. Is the Arctic Circle generally warmer or colder than Antarctica?

____

3. What is **permafrost**? ______________________________________

4. Many tall pine trees grow in the Arctic Circle. True False

Name ______________________________

Main Idea: The Polar Trail

Directions: Read the information about explorers to Antarctica.

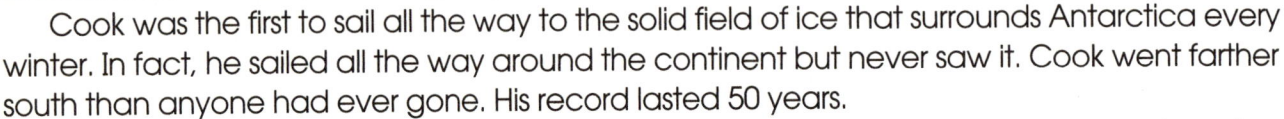

A recorded sighting of Antarctica, the last continent to be discovered, was not made until the early nineteenth century. Since then, many brave explorers and adventurers have sailed south to conquer the icy land. Their achievements once gained as much world attention as those of the first astronauts.

Long before the continent was first spotted, the ancient Greeks suspected there was a continent at the bottom of the earth. Over the centuries, legends of the undiscovered land spread. Some of the world's greatest seamen tried to find it, including Captain James Cook in 1772.

Cook was the first to sail all the way to the solid field of ice that surrounds Antarctica every winter. In fact, he sailed all the way around the continent but never saw it. Cook went farther south than anyone had ever gone. His record lasted 50 years.

Forty years after Cook, a new kind of seamen sailed the icy waters. They were hunters of seals and whales. Sailing through unknown waters in search of seals and whales, these men became explorers as well as hunters. The first person known to sight Antarctica was an American hunter, 21-year-old Nathaniel Brown Palmer in 1820.

Directions: Draw an **X** on the blank for the correct answer.

1. The main idea is:

____ Antarctica was not sighted until the early nineteenth century.

____ Many brave explorers and adventurers have sailed south to conquer the icy land.

2. The first person to sail to the ice field that surrounds Antarctica was

____ Nathaniel Brown Palmer.

____ Captain James Cook.

____ Neal Armstrong.

3. His record for sailing the farthest south stood for

____ 40 years.

____ 50 years.

____ 500 years.

4. The first person known to sight Antarctica was

____ an unknown ancient Greek.

____ Captain James Cook.

____ Nathaniel Brown Palmer.

5. His profession was

____ hunter.

____ ship captain.

____ explorer.

Name ______________________________

Comprehension: Polar Bears

Directions: Read the information about polar bears. Then, respond to the statements by circling **True** or **False**.

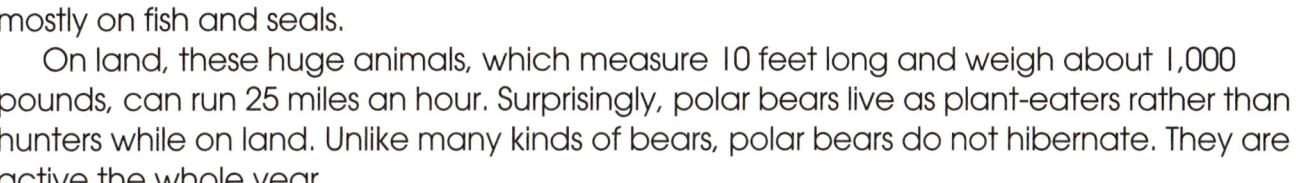

Some animals are able to survive the cold weather and difficult conditions of the snow and ice fields in the Arctic polar regions. One of the best known is the polar bear.

Polar bears live on the land and the sea. They may drift hundreds of miles from land on huge sheets of floating ice. They use their great paws to paddle the ice along. Polar bears are excellent swimmers, too. They can cross great distances of open water. While in the water, they feed mostly on fish and seals.

On land, these huge animals, which measure 10 feet long and weigh about 1,000 pounds, can run 25 miles an hour. Surprisingly, polar bears live as plant-eaters rather than hunters while on land. Unlike many kinds of bears, polar bears do not hibernate. They are active the whole year.

Baby polar bears are born during the winter. At birth, they are pink and almost hairless. These helpless cubs weigh only two pounds—less than one-third the size of most human infants. The mother bears raise their young in dens dug in snowbanks. By the time they are 10 weeks old, polar bear cubs are about the size of puppies and have enough white fur to protect them in the open air. The mothers give their cubs swimming, hunting, and fishing lessons. By the time autumn comes, the cubs are left to survive on their own.

1. Polar bears can live on the land and the sea. True False
2. Polar bears are excellent swimmers. True False
3. Polar bears hibernate in the winter. True False
4. A newborn polar bear weighs more than a newborn human baby. True False
5. Mother polar bears raise their babies in caves. True False
6. Father polar bears give the cubs swimming lessons. True False

Name ____________________

Comprehension: Walruses

Directions: Read the information about walruses. Then, respond to the statements by circling **True** or **False**.

A walrus is actually a type of seal that lives only in the Arctic Circle. It has two huge upper teeth, or tusks, which it uses to pull itself out of the water or to move over the rocks on land. It also uses its tusks to dig clams, one of its favorite foods, from the bottom of the sea. On an adult male walrus, the tusks may be three and a half feet long!

A walrus has an unusual face. Besides its long tusks, it has a big, bushy mustache made up of hundreds of movable, stiff bristles. These bristles also help the walrus push food into its mouth. Except for small wrinkles in the skin, a walrus has no outer ears.

Like a seal, the walrus uses its flippers to help it swim. Its front flippers serve as paddles, and while swimming, it swings the back of its huge body from side to side. A walrus looks awkward using its flippers to walk on land, but don't be fooled! A walrus can run as fast as a man.

Baby walruses are born in the early spring. They stay with their mothers until they are two years old. There is a good reason for this—they must grow little tusks, at least three or four inches long, before they can catch their own food from the bottom of the sea. Until then, they must stay close to their mothers to eat. A young walrus that is tired from swimming will climb onto its mother's back for a ride, holding onto her with its front flippers.

1. The walrus is a type of seal found only ____________________.
2. List two ways the walrus uses its tusks.

   ____________________ ____________________

3. A walrus cannot move quickly on land. True False
4. A walrus has a large, bushy mustache. True False
5. A baby walrus stays very close to its mother until it is two years old. True False
6. Baby walruses are born late in fall. True False

Name ______________________________

Comprehension: The Desert

Directions: Read the information about the desert. Then, respond to the statements by circling **True** or **False**.

Deserts are found where there is little rainfall or where the rainfall for a whole year falls in only a few weeks' time. Ten inches of rain may be enough for many plants to survive if the rain is spread throughout the year. If the 10 inches of rain falls during one or two months and the rest of the year is dry, those plants may not be able to survive and a desert may form.

When people think of deserts, they may think of long stretches of sand. Sand begins as tiny pieces of rock that get smaller and smaller as wind and weather wear them down. Sand dunes, or hills of drifting sand, are formed as winds move the sand across the desert. Grain by grain, the dunes grow over the years, always shifting with the winds and changing shape. Most dunes are only a few feet tall, but they can grow to be several hundred feet high.

There is, however, much more to a desert than sand. In the deserts of the southwestern United States, cliffs and canyons were formed from thick mud that once lay beneath a sea more than a hundred million years ago. Over the centuries, the water drained away. Wind, sand, rain, heat, and cold all wore away at the remaining rocks. The faces of the desert mountains are always changing—very, very slowly—as these forces of nature continue to work on the rock.

Most deserts have a surprising variety of life. There are plants, animals, and insects that have adapted to life in the desert. During the heat of the day, a visitor may see very few signs of living things, but as the air begins to cool in the evening, the desert comes to life. As the sun begins to rise again in the sky, the desert once again becomes quiet and lonely.

1. Deserts are found where there is little rainfall or where the rainfall for a whole year falls in only a few weeks. True False

2. Sand begins as tiny pieces of rock that get smaller and smaller as wind and weather wear them down. True False

3. Sand dunes were formed from thick mud that once lay beneath a sea more than a hundred million years ago. True False

4. The faces of the desert mountains can never change. True False

Name ______________________________

Comprehension: Desert Weather

Directions: Read the information about desert weather. Then, answer the questions.

One definition of a desert is an area that has, on average, less than 10 inches of rain a year. Many deserts have far less than that. Death Valley in California and Nevada, for example, averages fewer than 2 inches of rain each year. The driest of all deserts is the Atacama Desert in Chile, where no rain has been known to fall in 400 years!

Some deserts have a regular rainy season each year, but usually desert rainfall is totally unpredictable. An area may have no rainfall for many years. Sometimes a passing cloud may look like it will send relief to the waiting land, but only a "ghost rain" falls. This means that the hot, dry air dries up the raindrops long before they ever reach the ground.

The temperature in the desert varies greatly. The daytime temperatures in the desert frequently top 120 degrees. In Death Valley, temperatures have been known to reach 190 degrees! In most parts of the world, moisture in the air works like a blanket to hold the heat of the day close to the earth at night. But, because it has so little moisture, the desert has no such blanket. As a result, nighttime temperatures are very chilly. Temperatures have been known to drop 50 or even 100 degrees at night in the desert.

1. On the average, how much rainfall is there in a year in a desert?

____

2. Where is the driest desert in the world? ______________________________

3. What is a "ghost rain"? ______________________________

4. In other parts of the world, what works as a "blanket" to hold the heat of the day close to the earth at night? ______________________________

5. What happens to the temperature in the desert at night?

____

Name ______________________________

Context Clues: Desert Plants

Directions: Read the information about desert plants. Use context clues to determine the meaning of the bold words. Then, check the correct answers.

Desert plants have special features, or adaptations, that allow them to **survive** the harsh conditions of the desert. A cactus stores water in its tissues when it rains. It then uses this supply of water during the long dry season. The tiny needles on some kinds of **cacti** may number in the tens of thousands. These sharp thorns protect the cactus. They also form tiny shadows in the sunlight that help keep the plant from getting too hot.

Other plants are able to live by dropping their leaves. This cuts down on the **evaporation** of their water supply in the hot sun. Still other plants survive as seeds, protected from the sun and heat by tough seed coats. When it rains, the seeds **sprout** quickly, bloom, and produce more seeds that can **withstand** long dry spells.

Some plants spread their roots close to the earth's surface to quickly gather water when it does rain. Other plants, such as the mesquite, have roots that grow 50 or 60 feet below the ground to reach underground water supplies.

1. Based on the other words in the sentence, what is the correct definition of **survive**?

    ____ continue to live
    ____ bloom in the desert
    ____ flower

2. Based on the other words in the sentence, what is the correct definition of **evaporation**?

    ____ water loss from heat
    ____ much-needed rainfall
    ____ boiling

3. Based on the other words in the sentence, what is the correct definition of **withstand**?

    ____ put up with
    ____ stand with another
    ____ take from

4. Based on the other words in the sentence, what is the correct definition of **cacti**?

    ____ a type of sand dune
    ____ more than one cactus
    ____ a caravan of camels

5. Based on the other words in the sentence, what is the correct definition of **sprout**?

    ____ a type of bean that grows only in the desert
    ____ begin to grow
    ____ a small flower

Name ______________________________

Comprehension: Lizards

Directions: Read the information about lizards. Then, answer the questions.

Lizards are reptiles, related to snakes, turtles, alligators, and crocodiles. Like other reptiles, lizards are cold-blooded. This means their body temperature changes with that of their surroundings. However, by changing their behavior throughout the day, they can keep their temperature fairly constant.

Lizards are among the many animals that live in deserts. They usually come out of their burrows early in the morning. Most lizards lie in the sun to get warm before starting their daily activities. In mid-morning, they hunt for food. If it becomes too hot, lizards can raise their tails and bodies off the ground to help cool off. At mid-day, they return to their burrows or crawl under rocks for several hours. Late in the day, they again lie in the sun to absorb heat before the chilly desert night falls.

Like all animals, lizards have ways of protecting themselves. Some types of lizards have developed a most unusual defense. If a hawk or other animal grabs one of these lizards by its tail, the tail will break off. The tail will continue to wiggle around to distract the attacker while the lizard runs away. A month or two later, the lizard grows a new tail.

There are about 3,000 kinds of lizards, and all of them can bite, but only two types of lizards are poisonous: the Gila monster of the southwestern United States and the Mexican bearded lizard. Both are short-legged, thick-bodied reptiles with fat tails. These lizards do not attack people and will not bite them unless they are attacked.

1. What can a lizard do if it becomes too hot? ______________________________

____

2. What is an unusual defense some lizards have developed to protect themselves?

____

3. What two types of lizards are poisonous? ______________________________

____

Name ______________________________

Main Idea: People in the Desert

Directions: Read the information about people in the desert. Then, answer the questions.

Long before Europeans came to live in America, Native Americans had discovered ways of living in the desert. Some of these Native Americans were hunters or belonged to wandering tribes that stayed in the desert for only short periods of time. Others learned to farm and live in villages. They made their houses of trees, clay, and brush.

The desert met all of their needs for life: food, water, skins for clothing, materials for tools, weapons, and shelter. For meat, the desert offered deer, birds, and rabbits for hunting. When these animals were hard to find, the Native Americans would eat mice and lizards. Many desert plants, such as the prickly pear and mesquite, provided moisture, fruit, and seeds that could be eaten.

The first Europeans in the American deserts were searching for furs and metals, like silver and gold. They explored, but did not settle in the desert. The early pioneers were usually unsuccessful at living in the desert. They found the great heat and long dry periods too difficult. When they moved away, they left behind empty mining camps, houses, and sheds that slowly fell apart in the sun and wind.

1. What is the main idea of this selection?

   _____ Before Europeans came to live in America, Native Americans had discovered ways of successfully living in the desert.

   _____ Some Native Americans were hunters or belonged to wandering tribes who stayed in the desert for only short periods of time.

2. Who were the first people to live in the deserts of North America?

   ____

3. What did the Native Americans use to make their houses in the desert?

   ____

4. What kinds of food did the Native Americans find in the desert?

   ____

5. What were the first Europeans who came to the desert looking for?

   ____

Name ______________________________

Main Idea: Camels

Directions: Read the information about camels. Then, answer the questions.

Camels are well suited to desert life. They can cope with infrequent supplies of food and water, blazing heat during the day, low temperatures at night, and sand blown by high winds.

There are two kinds of camels: the two-humped bactrian and the one-humped dromedary. The dromedary is the larger of the two. It has coarse fur on its back that helps protect it from the sun's rays. The hair on its stomach and legs is short to prevent overheating. When camels **molt** in the spring, their wool can be collected in tufts from the bushes and ground.

The legs of the dromedary are much longer than those of the bactrian. Animals that live in very hot countries tend to have longer legs. This gives them a larger area of body surface from which heat can escape. Bactrian camels live in the deserts of central Asia where winters are bitterly cold, so they are not as tall as dromedaries.

Both kinds of camels have pads on their feet that keep them from sinking into the sand as they walk. A camel's long neck allows it to reach the ground to drink water and eat grass without having to bend its legs. It also can reach up to eat leaves from trees.

Camels do not store water in their humps as many people believe. The hump is for fat storage. When there is plenty of food, the camel's hump swells and feels firm. During the dry season when there is little food, the fat is used up and the hump shrinks and becomes soft.

1. What is the main idea of this selection?

   ____ Camels are well suited to desert life.

   ____ There are two kinds of camels.

2. Based on the other words in the sentence, what is the correct definition of **molt**?

   ____ turns into a butterfly

   ____ sheds its hair

   ____ becomes overheated

3. What are the two kinds of camels? ______________________________

4. Why don't camels sink into the sand when they walk? ______________________________

   ____

5. What is the purpose of a camel's hump? ______________________________

Name ______________________________

Comprehension: Desert Lakes

Directions: Read the information about lakes in the desert. Then, answer the questions.

A few deserts have small permanent lakes. While they may be a welcome sight in the desert, the water in them is not fit for drinking. They are salt lakes. Rain from nearby higher land keeps these lakes supplied with water, but the lakes are blocked in with nowhere to drain. Over the years, mineral salts collect in the water and build up to a high level, making the water undrinkable.

Most desert lakes are only temporary. Occasional rains may fill them to depths of several feet, but in a matter of weeks or months, all the water has been dried up by the heat and sun. The dried lake beds that remain are called **playas**. Some playas are simply areas of sun-baked mud; others are covered with a sparkling layer of salt.

Perhaps the most unusual desert lake is in central Australia. It is called Lake Eyre. It is a huge lake—nearly 3,600 square miles in area—but it is almost totally dry most of the time. Since it was discovered in 1840, it has been filled only two times. Both times, the lake completely dried up again within a few years.

1. Why is the water in a desert lake not fit for drinking?

____

2. Why are the lakes in the desert salt lakes?

____

3. Why are most desert lakes only temporary?

____

4. What is a **playa**? ______________________________

5. What is the name of the unusual desert lake in central Australia?

____

6. How big is this desert lake? ______________________________

Name ______________________________

Reading a Recipe

Directions: Read the recipe. Then, answer the questions.

Graham Cracker Smoothies

Graham crackers

Icing:
- 2 T. peanut butter
- 2 T. butter
- 2 c. powdered sugar
- milk

Break graham crackers in half. Mix peanut butter, butter, and powdered sugar with a spoon. Add enough milk to make creamy icing. Stir vigorously until no lumps remain. Spread on graham cracker half and top with another graham cracker half, sandwich style. Enjoy!
The smoothie icing will keep in the refrigerator for two days.

1. What do these abbreviations stand for?

T. ______________________________

c. ______________________________

2. Number the steps in the correct order.

___ Spread icing on graham crackers.

___ Add milk and stir until creamy.

___ Break graham crackers in half.

___ Eat and enjoy.

___ Mix the peanut butter, butter, and powdered sugar together.

3. Why is it important to follow the correct sequence when cooking?

____

Name ____________________

Reading Skills: Labels

Labels provide information about products.

Directions: Read the label on the medicine bottle. Then, answer the questions.

> **Remember:** Children should never take medicines without their parents' knowledge and consent.

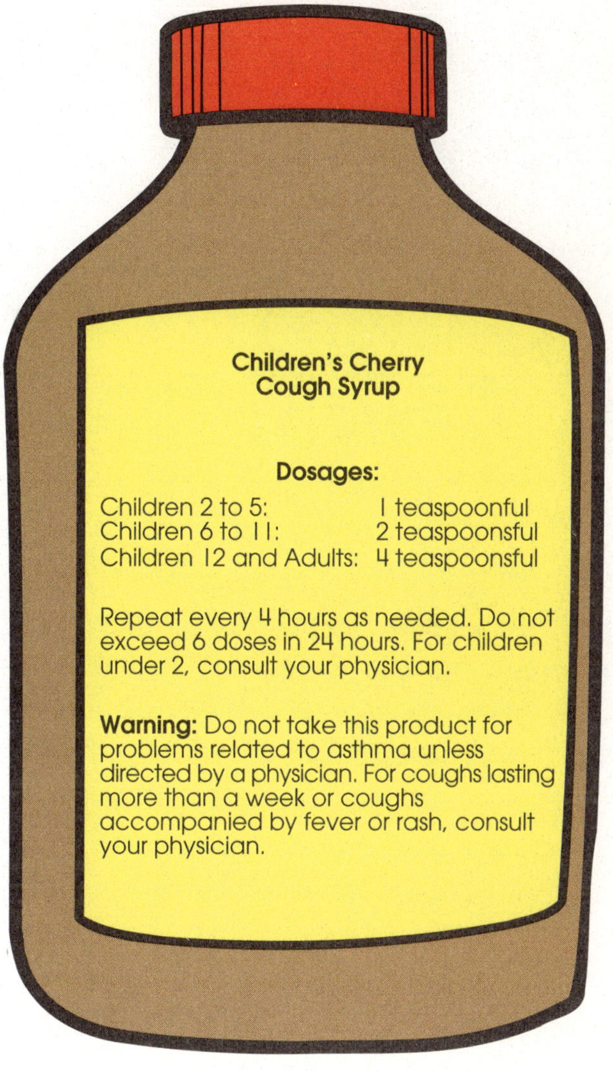

1. What is the dosage, or amount to be taken, for a three-year-old child?

2. How often can you take this medicine if it is needed?

3. How many times a day can you take this medicine?

4. What should you do before taking the medicine if you have a rash in addition to your cough?

5. Will this medicine help you if you are sneezing?

6. What is the dosage for an adult?

Name ______________________

Reading Skills: Newspapers

Directions: Write the answers to the following questions.

1. What is the name of your daily local newspaper?

2. List the sections included in your local newspaper.

3. What sections of the newspaper do you read on a regular basis?

4. Ask a parent which sections he or she reads on a regular basis.

5. Find the editorial section of your newspaper. An editorial is the opinion of one person. Write the main idea of one editorial. ______________________

6. If you could work at a newspaper, which job would you like? Why?

Directions: Read a copy of *USA Today*. You can find a copy in most libraries. Compare it to your local paper.

1. How are they alike? ______________________

2. How are they different? ______________________

Name ____________________

Reading Skills: A Newspaper Index

An **index** is a listing in a book, magazine, or newspaper that tells where to find items or information.

Newspapers provide many kinds of information. You can read about national events, local news, the weather, and sports. You will also find opinions, feature stories, advice columns, comics, entertainment, recipes, advertisements, and more. A guide that tells you where to find different types of information in a newspaper is called a **newspaper index**. An index of the newspaper usually appears on the front page.

Directions: Use the newspaper index to answer the questions.

Business	8	Local News	5–7
Classified Ads	18–19	National News	1–4
Comics	20	Radio-TV	17
Editorials	9	Sports	11–13
Entertainment	14–16	Weather	10

1. Where would you look for the results of last night's basketball games?
   Section: ____________________ Page(s) ____________
2. Where would you find your favorite cartoon strip?
   Section: ____________________ Page(s) ____________
3. Where would you find opinions of upcoming elections?
   Section: ____________________ Page(s) ____________
4. Where would you find a used bicycle to buy?
   Section: ____________________ Page(s) ____________
5. Where would you find out if you need to wear your raincoat tomorrow?
   Section: ____________________ Page(s) ____________
6. Where would you find the listing of tonight's TV shows?
   Section: ____________________ Page(s) ____________
7. Which would be first, a story about the president's trip to Europe or a review of the newest movie?
   ____

Name ________________________________

Reading Skills: Classified Ads

A **classified ad** is an advertisement in a newspaper or magazine offering a product or service for sale or rent.

Example: For Sale: Used 26″ 30-speed bike. $100. Call 555-5555.

Directions: Read these advertisements. Then, answer the questions.

1.

Yard Work
Breaking Your Back?
Give Mike and Jane a crack!
Mowing, raking, trash hauled.
References provided.
Call 555-9581.

2.

Pet Sitter
Going on vacation?
Away for the weekend?
I am 14 years old and have experience caring for dogs and cats.
Your home or mine.
Excellent references.
Call Sally Trent.
Phone: 555-8250.

3.

Singing Lessons
for All Ages!
Be popular at parties!
Fulfill your dreams!
20 years coaching experience.
Madame Rinaud . . .
Coach to the Stars.
555-5331.

1. What is promised in the third ad? ________________________________
2. Is it fact or opinion? ________________________________
3. What fact is offered in the third ad? ________________________________
4. Give an example of a slogan, or easy-to-remember phrase, that appears in one of the ads. ________________________________
5. Which ad gives the most facts? ________________________________
6. Which ad is based mostly on opinion? ________________________________

Name ______________________________

Reading Skills: Schedules

A **schedule** lists events or programs by time, date, and place or channel.

Example:

Packer Preseason Games

August 14	7 P.M.	NY Jets at Green Bay
August 23	7 P.M.	Denver Broncos at Madison
August 28	3 P.M.	Saints at New Orleans
September 2	Noon	Miami Dolphins at Green Bay

Directions: Use this newspaper television schedule to answer the questions.

Evening

6:00	3	Let's Talk! Guest: Animal expert, Jim Porter
	5	Cartoons
	8	News
	9	News
7:00	3	Farm Report
	5	Movie. *A Laugh a Minute* (1955) James Rayburn. Comedy about a boy who wants to join the circus.
	8	Spin for Dollars!
	9	Cooking With Cathy. Tonight: Chicken with mushrooms
7:30	3	Double Trouble (comedy). The twins disrupt the high school dance.
	8	Wall Street Today: Stock Market Report
8:00	3	NBA Basketball. Teams to be announced.
	8	News Special. "Saving Our Waterways: Pollution in the Mississippi."
	9	Movie. *At Day's End* (1981). Michael Collier, Julie Romer. Drama set in World War II.

1. What two stations have the news at 6:00? ______________________
2. What time would you turn on the television to watch a funny movie? ______________________
   What channel? ______________________
3. What could you watch if you are a sports fan? ______________________
   What time and channel is it on? ______________________
4. Which show title sounds like it could be a game show? ______________________
5. What show might you want to watch if you are interested in the environment?
   ____
   What time and channel is it on? ______________________

Name ______________________________

Comprehension: Facts About Folk Music

Folk music literally means music "of the folks," and it belongs to everyone. The names of the musicians who composed most folk music have long been forgotten. Even so, folk music has remained popular because it tells about the lives of people. Usually, the tune is simple, and even though folk songs often have many verses, the words are easy to remember. Do you know the words to "She'll Be Comin' 'Round the Mountain"?

Although no one ever says who "she" is, the verses tell you that she will be "riding six white horses" and that "we'll go out to greet her." The song also describes what will be eaten when she comes (chicken and dumplings) and what those singing will be wearing (red pajamas).

"Clementine" is a song that came out of the California gold rush in the mid-1800s. It tells the story of a woman who was "lost and gone forever" when she was killed. ("In a cavern, in a canyon, excavating for a mine/Met a miner '49er and his daughter, Clementine.")

Another famous folk song is "Swing Low, Sweet Chariot." This song was sung by slaves in the United States and today is sung by people of all races. The words "Swing low, sweet chariot, coming for to carry me home . . . " describe the soul being united with God after death. Like other folk songs that sprang from slaves, "Swing Low, Sweet Chariot" is simple, moving, and powerful.

Directions: Answer these questions about folk music.

1. What is the purpose of folk music? ______________________________

____

2. What food is sung about in "She'll Be Comin' 'Round the Mountain"? ______________________________

____

3. Where did Clementine live?

☐ Florida ☐ Mississippi ☐ California

4. Where in the United States do you think "Swing Low, Sweet Chariot" was first sung?

☐ the North ☐ the West ☐ the South

Name ______________________________

Recalling Details: Woodwinds

There are four kinds of woodwind instruments in modern bands. They are flutes, oboes, clarinets, and bassoons. They are called "woodwind" instruments for two sensible reasons. In the beginning, they were all made of wood. Also, the musician's breath, or "wind," was required to play them.

Although they are all woodwinds, these instruments look different and are played differently. To play an oboe, the musician blows through a mouthpiece on the front of the instrument. The mouthpiece, called a *reed,* is made of two flat pieces of a kind of wood called *cane*. Clarinet players also blow into a reed mouthpiece. The clarinet has only one reed in its mouthpiece.

To play the flute, the musician blows across a hole near one end of the instrument. The way the breath is aimed helps to make the flute's different sounds. The bassoon is the largest woodwind instrument. Bassoon players blow through a mouthpiece that goes through a short metal pipe before it goes into the body of the bassoon. It makes a very different sound from the clarinet or the oboe.

Woodwind instruments also have keys—but not the kind of keys that open locks. These keys are more like levers that the musician pushes up and down. The levers cover holes. When the musician pushes down on a lever, it closes that hole. When the player lifts his or her finger, it opens the hole. Different sounds are produced by controlling the amount of breath, or "wind," that goes through the holes.

Directions: Answer these questions about woodwind instruments.

1. What instruments are in the woodwind section? ______________________________

2. Why are some instruments called woodwinds? ______________________________

____

3. How is a flute different from the other woodwinds? ______________________________

4. What happens when a musician pushes down on a woodwind key? ______________________________

____

5. How would a woodwind musician open the holes on his or her instrument?

____

Name ______________________________

Comprehension: Harp Happenings

If you have ever heard a harpist play, you know what a lovely sound a harp makes. Music experts say the harp is among the oldest of instruments. It probably was invented several thousand years ago in or near Egypt.

The first harps are believed to have been made by stretching a string tightly between an empty tortoise shell and a curved pole. The empty shell magnified the sound the string made when it was plucked. More strings were added later so that more sounds could be made. Over the centuries, the shape of the harp gradually was changed into that of the large, graceful instruments we recognize today.

Here is how a harpist plays a harp. First, he or she leans the harp against his or her right shoulder. Then, the harpist puts his or her hands on either side of the harp and plucks its strings with both hands.

A harp has seven pedals on the bottom back. The audience usually cannot see these pedals. Most people are surprised to learn about them. The pedals are connected to the strings. Stepping on a particular pedal causes certain strings to tighten. The tightening and loosening of the strings makes different sounds; so does the way the strings are plucked with the hands.

At first glance, harps look like simple instruments. Actually, they are rather complicated and difficult to keep in tune. A harpist often spends as long as half an hour before a performance tuning his or her harp's strings so it produces the correct sounds.

Directions: Answer these questions about harps.

1. When were harps invented? ______________________________

2. Where were harps invented? ______________________________

3. What is a person who plays the harp called? ______________________________

4. The harpist leans the harp against his or her

☐ right shoulder. ☐ left shoulder. ☐ left knee.

5. How many pedals does a harp have?

☐ five ☐ six ☐ seven

6. Harps are easy to play.

☐ true ☐ false

Name ______________________________

Comprehension: Brass Shows Class

If you like band music, you probably love the music made by brass instruments. Bright, loud, moving, and magnificent—all these words describe the sounds made by brass.

Some of the earliest instruments were horns. Made from hollowed-out animal horns, these primitive instruments could not possibly have made the rich sounds of modern horns that are made of brass.

Most modern brass bands have three instruments—tubas, trombones, and trumpets. Combined, these instruments can produce stirring marches, as well as haunting melodies. The most famous composer for brass instruments was John Phillip Sousa. Born in Washington, D.C., in 1854, Sousa was a military band conductor and composer. He died in 1932, but his music is still very popular today. One of Sousa's most famous tunes for military bands is "Stars and Stripes Forever."

Besides composing band music, Sousa also invented a practical band instrument—the sousaphone. The sousaphone is a huge tuba that makes very low noises. Because of the way it curls around the body, a sousaphone is easier to carry than a tuba, especially when the musician must march. This is exactly why John Phillip Sousa invented it!

Directions: Answer these questions about brass instruments.

1. Who invented the sousaphone? ______________________________

2. What were the first horns made from? ______________________________

3. Where was John Phillip Sousa born? ______________________________

4. When did John Phillip Sousa die? ______________________________

5. Why did Sousa invent the sousaphone? ______________________________

____

6. What types of instruments make up a modern brass band? ______________________________

____

Name ______________________________

Comprehension: Violins

If you know anything about violin music, chances are you have heard the word *Stradivarius* (Strad-uh-vary-us). Stradivarius is the name for the world's most magnificent violins. They are named after their creator, Antonio Stradivari.

Stradivari was born in northern Italy and lived from 1644 to 1737. Cremona, the town he lived in, was a place where violins were manufactured. Stradivari was very young when he learned to play the violin. He grew to love the instrument so much that he began to make them himself.

Violins were new instruments during Stradivari's time. People made them in different sizes and shapes and of different types of wood. Stradivari is said to have been very particular about the wood he selected for his violins. He took long walks alone in the forest to find just the right tree. He is also said to have used a secret and special type of varnish to put on the wood. Whatever the reasons, his violins are the best in the world.

Stradivari put such care and love into his violins that they are still used today. Many of these are in museums. But some wealthy musicians, who can afford the thousands and thousands of dollars they cost, own Stradivarius violins.

Stradivari passed his methods on to his sons. But the secrets of making Stradivarius violins seem to have died out with the family. Their rarity, as well as their mellow sound, make Stradivarius violins among the most prized instruments in the world.

Directions: Answer these questions about Stradivarius violins.

1. Where did Stradivari live? ______________________________

2. Why did he begin making violins? ______________________________

3. Why are Stradivarius violins special? ______________________________

____

4. Where can Stradivarius violins be found today? ______________________________

____

5. How did Stradivari select the wood for his violins? ______________________________

____

6. Who else knew Stradivari's secrets for making such superior violins? ______________________________

Name ___________________________

Main Idea: Creating Art

No one knows exactly when the first human created the first painting. Crude drawings and paintings on the walls of caves show that humans have probably always expressed themselves through art. These early cave pictures show animals being hunted, people dancing, and other events of daily life. The simplicity of the paintings reflect the simple lifestyles of these primitive people.

The subjects of early paintings also help to make another important point. Art is not created out of nothing. The subjects an artist chooses to paint reflect the history, politics, and culture of the time and place in which he or she lives. An artist born and raised in New York City, for example, is not likely to paint scenes of the Rocky Mountains. An artist living in the Rockies is not likely to paint pictures of city life.

Of course, not all paintings are realistic. Many artists choose to paint pictures that show their own "inner vision" as opposed to what they see with their eyes. Many religious paintings of earlier centuries look realistic but contain figures of angels. These paintings combine the artist's inner vision of angels with other things, such as church buildings, that can be seen.

Directions: Answer these questions about creating art.

1. Circle the main idea:

Art was important to primitive people because it showed hunting and dancing scenes, and is still important today.

Through the ages, artists have created paintings that reflect the culture, history, and politics of the times, as well as their own inner visions.

2. Why is an artist living in the Rocky Mountains less likely to paint city scenes?

____

____

3. In addition to what they see with their eyes, what do some artists' paintings also show?

____

____

Name ______________________

Comprehension: Leonardo da Vinci

Many people believe that Leonardo da Vinci, an Italian artist and inventor who lived from 1452 to 1519, was the most brilliant person ever born. He was certainly a man ahead of his time! Records show that da Vinci loved the earth and was curious about everything on it.

To learn about the human body, he dissected corpses to find out what was inside. In the 15th and 16th centuries, dissecting the dead was against the laws of the Catholic church. Leonardo was a brave man!

He was also an inventor. Leonardo invented a parachute and designed a type of helicopter—5 centuries before airplanes were invented! Another of da Vinci's major talents was painting. You have probably seen a print, or copy, of one of his most famous paintings. It is called *The Last Supper*, and shows Jesus eating his final meal with his disciples. It took da Vinci 3 years to paint *The Last Supper*. The man who hired da Vinci to do the painting was upset. He went to da Vinci to ask why it was taking so long. The problem, said da Vinci, was that in the painting, Jesus has just told the disciples that one of them would betray him. He wanted to get their expressions exactly right as each cried out, "Lord, am I the one?"

Another famous painting by da Vinci is called the *Mona Lisa*. Have you seen a print of this painting? Maybe you have been lucky enough to see the original hanging in a Paris art museum called the Louvre (Loov). If so, you know that Mona Lisa has a wistful expression on her face. The painting is of a real woman, the wife of an Italian merchant. Art historians believe she looks wistful because one of her children had recently died.

Directions: Answer these questions about Leonardo da Vinci.

1. How old was da Vinci when he died? ______________________

2. Name two of da Vinci's inventions. ______________________

____

3. Name two famous paintings by da Vinci. ______________________

____

4. In which Paris museum does *Mona Lisa* hang? ☐ Lourre ☐ Loure ☐ Louvre

Name ______________________________

Comprehension: Michelangelo

Another famous painter of the late 14th and early 15th centuries was Michelangelo Buonarroti. Michelangelo, who lived from 1475 to 1564, was also an Italian. Like da Vinci, his genius was apparent at a young age. When he was 13, the ruler of his hometown of Florence, Lorenzo Medici (Muh-dee-chee), befriended Michelangelo and asked him to live in the palace. There, Michelangelo studied sculpture and met many artists.

By the time he was 18, Michelangelo was a respected sculptor. He created one of his most famous religious sculptures, the *Pieta* (pee-ay-tah), when he was only 21. Then, the Medici family abruptly fell from power and Michelangelo had to leave Florence.

Still, his work was well known and he was able to make a living. In 1503, Pope Julius II called Michelangelo to Rome. He wanted Michelangelo to paint the tomb where he would someday be buried. Michelangelo preferred sculpting to painting, but no one turned down the pope! Before Michelangelo finished his painting, however, the pope ordered Michelangelo to begin painting the ceiling of the Sistine Chapel inside the Vatican. (The Vatican is the palace and surrounding area where the pope lives in Rome.)

Michelangelo was very angry! He did not like to paint. He wanted to create sculptures. But no one turns down the pope. After much complaining, Michelangelo began work on what would be his most famous project.

Directions: Answer these questions about Michelangelo.

1. How old was Michelangelo when he died? ______________________________

2. What was the first project Pope Julius II asked Michelangelo to paint?

____

3. What is the Vatican? ______________________________

4. What was the second project the pope asked Michelangelo to do?

☐ paint his tomb's ceiling ☐ paint the Sistine Chapel's ceiling

Name ______________________________

Comprehension: Rembrandt

Most art critics agree that Rembrandt (Rem-brant) was one of the greatest painters of all time. This Dutch artist, who lived from 1606 to 1669, painted some of the world's finest portraits.

Rembrandt, whose full name was Rembrandt van Rijn, was born in Holland to a wealthy family. He was sent to a fine university, but he did not like his studies. He only wanted to paint. He sketched the faces of people around him. During his lifetime, Rembrandt painted eleven portraits of his father and nearly as many of his mother. From the beginning, the faces of old people fascinated him.

When he was 25, Rembrandt went to paint in Amsterdam, a large city in Holland where he lived for the rest of his life. There, he married a wealthy woman named Saskia, whom he loved deeply. She died from a disease called tuberculosis (ta-bur-ku-lo-sis) after only eight years of marriage, leaving behind a young son named Titus (Ty-tuss).

Rembrandt was heartbroken over his wife's death. He began to spend all his time painting. But instead of painting what his customers wanted, he painted exactly the way he wanted. Unsold pictures filled his house. They were wonderful paintings, but they were not the type of portraits people wanted. Rembrandt could not pay his debts. He and his son were thrown into the streets. The creditors took his home, his possessions, and his paintings. One of the finest painters on earth was treated like a criminal.

Directions: Answer these questions about Rembrandt.

1. How old was Rembrandt when he died? ______________________________

2. In what city did he spend most of his life? ______________________________

3. How many children did Rembrandt have? ______________________________

4. Rembrandt's wife was named

☐ Sasha. ☐ Saskia. ☐ Saksia.

5. These filled his house after his wife's death.

☐ friends ☐ customers ☐ unsold paintings

Name ____________________

Nouns

A **noun** is a word that names a person, place, or thing.

Examples:

person — friend
place — home
thing — desk

Nouns are used many ways in sentences. They can be the subjects of sentences.

Example: Noun as subject: Your high-topped **sneakers** look great with that outfit.

Nouns can be direct objects of a sentence. The **direct object** follows the verb and completes its meaning. It answers the question **who** or **what**.

Example: Noun as direct object: Shelly's family bought a new **car**.

Nouns can be indirect objects. An **indirect object** comes between the verb and the direct object and tells **to whom** or **for whom** something was done.

Example: Noun as indirect object: She gave **Tina** a big hug.

Directions: Underline all the nouns. Write **S** above the noun if it is a subject, **DO** if it is a direct object, or **IO** if it is an indirect object. The first one has been done for you.

1. Do alligators (S) eat people (DO)?
2. James hit a home run, and our team won the game.
3. The famous actor gave Susan his autograph.
4. Eric loaned Keith his bicycle.
5. The kindergarten children painted cute pictures.
6. Robin sold David some chocolate chip cookies.
7. The neighbors planned a going-away party and bought a gift.
8. The party and gift surprised Kurt and his family.
9. My scout leader told our group a funny joke.
10. Karen made her little sister a clown costume.

Name ______________________________

Nouns

Directions: Write 10 nouns for each category.

People

1. ______________________
2. ______________________
3. ______________________
4. ______________________
5. ______________________
6. ______________________
7. ______________________
8. ______________________
9. ______________________
10. ______________________

Places

1. ______________________
2. ______________________
3. ______________________
4. ______________________
5. ______________________
6. ______________________
7. ______________________
8. ______________________
9. ______________________
10. ______________________

Things

1. ______________________
2. ______________________
3. ______________________
4. ______________________
5. ______________________
6. ______________________
7. ______________________
8. ______________________
9. ______________________
10. ______________________

Name ______________________________

Proper and Common Nouns

Proper nouns name specific people, places, or things.

Examples: Washington, D.C., Thomas Jefferson, Red Sea

Common nouns name nonspecific people, places, or things.

Examples: man, fortress, dog

Directions: Underline the proper nouns and circle the common nouns in each sentence.

1. My friend, Josephine, loves to go to the docks to watch the boats sail into the harbor.
2. Josephine is especially interested in the boat named *Maiden Voyage*.
3. This boat is painted red with yellow stripes and has several large masts.
4. Its sails are white and billow in the wind.
5. At Misty Harbor, many boats are always sailing in and out.
6. The crews on the boats rush from bow to stern working diligently to keep the sailboats moving.
7. Josephine has been invited aboard *Maiden Voyage* by its captain.
8. Captain Ferdinand knew of her interest in sailboats, so he offered a tour.
9. Josephine was amazed at the gear aboard the boat and the skills of the crew.
10. It is Josephine's dream to sail the Atlantic Ocean on a boat similar to *Maiden Voyage*.
11. Her mother is not sure of this dangerous dream and urges Josephine to consider safer dreams.
12. Josephine thinks of early explorers like Christopher Columbus, Amerigo Vespucci, and Leif Ericson.
13. She thinks these men must have been brave to set out into the unknown waters of the world.
14. Their boats were often small and provided little protection from major ocean storms.
15. Josephine believes that if early explorers could challenge the rough ocean waters, she could, too.

Name ______________________________

Abstract and Concrete Nouns

Concrete nouns name something that can be touched or seen. **Abstract nouns** name an idea, a thought, or a feeling which cannot be touched or seen.

Examples:

concrete nouns: house, puppy, chair
abstract nouns: love, happiness, fear

Directions: Write **concrete** or **abstract** in the blank after each noun.

1. loyalty ____________________
2. lightbulb ____________________
3. quarter ____________________
4. hope ____________________
5. satellite ____________________
6. ability ____________________
7. patio ____________________
8. door ____________________
9. allegiance ____________________
10. Cuba ____________________
11. Michael Jordan ____________________
12. friendship ____________________
13. telephone ____________________
14. computer ____________________

Directions: Write eight nouns for each category.

Concrete	Abstract
1. ____________	1. ____________
2. ____________	2. ____________
3. ____________	3. ____________
4. ____________	4. ____________
5. ____________	5. ____________
6. ____________	6. ____________
7. ____________	7. ____________
8. ____________	8. ____________

Name ______________________________

For Sale

A **possessive noun** shows ownership. To make a singular noun possessive, add an **apostrophe** and an **s**.

To make a plural noun possessive, check the last letter—if the word ends in **s**, add an apostrophe after it to show posession. If it doesn't, add an apostrophe and an **s**.

Examples: my mother's friends   the parents' organization   the women's group

Directions: The Eastborough Youth Center is having its yearly rummage sale. Everyone in town has been asked to donate items to sell to raise money. Rewrite the missing noun from each sentence as a possessive.

1. ______________ (Carlos) feet had grown, so he brought his used inline skates.
2. ______________ (Jason) chess set was old but had all the pieces.
3. ______________ (Maddie) toy mouse was broken and no one wanted to buy it.
4. On the other hand, her ______________ (brother) teddy bear sold right away.
5. The ______________ (children) toys were all labeled with price tags.
6. The ______________ (parents) job was to take the money.
7. At 2:00, there was an announcement: "______________ (someone) car lights are on."
8. A little girl called out, "Hey, that's my ______________ (sisters) car!"
9. We were all surprised when one ______________ (table) leg gave out and all the donated books fell on the floor.
10. We propped the table back up with the ______________ (janitor) rope and picked up the books.
11. At 3:00, the ______________ (Director) husband brought cookies for the volunteers to enjoy.

Directions: Now, fill in the blanks with possessive nouns of your own.

1. Belinda was happy when a boy bought the old toys she had found in her ______________ garage.
2. At 5:00, the sale was over and ______________ hard work was finished for the day.
3. ______________ mother counted the proceeds from the sale; they had earned over $500!

Name ______________________________

A Thunk in the Night

An **interrogative pronoun** asks a question. **Who**, **what**, and **which** are all interrogative pronouns.

An **indefinite pronoun** does not refer to a specific person, place, or thing. **Somebody**, **anyone**, **all**, **everyone**, **something**, **anything**, **both**, **either**, **none**, and **nothing** are all indefinite pronouns.

Directions: Use the code below to fill in the missing interrogative and indefinite pronouns. Once you have finished, go back and circle all the interrogative pronouns.

a	b	c	d	e	f	g	h	i	j	k	l	m	n	o	p	q	r	s	t	u	v	w	x	y	z
z	y	x	w	v	u	t	s	r	q	p	o	n	m	l	k	j	i	h	g	f	e	d	c	b	a

It was midnight when I glanced at the clock. I had been asleep, but __________ (hlnvgsrmt) awakened me. THUNK! Didn't __________ (zmblmv) hear __________ (zmbgsrmt)? Apparently not, because __________ (vevibImv) was still sleeping soundly.

I decided to wake my sister. I shook her, saying, "There's __________ (hlnvlmv) outside. Listen!" She sat up slowly, rubbing her eyes. THUNK! There it was again.

"__________ (Dszg) is that? __________ (Dsl) could it be?" she asked.

__________ (Ylgs) of us ran to the window.

We saw __________ (mlgsrmt)! THUNK! There it was again.

"That's coming from the bird feeder!" she said.

"__________ (Dszg) birds come to the feeder at night?"

"__________ (Mlmv) that I know about," I said.

THUNK! We heard it again.

"Let's get the flashlights," my sister said.

"__________ (Dsrxs) do you want?" I asked.

"__________ (Vrgsvi) is fine," she answered. Guess what we saw. A raccoon! That's __________ (dszg) was making the thunking sound. __________ (zoo) I can say is that I'm glad the mystery is solved!

Name ______________________________

Do You Agree?

A pronoun must agree with its **antecedent**, the word to which it refers. Choosing the correct pronoun can be tricky when your antecedent is an **indefinite pronoun** such as **someone**, **nobody**, **several**, **few**, and **most**. These rules can help:

- Use **his** or **her** if the antecedent is a singular pronoun.
- Use **their** if the antecedent is plural.

Some indefinite pronouns like **most** and **none** can be singular or plural depending on how they are used in the sentence. If it has more than one antecedent joined by **or** or **nor**, the pronoun should agree with the antecedent that is closer to it.

Directions: Underline the pronoun in parentheses that agrees with its antecedent. Give yourself 3 points for each correct item. Then, add up your total points and check the score card at the bottom of the page.

1. ___ Someone left (their, his or her) backpack on the bus.
2. ___ Most of my friends like (their, his or her) classes.
3. ___ She should have had each guest bring (their, his or her) own lunch.
4. ___ Linda and Andy found (their, her or her) notebooks.
5. ___ One of my brothers lost (their, his) baseball mitt.
6. ___ Neither Ann nor Jackie brought (their, her) sneakers.
7. ___ Anyone who wants to go should ask (their, his or her) parents.
8. ___ A few of the parents drove (their, his or her) vans.
9. ___ Each of the boys took (their, his) jacket.
10. ___ Beth or Angie rode (their, her) bike today.
11. ___ Dave and Mark ran into (their, his) friends at the park.
12. ___ None of the girls brought along (their, her) lunch.
13. ___ Does anybody want to read (their, his or her) report?
14. ___ No one has finished (their, his or her) science project yet.
15. ___ Several of the neighbors left (their, his or her) lights on all night.
16. ___ Both of my parents like (their, his or her) job.
17. ___ No one has taken (their, his or her) seat yet.
18. ___ Others are in (their, his or her) room.

_______ = total points

45 – 54	30 – 42	18 – 27	3 – 15
Great job! You know your stuff!	Good going! You're on your way.	Good try! Keep at it.	Reread the rules and try again.

Name ______________________________

Singular or Plural?

A **singular noun** names one person, place, or thing. A **plural noun** names more than one person, place, or thing.

Directions: First, read the rules for making plural nouns. Next, cover the rules with a sheet of paper. Write the plural for each verb listed at the bottom of the page. Finally, compare your answers to the rules. How did you do?

For regular nouns:

- Add **s** to most singular nouns to make them plural: dog/dogs, restaurant/restaurants, crayon/crayons.
- If a word ends in **s**, **sh**, **ch**, or **x**, add **es** to make it plural: class/classes, beach/beaches, fox/foxes.
- If a noun ends in a **consonant** and **y**, change the **y** to **i** and add **es**: party/parties, jelly/jellies, lady/ladies.

For irregular nouns:

- Some nouns have the same singular and plural form: fish/fish, deer/deer.
- Some nouns change spelling completely when they become plural: child/children, goose/geese.
- Some nouns that end in **f** or **fe** can be made plural by replacing the **f** or **fe** with **v** and adding **es**: leaf/leaves, wife/wives.
- Other nouns that end in **f** can be made plural simply by adding **s**: chief/chiefs, oaf/oafs.
- If a noun ends in a consonant followed by **o**, check the dictionary to find out the plural form. Some end in **s** and some end in **es**: cello/cellos, tomato/tomatoes.

1. wolf ______________________

2. cheese ______________________

3. baby ______________________

4. buffalo ______________________

5. Walsh ______________________

6. idea ______________________

7. knife ______________________

8. piano ______________________

9. jetty ______________________

10. galosh ______________________

11. Johnson ______________________

12. bus ______________________

13. county ______________________

14. sandwich ______________________

15. sheriff ______________________

16. life ______________________

Name ______________________________

Perplexing Plurals

calves
echoes
elves
geese
halves
handkerchiefs
heroes
leaves
moose
potatoes
scarves
shelves
thieves
tomatoes
wives
wolves
women
yourselves

Some plurals involve changes in vowels or even consonants. These are called **irregular plurals**. Here are some common rules for spelling plurals.

Most words ending in **f** or **fe** form the plural by changing the **f** or **fe** to **v** and adding **es**. **Example:** wolf–wolves

A few words ending in **f** just add **s**. **Example:** chief–chiefs

Words ending in **o** add **s** or **es**. **Example:** buffalo–buffaloes

Some plurals involve changes within the word.
Examples: foot–feet   mouse–mice

Some singular and plural forms have the same spelling.
Examples: deer–deer   sheep–sheep

Directions: Write the plural form of each word from the word list in the appropriate category.

f to **v**, add **es**

______________________ ______________________
______________________ ______________________
______________________ ______________________
______________________ ______________________
______________________ ______________________

same singular and plural

____

add **s** only

____

vowel change

____
____

end in **o**, add **es**

______________________ ______________________
______________________ ______________________

Directions: Complete the following analogies using the words from the word list.

1. **Snow** is to **shovel** as ______________ are to **rake**.
2. **Boys** are to **men** as **girls** are to ______________ .
3. ______________ are to **neck** as **belts** are to **waist**.
4. **Lives** are to **life** as ______________ are to **calf**.
5. **Mouse** is to **mice** as **goose** is to ______________ .

Name ______________________________

Persistent Plurals

anniversary
beauty
birthday
chimney
decoy
dictionary
highway
holiday
industry
monkey
mortuary
party
quantity
salary
strawberry
survey
turkey
valley

Words ending in **y**, preceded by a vowel, form the plural by adding **s** to the singular. **Example:** boy → boys

Words ending in **y**, preceded by a consonant, form the plural by changing the **y** to **i** and adding **es**.
Example: bunny → bunnies

Directions: Using the rules above, write the **singular** and **plural** forms of each word from the word list in the appropriate category.

vowel **y** = add **s**

1. ______________ ______________
2. ______________ ______________
3. ______________ ______________
4. ______________ ______________
5. ______________ ______________
6. ______________ ______________
7. ______________ ______________
8. ______________ ______________
9. ______________ ______________

consonant **y** = change **y** to **i** + **es**

1. ______________ ______________
2. ______________ ______________
3. ______________ ______________
4. ______________ ______________
5. ______________ ______________
6. ______________ ______________
7. ______________ ______________
8. ______________ ______________
9. ______________ ______________

Directions: On the lines below, rewrite the two rules above in your own words.

____

____

____

Name ______________________________

Transitive Tongue Twisters

A **transitive verb** is an action verb that needs a direct object to complete a sentence's meaning.

Directions: Use the pattern **noun–transitive verb–noun** to write some tongue twisters in alphabetical order. The nouns and verb in each tongue twister must begin with the same letter. **Hint:** Think of your transitive verbs first!

A Apples attract ants.

B Betty bothered the bears.

C Cathy caught a cab.

D ______________________________

E ______________________________

F ______________________________

G ______________________________

H ______________________________

I ______________________________

J ______________________________

K ______________________________

L ______________________________

M ______________________________

N ______________________________

O ______________________________

P ______________________________

Q ______________________________

R ______________________________

S ______________________________

T ______________________________

U ______________________________

V ______________________________

W ______________________________

X ______________________________

Y ______________________________

Z ______________________________

Name ____________________________

The Art Exhibit

A **verb phrase** consists of one **main verb** and one or more **helping verbs**. The main verb is the most important verb in a verb phrase.

Directions: The following is a list of quotes overheard at Lincoln School's Fall Art Exhibit. Find the verb phrase in each quote. Then, circle the main verb and underline the helping verbs. The first one has been done for you.

1. "Who could have drawn that picture?"
2. "Bobby must have been the artist. He has been drawing since the third grade."
3. "My daughter painted that picture. I will be having it framed as soon as the exhibit is over."
4. "The art department said that they will be organizing another exhibit soon."
5. "I am going to draw something for the next exhibit."
6. "Eric will show his painting, too. He has been working on it for the past few weeks."
7. "Any student can be considered for one of the exhibits. But only the best work is shown."
8. "We must not bring food or drinks to the room; if someone spilled, the artwork could be ruined."
9. "That's Mr. Franklin, the art teacher. He will be showing off the artwork once everyone is here."
10. "The name of the artist must be written on each work."
11. "You will recognize many of the artists' names."
12. "This is the best exhibit the school has put on in two years!"

Name ____________________

Linking Verbs

Linking verbs link the subject to a word in the predicate. The linking verbs most often used are **am**, **is**, **are**, **was**, and **were**.

Example:
We were **happy** about the outcome.

A linking verb may be followed by a **predicate noun**, which renames the subject, or a **predicate adjective**, which describes the subject.

Examples:
Harry is a **teacher**. (predicate noun)
Harry is **confident**. (predicate adjective)

Directions: Complete each sentence with a predicate noun.

1. Sarah is a ________________ .   **2.** Her best friend is a ________________ .

Directions: Circle each predicate noun. Underline the noun or pronoun in the subject that is renamed.

1. The children were actors.

2. The setting of the play was a garden.

3. Butterflies are main characters in the play.

4. Ralph is the star.

Directions: Complete each sentence with a predicate adjective.

1. Today's weather is ________________ .   **2.** Tom will be ________________ .

Directions: Circle each predicate adjective. Underline the noun or pronoun in the subject that is described.

1. The trap-door spider is clever.

2. Its building skills are amazing.

3. The webs covering the walls were soft and silky.

4. The trap was invisible.

Name ______________________________

Irregular Verbs

Verbs that do not add **ed** to show the past tense are called **irregular verbs**. Irregular verbs change in spelling in the past tense.

Examples:

Present	**Past**	**Past With Helpers**
begin	began	(has, have) begun
see	saw	(has, have) seen
drive	drove	(has, have) driven

Directions: Fill in the blanks on the chart. You may refer to a dictionary.

Present	Past	Past With Helpers
speak		
		taken
		ridden
choose		
	rang	
	went	
drink		
		driven
	drew	
know		
		eaten
do		

Directions: Underline the correct verb in each sentence below.

1. Martha has (began, begun) her research project.
2. First, she (chose, chosen) the topic.
3. She (drove, driven) many places to locate information.
4. Martha made a list of the interviews she had (did, done).
5. She (spoke, spoken) to people of many ages.
6. Many (knew, known) a great deal about the subject.
7. While interviewing people, Martha had (took, taken) notes.
8. Diagrams were (drew, drawn) for the project.

Name ______________________________

Forms of Be, Do, and Have

Some forms of the verb **be** can be used as linking or helping verbs. Three forms of **be** cannot be used alone as verbs: **be**, **being**, and **been**. These must always be used with helping verbs.

Examples:
Polar bears **are** carnivores. (**be** as linking verb)
The polar bear **is** hunting the seal. (**be** as helping verb)
A polar bear **has been** seen near here. (**be** with helping verb)
Forms of **be**: am, is, are, was, were, be, being, been

Directions: Complete each sentence below with the correct form of the verb **be** found in parentheses. Add helping verbs where needed.

1. Polar bears ______________ excellent swimmers. (is, are)
2. The polar bear ________________ seen running at a speed of 35 miles per hour. (was, being)
3. I ______________ sure I saw a polar bear swimming in the water. (am, are)
4. Polar bears ______________________ seen swimming many miles from shore. (been, have been)

The verbs **do** and **have** can be used as main verbs or as helping verbs.

Examples:
I **have** traveled to Canada to see polar bears. (helping verb)
I **did** my report on polar bears yesterday. (main verb)
Forms of **do**: do, did, done   Forms of **have**: have, has, had

Directions: Complete the story below using the correct forms of the verbs **do** and **have**.

I ____________ believe polar bears are very beautiful. I ______________ seen them along the coast of Alaska. I ________________ see one come up to our tour bus. By the age of 10 years, a male polar bear ____________________ grown to its full size. Countries around the Arctic have _________________ a very good job of trying to save the polar bear from extinction. Polar bears _______________ beautiful coats which _____________ attracted hunters. Now, the bears ________________ protection from hunters by law.

Name ______________________________

Troublesome Verb Pairs

Don't confuse verbs that have similar meanings.

Lay means *put* or *place*.
Lie means *rest* or *recline*.

Set means *put something somewhere*.
Sit means *sit down*.

Let means *allow*.
Leave means *allow to remain*.

Teach means *show how*.
Learn means *find out*.

Lend means *give to someone*.
Borrow means *get from someone*.

Directions: Write the correct verb on each blank below.

"Mark, did you ________________ (set, sit) the saddle on the fence?" David asked. "Yes, David. I was going to ______________ (let, leave) it in the barn, but it was heavy."

Did you ________________ (teach, learn) how to throw the saddle onto your horse's back yet?" Mark asked.

"Yes, and then I needed to ______________ (lay, lie) down and rest," David answered. "I was going to ______________ (lend, borrow) you a hand, but I was too busy trying to ______________ (teach, learn) how to rope," David remarked.

"Will you ______________ (let, leave) me ______________ (lend, borrow) your horse tomorrow morning?" Mark inquired.

"Sure, Mark. I'm going to just ______________ (set, sit) under a tree and read a book tomorrow morning," David responded.

Directions: Write the correct verb from the parentheses for each sentence.

1. Tell your dog to ________________ (lay, lie) down in front of the barn.
2. Please, ______________________ (lay, lie) that saddle down in front of the stall and ______________________ (set, sit) the bridle on the table.
3. ______________________ (Set, Sit) on that bale of hay and rest your tired legs.
4. Will you ______________________ (let, leave) me wear your boots tomorrow?
5. Don't ______________________ (let, leave) those oats there.
6. I want to ______________________ (teach, learn) how to trim my horse's hooves.
7. We will certainly be happy to ______________________ (teach, learn) you.

Name ______________________________

Review of Verbs

Directions: Underline the complete verb in the following sentences. Be sure to include any helping verbs. Write if the verb is an **action** verb or **being** verb and whether the main verb is **regular** or **irregular**.

action *regular* **He stepped onto the plane.**

________ ________ **1.** Black soot and brilliant diamonds are both carbon.

________ ________ **2.** Diamonds are crystals of carbon.

________ ________ **3.** The carbon must be pressed very hard.

________ ________ **4.** It must be heated to a high temperature at the same time.

________ ________ **5.** Miners usually find diamonds deep in the ground.

________ ________ **6.** For centuries, most diamond mines were in India.

________ ________ **7.** Now the biggest diamond mines are found in Africa.

________ ________ **8.** One day in 1866, some children saw a pretty pebble in a river near Hopetown, South Africa.

________ ________ **9.** It looked like frosted glass.

________ ________ **10.** The children brought it home with them.

________ ________ **11.** One day, a neighbor offered money for it.

________ ________ **12.** The children gave it to him for nothing.

________ ________ **13.** The children did not know the value of the stone.

________ ________ **14.** It was a diamond.

________ ________ **15.** Word about this discovery spread quickly.

________ ________ **16.** Other people hunted for diamonds nearby.

________ ________ **17.** Many of them were disappointed.

________ ________ **18.** However, some people found diamonds in the area.

________ ________ **19.** They were blessed with good fortune.

________ ________ **20.** Diamonds were discovered in other parts of Africa as well.

Name ______________________________

Where in the World?

A **verb** expresses an action or a state of being. The **tense** of a verb tells whether that action or state of being is taking place in the present, the past, or the future.

present tense = happening now
past tense = already happened
future tense = will happen

Directions: Underline the verb or verbs in each sentence and write whether they are past tense, present tense, or future tense on the line. Then, tell where you think the writer is going.

1. ____________ My best friend, Jake, moved to the East Coast last summer.
2. ____________ This afternoon we will see each other for the first time in a year.
3. ____________ My parents surprised me with a plane ticket for my birthday.
4. ____________ Jake and his parents live in the Empire State now.
5. ____________ His mom has a cool job as a translator at the U.N.
6. ____________ I packed all my stuff last night, except for my Yankees cap Jake sent me.
7. ____________ I am excited about seeing Jake after so long.
8. ____________ I hardly slept at all last night.
9. ____________ My dad says it is time to leave for the airport.
10. ____________ The flight will take about four hours.
11. ____________ I will bring along a book and a couple of games to play.
12. ____________ I will call my parents as soon as the plane lands at La Guardia Airport.
13. ____________ I promised my mom three times already.
14. ____________ On Friday, Jake and I will visit the "Lady With the Lamp" and Ellis Island.
15. ____________ Jake's dad also has tickets for a Yankees game.
16. Where is the writer going?

____

____

Name ______________________________

Manuel the Magnificent

The **present tense** tells about something that exists or is happening now. Sometimes you add **s** or **es** to a base verb when the subject is singular.

The **past tense** tells about something that has happened or existed in the past. Most regular verbs in the past tense end in **d** or **ed**.

The **future tense** tells about something that will exist or take place in the future. You usually use the helping verbs **will** or **shall** with the main verb.

Directions: Use a verb from the box in the indicated tense to correctly complete each sentence.

place	applaud	perform	borrow	move	observe	plan
volunteer	hope	select	reveal	climb	amaze	attend

1. Manuel the Magnificent ______________________ you with his act. **future**
2. He ______________________ some of the coolest tricks I've ever seen. **present**
3. I ______________________ his matinee and evening performances today. **future**
4. One time, Manuel ______________________ a dollar bill from an audience member and ____________________________ it at one end of the table. **past**
5. After saying the word "Manuelmagnifico," the dollar bill slowly and mysteriously ____________________________ toward his hand! **past**
6. This afternoon I ______________________ much more carefully to figure out how he does it. **future**
7. A good magician rarely ______________________ how a trick is done. **present**
8. Last year, I ______________________ to let him saw me in half. **past**
9. When I ______________________ from the box unharmed, everyone ____________________________ enthusiastically. **past**
10. Manuel ______________________ to do my favorite trick tonight—making someone disappear right before your eyes. **present**
11. Perhaps he ______________________ me to be the one who disappears. **future**
12. Someday I ______________________ to become as good a magician as Manuel. **present**

Name ______________________________

As a Matter of Fact . . .

An **adjective** is a word that describes a noun or a pronoun. It answers questions such as which one, how many, or what kind of?

Directions: Read the facts below. Circle each adjective and draw an arrow to the noun it describes. Then, write the adjective where it belongs on the chart.

1. The "red eye" is not a terrible disease but an overnight flight.
2. The human body contains eight pints of blood.
3. A bald eagle is not really bald; it has white feathers on its head.
4. Presidents of the United States have had many unusual pets, including an alligator, a turkey, a parrot, raccoons, and a donkey.
5. The imaginary lines that mark the time zones are called meridians.
6. At night, sea otters wrap themselves in beds of kelp, a type of large seaweed, so the currents do not take them out to sea.
7. Mount McKinley is the highest mountain in the United States and is located in Alaska, the biggest and coldest state.
8. On a ship, the day is divided into five watches of four hours each and two watches of two hours each.
9. Among those astronauts who walked on the Moon, Neil Armstrong was first.
10. The eye of the giant squid is reported to be up to 15 inches across.

How Many?	What Kind Of?		Which One?

Name ______________________________

This and That

A **demonstrative adjective** points out a specific person or thing and answers the question which one or which ones.

This and **these** point out nearby people or things. **That** and **those** point out people or things farther away. Use **these** and **those** with plural nouns. Use **this** and **that** with singular nouns.

Directions: Help Clarence the Cartoonist meet his deadline by writing **this**, **that**, **these**, or **those** to complete the sentence in each speech balloon.

If you give me __________ magazine, I'll give you __________ book.
SCIENCE MAGAZINE
I think __________ grapes are much sweeter than __________ over there.
I like __________ sweater better than all of __________ other jackets over there.
Try one of __________ cookies and a piece of __________ pie.

Name ______________________________

Proper Adjectives

Adjectives are words that describe nouns. **Proper adjectives** are formed from proper nouns, and they must be capitalized. Other adjectives are called **common adjectives**.

Examples:

proper adjectives: French toast, **American** flag
common adjectives: cold toast, **waving** flag

Directions: Circle all the adjectives in the sentences below.

1. Camels have carried loads across desert sands for centuries.
2. They were once the only means of transporting goods across the Sahara Desert and Middle Eastern deserts.
3. The Sahara Desert is in the North African desert region.
4. The Arabian camel has one hump, while the Bactrian camel has two humps.
5. The Bactrian camel got its name long ago from a Central Asian country known as Bactria.
6. Both types of camels are used in some Asian regions.
7. In wars, fighting men have ridden the faithful camel.
8. The camel Napoleon rode during his Egyptian campaign was later put in an exhibit.

Directions: Write each circled adjective under the proper heading.

Proper Adjectives

1. ______________________
2. ______________________
3. ______________________
4. ______________________
5. ______________________
6. ______________________
7. ______________________
8. ______________________
9. ______________________
10. ______________________

Common Adjectives

1. ______________________
2. ______________________
3. ______________________
4. ______________________
5. ______________________
6. ______________________
7. ______________________
8. ______________________

Name ______________________________

Adverbs Modify

You have learned that adverbs modify verbs. An **adverb** can also modify **adjectives** and **other adverbs**. These adverbs usually tell **how much** or **to what degree**.

Examples:

The eagle's descent was **very** steep.
(modifies "steep," an adjective)
The eagle attacked the fish **quite** suddenly.
(modifies "suddenly," an adverb)

Directions: Underline only the adverbs in the sentences below that modify an adjective or another adverb. Draw an arrow to the word that each modifies. In the blank, write if the modified word is an adjective or an adverb.

1. The eagle spread its wings <u>very</u> wide. ___*adverb*___
2. It had to fly quite far to the lake. ______________
3. The eagle is an extremely graceful bird. ______________
4. It is much larger than most birds. ______________
5. Its hooked beak is rather sharp. ______________
6. The eagle watched the lake very carefully. ______________
7. A large trout is really tasty food for the eagle. ______________
8. A beautiful rainbow trout jumped quite suddenly out of the water. ______________
9. The eagle has extremely sharp eyesight. ______________
10. It swooped almost instantly toward the fish. ______________

Directions: Complete each sentence with an adverb that modifies the adjective or adverb.

1. The eagle flew ______________ low over the water's surface.
2. Then, it flew ______________ high into the blue summer sky.
3. It landed in its nest ______________ gently.
4. The eagle is a ______________ majestic bird.
5. It has to be ______________ patient as it hunts for food.

Name ______________________________

What's Missing?

Adverbs are words that describe or modify verbs, adjectives, or other adverbs. They answer questions like **when? where? how? how much?**

Directions: Write the correct adverb in each sentence. Use the words in the box. Time yourself. Can you do it in four minutes?

closely	cleverly
little	quite
instantly	carefully
thoroughly	easily
rather	mainly
suddenly	rarely

1. The detectives ______________ searched the crime scene for clues.
2. Just glancing at my mother's face, I knew ______________ that she was upset about something.
3. After working for eight hours we were ______________ tired.
4. No one knows what to wear because the weather has been ______________ unpredictable.
5. ______________ do our parents know about plans for their surprise party.
6. My father has ______________ if ever been late to work, even though he commutes over an hour each morning.
7. The children ______________ disguised themselves so that not even their friends recognized them.
8. The storm hit ______________, leaving many unsuspecting residents stranded.
9. My brother is ______________ interested in music and spends most of his spare time playing his guitar.
10. I ______________ rechecked my calculations to make sure I hadn't made any mistakes.
11. Some people confuse me with my sister because we ______________ resemble each other.
12. We ______________ finished the test in no time at all.

Name ______________________________

Tongue Twisters

Directions: Theodore Thistle loves tongue twisters. Here are a few of them, but he put the adverbs in the wrong places. Underline the adverbs. Next, rewrite each tongue twister, placing the adverbs where they make the most sense. Then, try to say each sentence five times as fast as you can!

1. Peter Piper picked a pluckily peck of pickled peppers.

____

2. Six slowly striped snakes slithered southward.

____

3. Betty Botter boasted 'bout her buttery boldly batter.

____

4. Noisy annoyingly noises annoy Mrs. always Lloyd.

____

5. Fast always Bo-Peep's sleepy sheep fall asleep.

____

6. Bradley Baker burned the brown badly bread.

____

7. A gaggle of ganders gobbled gobs of goober gloriously peas.

____

8. Sherry Shiffler's selfish sister seldom Shelly's shellfish sell.

____

9. Oodles of noisily poodles nibble oodles of noodles.

____

10. Shy Sam Phipps sips Sally's salty silently soup.

____

GRADE 5

Name ______________________________

Spicy Hot!

A **simple subject** is the main noun or pronoun in the subject of a sentence.

A **complete subject** includes the simple subject and all words that modify it.

A **simple predicate** is the verb in the complete predicate.

A **complete predicate** includes the verb and all the words that modify it.

Directions: Which word is missing from each sentence? Is it the simple subject or the simple predicate? Insert a word from the box into the correct sentence, and use the ^ symbol. Then, draw a vertical line between the complete subject and complete predicate in each sentence. The first one has been done for you.

recipes	causes	spices	spoiled	problem
evaporates	consume	curries	reason	helps

1. People who live in hotter climates | typically ^consume spicy, hot foods.

2. Many Mexican and South American call for hot chili peppers.

3. Hot are used in East Indian recipes.

4. The for this is really quite simple.

5. Eating foods with hot spices a person stay cool.

6. Particularly spicy food the body to perspire.

7. Then, the perspiration and cools off the body.

8. Before the days of refrigeration, food quickly.

9. The was especially bad in hot climates.

10. The hot made the food last longer and hid the bad taste of spoiled food.

Name ______________________________

Simon's Silly Sentences

A **simple subject** is the main noun or pronoun in the subject of a sentence.
A **compound subject** consists of two or more simple subjects joined by the conjunctions **and** or **or**.
A **simple predicate** is the verb in the complete predicate.
A **compound predicate** is two or more verbs joined by the conjunctions **and**, **or**, or **but**.

Directions: Simon wants to play a game. In his game, each player has to write four silly sentences using nonsense words. Here's how the game is scored:

1 point for a sentence with a simple subject and a simple predicate
3 points for a sentence with a compound subject or a compound predicate
5 points for a sentence with a compound subject and a compound predicate

Simon has written the following nonsense sentences. Underline each simple subject and predicate. Then, circle the compound subjects and predicates. Determine Simon's score. Finally, see if you can top it by writing four nonsense sentences of your own!

Simon's Sentences **Simon's Score:** _____ points

1. Slipperty Hibbert, Flapperty Flip, and Hippity Pip pluckered Flipperty Gip's pretty purple plips. _____
2. You and Mickety Flickety can flipper and flapper with Dippity Ditz and me on the grippity grop. _____
3. The flippity mip with the frizzy wizzy wuzzies is zippiting zoo dahs today. _____
4. The bibbity mibbity flapmoddle and I gribbled through the hablet but didn't briggle the biblet. _____

Your Sentences **Your Score:** _____ points

____
______________________________ _____
____
______________________________ _____
____
______________________________ _____
____
______________________________ _____

Name ______________________________

Do the Twist

A **direct object** is a noun or pronoun that receives the action of a verb.

Directions: As you read each sentence, underline the direct object. Then, use a sheet of paper, tape, a pencil, and a pair of scissors to find out what the surprise is.

1. Nikki showed me a really neat trick.
2. She found the directions in her math book.
3. First, she took a sheet of notebook paper.
4. Next, she cut a strip about 1 inch wide and 11 inches long.
5. Then, she started to make a loop.
6. Just before Nikki taped the ends together, she made one twist.
7. Now, she had a model of an endless belt, or Mobius strip.
8. Nikki took a pencil, started to draw a line down the middle of the strip, and ended up where she started!
9. Then, she gave me a pair of scissors, so I could cut along the line.
10. Try the activity yourself to see why I was so surprised.

Name ______________________________

Object-ively Speaking

A **direct object** is a noun or pronoun that receives the action of a verb. An **indirect object** is a word or words that come between a verb and its direct object, telling **to whom** or **for whom** something is done.

Directions: Say each of the following tongue twisters five times, as fast as you can, without making a mistake. Then, underline each direct object and circle each indirect object.

1. Betty Blake baked Blake Baker a batch of baked beans.
2. Tad told Todd two tall tales.
3. Will Willa whittle Wally a little wooden whistle?
4. Nate's nice niece Nell knit Nancy a fancy cap.
5. Did Dudley Dooley draw Dewey a doodle?
6. Lilah loaned Lola Layla's lovely lilac leggings.
7. Suki Suzuki saved Celia six seats.
8. Simon Shiller sold Sheila Shiffler shiny silver slippers.
9. Bart bought Bertie a buttery blueberry bagel.
10. Harry handed Harvey Harley's heavy hammer.

Challenge: Now, write some tongue twisters of your own! Be sure to include and underline a direct object and an indirect object in each one.

____

____

____

____

____

____

____

____

____

Name ______________________________

Conjunctions

A conjunction joins words, groups of words, or entire sentences. The most common conjunctions are **and**, **or**, **but**.

Examples:

Christian Huygens **and** Jean Cassini made discoveries about Saturn. (joins subjects)

The Italian astronomer Galileo first saw Saturn's rings through a telescope, **but** the rings weren't very clear. (joins sentences)

He discovered the rings in the early 1600s **and** thought they were large satellites. (joins predicates)

Directions: Add a conjunction to each sentence below.

1. Did you know that Saturn takes about $29\frac{1}{2}$ Earth-years to orbit the Sun, ______________ are you still looking up that fact?
2. Saturn ______________ Earth have very different day lengths.
3. Earth's day is about 24 hours, ______________ Saturn's is only about $10\frac{1}{2}$ hours.
4. Saturn has 23 satellites that have been discovered, ______________ Earth has only one.
5. Saturn's natural satellites all have different names, ______________ Earth's satellite is just called "the Moon."
6. Saturn has many rings that surround it, ______________ Earth has none.

Directions: Add a conjunction to each phrase below that describes Saturn.

1. beautiful ______________ majestic
2. far away, ______________ gigantic
3. larger than Earth, ______________ lighter in comparison
4. shorter days than Earth ______________ faster rotation
5. atmosphere of mostly hydrogen ______________ helium
6. beautiful rings ______________ not the only planet with them

Name ______________________________

The Conjunction Code

Conjunctions are words that join other words, phrases, and sentences.

Directions: Find the pattern in this conjunction code to discover 18 common conjunctions. Use these conjunctions to complete the sentences below. Each conjunction is used only once.

a i n f d b a u f t t o e r r u w n h t i i l l

e u w n h l e e t s h s e w r h b e e n c n

a o u r s e e i a t l h t e h r o b u e g f h o

f r o e r a w s h s e o n o e n v a e s r

1. ______________ you study for your test, I'm going to finish my math homework.
2. I'll tell Mom ______________ you don't give back my CD right now!
3. ______________ you stay ______________ go is completely up to you.
4. We can't go swimming yet, ______________ the surf is too rough.
5. ______________ it rained all night, the field should be dry by game time.
6. We were just about to eat ______________ the phone rang.
7. My friends will wait for me ______________ I get there.
8. We aren't going ______________ you can go, too.
9. Neither my brother ______________ my sister wants to practice right now.
10. We have both math ______________ English homework tonight.
11. ______________ we hear anything, we'll call you immediately.
12. We have to straighten up our room ______________ we can come over.
13. ______________ we plan a picnic, it always rains.
14. I ran as fast as I could ______________ I didn't want to miss the bus.
15. You can go to the dance, ______________ you have to be home by ten o'clock.
16. We will ______________ go to the mall ______________ to a movie tonight.
17. ______________ I return this book to the library, I have to stop at the store.

Name ______________________________

Prepositional Phrases

A **prepositional phrase** is a group of words that begins with a preposition and ends with the object of the preposition.

Example: Water makes up about 65 percent **of the human body**.

Directions: Circle the prepositional phrases in the sentences.

1. An adult skeleton consists of about 200 bones.
2. The body of a 160-pound man contains about 5 quarts of blood.
3. People who live in high altitudes may have more blood flowing in their veins.
4. Our skin helps protect our inner tissues from the outside world.

If a prepositional phrase modifies a noun or pronoun, it acts as an **adjective**.
If a prepositional phrase modifies a verb, it acts as an **adverb**.

Examples: *Fluids* ***in the inner ear*** *help us maintain our balance.* (adjective)
The doctors talked ***in loud voices****.* (adverb)

Directions: Circle the prepositional phrase in each sentence. Then, identify it as an **adjective** or **adverb** on the line.

1. The muscles in the human body number 600. ____________________
2. All adults should brush their 32 teeth with great care. ____________________
3. Our skin might burn in the hot sun. ____________________
4. Every person on the earth is warm-blooded. ____________________
5. The man went through the hospital doors. ____________________
6. The temperature inside the body is about 98.6° F. ____________________
7. The dentist looked inside my mouth. ____________________

Name ________________________________

Is That a Fact?

A **preposition** is a word that shows how one word is related to another in a sentence.

A **prepositional phrase** is a group of words that begins with a preposition and ends with a noun or pronoun. This noun or pronoun is called the **object of the preposition**.

Directions: Each fact below is missing a prepositional phrase. Use the code to figure out each one. Write the phrase, underline the preposition, and circle the object of the preposition.

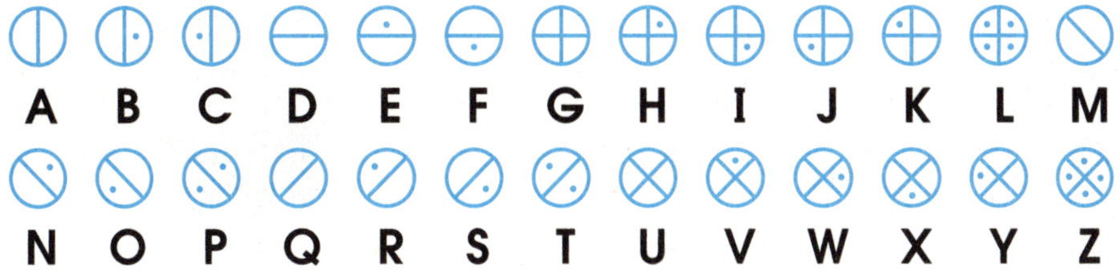

1. The Iditarod is a 1200-mile dogsled race

____

2. Air rushes  at 100 miles per hour when you sneeze.

____

3. Red is the most commonly found color

____

4. The Islands of Hawaii evolved as volcanoes erupted

____

5. French fries are not really  but 

____

6. Bertrand Piccard and Brian Jones were the first to fly   nonstop 

____

Name ______________________

Kinds of Sentences

There are four kinds of sentences.
A **declarative sentence** makes a statement.
Tuesday was a chilly day.
An **interrogative sentence** asks a question.
Was Tuesday a chilly day?
An **imperative sentence** gives a command or makes a request.
Be at my house at 11 o'clock.
An **exclamatory sentence** expresses excitement or strong feeling.
What a terrible storm!

Directions: Identify each type of sentence.

1. The Hawaiian Islands are really mountaintops. ______________________
2. Were those mountains once active volcanoes? ______________________
3. Read the article in the magazine that Sid brought. ______________________
4. What beautiful pictures that article has! ______________________
5. Hawaii is made up of a chain of 132 islands in the Pacific Ocean.
   ____
6. Bring your lei to school tomorrow. ______________________
7. Which island has the most people living on it? ______________________
8. I just can't believe that the small island of Oahu does! ______________________
9. I'm astonished that the average temperature is 75° F! ______________________

Directions: Rewrite each sentence as the type suggested in parentheses.

1. Were the Polynesians the first people on Hawaii? (declarative)
   ____
2. An English explorer, Captain Cook, named the islands the "Sandwich Islands." (interrogative) ____
   ____
3. Will you bring me a present from Hawaii? (imperative)
   ____

Name ______________________________

Interjections and Direct Address

Strong interjections, which show great feeling, are followed by exclamation points.

Mild interjections, such as **now**, **well**, and **yes**, are set apart by commas.

A comma or commas are used to set apart the name of a person being directly spoken to, or addressed, in a sentence. This is called **direct address**.

Examples:

Ugh! That soup is horrible. (strong interjection)
No, I haven't finished my homework yet. (mild interjection)
Sue, please hand me the pencil. (direct address)
Thank you, **Jean**, for your contribution. (direct address)

Directions: Add commas and exclamation points where they are needed in the following sentences.

1. Yes we will finish the science project soon.
2. Wow I forgot that it must be completed by Friday.
3. Oh I forgot that the materials for the experiment are at home.
4. Jim bring the microscope to the science lab.
5. Now Leonard it's your turn to work on the experiment.
6. Will the research for the project be completed soon Amy?
7. No Mrs. Clarke it will take at least another week.
8. Yikes That was a scary experiment you did Mark.

Directions: Add commas and exclamation points where they are needed in the following sentences. In the blank, write the letter of the reason each punctuation mark is used. Some have two answers.

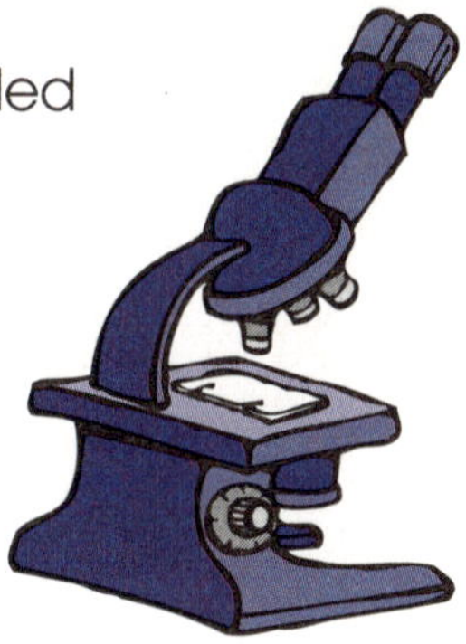

A. Interjection **B.** Direct Address

1. ____ Lewis will you attempt this experiment on air pressure?
2. ____ No I need to work on my electricity project Sam.
3. ____ I need some help Mr. Johnson with my electrical circuit.
4. ____ The science lab is too crowded to set up the project Ms. Chang.
5. ____ Cool I would love to use the other lab.
6. ____ Yes I'll try to set up the project in that room Sarah.
7. ____ Well that solved my problem.

Name ______________________________

Out of Order

To build a good sentence, you must know all the parts of speech and how they function together. For example, adjectives belong before the nouns and pronouns they modify. Adverbs should come as close as possible to the verbs, adjectives, or other adverbs they modify. Interjections usually come at the beginning of a sentence.

Directions: Here are some sentences that Ed wrote. Unfortunately, he misplaced some words or phrases in each one. Rewrite Ed's sentences, correctly placing all the words and phrases where they belong.

1. Would you call kindly me and my brother at your earliest convenience? ______________________________

2. The woman who across the street lives bakes the chocolate cakes most delicious in the world. ______________________________

3. Is the little black dog with spots white, long ears floppy, and stubby tail yours really? ______________________________

4. Hysterically my older sister laughed when she saw my hair how I had fixed for the dance. ______________________________

5. The homemade bread and soup so smelled delicious that hardly we could wait to eat. ______________________________

6. Was that the most terrifying movie ever I've seen. Wow! ______________________________

7. A squirrel our cat chased and was hit by a car almost. ______________________________

8. Read first the book and tell then what you think about me the author. ______________________________

Name ______________________________

Batter Up!

Remember: a sentence is a group of words that expresses a complete thought.

A **simple sentence** consists of a complete subject and a complete predicate. It can have a simple subject or a compound subject and a simple verb or a compound verb.

A **compound sentence** consists of two or more simple sentences joined by a semicolon or by a comma and a coordinating conjunction.

A **complex sentence** consists of one simple sentence and one or more dependent clauses introduced by a subordinating conjunction.

Directions: Rewrite the following story, changing as many simple sentences as you can into compound or complex sentences. You can add your own words or use the coordinating or subordinating conjunctions in the box. Once you have finished, underline each compound sentence and circle each complex sentence.

and	after	before	because	since	but
if	although	until	whenever	or	while
unless	yet	so	when	just as	even though

It's April. It's also a perfect Saturday afternoon for a game of baseball. It's not too hot or humid. No one is using the old vacant lot at the moment. Jeremy and some of his friends decide to organize a neighborhood game. Luis runs home to get his bat, glove, and a couple of baseballs. Luke is the resourceful one of the group. His job is to come up with something for bases. Yuki gets his brother Yuichi and his glove. Tomas and Ricardo look for Jelani and Devon. Jeremy sees Sammy and Eugene down the street and whistles for them to come.

Most of the neighborhood boys gather at the lot in no time. They begin to choose sides. Jeremy's sisters Lisa and Tina happen to show up. They ask to play too. The boys aren't too crazy about that idea. Lisa convinces them otherwise. They need 18 players for two teams. There are only 16 boys. The boys agree. It's a good thing. Lisa hit a home run in the second inning. Tina drove two runners home in the third inning! It was the perfect Saturday afternoon for a game of baseball.

Name ______________________

Contraction Action

aren't
can't
couldn't
didn't
hasn't
he's
I'd
isn't
let's
shouldn't
they're
they've
wasn't
weren't
we've
wouldn't
you'd
you're

Contractions are a shortened form of two words. Missing letters are replaced by an apostrophe.

Directions: Write the correct contraction for each word pair.

you are ______________	should not ______________
would not ______________	did not ______________
I had ______________	could not ______________
let us ______________	was not ______________
we have ______________	are not ______________
you had ______________	is not ______________
has not ______________	they have ______________
he is ______________	can not ______________
they are ______________	were not ______________

Now, put the contractions into word families.

(n't)
not family

______________ ______________
______________ ______________
______________ ______________
______________ ______________
______________ ______________

('s)
is family

____

('s)
us family

____

('re)
are family

____
____

('d)
would/had family

____
____

('ve)
have family

____
____

Name ______________________________

Shorten the Conversation

Directions: Read the conversation below. Circle all the words that can be shortened into contractions. Then, rewrite the sentences using contractions.

1. I have never had so much fun in a class before.

____

2. Luckily, the windy day was not a problem.

____

3. Our teacher was a great skater. Can you believe how many competitions she has won?

____

4. A lot, that is for sure.

____

5. I wanted to show her I could go fast. She said, "Do not go out so fast."

____

6. You will do better if you take your time.

____

7. I could not skate backwards.

____

8. It is hard to do.

____

9. I know we will improve.

____

10. Let us meet here tomorrow to practice.

____

Name ________________________________

More Contraction Action

It's and **its** sound the same, but they have different spellings and meanings. **It's** is a contraction that means *it is*. **Its** means *belonging to*.

Directions: Marla and Darla opened an ice cream parlor. Here's a conversation they had on their first day in business. Write **it's** or **its** to correctly complete each sentence.

1. I hope ________ a busy day with lots of customers.
2. The store is on a good street. ________ location is perfect.
3. ________ going to be a success because of the unusual flavors we offer.
4. Summer is coming. ________ going to be a busy time for us.
5. ________ the best hot weather treat I know.
6. ________ time to unlock the door.
7. I love the bell on the door. ________ sound will ring each time someone comes in.
8. Remember to use the newest scoop. ________ handle is blue.
9. We can't forget to thank everyone. ________ important to be polite.
10. ________ cozy feeling will bring everyone back for more.

Directions: Combine each pronoun with verbs from the box to form contractions. See how many contractions you can make.

will	had	have	am	are	is

1. I ________________________________
2. she ________________________________
3. he ________________________________
4. we ________________________________
5. they ________________________________
6. it ________________________________

Name ______________________________

Capitals

Always remember to capitalize the following:

- first word in a sentence
- first word in a direct quotation
- first word in every line of poetry
- pronoun **I**
- initials
- proper nouns
- proper adjectives

Directions: Underline each word that should begin with a capital letter.

one summer night, seth and tony noticed a bat flying overhead.
"did you know that bats help control insects?" remarked tony.
seth replied, "somehow i always think of dracula when i see a bat."
"long ago, people of slavic countries believed in vampires, but a bat isn't really scary," laughed tony. "a brown bat weighs only about half an ounce." "i haven't seen one up close," admitted seth.
"a good place to see bats is carlsbad caverns in new mexico. a colony of mexican free-tailed bats lives in one of the caves. at dusk, hundreds of thousands of bats fly out to hunt. many american tourists visit there to see this amazing sight."

edwin gould studied the eating habits of bats in cape cod, massachusetts. donald r. griffin photographed bats eating. one tiny bat caught 175 mosquitoes in fifteen minutes of hunting! fredric a. webster discovered that bats catch insects with their tail membranes.

most north american bats hibernate during december, january, and february. when early insects come out in march or april, the bats awaken.

Bats

Bats come out at night,
Catching insects in their flight.
Furry little mammal brown,
Found in country, village, and town.

Name ________________________________

A Comma Conundrum

The **comma (,)** is a punctuation mark that is usually used in a sentence where a pause would be made if you were reading aloud. Commas are always found inside quotation marks.

Directions: There are lots of rules for where to put commas. Connie is making a list of these rules with an example for each one, but she hasn't added the commas yet. Can you help her out? Read the rules. Then, insert commas where they belong.

Always use a comma:

- *before a conjunction when you join an independent clause in a compound sentence.*
  The Sun may be 93 million miles from Earth but it is more than 200,000 times closer than the next nearest star.
- *after a dependent clause that comes at the beginning of a sentence.*
  Even though there are 30,000 species of plants 90% of the world's food comes from just 20 species.
- *between a city and a state.*
  We recently moved to San Francisco California.
- *between the day and year in a date.*
  The Northwest Territories of Canada split in two on April 1 1999.
- *to separate three or more words or phrases in a series.*
  Dinosaur experts use footprints as clues to tell how fast a dinosaur traveled if it ate alone or in a pack and if it was a meat-eater or a plant-eater.
- *after introductory words or phrases and mild interjections.*
  By the way there are over 250,000 species of beetles.
  Yes there are more kinds of beetles than any other animal.
- *to set off the person being directly spoken to.*
  Mike you really ought to check out this book.
  Thanks for the suggestion Beth.
- *to set off appositives, which stand beside a noun and rename it.*
  San Francisco's Lombard Street the most crooked street in the world has ten sharp turns in one block.
- *with words or phrases that interrupt the main idea of a sentence.*
  This symphony in my opinion is Beethoven's best.
- *before a direct quotation in the middle of a sentence.*
  Our teacher asked "How old was Chester Greenwood when he developed his idea for earmuffs?"
- *at the end of a direct quotation that is a statement when it is at the beginning of a sentence.*
  "Chester Greenwood was just 15 years old when he came up with the idea" I answered.

Name ____________________________

Using Commas

Use commas to set off an **appositive**, a noun or phrase that explains or identifies the noun it follows.
Example: Jack, the janitor, walked down the hall.

Use commas to separate words or phrases in a **series**.
Example: He ate the apple, the peach, and the plum.

Use commas after **introductory** words or phrases.
Examples: Yes, I'm going to the fair.
By the way, did you bring a camera?

Use commas to set off a **noun of address**, the name of the person being addressed or spoken to.
Example: Caroline, will you come with me?

Use commas to set off **interrupting** words or phrases.
Example: He was, as you know, an actor before he was elected.

Directions: Add commas to the sentences where they are needed. On each line, explain why you added the comma by writing **appositive**, **series**, **introductory**, **noun of address**, or **interrupting**.

1. Maryanne the new girl in school is a very good cook. ____________________
2. My favorite snacks are red apples pretzels and popcorn. ____________________
3. My skills however do not include cooking. ____________________
4. I know Sally that you love to cook. ____________________
5. That was in my opinion the best meal ever served. ____________________
6. After they finished the books Tom and Larry wrote the report. ____________________
7. Thomas Edison an inventor had failures before each success. ____________________
8. Pete our best soccer player won't be here for the big game. ____________________
9. No I won't be seeing the movie. ____________________
10. The coating on the pecans was sweet sugary and crisp. ____________________
11. That is if I'm not mistaken my yellow and green pencil. ____________________
12. Sam would you please pass me my pen? ____________________

Name ____________________________

Proofreading for Punctuation

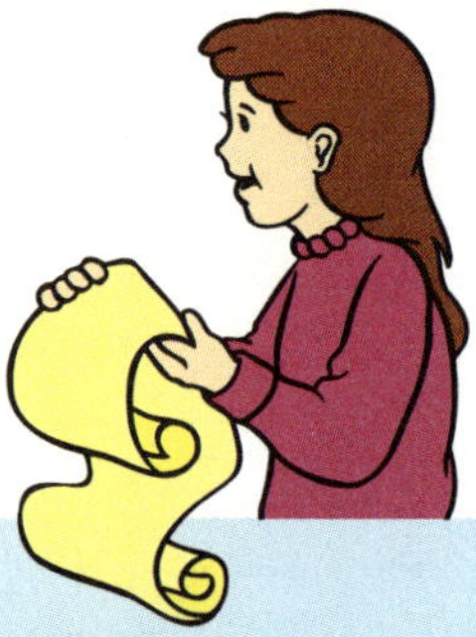

Anna is running for class president. She has written her last campaign speech before the election but has not done a very good job of punctuating it.

Directions: Read her speech. Write in capital letters where needed and add correct punctuation.

> tomorrow you will choose one of five candidates as your class president i want to be the one you choose. why should you vote for me As class president I will collect twenty-five cents a month from every class member The money will be used for a party at the end of the school year I will listen to your suggestions and try to do something about them As president of our class I will go to teachers' meetings I will try to have homework assignments over weekends reduced Vote for me I know I will make the next year the best one for you and our class. it will be a year to remember thank you for your support

Anna did not win the election, but she was a good sport. She wrote a message to Kim, the winner, in the school newspaper. The editor did not proofread Anna's message, and it got published just as she wrote it.

Directions: Correct Anna's work once more.

> I want to congratulate Kim i know she will make a fine class president i am sorry I did not win, but I want Kim and everyone else to know I support her Now that the election is over and the class showed their preference, let's all join together and support Kim congratulations Kim

Name ______________________________

Dolphins

Sometimes the main idea of a paragraph is stated in one sentence. This sentence is called the **topic sentence**. It can be found anywhere in the paragraph, but it usually comes at the beginning or end of the paragraph.

Directions: Underline the topic sentence of each paragraph. Add the missing punctuation.

Dolphins are among the most intelligent animals on Earth. They are playful as well as smart and are easily trained for zoo and aquarium shows. They jump through hoops and fetch and grab objects from the trainer's hands Dolphins communicate with each other in a variety of ways using clicking whistling and slapping sounds.

Dolphins can locate objects easily under the water through a system called *echolocation* This is like a built-in sonar system. The dolphin makes a series of clicking sounds then listens for the sounds as echoes bounce back from the underwater object.

Many dolphins are caught and killed. These friendly mammals are killed by hunters of several nations for their meat and oils and are often caught in fishing nets intended to catch tuna cod and other fish. Steps have been taken to try to limit the number of dolphins killed

Name ______________________________

What's the Problem?

Use a **hyphen** (-) to write two-part numbers from twenty-one to ninety-nine, to write fractions as words, and in some compound nouns and adjectives.

Directions: Willis was in a big hurry to write math word problems for his study group, and he forgot to add hyphens where they belong. Help Willis figure out where the hyphens belong and add them. Then, solve the word problems and write the answers. Use hyphens as needed in your answers.

1. Maxwell bought the latest best selling kids' book by well known author Morris Madison. Yesterday, Maxwell read eighty nine pages, or one third of the book. It took him an hour and forty four minutes. How many pages are in the book? How much longer will it take Maxwell to finish the book if he reads nonstop? What time will he finish the book if he begins reading at 7:15 P.M. tonight?

   There are ______________________________ pages in the book.

   It will take Maxwell ______________________________ to finish the book.

   It will be ______________________________ when he finishes the book.

2. Millicent has twenty one four by six inch index cards. Two thirds of the cards are off white. The rest of the cards are yellow. Millicent decides to cut the large sized cards in half to use for a project. How many small sized cards does she have in all, and what are the dimensions? How many cards of each color does she have?

   Millicent has ______________ ______________________ in all.

   She has ______________________ cards and ______________ cards.

3. Marvin has always been a bit of a know it all. He felt sure that he had enough gas to drive home last night, even though he had to drive fifteen miles and the gas gauge was almost empty. About three fourths of the way home, his car sputtered to a stop. How many miles had Marvin driven already? How far was Marvin from home?

   Marvin had already driven ______________________________ miles.

   Marvin was ______________________________ miles from home.

Name ______________________________

Editing

To **edit** means to revise and correct written work. Learning how to edit your work will help you become a better writer. First, you should write a rough draft of your paper, then edit it to make it better. Remember these things when writing your rough draft:

- **Do not overcrowd your page.** Leave space between every line and at the sides of your pages to make notes and changes.
- **Write so you can read it.** Don't be sloppy just because you're only writing a rough draft.
- **Number your pages.** This will help you keep everything in order.
- **Write on only one side of the page.** This gives you plenty of space if you want to make changes or add information between paragraphs.
- **Use the same size notebook paper for all drafts.** If all pages are the same size, you're less likely to lose any.

Before turning in your report or paper, ask yourself these questions:

- **Have I followed my outline?**
- **Have I told the who, what, when, where, why, and how?**
- **Have I provided too much information?** (Good writers are concise. Don't repeat yourself after you have made a point.)
- **Do I still have unanswered questions?** (If you have questions, you can bet your readers will also. Add the missing information.)

It is always a good idea to let a day or so pass before rereading your paper and making final corrections. That way you will see what you actually wrote, instead of what you **think** you wrote.

When you edit your work, look for:

- **Correct grammar.**
- **Correct spelling.** Use the dictionary if you are not 100 percent sure.
- **Correct punctuation.**
- **Complete sentences.** Each should contain a complete thought.

Directions: Answer these questions about editing by writing **T** for true or **F** for false.

___ **1.** When you are editing, you should look for correct grammar and spelling.

___ **2.** Editors do not look for complete sentences.

___ **3.** Editors do not have to read each word of a story.

___ **4.** It is best to use both sides of a sheet of paper when writing the rough draft of your report.

___ **5.** It does not matter how neat your first draft is.

___ **6.** Editors make sure that sentences are punctuated correctly.

Name ______________________________

Editing

Editors and proofreaders use certain marks to note the changes that need to be made. In addition to circling spelling errors and fixing capitalization mistakes, editors and proofreaders also use the following marks to indicate other mistakes that need to be corrected.

~~the~~	Delete.	^	Insert a comma.
a ⁀ nt	Remove the space.	∨	Insert an apostrophe.
In # this	Insert a space.	∨	Insert quotation marks.
^ is	Insert a word.	⊙	Insert a period.

Directions: Use editing marks to correct the errors in these sentences. Then, write the sentences correctly on the lines.

1. Mr. Ramsey was a man who liked to do nothing

____

2. Lili a young hawaiian girl, liked to swim in the sea.

____

3. Youngsters who play baseballalways have a favorite player.

____

4. Too many people said, That movie was terrible."

____

5. I didn't wantto go to the movie with sally

____

6. Prince charles always wants to play polo

____

7. The little boy's name was albert leonard longfellow

____

Proofreading

Proofreading or "proofing" means to carefully look over what has been written, checking for spelling, grammar, punctuation, and other errors. At a newspaper, this is the job of a copyeditor. All good writers carefully proofread and correct their own work before turning it in to a copyeditor—or a teacher.

Here are three common proofreading marks:

Correct spelling   ~~dot~~ dog

Replace with lower-case letter   A (with slash)

Replace with upper-case letter   a (triple underline)

Directions: Carefully read the following paragraphs. Use proofreading marks to correct all of the errors. The first sentence has been done for you.

A six-~~alurm~~ alarm fire at 2121 windsor (triple underline) Terrace on the northeast side awoke apartment Residents (slash) at 3 A.M. yesterday morning. Elven people were in the biulding. No one was hurt in the blase, which caused $200,000 of property damage.

Proporty manager Jim smith credits a perfectly Functioning smoke alurm system for waking residents so they could get out safely. A springkler system were also in plase. "There was No panick," Smith said proudly. "Everone was calm and Orderly."

Name ______________________________

More Proofreading

Directions: Proofread the news article. Mark and correct the 20 errors in capitalization and spelling.

Be Wise When Buying a Car

Each year, about five percent of the U.S. popalation buys a new car, acording to J.D. Link and Associates, a New York-based auto industry reseerch company.

"A new car is the second most expenseve purchase most people Ever make," says Link. "it's amazing how litle reseerch people do before they enter the car showroom."

Link says reseerch is the most impotant Thing a new car buyer can do to pertect himself or herself. That way, he or she wil get the Best car at the best price.

"the salesman is not trying to get You the best deal," says Link. "he's trying to get himself the best deal. Bee smart! Read up on new cars in magazines like *Car and Driver* and *motortrend* before you talk to a saleman!"

Name ____________________________________

Tim Burr, Tall Tale Hero

Directions: Read the following tall tale about Tim Burr. Use proofreading marks to edit the paragraphs and correct the sentence fragments. Write the quotations correctly. Use proper capitalization and the appropriate homophones (words that sound alike but have different spellings and meanings).

far up north, in the rugged, wooded regions of canada, their lived the famous lumberjack tim burr. his trusty sidekick, saw mills, lived there to. one day, saw and tim loaded up their axes and set off four the woods. To fell more trees. For the local mill, Log Lagoon. they took along they're pack mules, beauty and beast. they chopped so fast that the trees began falling onto each other. Creating quite a logjam. its knot my fault yelled saw. i can't see where you are cutting.

the problem grew worse. beauty, tim's beloved mule, almost got his tale sliced off. Buy a falling tree trunk. that does it yelled tim angrily when you cut down a tree. call for me. So i no where you are.

saw obeyed tim's wishes. From that day on. as each tree was felled, saw cried "TIM BURR!"

Name ______________________________

Jazz It Up!

Directions: Find the eight missing adjectives and adverbs in the puzzle below. Circle them going across, down, or diagonally, and write them on the lines. Then, insert them into the paragraph where they belong.

G	O	Z	W	Q	R	E	T	G	K	P	M
P	W	F	S	C	T	A	L	L	I	D	A
R	M	H	R	U	B	I	V	S	T	Q	E
I	E	L	O	U	D	L	Y	S	G	U	L
N	A	D	M	R	A	D	J	H	K	I	T
J	B	D	R	E	P	K	E	I	A	C	Z
T	I	G	H	T	L	Y	S	N	H	K	M
Y	G	R	O	E	R	P	D	Y	L	L	E
Q	A	G	F	A	O	M	T	N	N	Y	A

____

____

____

____

____

____

____

____

Trouble for Tuba Thief

A ____________________ man wearing a ____________________ shirt entered Noted for Music, on 5th and Main Street, yesterday. He told the owner he wanted a ____________________ tuba. When the owner took a tuba out of its case, the man ____________________ grabbed it. Then, he ran ____________________ out of the store. But the man couldn't see where he was going because the tuba was so ____________________. He tripped on the sidewalk and got his head stuck ____________________ inside the tuba! The owner yelled ____________________ for the police and the man was arrested.

Name ______________________________

Some Tasty Details

Some words and phrases are used so often they lose their meaning. Commonly overused words are *good, great, nice, really, very, a lot,* and *some*. You can often replace overused words with more descriptive ones.

Example: Luis did a **very nice** job on his report.
Luis did a **spectacular** job on his report.

Including adjectives, adverbs, and specific details can also improve your writing.

Example: His mom gave him **a reward**.
His mom gave him **a brand new basketball as a reward**.

Directions: Read the following paragraph. Then, rewrite the paragraph to make it more interesting. Replace any overused words you see with more descriptive ones and add specific details wherever you can. Make the paragraph as exciting as possible without changing its meaning.

My brother, Terence, is a good cook. He makes some nice dishes. Last night, for example, Terence made dinner for the whole family. We had a salad with lots of things in it. Then, he brought out bread, beans, and spaghetti with meatballs. The sauce on the meatballs was really good. Everyone liked it a lot. After we ate, we were full. But we always know to save room for Terence's desserts. This time, he made a chocolate cream pie with all the trimmings. My mom was happy because she likes chocolate cream pie. Usually, dinnertime is the noisiest time of day at our house— but when Terence cooks, we're all too busy eating to say a word!

Name ____________________________

Combining Sentences

Not every pair of sentences can be combined with "who," "which," or "that" clauses. These sentences can be combined in other ways, either with a conjunction or by renaming the subject.

Examples:

Tim couldn't go to sleep. Todd was sleeping soundly.
Tim couldn't go to sleep, **but** Todd was sleeping soundly.

The zoo keeper fed the baby ape. A crowd gathered to watch.
When the zoo keeper fed the baby ape, a crowd gathered to watch.

Directions: Combine each pair of sentences using "who," "which," or "that" clauses, by using a conjunction or by renaming the subject.

1. The box slipped off the truck. The box was filled with bottles.

____

2. Carolyn is our scout leader. Carolyn taught us a new game.

____

3. The girl is 8 years old. The girl called the emergency number when her grandmother fell.

____

4. The meatloaf is ready to eat. The salad isn't made yet.

____

5. The rain poured down. The rain canceled our picnic.

____

6. The sixth grade class went on a field trip. The school was much quieter.

____

Name ______________________________

Transformations!

When you combine sentences, make sure to use the correct punctuation. Also, make sure not to change the meaning of the sentences.

Directions: Circle the best combination for each set of sentences below.

1. *I like to use rabbits in my magic show. They are easy to take care of. Everyone likes them.*
   - I like to use rabbits in my magic show but they are easy to take care of; but everyone likes them.
   - I like to use rabbits in my magic show but they are easy to take care of because everyone likes them.
   - I like to use rabbits in my magic show they are easy to take care of everyone likes them.
   - I like to use rabbits in my magic show because they are easy to take care of and everyone likes them.
2. *Wanda has two sisters. Their names are Abra and Cadabra.*
   - Wanda has Abra and Cadabra; two sisters.
   - Wanda has two sisters; Wanda's two sisters are named Abra and Cadabra.
   - Wanda has two sisters named Abra and Cadabra.
   - Wanda's sisters are named Abra and Cadabra, and there are two of them.
3. *Abra is black. Oops, I mean, she is white!*
   - Abra is black—oops, I mean, she is white!
   - Abra is black oops I mean— she is white!
   - Abra is black oops I mean, she is white!
   - Abra is black so oops, I mean she is white!
4. *That means Cadabra is the black one. Probably.*
   - That means Cadabra is the black one and probably.
   - That means; Cadabra is the black one—probably.
   - That means that the one that probably is black is Cadabra.
   - That means Cadabra is probably the black one.
5. *The problem is keeping the rabbits straight. I always get mixed up!*
   - The problem is keeping the rabbits straight I always get mixed up!
   - The problem is keeping the rabbits straight and mixed up!
   - The problem is keeping mixed up and always get the rabbits straight!
   - The problem is keeping the rabbits straight; I always get mixed up!
6. *Maybe I should give them name tags. Then my magic tricks might turn out right.*
   - Maybe I should give them name tags, and then—my magic tricks might turn out right.
   - Maybe I should give them name tags but then my magic tricks might turn out right.
   - Maybe I should give them name tags; then my magic tricks might turn out right.
   - Maybe I should give them name tags after my magic tricks turn out right.

Name ____________________

Putting It All Together

Directions: Rewrite this report on the lines below. Combine sentences where it makes the most sense. Remember: A sentence must include a noun and a verb and must express a clear thought.

Earthquakes occur. It happens when plates under the Earth's crust move. The plates bump. They bump against each other along fault lines. This causes the ground to shake violently. Some earthquakes can cause damage. They can especially cause damage to buildings. And earthquakes can kill and injure many people.

There is a scale called the Richter scale. This scale measures how strong an earthquake is. The worst earthquake was in the United States. It occurred on March 27, 1964. It occurred in Alaska. That earthquake measured 8.4 on the Richter scale.

____

____

____

____

____

____

____

____

____

____

Name ______________________________

A Little Support

Directions: Read the following article, and fill in the subject and the topic sentence. Then, fill in the supporting details and other details.

Have you ever seen a platypus? Platypuses are unusual creatures. First, they are strange-looking. A playtypus looks like several animals joined together; it has webbed feet like a duck, a flat tail like a beaver, and a long, furry body like an otter. It appears to have no neck. Even more unusual is that the platypus has a snout that looks just like a duck's bill, which it uses to hunt for the worms and bugs that it eats.

The platypus is also one of only two mammals in the world that lays eggs. A mother platypus may lay 2–4 eggs at a time; a group of baby platypuses is called a *clutch*. Platypuses burrow through banks of rivers and streams to make their homes. They are excellent swimmers and divers, and their senses of sight and hearing are unbelievably strong!

Subject of Passage: ______________________________

Topic Sentence: ______________________________

____

Supporting Details: ______________________________

____

____

____

____

____

Other Details: ______________________________

____

____

____

____

Name ______________________________

It's All a Jumble, Part 1

An **outline** is a plan of important ideas and information that a writer wants to include in a story, report, or article. Making an outline can help you organize your thoughts before you begin writing.

In an outline, each Roman numeral stands for a main idea. Capital letters underneath the Roman numerals set off phrases that support the main ideas. Numbers under the capital letters indicate information that supports the phrases.

Directions: Troy has prepared the following outline for his science report, "Life in the World's Deserts." Look at his outline.

I. Introduction
  A. What is a desert?
  B. Where are the world's deserts located?
    1. "hot" deserts found in Africa, Asia, the Americas, and Australia
    2. "cold" deserts found in Asia and Antarctica
  C. Deserts are rich ecosystems
II. Desert Plants
  A. How they get water
    1. plants with intricate root systems
    2. plants with deep taproots
  B. How they store water
    1. in roots
    2. in leaves
  C. Some unusual desert plants
III. Desert Animals
  A. Where they find shelter from heat and cold
    1. underground
    2. under rocks and plants
  B. How they find food and water
    1. eating desert plants and other animals
    2. traveling long distances for water
  C. Some unusual desert animals
  D. Can people live in the desert, too?
IV. Threats to the World's Deserts
  A. Natural dangers
  B. Dangers posed by people
    1. habitat threatened by mining
    2. habitat threatened by farming
V. Conclusion
  A. Deserts contain wide variety of life that must be protected
  B. Things people can do to help protect our deserts

Name ______________________________

It's All a Jumble, Part 2

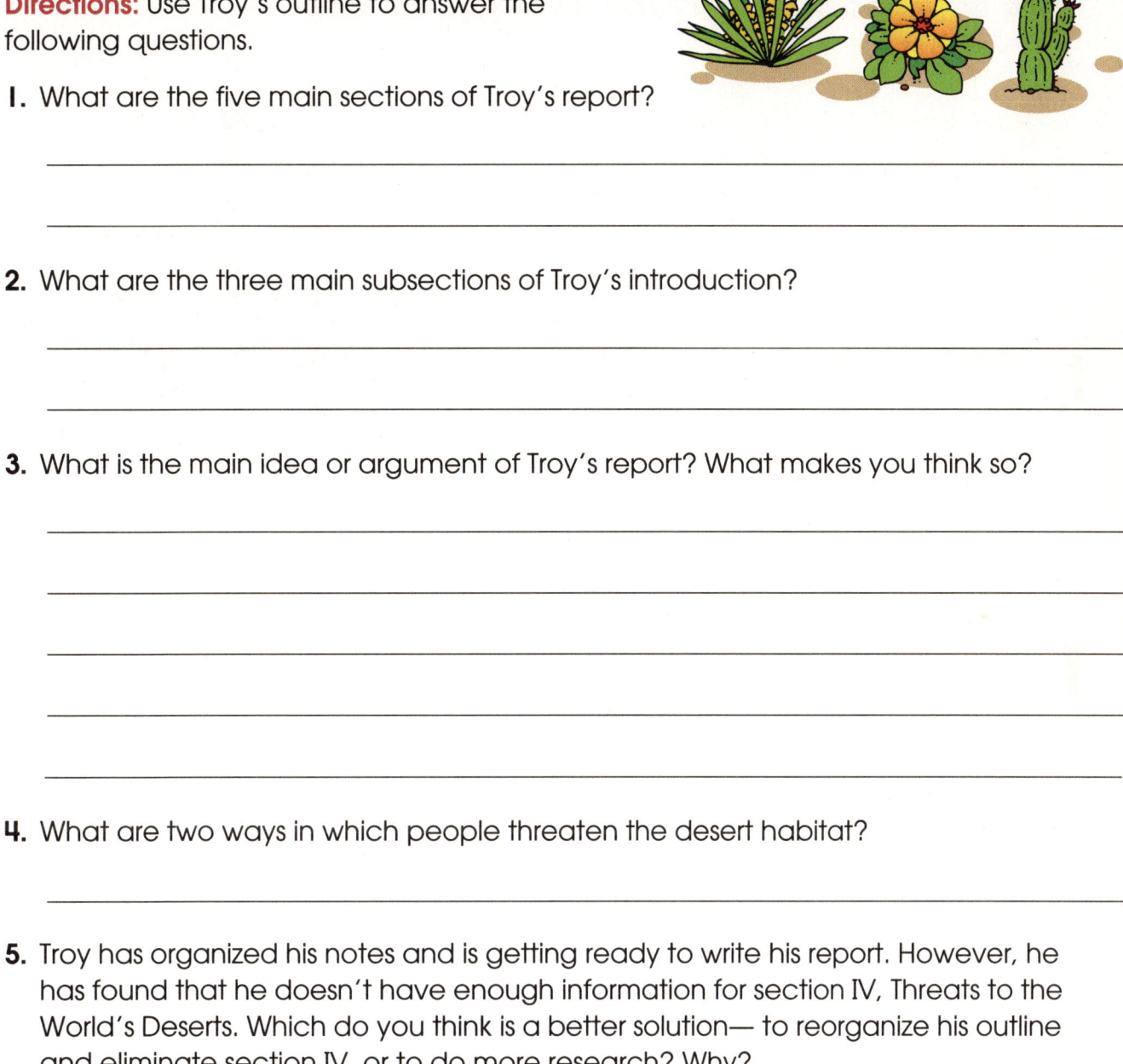

Directions: Use Troy's outline to answer the following questions.

1. What are the five main sections of Troy's report?

____

____

2. What are the three main subsections of Troy's introduction?

____

____

3. What is the main idea or argument of Troy's report? What makes you think so?

____

____

____

____

____

4. What are two ways in which people threaten the desert habitat?

____

5. Troy has organized his notes and is getting ready to write his report. However, he has found that he doesn't have enough information for section IV, Threats to the World's Deserts. Which do you think is a better solution— to reorganize his outline and eliminate section IV, or to do more research? Why?

____

____

____

____

Name ______________________________

Give Me One Reason

Directions: Place each line of information below in the correct spot on the outline. A few are already done for you. Check off the information as you use it.

I would be supervising other children	Program offers tutoring for younger kids
I would be working as a member of a team	Reading
To keep busy after school	Math
To help other children	Science
Program offers activities for younger kids	You wouldn't have to worry about me while you're at work
To gain responsibility	Arts and crafts
Program runs until 5:00	Playground games

Reasons I Should Join the After-School Program

I. To Help Other Children

A. ______________________________

1. ______________________________

2. ______________________________

3. Math

B. Program offers activities for younger kids

1. Arts and crafts

2. ______________________________

II. To Gain Responsibility

A. I would be supervising other children

B. ______________________________

III. ______________________________

A. Program runs until 5:00

B. ______________________________

Name ______________________________

Writing: Topic Sentences

The topic sentence in a paragraph usually comes first. Sometimes, however, the topic sentence can come at the end or even in the middle of a paragraph. When looking for the topic sentence, try to find the one that tells the main idea of a paragraph.

Directions: Read the following paragraphs and underline the topic sentence in each.

The maple tree sheds its leaves every year. The oak and elm trees shed their leaves, too. Every autumn, the leaves on these trees begin changing color. Then, as the leaves gradually begin to die, they fall from the trees. Trees that shed their leaves annually are called deciduous trees.

When our family goes skiing, my brother enjoys the thrill of going down the steepest hill as fast as he can. Mom and Dad like to ski because it gets them out of the house and into the fresh air. I enjoy looking at the trees and birds and the sun shining on the snow. There is something about skiing that appeals to everyone in my family. Even the dog came along on our last skiing trip!

If you are outdoors at night and there is traffic around, you should always wear bright clothing so that cars can see you. White is a good color to wear at night. If you are riding a bicycle, be sure it has plenty of reflectors, and if possible, headlamps as well. Be especially careful when crossing the street, because sometimes drivers cannot see you in the glare of their headlights. Being outdoors at night can be dangerous, and it is best to be prepared!

Name ______________________

Writing: Supporting Sentences

A **paragraph** is a group of sentences that tell about one topic. The **topic sentence** in a paragraph usually comes first and tells the main idea of the paragraph. **Supporting sentences** follow the topic sentence and provide details about the topic.

Directions: Write at least three supporting sentences for each topic sentence below.

Example: **Topic Sentence:** Carly had an accident on her bike.
Supporting Sentences: She was on her way to the store to buy some bread. A car came weaving down the road and scared her. She rode her bike off the road so the car wouldn't hit her. Now, her knee is scraped, but she's all right.

1. I've been thinking of ways I could make some more money after school.

____

____

____

2. In my opinion, cats (dogs, fish, etc.) make the best pets.

____

____

____

3. My life would be better if I had a(n) (younger sister, younger brother, older sister, older brother).

____

____

____

4. I'd like to live next door to a (swimming pool, video store, movie theater, etc.).

____

____

____

Name ______________________________

Writing: Building Paragraphs

Directions: Read the groups of topic sentences and questions below. On another sheet of paper, write supporting sentences that answer the questions. Use your imagination! Write the supporting sentences in order, and copy them on this page after the topic sentence.

1. On her way home from school, Mariko made a difficult decision.

Questions: What was Mariko's decision? Why did she decide that? Why was the decision hard to make?

2. Suddenly, Conrad thought of a way to clear up all the confusion.

Questions: What was the confusion about? How was Conrad involved in it? What did he do to clear it up?

3. Bethany used to feel awkward at the school social activities.

Questions: Why did Bethany feel awkward before? How does she feel now? What happened to change the way she feels?

Name ______________________________

Writing: Sequencing

When writing paragraphs, it is important to write events in the correct order. Think about what happens first, next, later, and last.

Directions: The following sentences tell about Chandra's day, but they are all mixed up. Read each sentence and number them in the order in which they happened.

_____ She arrived at school and went to her locker to get her books.

_____ After dinner, she did the dishes, then read a book for a while.

_____ Chandra brushed her teeth and put on her pajamas.

_____ She rode the bus home, then she fixed herself a snack.

_____ She ate breakfast and went out to wait for the bus.

_____ Chandra woke up and picked out her clothes for school.

_____ She met her friend Sarah on the way to the cafeteria.

_____ She worked on homework and watched TV until her mom called her for dinner.

Directions: Write a short paragraph about what you did today. Use words like **first**, **next**, **then**, **later**, and **finally** to indicate the order in which you did things.

Name ____________________

Descriptive Sentences

Descriptive sentences give readers a vivid image and enable them to imagine a scene clearly.

Example:

Nondescriptive sentence: There were grapes in the bowl.
Descriptive sentence: The plump purple grapes in the bowl looked tantalizing.

Directions: Rewrite these sentences using descriptive language.

1. The dog walked in its pen.

____

2. The turkey was almost done.

____

3. I became upset when my computer wouldn't work.

____

4. Jared and Michelle went to the ice-cream parlor.

____

5. The telephone kept ringing.

____

6. I wrote a story.

____

7. The movie was excellent.

____

8. Dominique was upset that her friend was ill.

____

Name ______________________________

Writing: Descriptive Details

A writer creates pictures in a reader's mind by telling him or her how something looks, sounds, feels, smells, or tastes. For example, compare **A** and **B** below. Notice how the description in **B** makes you imagine how the heavy door and the cobweb would feel and how the broken glass would look and sound as someone walked on it.

A. I walked into the house.

B. I pushed open the heavy wooden door of the old house. A cobweb brushed my face, and broken glass, sparkling like ice, crushed under my feet.

Directions: Write one or two sentences about each topic below. Add details that will help your reader see, hear, feel, smell, or taste what you are describing.

1. Your favorite dinner cooking

____

____

2. Old furniture

____

____

3. Wind blowing in the trees

____

____

4. A tired stranger

____

____

5. Wearing wet clothes

____

____

6. A strange noise somewhere in the house

____

____

Name ______________________________

Complete the Story

Directions: Read the beginning of this story. Then, complete the story with your own ideas.

It was a beautiful summer day in June when my family and I set off on vacation. We were headed for Portsmouth, New Hampshire. There we planned to go on a whale-watching ship and perhaps spy a humpback whale or two. However, there were many miles between our home and Portsmouth.

We camped at many lovely parks along the way to New Hampshire. We stayed in the Adirondack Mountains for a few days and then visited the Green Mountains of Vermont before crossing into New Hampshire.

My family enjoys tent camping. My dad says you can't really get a taste of the great outdoors in a pop-up camper or RV. I love sitting by the fire at night, gazing at the stars, and listening to the animal noises.

The trip was going well, and everyone was enjoying our vacation. We made it to Portsmouth and were looking forward to the whale-watching adventure. We arrived at the dock a few minutes early. The ocean looked rough, but we had taken seasickness medication. We thought we were prepared for any kind of weather.

____

____

____

____

____

____

____

____

____

____

Name ______________________________

Writing Fiction

Directions: Use descriptive writing to complete each story. Write at least five sentences.

1. It was a cold, wintry morning in January. Snow had fallen steadily for 4 days. I was staring out my bedroom window when I saw the bedraggled dog staggering through the snow.

____

____

____

____

____

____

2. Mindy was home Saturday studying for a big science test. Report cards were due next Friday, and the test on Monday would be on the report card. Mindy needed to do well on the test to get an "A" in Science. The phone rang. It was her best friend, Jenny.

____

____

____

____

____

____

3. Martin works every weekend delivering newspapers. He wakes up at 5:30 A.M. and begins his route at 6:00 A.M. He delivers 150 newspapers on his bike. He enjoys his weekend job because he is working toward a goal.

____

____

____

____

____

____

Name ________________________________

Writing: Point of View

People often have different opinions about the same thing. This is because each of us has a different "point of view." **Point of view** is the attitude someone has about a particular topic as a result of his or her personal experience or knowledge.

Directions: Read the topic sentence below about the outcome of a basketball game. Then, write two short paragraphs, one from the point of view of a player for the Reds and one from the point of view of a player for the Cowboys. Be sure to give each person's opinion of the outcome of the game.

Topic Sentence: In the last second of the basketball game between the Reds and the Cowboys, the Reds scored and won the game.

Terry, a player for the Reds . . . ________________________________

____

____

Chris, a player for the Cowboys . . . ________________________________

____

____

Directions: Here's a different situation. Read the topic sentence, and then write three short paragraphs from the points of view of Katie, her dad, and her brother.

Topic Sentence: Katie's dog had chewed up another one of her father's shoes.

Katie . . . ________________________________

____

Katie's father . . . ________________________________

____

Katie's brother Mark, who would rather have a cat . . . ________________________________

____

Name ________________________________

Writing: Personification

Sometimes writers use descriptions like: The fire engine **screamed** as it rushed down the street. The sun **crawled** slowly across the sky. We know that fire engines do not really scream, and the sun does not really crawl. Writers use descriptions like these to make their writing more interesting and vivid. When a writer gives an object or animal human qualities, it is called **personification**.

Directions: For each object below, write a sentence using personification. The first one has been done for you.

1. the barn door

   The old, rusty barn door groaned loudly when I pushed it open.

2. the rain

   ____

3. the pickup truck

   ____

4. the radiator

   ____

5. the leaves

   ____

6. the television

   ____

7. the kite

   ____

8. the river

   ____

Name ______________________________

Writing: Common Similes

There are many similes that are used often in the English language. For example, "as frightened as a mouse" is a very common simile. Can you think of others?

Directions: Match the first part of each common simile to the second part. The first one has been done for you.

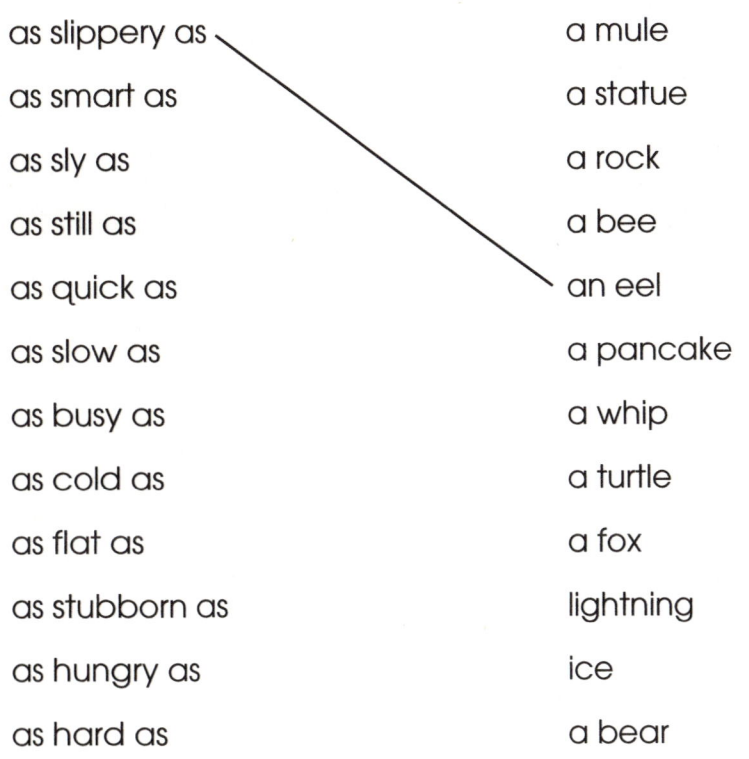

as slippery as	a mule
as smart as	a statue
as sly as	a rock
as still as	a bee
as quick as	an eel
as slow as	a pancake
as busy as	a whip
as cold as	a turtle
as flat as	a fox
as stubborn as	lightning
as hungry as	ice
as hard as	a bear

Directions: Write sentences using these common similes.

1. eats like a bird

____

2. fits like a glove

____

3. sits there like a bump on a log

____

4. like a bull in a china shop

____

5. works like a charm

____

Name ______________________________

Similes

A **simile** is a comparison of two things that have something in common but are really very different. The words **like** and **as** are used in similes.

Examples:

The baby was **as** happy **as** a lark.
She is **like** a ray of sunshine to my tired eyes.

Directions: Choose a word from the box to complete each comparison. The first one has been done for you.

tack	grass	fish	mule	ox	rail	hornet	monkey

1. as stubborn as a mule
2. as strong as an ____________
3. swims like a ____________
4. as sharp as a ____________
5. as thin as a ____________
6. as mad as a ____________
7. climbs like a ____________
8. as green as ____________

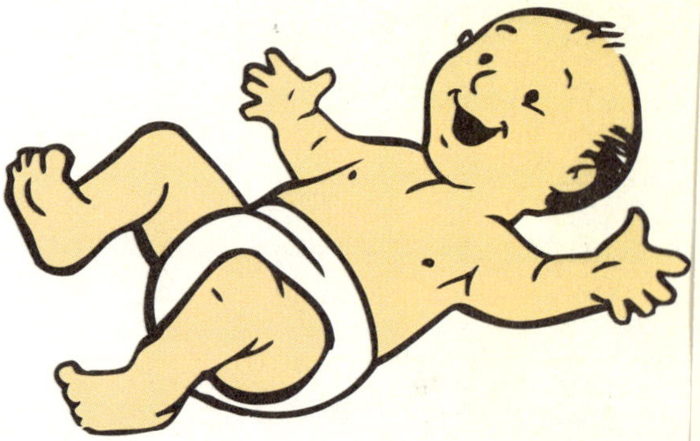

Directions: Use your own words to complete these similes.

1. as ____________ as a tack
2. ____________ like a bird
3. as hungry as a ____________
4. as white as ____________
5. as light as a ____________
6. as ____________ as honey
7. ____________ like a snake
8. as cold as ____________

Directions: Use your own similes to complete these sentences.

1. Our new puppy sounded ____________
2. The clouds were ____________
3. Our new car is ____________
4. The watermelon tasted ____________

Name ______________________________

Metaphors

A **metaphor** makes a direct comparison between two unlike things. A noun must be used in the comparison. The words **like** and **as** are not used.

Examples:

Correct: The exuberant puppy was a **bundle of energy**.
Incorrect: The dog is **happy**. (**Happy** is an adjective.)

Directions: Circle the two objects being compared.

1. The old truck was a heap of rusty metal.
2. The moon was a silver dollar in the sky.
3. Their vacation was a nightmare.
4. That wasp is a flying menace.
5. The prairie was a carpet of green.
6. The flowers were jewels on stems.
7. This winter, our pond is glass.
8. The clouds were marshmallows.

Directions: Complete the metaphor in each sentence.

1. The ruby was ______________________________.
2. The hospital is ______________________________.
3. The car was ______________________________.
4. This morning when I awoke, I was ______________________________.
5. When my brother is grumpy, he is ______________________________.
6. Her fingers on the piano keys were ______________________________.

Name ______________________________

Writing: Similes and Metaphors

Using **similes** and **metaphors** makes writing interesting. They are ways of describing things. Similes are comparisons that use **like** or **as**.

Examples: She looked like a frightened mouse.
She looked as frightened as a mouse.

Metaphors are direct comparisons that do not use **like** or **as**.

Example: She was a frightened mouse.

Directions: Rewrite each sentence two different ways to make them more interesting. In the first sentence (a), add at least one adjective and one adverb. In the second sentence (b), compare something in the sentence to something else, using a simile or metaphor.

Example: The baby cried.
a. The sick baby cried softly all night.
b. The baby cried louder and louder, like a storm gaining strength.

1. The stranger arrived.

a. ______________________________

b. ______________________________

2. The dog barked.

a. ______________________________

b. ______________________________

3. The children danced.

a. ______________________________

b. ______________________________

4. The moon rose.

a. ______________________________

b. ______________________________

Name ____________________________

Why Write?

There are four main purposes for writing: to **inform**, to **entertain**, to **persuade**, and to **express** feelings, opinions, or beliefs.

Directions: Think about the writing that you have read. Then, decide whether each of the following statements is true or false. Follow the directions.

1. Writers can write only for one purpose at a time.
If true, circle the letter in box # 16.
If false, circle the letter in box # 18.

2. Informative writing is always the most fun to read.
If true, circle the letter in box # 14.
If false, circle the letter in box # 4.

3. Writers who write to inform their readers don't ever try to write to entertain.
If true, circle the letter in box # 25.
If false, circle the letter in box # 12.

4. Writers who write to inform include many facts in their work.
If true, circle the letter in box # 20.
If false, circle the letter in box # 3.

5. Writers who write to inform should never express opinions in their work.
If true, circle the letter in box # 8.
If false, circle the letter in box # 1.

6. Good persuasive writers also provide information on their topics.
If true, circle the letter in box # 7.
If false, circle the letter in box # 21.

7. It is easier to write to entertain people than it is to write to inform them.
If true, circle the letter in box # 15.
If false, circle the letter in box # 11.

8. When writers write to inform their readers, they can also entertain them with interesting facts and stories.
If true, circle the letter in box # 22.
If false, circle the letter in box # 5.

9. A story about a struggle with illness is a good example of writing with a main purpose of expressing feelings, opinions, or beliefs.
If true, circle the letter in box # 10.
If false, circle the letter in box # 25.

1 E	2 A	3 T	4 X	5 N
6 H	7 C	8 S	9 M	10 E
11 L	12 L	13 R	14 A	15 I
16 V	17 B	18 E	19 D	20 N
21 U	22 T	23 R	24 O	25 G

Now, write all the circled letters, in order, to complete this sentence:

If you set your mind to it,
you can be an ☐☐☐☐☐☐☐☐☐ writer!

Name ______________________________

Personal Narratives

A **narrative** is a spoken or written account of an actual event. A **personal narrative** tells about your own experience. It can be written about any event in your life and may be serious or comical.

When writing a personal narrative, remember to use correct sentence structure and punctuation. Include important dates, sights, sounds, smells, tastes, and feelings to give your reader a clear picture of the event.

Directions: Write a personal narrative about an event in your life that was funny.

Name ______________________________

Writing: Supporting Your Opinion

Directions: Decide what your opinion is on each topic below. Then, write a paragraph supporting your opinion. Begin with a topic sentence that tells the reader what you think. Add details in the next three or four sentences that show why you are right.

Example: Whether kids should listen to music while they do homework

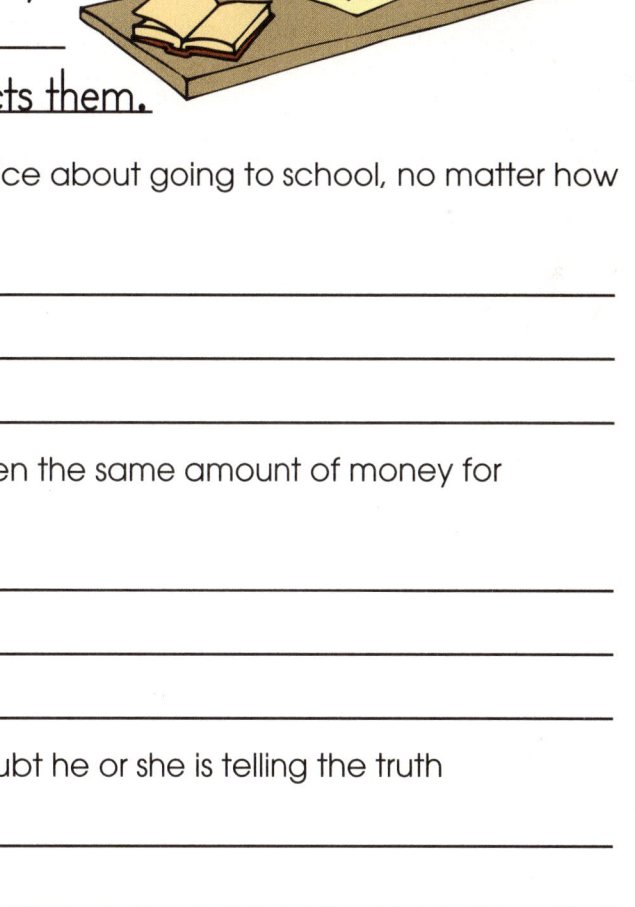

Kids do a better job on their homework if they listen to music. The music makes the time more enjoyable. It also drowns out the sounds of the rest of the family. If things are too quiet while kids do homework, every little sound distracts them.

1. Whether young people should have a choice about going to school, no matter how old they are

____

____

____

2. Whether all parents should give their children the same amount of money for an allowance

____

____

____

3. Whether you should tell someone if you doubt he or she is telling the truth

____

____

____

Name ___________________________

Newswriting

Newswriting is a style of writing used by newspaper reporters and other journalists who write for periodicals. **Periodicals** are newspapers, magazines, and newsletters that are published regularly.

Magazine and newspaper writers organize their ideas and their writing around what is called "the five W's and the H" — who, what, when, where, why, and how. As they conduct research and interview people for articles, journalists keep these questions in mind.

Directions: Read a newspaper article of your choice. Use the information you read to answer the questions.

Who

Who is involved? ___________________________

Who is affected? ___________________________

Who is responsible? ___________________________

What

What is the event or subject? ___________________________

What exactly has happened? ___________________________

____

When

When did this happen? ___________________________

Where

Where did it happen? ___________________________

____

Why

Why did it happen? ___________________________

Why will readers care? ___________________________

____

How

How did it happen? ___________________________

____

Name ______________________________

Writing: Just the Facts

Some forms of writing, such as reports and essays, contain opinions that are supported by the writer. In other kinds of writing, however, it is important to stick to the facts. Newspaper reporters, for example, must use only facts when they write their stories.

Directions: Read the following newspaper story about a fire, and underline the sentences or parts of sentences that are opinions. Then, rewrite the story in your own words, giving only the facts.

At around 10:30 P.M. last night, a fire broke out in a house at 413 Wilshire Boulevard. The house is in a very nice neighborhood, surrounded by beautiful trees. The family of four who lives in the house was alerted by smoke alarms, and they all exited the house safely, although they must have been very frightened. Firefighters arrived on the scene at approximately 10:45 P.M., and it took them over 3 hours to extinguish the blaze. The firefighters were very courageous. The cause of the fire has not yet been determined, although faulty electric wiring is suspected. People should have their electric wiring checked regularly. The family is staying with relatives until repairs to their home can be made, and they are probably very anxious to move back into their house.

____

____

____

____

____

____

____

____

____

____

____

____

Name ______________________________

Help Me!

Directions: Circle the reference source you would use to answer each question below.

1. Which source would you use to learn how to make pancakes?

   dictionary   atlas   cookbook

2. Which source might show where Treegap is?

   dictionary   atlas   thesaurus

3. Which source would describe the peacock?

   book on insects   encyclopedia   newspaper

4. Which source would describe the sounds a cricket makes?

   book on insects   thesaurus   atlas

5. Which source would give the meaning of "constable"?

   newspaper   dictionary   atlas

6. Which source would describe the most recent world events?

   newspaper   encyclopedia   thesaurus

7. Which source would tell how to divide "accommodations" into syllables?

   thesaurus   book on insects   dictionary

8. Which source could give a synonym for "push"?

   thesaurus   cookbook   encyclopedia

9. Which source might best forecast tomorrow's weather?

   encyclopedia   atlas   newspaper

Use references to answer the following questions:

Which countries border Nepal?

Answer: ______________________________

Source: ______________________________

Page #: ____________

What are the headlines in today's paper?

Answer: ______________________________

Source: ______________________________

Page #: ____________

Name ______________________________

Writing: Just the Facts

Directions: Unscramble the words in the box below. Each one is the name for one of the sections of your local library. Then, look at the list of books. Next to each one, write the section of the library where it would be located.

nitofniocn	____________________
freerceen	____________________
noticif	____________________
ciolasredip	____________________

Book Titles:

Encyclopedia of Dogs	____________________
Hound Dog Journal	____________________
Private Eye Pooch—A Novel	____________________
The Old Dog's New Almanac	____________________
Marvelous Mutts—Doggie Olympic Heroes	____________________
Tough Mutts, a Doggie Romance	____________________
Sit! Stay! Dog Training for Dodos	____________________
Grr! Bark! Woof! A Doggie Thesaurus	____________________
The Hooperville Daily Hound	____________________
Wonderful Working Dogs	____________________
The Complete List of Dog Names	____________________
The Mongrel Monthly	____________________
Raising Happy Puppies	____________________
The Poodles Play Ping-Pong	____________________

Name ______________________________

Magazine Material

Magazines can be useful sources of information for research reports. When you use a magazine, you need to know how to write it correctly in your bibliography. The following information is important to include in your citation: author, article title, magazine title, magazine date, and pages the article is located on.

Directions: Mary Magazine is a very careful student. She is writing a report about aliens, and she has found a magazine article to use as a source. Use Mary's source to answer the questions below. Circle the letter of your answer.

Nokidding, Joe. "Famous People Who Are Actually Space Aliens." Unreal Truth June 2000: 36–54.

1. The title of the article is
   (a) Joe Nokidding
   (b) Famous People Who Are Actually Space Aliens
   (c) Unreal Truth
2. The name of the magazine is
   (a) Joe Nokidding
   (b) Famous People Who Are Actually Space Aliens
   (c) Unreal Truth
3. The author of the article is
   (a) Joe Nokidding
   (b) Famous People Who Are Actually Space Aliens
   (c) Real Truth
4. The article is on pages
   (a) 2000
   (b) 36–54
   (c) 2
5. The date of the magazine is
   (a) 2000
   (b) June 2000
   (c) June
6. What punctuation mark follows the date?
   (a) comma
   (b) period
   (c) colon

Name ______________________________

Online Odyssey

When using the Internet, it is important to be able to tell which sites are reliable and contain accurate information.

Directions: Connie Confused is looking for information about the early frontiersman, Daniel Boone, on the Internet. Help Connie by underlining the Web sites you think might contain relevant and reliable information.

1. the Daniel Boone page of the University of Kentucky Library Web site
2. home page for Daniel Boone High School
3. Danny Loone's own Daniel Boone-themed Web site
4. an article on Daniel Boone from the American Heritage Articles on Frontiersman Web site
5. the home page of the Daniel Boone Coin Club
6. the Daniel Boone page of the Kentucky Historical Society Web site
7. a Web site containing Mrs. Bea Quiet's 5th grade class reports on Daniel Boone
8. the Realsmart family home page containing Timmy Realsmart's research report on Daniel Boone for Mrs. Bea Quiet's 5th grade class

Directions: The Internet makes doing research convenient, but sometimes you must use other resource materials to find your information. Name at least two other sources, besides the Internet, where you might find reliable information for a report on Daniel Boone.

____

____

____

____

Name ______________________________

Library Research

Directions: Read about doing research in a library. Then, answer the questions.

Step 1: Look in a general encyclopedia, such as *Encyclopedia Americana* or *World Book*, for background information on your topic. Use the index volume to locate the main article and all related articles. Look at the suggested cross-references that direct you to other sources. Also, check for a bibliography at the end of the article for clues to other sources. A **bibliography** lists all the books and magazines used to write the article.

Step 2: Use a special encyclopedia for more specific information or for definitions of special terms. The *Encyclopedia of Education, International Encyclopedia of the Social Sciences,* and the *Encyclopedia of Bioethics* are examples of special encyclopedias.

Step 3: Look for a general book on your topic using the subject headings in the library catalog. Be sure to note the copyright date (date published) on all books you select. For current topics such as medical research or computers, you will want to use only the most recently published and up-to-date sources.

Step 4: Use *Facts on File* to pinpoint specific facts or statistics related to your topic. *Facts on File* is a weekly summary of national and international news.

Step 5: An index helps you locate magazine articles on your topic. To find the most current information, try the *Reader's Guide to Periodical Literature*. The *Guide* lists articles by subject published during a particular month, the magazines containing the articles, and the date and page numbers of the articles.

1. Name two general encyclopedias. ______________________________

____

2. Name three special encyclopedias. ______________________________

____

____

3. Which reference book contains a weekly summary of national and international news?

____

Test Practice Table of Contents

About the Tests

What Are Standardized Achievement Tests?

Achievement tests measure what children know in particular subject areas such as reading, language arts, and mathematics. They do not measure your child's intelligence or ability to learn.

When tests are standardized, or *normed,* children's test results are compared with those of a specific group who have taken the test, usually at the same age or grade.

Standardized achievement tests measure what children around the country are learning. The test makers survey popular textbook series, as well as state curriculum frameworks and other professional sources, to determine what content is covered widely.

Because of variations in state frameworks and textbook series, as well as grade ranges on some test levels, the tests may cover some material that children have not yet learned. This is especially true if the test is offered early in the school year. However, test scores are compared to those of other children who take the test at the same time of year, so your child will not be at a disadvantage if his or her class has not covered specific material yet.

Different School Districts, Different Tests

There are many flexible options for districts when offering standardized tests. Many school districts choose not to give the full test battery, but select certain content and scoring options. For example, many schools may test only in the areas of reading and mathematics. Similarly, a state or district may use one test for certain grades and another test for other grades. These decisions are often based on the amount of time and money a district wishes to spend on test administration. Some states choose to develop their own statewide assessment tests.

On pages 255-257 you will find information about these five widely used standardized achievement tests:

- California Achievement Tests (CAT)
- Terra Nova/CTBS
- Iowa Test of Basic Skills (ITBS)
- Stanford Achievement Test (SAT9)
- Metropolitan Achievement Test (MAT).

However, this book contains strategies and practice questions for use with a variety of tests. Even if your state does not give one of the five tests listed above, your child will benefit from doing the practice questions in this book. If you're unsure about which test your child takes, contact your local school district to find out which tests are given.

Types of Test Questions

Traditionally, standardized achievement tests have used only multiple choice questions. Today, many tests may include constructed response (short answer) and extended response (essay) questions as well.

In addition, many tests include questions that tap students' higher-order thinking skills. Instead of simple recall questions, such as identifying a date in history, questions may require students to make comparisons and contrasts or analyze results among other skills.

What the Tests Measure

These tests do not measure your child's level of intelligence, but they do show how well your child knows material that he or she has learned and that

is also covered on the tests. It's important to remember that some tests cover content that is not taught in your child's school or grade. In other instances, depending on when in the year the test is given, your child may not yet have covered the material.

If the test reports you receive show that your child needs improvement in one or more skill areas, you may want to seek help from your child's teacher and find out how you can work with your child to improve his or her skills.

California Achievement Test (CAT/5)

What Is the *California Achievement Test?*

The *California Achievement Test* is a standardized achievement test battery that is widely used with elementary through high school students.

Parts of the Test

The CAT includes tests in the following content areas:

Reading
- Word Analysis
- Vocabulary
- Comprehension

Spelling

Language Arts
- Language Mechanics
- Language Usage

Mathematics

Science

Social Studies

Your child may take some or all of these subtests if your district uses the *California Achievement Test.*

Terra Nova/CTBS (Comprehensive Tests of Basic Skills)

What Is the *Terra Nova/CTBS?*

The *Terra Nova/Comprehensive Tests of Basic Skills* is a standardized achievement test battery used in elementary through high school grades.

While many of the test questions on the *Terra Nova* are in the traditional multiple choice form, your child may take parts of the *Terra Nova* that include some open-ended questions (constructed-response items).

Parts of the Test

Your child may take some or all of the following subtests if your district uses the *Terra Nova/CTBS:*

Reading/Language Arts

Mathematics

Science

Social Studies

Supplementary tests include:
- Word Analysis
- Vocabulary
- Language Mechanics
- Spelling
- Mathematics Computation

Critical thinking skills may also be tested.

Iowa Test of Basic Skills (ITBS)

What Is the *ITBS?*

The *Iowa Test of Basic Skills* is a standardized achievement test battery used in elementary through high school grades.

Parts of the Test

Your child may take some or all of these subtests if your district uses the *ITBS*, also known as the *Iowa:*

Reading
- Vocabulary
- Reading Comprehension

Language Arts
- Spelling
- Capitalization
- Punctuation
- Usage and Expression

Math
- Concepts/Estimate
- Problems/Data Interpretation

Social Studies

Science

Sources of Information

Stanford Achievement Test (SAT9)

What Is the *Stanford Achievement Test?*

The *Stanford Achievement Test, Ninth Edition (SAT9)* is a standardized achievement test battery used in elementary through high school grades.

Note that the *Stanford Achievement Test (SAT9)* is a different test from the *SAT* used by high school students for college admissions.

While many of the test questions on the *SAT9* are in traditional multiple choice form, your child may take parts of the *SAT9* that include some open-ended questions (constructed-response items).

Parts of the Test

Your child may take some or all of these subtests if your district uses the *Stanford Achievement Test.*

Reading
- Vocabulary
- Reading Comprehension

Mathematics
- Problem Solving
- Procedures

Language Arts

Spelling

Study Skills

Listening

Critical thinking skills may also be tested.

Metropolitan Achievement Test (MAT7 and MAT8)

What Is the *Metropolitan Achievement Test*?

The *Metropolitan Achievement Test* is a standardized achievement test battery used in elementary through high school grades.

Parts of the Test

Your child may take some or all of these subtests if your district uses the *Metropolitan Achievement Test*.

Reading
- Vocabulary
- Reading Comprehension

Math
- Concepts and Problem Solving
- Computation

Language Arts
- Pre-writing
- Composing
- Editing

Science

Social Studies

Research Skills

Thinking Skills

Spelling

Statewide Assessments

Today, the majority of states give statewide assessments. In some cases, these tests are known as *high-stakes assessments*. This means that students must score at a certain level in order to be promoted. Some states use minimum competency or proficiency tests. Often, these tests measure more basic skills than other types of statewide assessments.

Statewide assessments are generally linked to state curriculum frameworks. Frameworks provide a blueprint, or outline, to ensure that teachers are covering the same curriculum topics as other teachers in the same grade level in the state. In some states, standardized achievement tests (such as the five described in this book) are used in connection with statewide assessments.

When Statewide Assessments Are Given

Statewide assessments may not be given at every grade level. Generally, they are offered at one or more grades in elementary school, middle school, and high school. Many states test at grades 4, 8, and 10.

State-by-State Information

You can find information about statewide assessments and curriculum frameworks at your state Department of Education Web site. To find the address for your individual state go to www.ed.gov, click on Topics A–Z, and then click on State Departments of Education. You will find a list of all the state departments of education, mailing addresses, and Web sites.

How to Help Your Child Prepare for Standardized Testing

Preparing All Year Round

Perhaps the most valuable way you can help your child prepare for standardized achievement tests is by providing enriching experiences. Keep in mind also, that test results for younger children are not as reliable as for older students. If a child is hungry, tired, or upset, this may result in a poor test score. Here are some tips on how you can help your child do his or her best on standardized tests.

Read aloud with your child. Reading aloud helps develop vocabulary and fosters a positive attitude toward reading. Reading together is one of the most effective ways you can help your child succeed in school.

Share experiences. Baking cookies together, planting a garden, or making a map of your neighborhood are examples of activities that help build skills that are measured on the tests such as sequencing and following directions.

Become informed about your state's testing procedures. Ask about or watch for announcements of meetings that explain about standardized tests and statewide assessments in your school district. Talk to your child's teacher about your child's individual performance on these state tests during a parent-teacher conference.

Help your child know what to expect. Read and discuss with your child the test-taking tips in this book. Your child can prepare by working through a couple of strategies a day so that no practice session takes too long.

Help your child with his or her regular school assignments. Set up a quiet study area for homework. Supply this area with pencils, paper, markers, a calculator, a ruler, a dictionary, scissors, glue, and so on. Check your child's homework and offer to help if he or she gets stuck. But remember, it's your child's homework, not yours. If you help too much, your child will not benefit from the activity.

Keep in regular contact with your child's teacher. Attend parent-teacher conferences, school functions, PTA or PTO meetings, and school board meetings. This will help you get to know the educators in your district and the families of your child's classmates.

Learn to use computers as an educational resource. If you do not have a computer and Internet access at home, try your local library.

Remember—simply getting your child comfortable with testing procedures and helping him or her know what to expect can improve test scores!

Getting Ready for the Big Day

There are lots of things you can do on or immediately before test day to improve your child's chances of testing success. What's more, these strategies will help your child prepare him, or herself for school tests, too, and promote general study skills that can last a lifetime.

Provide a good breakfast on test day. Instead of sugar cereal, which provides immediate but not long-term energy, have your child eat a breakfast with protein or complex carbohydrates such as an egg, whole grain cereal or toast, or a banana-yogurt shake.

Promote a good night's sleep. A good night's sleep before the test is essential. Try not to overstress the importance of the test. This may cause your child to lose sleep because of anxiety. Doing some exercise after school and having a quiet evening routine will help your child sleep well the night before the test.

Assure your child that he or she is not expected to know all of the answers on the test. Explain that other children in higher grades may take the same test, and that the test may measure things your child has not yet learned in school. Help your child understand that you expect him or her to put forth a good effort—and that this is enough. Your child should not try to cram for these tests. Also avoid threats or bribes; these put undue pressure on children and may interfere with their best performance.

Keep the mood light and offer encouragement. To provide a break on test days, do something fun and special after school—take a walk around the neighborhood, play a game, read a favorite book, or prepare a special snack together. These activities keep your child's mood light—even if the testing sessions have been difficult—and show how much you appreciate your child's effort.

Taking Standardized Tests

No matter what grade you're in, this is information you can use to prepare for standardized tests. Here is what you'll find:

- Test-taking tips and strategies to use on test day and year-round.
- Important terms to know for Language Arts and Reading.
- General study/homework tips.

By opening this book, you've already taken your first step towards test success. The rest is easy—all you have to do is get started!

What You Need to Know

There are many things you can do to increase your test success. Here's a list of tips to keep in mind when you take standardized tests—and when you study for them, too.

Keep up with your school work. One way you can succeed in school and on tests is by studying and doing your homework regularly. Studies show that you remember only about one-fifth of what you memorize the night before a test. That's one good reason not to try to learn it all at once! Keeping up with your work throughout the year will help you remember the material better. You also won't be as tired or nervous as if you try to learn everything at once.

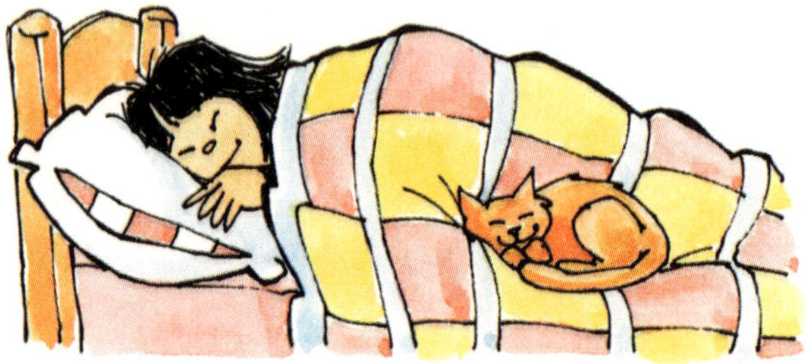

Feel your best. One of the ways you can do your best on tests and in school is to make sure your body is ready. To do this, get a good night's sleep each night and eat a healthy breakfast (not sugary cereal that will leave you tired by the middle of the morning). An egg or a milkshake with yogurt and fresh fruit will give you lasting energy. Also, wear comfortable clothes, maybe your lucky shirt or your favorite color on test day. It can't hurt, and it may even help you relax.

Be prepared. Do practice questions and learn about how standardized tests are organized. Books like this one will help you know what to expect when you take a standardized test.

When you are taking the test, follow the directions. It is important to listen carefully to the directions your teacher gives and to read the written instructions carefully. Words like *not, none, rarely, never,* and *always* are very important in test directions and questions. You may want to circle words like these.

Look at each page carefully before you start answering. In school you usually read a passage and then answer questions about it. But when you take a test, it's helpful to follow a different order.

If you are taking a Reading test, first read the directions. Then read the questions before you read the passage. This way you will know exactly what kind of information to look for as you read. Next, read the passage carefully. Finally, answer the questions.

On math and science tests, look at the labels on graphs and charts. Think about what each graph or chart shows. Questions often will ask you to draw conclusions about the information.

Manage your time. *Time management* means using your time wisely on a test so that you can finish as much of it as possible and do your best. Look over the test or the parts that you are allowed to do at one time. Sometimes you may want to do the easier parts first. This way, if you run out of time before you finish, you will have completed a good chunk of the work.

For tests that have a time limit, notice what time it is when the test begins and figure out when you need to stop. Check a few times as you work through the test to be sure you are making good progress and not spending too much time on any particular section.

You don't have to keep up with everyone else. You may notice other students in the class finishing before you do. Don't worry about this. Everyone works at a different pace. Just keep going, trying not to spend too long on any one question.

Fill in answer circles properly. Even if you know every answer on a test, you won't do well unless you fill in the circle next to the correct answer.

Fill in the entire circle, but don't spend too much time making it perfect. Make your mark dark, but not so dark that it goes through the paper! And be sure you only choose one answer for each question, even if you are not sure. If you choose two answers, both will be marked as wrong.

It's usually not a good idea to change your answers. Usually your first choice is the right one. Unless you realize that you misread the question, the directions, or some facts in a passage, it's usually safer to stay with your first answer. If you are pretty sure it's wrong, of course, go ahead and change it. Make sure you completely erase the first choice and neatly fill in your new choice.

Use context clues to figure out tough questions. If you come across a word or idea you don't understand, use context clues—the words in the sentences nearby— to help you figure out its meaning.

Sometimes it's good to guess. Should you guess when you don't know an answer on a test? That depends. If your teacher has made the test, usually you will score better if you answer as many questions as possible, even if you don't really know the answers.

On standardized tests, here's what to do to score your best. For each question, most of these tests let you choose from four or five answer choices. If you decide that a couple of answers are clearly wrong but you're still not sure about the answer, go ahead and make your best guess. If you can't narrow down the choices at all, then you may be better off skipping the question. Tests like these take away extra points for wrong answers, so it's better to leave them blank. Be sure you skip over the answer space for these questions on the answer sheet, though, so you don't fill in the wrong spaces.

Sometimes you should skip a question and come back to it. On many tests, you will score better if you answer more questions. This means that you should not spend too much time on any single question. Sometimes it gets tricky, though, keeping track of questions you skipped on your answer sheet.

If you want to skip a question because you don't know the answer, put a very light pencil mark next to the question in the test booklet. Try to choose an answer, even if you're not sure of it. Fill in the answer lightly on the answer sheet.

Check your work. On a standardized test, you can't go ahead or skip back to another section of the test. But you may go back and review your answers on the section you just worked on if you have extra time.

First, scan your answer sheet. Make sure that you answered every question you could. Also, if you are using a bubble-type answer sheet, make sure that you filled in only one bubble for each question. Erase any extra marks on the page.

Finally—avoid test anxiety! If you get nervous about tests, don't worry. *Test anxiety* happens to lots of good students. Being a little nervous actually sharpens your mind. But if you get very nervous about tests, take a few minutes to relax the night before or the day of the test. One good way to relax is to get some exercise, even if you just have time to stretch, shake out your fingers, and wiggle your toes. If you can't move around, it helps just to take a few slow, deep breaths and picture yourself doing a great job!

Name ____________________

READING: VOCABULARY

Lesson 1: Synonyms

Directions: Read each item. Fill in the circle next to the word that means the same or about the same as the underlined word.

Examples

A. **a small dwelling**
- Ⓐ school
- Ⓑ home
- Ⓒ suburb
- Ⓓ tribe

B. **Fascinating means —**
- Ⓕ disturbing
- Ⓖ annoying
- Ⓗ pleasant
- Ⓙ interesting

Clue: **Choose only one answer. Be sure to fill in the circle completely.**

Practice

1. **successful corporation**
- Ⓐ business
- Ⓑ team
- Ⓒ person
- Ⓓ country

2. **skilled laborer**
- Ⓕ musician
- Ⓖ professor
- Ⓗ worker
- Ⓙ relative

3. **tiny particle**
- Ⓐ animal
- Ⓑ package
- Ⓒ piece
- Ⓓ gift

4. **a desert region**
- Ⓕ area
- Ⓖ culture
- Ⓗ religion
- Ⓙ plant

5. **An imaginary story is —**
- Ⓐ biographical.
- Ⓑ fictional.
- Ⓒ actual.
- Ⓓ humorous.

6. **To interpret is to —**
- Ⓕ organize.
- Ⓖ adjust.
- Ⓗ catch.
- Ⓙ explain.

7. **To pave is to —**
- Ⓐ cover.
- Ⓑ hide.
- Ⓒ recycle.
- Ⓓ fly.

8. **An affectionate person is —**
- Ⓕ hostile.
- Ⓖ adorable.
- Ⓗ loving.
- Ⓙ ill.

STOP

Name ______________________________

READING: VOCABULARY

● Lesson 2: Vocabulary Skills

Directions: Read each item. Fill in the circle next to the word that means the same or about the same as the underlined word.

Examples

A. admire a leader

- Ⓐ advise
- Ⓑ detest
- Ⓒ trust
- Ⓓ respect

B. A journalist interviewed the athlete. Journalist means —

- Ⓕ referee
- Ⓖ reporter
- Ⓗ collector
- Ⓙ scientist

Clue If you are not sure which answer is correct, take your best guess. Eliminate answer choices you know are wrong.

● Practice

1. Complete the assignment.

- Ⓐ task
- Ⓑ assistant
- Ⓒ design
- Ⓓ office

2. Focus your attention.

- Ⓕ fluctuate
- Ⓖ irritate
- Ⓗ compile
- Ⓙ concentrate

3. good publicity

- Ⓐ appreciation
- Ⓑ public attention
- Ⓒ publisher
- Ⓓ celebrity

4. Tom waited anxiously for the announcement. Anxiously means —

- Ⓕ nervously
- Ⓖ without concern
- Ⓗ quickly
- Ⓙ with anger

5. The story was about children who benefit from the fundraiser. Benefit means —

- Ⓐ to volunteer.
- Ⓑ to serve.
- Ⓒ to raise money.
- Ⓓ to receive help.

6. Her hard work was complimented. Complimented means —

- Ⓕ disliked.
- Ⓖ given away freely.
- Ⓗ praised.
- Ⓙ completed.

7. The workers went on strike. Strike means —

- Ⓐ to take a vacation.
- Ⓑ to hit.
- Ⓒ to stop working in order to protest.
- Ⓓ to throw a ball.

STOP

Name ______________________

READING: VOCABULARY

Lesson 3: Antonyms

Directions: Read each item. Fill in the circle next to the word that means the opposite of the underlined word.

Examples

A. departed guests
- (A) honored
- (B) excited
- (C) gathered
- (D) neglected

B. rare appearances
- (F) frequent
- (G) old
- (H) uncommon
- (J) distant

Read each item carefully. Choose the answer that means the opposite.

Practice

1. Accept the truth.
- (A) deny
- (B) understand
- (C) illustrate
- (D) respect

2. attentive people
- (F) beautiful
- (G) prosperous
- (H) messy
- (J) heedless

3. an absurd story
- (A) logical
- (B) exciting
- (C) rewarding
- (D) fanciful

4. generous servings
- (F) large
- (G) grateful
- (H) small
- (J) general

5. brief description
- (A) important
- (B) lengthy
- (C) short
- (D) casual

6. employ the workers
- (F) befriend
- (G) manage
- (H) argue with
- (J) dismiss

7. confident in your abilities
- (A) uncertain
- (B) assured
- (C) proud
- (D) neglectful

8. superior attitude
- (F) extreme
- (G) inferior
- (H) great
- (J) focused

Name ______________________

READING: VOCABULARY

● Lesson 4: Multi-Meaning Words

Directions: Read each item. Fill in the circle next to the answer you think is correct.

Examples

A. Unemployment is running high here since the factory closed.

In which sentence does the word running mean the same thing as in the sentence above?

- Ⓐ Tracy saw the horse running through the field.
- Ⓑ Beth was running the lawn mower.
- Ⓒ Club attendance was running low due to heavy snow.
- Ⓓ Peter is running for class president.

B. Choose the word that fits in both the blanks.

Set the package _______ to the side.

We had the day _______.

- Ⓕ over
- Ⓖ off
- Ⓗ apart
- Ⓙ away

Clue: **Read the question carefully. Use the meaning of the sentences to help you choose the right answer.**

● Practice

1. Groaning, he rolled over and planted his feet firmly on the floor.

In which sentence does the word planted mean the same thing as in the sentence above?

- Ⓐ Jean planted four rows of cucumbers.
- Ⓑ The lawyer claimed that the evidence had been planted.
- Ⓒ The settlers planted new crops.
- Ⓓ Jo planted her feet in the dirt before swinging the bat.

2. Barb put a clean _______ on the bed.

Jason washed the cookie _______ after he finished baking.

- Ⓕ pillow
- Ⓖ tray
- Ⓗ sheet
- Ⓙ cover

3. We _______ nearer to the warmth of the campfire.

He _______ the wrong conclusion from the facts that were presented.

- Ⓐ drew
- Ⓑ moved
- Ⓒ identified
- Ⓓ illustrated

STOP

Name ______________________________

READING: VOCABULARY

Lesson 5: Words in Context

Directions: Read the paragraph. Find the word below that fits best in each numbered blank.

Examples

The United States Capitol is well known for its __(A)__, or round room. The room has a large dome. A bronze Statue of Freedom __(B)__ on top of the dome.

A.
- (A) parlor
- (B) library
- (C) rotunda
- (D) media center

B.
- (F) stands
- (G) centered
- (H) flies
- (J) bends

Look carefully at each answer. Choose the word that sounds best in the sentence.

Practice

The Montgolfier brothers __(1)__ the hot-air balloon in 1783. However, they __(2)__ never guessed how high or how far one of these balloons could go. In the brothers' first __(3)__, they used a huge bag made of paper and __(4)__. They held its open end over a __(5)__. The bag filled with smoke and hot air. Then it rose into the air and __(6)__ for a mile and a half.

1.
- (A) discovered
- (B) invented
- (C) explored
- (D) arranged

2.
- (F) probably
- (G) randomly
- (H) rarely
- (J) frequently

3.
- (A) grade
- (B) demonstration
- (C) hope
- (D) suggestion

4.
- (F) steel
- (G) bricks
- (H) mortar
- (J) fabric

5.
- (A) pool
- (B) puddle
- (C) fire
- (D) engine

6.
- (F) dropped
- (G) recorded
- (H) sank
- (J) floated

STOP

Name ____________________

READING: VOCABULARY

● Lesson 6: Word Study

Directions: Read each item. Fill in the circle for the answer you think is correct.

Examples

A. **Which of these words probably comes from the Latin word *albus*, meaning "white"?**

- Ⓐ albino
- Ⓑ album
- Ⓒ algebra
- Ⓓ alchemy

B. **Margo was _______ that her team lost the game.**

Which of these words would indicate that Margo felt sad?

- Ⓕ elated
- Ⓖ frustrated
- Ⓗ disappointed
- Ⓙ angry

Clue **Look for key words in the question. The key words will help you choose the right answer.**

● Practice

1. **Which of these words probably comes from the Greek word *demos kratos* meaning "rule of the people"?**

- Ⓐ demolish
- Ⓑ democracy
- Ⓒ demote
- Ⓓ demonstration

2. **Which of these words probably comes from the Latin word *audire* meaning "to hear"?**

- Ⓕ audit
- Ⓖ auburn
- Ⓗ auction
- Ⓙ audio

3. **The stadium was filled with _______. Which of these words would indicate that there was an audience at the stadium?**

- Ⓐ spectators
- Ⓑ performers
- Ⓒ soldiers
- Ⓓ employees

4. **Ramon's grandfather stored family _______ in the attic.**

Which of these words means there were heirlooms in the attic?

- Ⓕ antiques
- Ⓖ pets
- Ⓗ chores
- Ⓙ rubbish

For numbers 5 and 6, choose the answer that best defines the underlined part.

5. **precede   predict**

- Ⓐ after
- Ⓑ around
- Ⓒ before
- Ⓓ between

6. **biology   geology**

- Ⓕ person who
- Ⓖ study of
- Ⓗ quality of being
- Ⓙ full of

STOP

Name ______________________________

READING: VOCABULARY

SAMPLE TEST

● **Directions:** Read each item. Fill in the circle next to the word that means the same or about the same as the underlined word.

Examples

A. spoiled fruit

- Ⓐ citrus
- Ⓑ yellow
- Ⓒ fresh
- Ⓓ rotten

B. A helper is the same as an —

- Ⓕ adviser
- Ⓖ assistant
- Ⓗ elevator
- Ⓙ organizer

For numbers 1–13, fill in the circle next to the word that means the same or about the same as the underlined word.

1. Do it now.

- Ⓐ immediately
- Ⓑ later
- Ⓒ soon
- Ⓓ slowly

2. artistic film

- Ⓕ play
- Ⓖ drama
- Ⓗ movie
- Ⓙ episode

3. in the cellar

- Ⓐ attic
- Ⓑ basement
- Ⓒ garage
- Ⓓ workshop

4. newspaper article

- Ⓕ story
- Ⓖ novel
- Ⓗ journal
- Ⓙ book

5. Something that has concluded is —

- Ⓐ in progress.
- Ⓑ continuing.
- Ⓒ beginning.
- Ⓓ finished.

6. An irregular shape is —

- Ⓕ symmetrical.
- Ⓖ uneven.
- Ⓗ balanced.
- Ⓙ broken.

7. A career is —

- Ⓐ a hobby.
- Ⓑ a university.
- Ⓒ an occupation.
- Ⓓ a library.

8. To take a brisk walk means to walk —

- Ⓕ quickly.
- Ⓖ leisurely.
- Ⓗ by yourself.
- Ⓙ with others.

GO ON

Name ______________________________

READING: VOCABULARY

SAMPLE TEST (cont.)

9. The association works to help animals.
Association means —

- Ⓐ occupation.
- Ⓑ college.
- Ⓒ friendship.
- Ⓓ organization.

10. You can see the sunlight through the sheer curtains.
Sheer means —

- Ⓕ white.
- Ⓖ thick.
- Ⓗ transparent.
- Ⓙ open.

11. Helga is a loyal friend.
Loyal means —

- Ⓐ devoted.
- Ⓑ dangerous.
- Ⓒ good.
- Ⓓ dishonest.

12. The timeline marked the milestones of the Civil War.
Milestones means —

- Ⓕ speeches.
- Ⓖ roads.
- Ⓗ events.
- Ⓙ conditions.

13. Jacob corresponded with his pen pal.

Corresponded means he —

- Ⓐ played.
- Ⓑ visited.
- Ⓒ telephoned.
- Ⓓ wrote.

For numbers 14–19, fill in the circle next to the word that means the opposite of the underlined word.

14. express your thoughts

- Ⓕ yell
- Ⓖ withhold
- Ⓗ summarize
- Ⓙ tell

15. obvious signs

- Ⓐ unclear
- Ⓑ apparent
- Ⓒ momentary
- Ⓓ secondary

16. ignore the noise

- Ⓕ contribute to
- Ⓖ notice
- Ⓗ overlook
- Ⓙ behave

17. respect for the law

- Ⓐ obedience
- Ⓑ trust
- Ⓒ honor
- Ⓓ contempt

18. with regret

- Ⓕ happiness
- Ⓖ sorrow
- Ⓗ fear
- Ⓙ bravery

19. a great achievement

- Ⓐ victory
- Ⓑ failure
- Ⓒ mistake
- Ⓓ accomplishment

GO ON

Name ______________________

READING: VOCABULARY

SAMPLE TEST (cont.)

For numbers 20–23, choose the word that best completes both sentences.

20. Please _______ my coat to the bus. An actor's voice must _______ to the last row of seats.

- (F) deliver
- (G) reach
- (H) take
- (J) carry

21. Throw the _______ to me. Sheila wore a formal dress to the _______.

- (A) party
- (B) ball
- (C) coat
- (D) dance

22. Reach out with your _______. The soldiers gathered _______ for the battle.

- (F) arms
- (G) legs
- (H) supplies
- (J) muskets

23. The class visited a _______ art museum. He had to pay a _______ for speeding.

- (A) modern
- (B) charge
- (C) quality
- (D) fine

For numbers 24 and 25, fill in the circle next to the answer that you think is correct.

24. I tied the key on a string. In which sentence does the word *key* mean the same thing as in the sentence above?

- (F) The key to a riddle provides the answer.
- (G) I sailed around the key.
- (H) I opened the door with my key.
- (J) The choir sang in key.

25. I opened a savings account at the bank. In which sentence does the word *bank* mean the same thing as in the sentence above?

- (A) The pilot flew through a bank of clouds.
- (B) My mom is a bank manager.
- (C) My house sits on the bank of a river.
- (D) Bank to the left at the intersection.

For numbers 26 and 27, choose the answer that best defines the underlined part.

26. subway submarine

- (F) under
- (G) over
- (H) apart
- (J) backward

27. careless thoughtless

- (A) less than one
- (B) full of
- (C) without
- (D) forward

GO ON

Name ______________________________

READING: VOCABULARY

SAMPLE TEST (cont.)

For numbers 28–31, fill in the circle next to the correct answer.

28. Which of these words probably comes from the Latin word *barba,* meaning "beard"?

- (F) barb
- (G) barbarian
- (H) barber
- (J) bargain

29. Which of these words probably comes from the Greek word *kolla,* meaning "glue"?

- (A) college
- (B) collage
- (C) collide
- (D) collar

30. The pioneers moved west to settle the _______.

Which of these words means the settlers moved to the border of their country?

- (F) soil
- (G) state
- (H) suburb
- (J) frontier

31. The police officer inspected the accident _______.

Which of these words means the officer inspected the location of the accident?

- (A) site
- (B) situation
- (C) victims
- (D) problem

For numbers 32–35, read the paragraph. Find the word below that fits best in each numbered blank.

Wang Yani was born in a small town in southern China. Her father, an art teacher, recognized her interest and _________**(32)** in art very early in her life. Her first art _________**(33)** was held in Shanghai when Yani was only four years old. Yani paints using traditional Chinese _________**(34)**, but her style of broad brush strokes, say her critics, is refreshingly _________**(35)**.

32.
- (F) disgust
- (G) personality
- (H) talent
- (J) charm

33.
- (A) exhibition
- (B) experience
- (C) school
- (D) project

34.
- (F) containers
- (G) wood
- (H) homes
- (J) materials

35.
- (A) stale
- (B) unique
- (C) menacing
- (D) undeveloped

STOP

Name ______________________________

READING: COMPREHENSION

Lesson 7: Main Idea

Directions: Read each item. Fill in the circle next to the answer you think is correct.

Example

In school, veterinarians learn about animals' bodies, animal diseases, and the medicines used to treat them. They also learn how to perform surgeries.

A. What is this passage about?

- Ⓐ how veterinarians are trained
- Ⓑ the duties of a veterinarian
- Ⓒ equipment that veterinarians use
- Ⓓ the clothing that veterinarians wear

Clue

Look for a topic sentence in the passage. This will help you understand the main idea.

Practice

An urban habitat is home to many animals. Birds like pigeons and starlings nest on tall buildings. Mice and rats build their nests in or near buildings. Squirrels, rabbits, and opossums make their homes in the wide-open spaces of city parks. Timid animals like foxes and raccoons search for food in neighborhood garbage cans at night. Perhaps the favorite city animals, though, are the ones that live in the homes of people—cats, dogs, and other animal friends we call pets.

1. What would be a good title for this passage?

- Ⓐ Pests Among Us
- Ⓑ City Critters
- Ⓒ A Nocturnal Nuisance
- Ⓓ An Urban Legend

2. What is the main idea of this passage?

- Ⓕ People should protect city animals.
- Ⓖ Urban animals cause many problems.
- Ⓗ Many animals live in the city.
- Ⓙ People who live in cities should not have pets.

3. If the author wanted to continue describing urban habitats, what would be a good topic for the next paragraph?

- Ⓐ career opportunities in cities
- Ⓑ urban crime
- Ⓒ city schools
- Ⓓ plants that can be found in cities

4. What is the author's purpose for writing this passage?

- Ⓕ to tell people about animals that live in urban habitats
- Ⓖ to warn people about urban animals
- Ⓗ to present a plan to city officials about protecting animals
- Ⓙ to explain how people and animals work together

STOP

Name ______________________________

READING: COMPREHENSION

● Lesson 8: Recalling Details

Directions: Read each item. Fill in the circle next to the answer you think is correct.

Example

People laugh when I tell them what kind of farm we have. My family raises catfish! The fish live in ponds on our farm. We feed them pellets that look almost like the food you feed cats or dogs.

A. What does the food for the catfish look like?

- (A) birdseed
- (B) dog food
- (C) pebbles
- (D) sand

Read the questions first. Then, while you read the passage, you can look for the information that you will be asked about.

● Practice

Today was very busy. Jane, Carl, and I went out around 8:00 to fill our buckets with blackberries. It was hard work, and we didn't get back until it was time for lunch. This afternoon, Aunt Mara showed us how to wash and sort the berries. When it was time to make jam, Aunt Mara did the cooking part. Then she let us fill the jars and decorate the labels. Now Aunt Mara is letting me take a jar of jam home for Mom. She'll be surprised that I helped make it. I hope the rest of my stay here is as much fun as today was.

1. What was the first thing the narrator did?

- (A) picked blackberries
- (B) ate lunch
- (C) decorated labels
- (D) washed berries

2. Who cooked the berries?

- (F) the narrator
- (G) Jane
- (H) Carl
- (J) Aunt Mara

3. How does the narrator feel about this experience?

- (A) frustrated
- (B) surprised
- (C) happy
- (D) angry

4. When did the children pick the berries?

- (F) at night
- (G) in the afternoon
- (H) in the evening
- (J) in the morning

READING: COMPREHENSION

Lesson 9: Making Inferences/Drawing Conclusions

Directions: Read each item. Fill in the circle next to the answer you think is correct.

Example

Police officers carry equipment that helps them to protect themselves and other people. They carry guns, nightsticks, flashlights, and handcuffs on their belts. Some wear bullet-proof vests. They also carry two-way radios so they can call other officers for assistance.

A. Why would police officers need equipment for protection?

- Ⓐ because they teach people about the laws
- Ⓑ because they are trained to use the equipment
- Ⓒ because sometimes their work can be dangerous
- Ⓓ because they need to write reports

Clue Look carefully at all the answer choices before you choose your answer.

Practice

I was so nervous. I hadn't seen Abbie in three years, not since my mom got that new job. I remember the day we moved away. Abbie brought me our photograph in a frame. I gave her a necklace with a friendship charm on it. We promised to stay friends forever. Now that I was finally going to see her again, I wondered if we would still like the same kinds of things and laugh at the same kinds of jokes. I rubbed my sweaty palms on my jeans as we pulled into Abbie's driveway.

1. Why hasn't the narrator seen Abbie for three years?

- Ⓐ they were best friends
- Ⓑ because they didn't like each other's gifts
- Ⓒ because they had a fight
- Ⓓ because the narrator had to move away

2. Why are the narrator's palms sweaty?

- Ⓕ because she is nervous
- Ⓖ because she has a fever
- Ⓗ because she feels sick
- Ⓙ because she doesn't want to move

3. The passage gives you enough information to believe that the narrator —

- Ⓐ was angry at her mom for making her move.
- Ⓑ had a special friendship with Abbie.
- Ⓒ liked her new school.
- Ⓓ doesn't keep her promises.

4. The narrator will feel happy if —

- Ⓕ Abbie is not home.
- Ⓖ Abbie has changed a lot.
- Ⓗ she gets to move again.
- Ⓙ she and Abbie still get along.

STOP

Name ______________________________

READING: COMPREHENSION

Lesson 10: Fact and Opinion/Cause and Effect

Directions: Read each item. Fill in the circle next to the answer you think is correct.

Example

To pay off its national debts, the British government increased the taxes paid on its products by its colonists. The American colonists thought this was very unfair. They protested by throwing British tea and merchandise into Boston Harbor.

A. Why did the American colonists throw tea into Boston Harbor?

- Ⓐ because the British had too many debts
- Ⓑ because they wanted coffee instead of tea
- Ⓒ because they didn't like tea
- Ⓓ because they thought the tax increase was unfair

Clue **Look for key words in the question and find the words in the passage. This will help you locate the correct answer.**

Practice

The legend of Santa Clause started with stories about a fourth-century bishop. This bishop, Nicholas, was said to be kind, generous, and fond of children. In one story, Nicholas threw a bag of coins down the chimney of a needy family. Long after his death, Nicholas was named a saint. On his saint's day in December, Dutch children would place their shoes by the family hearth, hoping that St. Nicholas would leave treats in them. The Dutch called the saint "Sinter Klaas." When Dutch colonists settled in America, they continued this tradition. "Sinter Klaas" became known as Santa Claus.

1. What legend started the Dutch tradition of placing shoes by the family hearth?

- Ⓐ Bishop Nicholas living in the fourth century
- Ⓑ Bishop Nicholas throwing a bag of coins down a chimney
- Ⓒ Bishop Nicholas being named a saint
- Ⓓ the Dutch settling in America

2. Which one of these is an opinion?

- Ⓕ Life would be dull without Santa Claus.
- Ⓖ Nicholas was named a saint.
- Ⓗ The Dutch children placed their shoes on the hearth.
- Ⓙ The name "Sinter Klaas" became Santa Claus.

3. This passage would be considered —

- Ⓐ science fiction.
- Ⓑ historical fiction.
- Ⓒ nonfiction.
- Ⓓ fantasy.

STOP

Name ______________________________

READING: COMPREHENSION

● Lesson 11: Parts of a Story

Directions: Read each item. Fill in the circle next to the answer you think is correct.

Example

It was Saturday morning. All the world was smiling and bright—all, that is, except Tom Sawyer. With his pail of whitewash and a large brush, Tom stared sadly at the long fence. He dipped his brush into the white glop and began the job of whitewashing the fence.

A. This passage tells us about a boy named Tom Sawyer. How does Tom feel about whitewashing the fence?

- Ⓐ glum
- Ⓑ joyful
- Ⓒ excited
- Ⓓ cheerful

Clue

Skim the passage then read the questions. Go back to the passage to find the answers to the questions.

● Practice

One day, just as the leaves were beginning to change color, Rip Van Winkle walked through the woods and up the mountains. By early afternoon he found himself on one of the highest points of the Catskill Mountains. By late afternoon Rip was tired and panting, so he found a spot with a beautiful view where he could lay down and rest. Through an opening in the trees, Rip could see miles and miles of lower country and rich woodland. In the distance he could view the mighty Hudson River. It was moving calmly along its course, showing reflections of the soft white clouds in the sky.

1. What part of a story does this passage tell about?

- Ⓐ the setting
- Ⓑ the plot
- Ⓒ the conflict
- Ⓓ the characters

2. How do you think Rip feels about where he is?

- Ⓕ He thinks it is exciting.
- Ⓖ He thinks it is annoying.
- Ⓗ He thinks it is peaceful.
- Ⓙ He thinks it is dangerous.

3. Where in a story would you most likely find this passage?

- Ⓐ near the beginning
- Ⓑ in the middle
- Ⓒ near the end
- Ⓓ in the table of contents

4. At what time of year does this passage take place?

- Ⓕ winter
- Ⓖ spring
- Ⓗ summer
- Ⓙ fall

STOP

GRADE 5

Name ______________________________

READING: COMPREHENSION

Lesson 12: Fiction

Directions: Read the passage. Choose the answer for each question that follows the passage.

Example

Misha stood on the stage. His hands shook so hard that he could barely hold his violin. A hush fell over the audience. He shut his eyes tight and remembered what his music teacher had told him—"You can do it. Take a deep breath and pretend that you're standing in your living room." Misha lifted his violin to his chin and played his solo perfectly from beginning to end.

A. From this passage, what do you know about Misha?

- (A) He has been playing the violin for many years.
- (B) He likes to play his violin in front of an audience.
- (C) He gets nervous when he is performing in front of others.
- (D) He and his music teacher are friends.

Clue

Read the questions first. Think about them as you read the passage.

Practice

Floating the River

"Aren't we there yet?" Shiloh asked. At last, she and her family were on their way to their annual tubing trip. Floating down Glenn River on an inner tube was one of Shiloh's favorite things. This year they would float five whole miles, all the way to Glenn Fork.

With each passing mile, Shiloh smiled more and more as she thought of the fun they would have. When they finally reached Glenn Fork and parked the car, she jumped out, all ready to go.

"Not so fast, Shiloh," said her mother. "Remember, we're just here to leave the car. We still have to drive up the river. After we float back here, we'll be able to drive the car upstream to the truck. Otherwise, we won't have any way to get home."

"Oh, yeah, false alarm," Shiloh said. She had forgotten the family's plan to leave one car at each end of the float.

The whole family piled into the truck and drove to Jenkins Landing. Shiloh's father helped her unload her backpack and shiny tube from the truck. They walked down to the river's bank and put their toes in the water. Shiloh gasped as she felt how cold the water was. She took a deep breath and pushed herself out into the river. As Shiloh followed her family downstream, she thought to herself, "This will be the best tubing trip ever!"

GO ON

Name ______________________________

READING: COMPREHENSION

● Lesson 12: Fiction (cont.)

1. **This story is mostly about —**
   - (A) driving a truck.
   - (B) a family's adventure.
   - (C) a family's argument.
   - (D) a family's business.

2. **The family will float between which two points?**
   - (F) from Jenkins Landing to Glenn Fork
   - (G) from Glenn Fork to Glenn River
   - (H) from Glenn River to Jenkins Landing
   - (J) from Glenn Fork to Jenkins Landing

3. **How do you think Shiloh's parents feel about the tubing trip?**
   - (A) bored
   - (B) disappointed
   - (C) frustrated
   - (D) excited

4. **Why is the family driving both a car and a truck?**
   - (F) so they don't get the truck wet and muddy
   - (G) so they can show that they have a lot of money
   - (H) so they can all have a ride to the river
   - (J) so they can have transportation back to where they started

5. **Which character do you learn the most about in this passage?**
   - (A) Shiloh's mother
   - (B) Shiloh
   - (C) Shiloh's father
   - (D) Shiloh's sister

6. **When Shiloh says, "false alarm," she means —**
   - (F) she didn't tell the truth.
   - (G) that there is no danger.
   - (H) she made a mistake.
   - (J) there's been a warning.

STOP

Name ______________________________

READING: COMPREHENSION

● Lesson 13: Fiction

Directions: Read the passage. Choose the answer for each question that follows the passage.

Example

Skyler had never been as scared as he was the first time he tried to go inline skating. His legs felt like jelly. The skates kept slipping out from under him. He had thought it would be a snap to soar through the air in jumps and spins, but he found out that skating isn't as easy as it looks. Skyler wasn't going to give up. He practiced and practiced until he started to improve. Finally he was able to skate without falling down. Skyler knew if he kept practicing that some day he would be able to do some jumps and spins too.

A. By the end of the passage, Skyler's feelings have changed from —

Ⓐ proud ⟶ ashamed

Ⓑ frightened ⟶ determined

Ⓒ impatience ⟶ acceptance

Ⓓ sadness ⟶ happiness

Clue **If you don't know the answer to a question, skip it and come back to it later.**

● Practice

Survivors

As far as Kiki was concerned, the island had always been her home, and she loved it. She had been just about a year old when the ship she and her family had been on was caught in a great storm. She didn't remember their home in England, where she had been born, or boarding the ship for Australia. Kiki certainly didn't remember how her family and a few dozen others had arrived on the island in lifeboats, or even how they had built houses and made new lives.

The Martin family and the others who had survived the shipwreck had worked hard to make the island livable. In the weeks following the wreck, chests of seeds, tools, and food washed up on the beach. These chests gave the survivors a chance to build a new life on the island. Now, ten years after the disaster, the island was a wonderful place to live. Everyone had a comfortable home and there was plenty of food.

Kiki and the other children explored the island every day. It was on one of these outings that they saw the great ships. The children had climbed to the top of the highest peak on the island to study the sea birds that nested on the cliffs below. When they reached the top of the peak, Kiki spotted the four ships sailing toward the island.

GO ON

Name ____________________

READING: COMPREHENSION

● Lesson 13: Fiction (cont.)

By the time Kiki and her friends climbed down the mountain, the ships had reached the island and the captain and crew were surprised to find other English settlers there. They had known about the shipwreck, of course, but they had no idea there were survivors. The ships were heading to Australia, and the survivors were welcomed to join the crew on board.

That, however, was the problem. Almost all the survivors didn't want to leave the island, especially the children like Kiki who had spent most of their lives there or the dozen who had been born there. For them, the island was their world, and they couldn't imagine leaving it.

1. What is the main idea of this story?

Ⓐ how people lived after a shipwreck
Ⓑ explorers discovering a deserted island
Ⓒ children studying sea birds
Ⓓ a family's journey to Australia

2. What helped the survivors begin their new lives on the island?

Ⓕ having the children explore the island
Ⓖ memories of England
Ⓗ the captain and crew of the ships sailing to Australia
Ⓙ supplies that washed up on the beach

3. If the children could vote on whether to leave the island or to stay, which of these would probably happen?

Ⓐ Most would vote to leave.
Ⓑ Most would vote to stay.
Ⓒ Most would not vote.
Ⓓ There would be a tie.

4. Which of the following sentences expresses an opinion?

Ⓕ Kiki didn't remember their home in England.
Ⓖ The children had climbed to the top of the highest peak.
Ⓗ The island was a wonderful place to live.
Ⓙ The captain and crew were surprised to find other English settlers there.

5. What do you know about the island from reading this passage?

Ⓐ The island has a desert climate.
Ⓑ There are cliffs on the island.
Ⓒ There are palm trees on the island.
Ⓓ Dangerous animals live on the island.

6. How do you suppose Kiki will feel if her family decides to leave the island?

Ⓕ disappointed
Ⓖ excited
Ⓗ proud
Ⓙ happy

STOP

Name ______________________________

READING: COMPREHENSION

● Lesson 14: Fiction

Directions: Read the passage. Choose the answer for each question that follows the passage.

Example

Leo wrote an article called "Lizards" for the school paper. He didn't expect anyone to get excited about it, but they did. His teacher was pleased that Leo had done such a good job. "This was the best story you ever wrote," she said. "I'm going to enter it in the state writing competition for you. Maybe you'll win a prize!"

A. How do you think Leo felt about his teacher's reaction to his article?

- (A) afraid
- (B) unhappy
- (C) embarrassed
- (D) surprised

Clue **If you know which answer is correct, mark it and move on to the next questions.**

● Practice

The Story of Arachne

Long ago in a far away country lived a young woman named Arachne. She was not rich or beautiful, but she had one great talent. Arachne could weave the most beautiful cloth anyone had ever seen. Everyone in Arachne's village talked about her wonderful cloth, and soon she became famous. But as her fame grew, so did her pride.

"No one else can weave as well as I can," Arachne boasted. "Not even the goddess Minerva could make anything so lovely and fine."

Now Minerva wove cloth for all the gods. She was proud of her weaving too and thought that no human could ever match her skills. Soon Arachne's words reached Minerva's ears and the goddess became angry.

"So the human woman thinks she is better than I!" Minerva roared. "We will see about that!"

Minerva searched the countryside until she came upon Arachne's home. Minerva called to Arachne and challenged her to a contest. "Let us both weave a length of cloth. We will see whose is the most beautiful."

GO ON

Name ______________________________

READING: COMPREHENSION

● Lesson 14: Fiction (cont.)

Arachne agreed. She set up two looms, and she and Minerva went to work. The goddess wove cloth of all the colors of the rainbow. It sparkled in the sun and floated on the breeze like a butterfly. But Arachne wove cloth that sparkled like gold and jewels. The villagers were dazzled by Arachne's cloth. When Minerva inspected it, she knew Arachne was the best weaver.

Minerva was enraged. She took out a jar of magic water and sprinkled it on Arachne. Instantly, poor Arachne began to change. She shrank smaller and smaller until she could almost not be seen. She grew more arms and became covered in fine brown hair. When it was all over, Arachne had become a tiny brown spider. Arachne would never boast again, but she would spend the rest of her life weaving fine webs.

1. People in ancient times made up stories, or myths, to explain things in their world that they did not understand. This myth explains —

- (A) how to weave cloth.
- (B) why spiders weave webs.
- (C) how to turn a person into a spider.
- (D) why it is wrong to be boastful.

Here is a sequence of events that happens in the passage.

Arachne becomes a famous weaver.
Arachne brags that her skills are better than the goddess Minerva's.
Minerva realizes that Arachne is the better weaver.

2. Which of these events should go in the empty box?

- (F) Minerva sprinkles water on Arachne.
- (G) Minerva changes Arachne into a spider.
- (H) Minerva challenges Arachne to a weaving contest.
- (J) Arachne weaves webs.

3. What might have happened if Arachne had not bragged about her talents?

- (A) Minerva would have left her alone.
- (B) Arachne would not have become famous.
- (C) The villagers would not have appreciated Arachne's weaving.
- (D) Minerva would not be allowed to make cloth for the gods anymore.

4. What caused Minerva to challenge Arachne to the contest?

- (F) boredom and skill
- (G) contentment and humility
- (H) fear and confusion
- (J) pride and jealousy

5. This passage tells us the most about the —

- (A) plot.
- (B) mood.
- (C) characters.
- (D) setting.

6. This story might have been told to remind people not to —

- (F) brag about their talents.
- (G) weave cloth.
- (H) enter competitions.
- (J) kill spiders.

STOP

Name ______________________

READING: COMPREHENSION

Lesson 15: Nonfiction

Directions: Read the passage. Choose the answer for each question that follows the passage.

Example

Wasps build new nests every year. The potter wasp creates a mud "jar" nest for each of its eggs. The wasp then stings caterpillars to paralyze them and places them in the jar nests. The nests are sealed and the caterpillars are used as food for the developing wasps.

A. How does the potter wasp paralyze caterpillars?

- (A) by stinging them
- (B) by spitting on them
- (C) by biting them
- (D) by sealing them in jars

Clue **Look for important facts in the passage. These facts may be used in the questions that follow.**

Practice

Exploring a Coral Reef

A coral reef is a beautiful undersea wilderness filled with fascinating plants and animals. It is one of the most populated environments on Earth. Coral reefs are found where ocean water is warm, clean, and shallow.

For hundreds of years, people thought that coral was a type of flowering plant. Amazingly, coral reefs are actually formed by little tube-shaped animals called coral polyps. Coral polyps have hard outer skeletons that cover and protect their soft bodies. Most coral polyps stay within their protective skeletons during the day. At night, fingerlike tentacles emerge from the skeleton and pull tiny animals into the coral's mouth. When the coral polyps die, their skeletons remain in place. New polyps make their homes on the rocky foundations of the skeletons. In this way, the reef grows larger and larger.

Living things take up every bit of space on a coral reef. Beautiful tropical fish swim among sea turtles, colorful marine worms, and giant clams. Sharks patrol the water looking for food. Sea cucumbers share the rocky, sandy bottom of the reef with sea urchins. At dusk, octopuses come out of their caves and begin searching for food.

Many people come to coral reefs to snorkel or scuba dive. They swim in the water and explore the beauty of the reef. Unfortunately, some people damage the reefs by handling the coral. It may take hundreds of years for a reef to restore itself after a careless person damages it.

GO ON

Name ______________________________

READING: COMPREHENSION

● Lesson 15: Nonfiction (cont.)

1. What is the main idea of this passage?

Ⓐ Coral polyps are animals, not plants.
Ⓑ People should handle coral.
Ⓒ A coral reef is a delicate habitat populated by a wide array of animals.
Ⓓ Coral reefs need warm, clean, and shallow ocean water to survive.

2. How do coral polyps eat?

Ⓕ Tentacles emerge and capture tiny animals.
Ⓖ Tropical fish bring them food.
Ⓗ Tiny animals cling to the skeletons.
Ⓙ They are hand-fed by people.

3. How does the author of this passage feel about coral reefs?

Ⓐ The author would not want to visit a coral reef.
Ⓑ The author thinks reefs are easily replaced.
Ⓒ The author thinks reefs are hideous.
Ⓓ The author thinks reefs are beautiful.

4. Which of these sentences expresses an opinion?

Ⓕ Coral polyps have hard outer skeletons that cover and protect their soft bodies.
Ⓖ Some people damage the reefs by handling the coral.
Ⓗ A coral reef is a beautiful undersea wilderness.
Ⓙ Coral reefs are found where ocean water is warm, clean, and shallow.

5. Where would a passage like this be most likely to appear?

Ⓐ in a nature magazine
Ⓑ in an almanac
Ⓒ in a thesaurus
Ⓓ in a biography

6. Which of these is not explained in the passage?

Ⓕ how coral polyps eat
Ⓖ that people used to think coral was a plant
Ⓗ how pollution damages reefs
Ⓙ other types of animals that live in and around reefs

STOP

Name ____________________

READING: COMPREHENSION

Lesson 16: Nonfiction

Directions: Read the passage. Choose the answer for each question that follows the passage.

Example

Laura Ingalls Wilder wrote a series of nine children's books about her life as a pioneer. The first book was titled *Little House in the Big Woods*. Laura's books have been praised for their portrayals of life on the American frontier.

A. What would be a good title for this passage?

- (A) Little Laura
- (B) The American Frontier
- (C) Writing Children's Books
- (D) Laura Ingalls Wilder: Pioneer and Author

Clue: **Skim the passage, then read the questions. Refer back to the passage to find the answers. You don't have to read the story over again for each question.**

Practice

Swimming Star

Every day, thousands of people cross the channel of water between France and England in planes, ferries, and even trains. An American athlete, Gertrude Caroline Ederle, however, used a different method. She was the first woman to swim across the English Channel.

Gertrude Ederle was born in New York City in 1906. She dedicated herself to the sport of swimming at an early age and enjoyed great success. Before long, she was on her way to becoming one of the most famous American swimmers of her time. When she was sixteen, Ederle broke seven records in one day at a swimming competition in New York. Two years later, in 1924, she represented the United States at the Olympic Games, winning a gold medal in the 400-meter freestyle relay.

After her Olympic victory, she looked for an even greater challenge. One of the most difficult swims is to cross the 21-mile wide English Channel. The seas in the channel can be rough, and the water is cold. In the past, the feat had only been accomplished by male swimmers. Most people believed that the swim was too difficult for a woman, but Ederle wanted to prove them wrong. She didn't make it on her first attempt, but in 1926 she tried again. Leaving from the coast of France, Ederle had to swim even longer than planned because of heavy seas. She went an extra fourteen miles and still managed to beat the world record by almost two hours. This accomplishment made her an instant heroine at the age of twenty.

GO ON

Name ______________________________

READING: COMPREHENSION

● Lesson 16: Nonfiction (cont.)

1. What is the main idea of the passage?

Ⓐ Swimming is a fun sport.
Ⓑ Winning an Olympic medal will make you wealthy.
Ⓒ If you want to be very successful at something, you have to start at a young age.
Ⓓ Hard work and dedication can lead to great success.

2. Which event happened first in the passage about Ederle's life?

Ⓕ She swam across the English Channel.
Ⓖ She broke seven swimming records in a single day of competition.
Ⓗ She won an Olympic gold medal.
Ⓙ She looked for more challenges.

3. Based on the information in the passage, what word probably describes Ederle's personality?

Ⓐ imaginative
Ⓑ passive
Ⓒ lazy
Ⓓ determined

4. Why did Ederle decide to swim across the English Channel?

Ⓕ someone dared her to
Ⓖ to earn a lot of money
Ⓗ to prove that women could to do it
Ⓙ to win a gold medal

5. Which sentence would describe what the water was like on the day Ederle swam across the channel?

Ⓐ The water was cold and choppy.
Ⓑ The water was calm and warm.
Ⓒ The water was shallow.
Ⓓ The water was frozen.

6. According to the passage, why was Ederle considered a heroine?

Ⓕ because she was a generous person
Ⓖ because she had done something that no other woman had ever done
Ⓗ because she was a great swimmer
Ⓙ because she rescued someone

STOP

Name ____________________________

READING: COMPREHENSION

Lesson 17: Nonfiction

Directions: Read the passage. Choose the answer for each question that follows the passage.

Example

Ice hockey originated in the mid-1800s, when British troops played games of field hockey on the frozen lakes and ponds of Canada's provinces of Ontario and Nova Scotia. It became Canada's national sport by the early 1900s. Since then, the sport has become popular in European countries such as Russia and Sweden, as well as in the United States.

A. Where would a passage like this be most likely to appear?

- (A) in an atlas
- (B) in a medical journal
- (C) in a dictionary
- (D) in a book on the history of sports

Clue: **Once you have chosen an answer, move on to the next question. Only change an answer if you are certain that it is wrong.**

Practice

Jackie Robinson

Jackie Robinson, born in 1919, was the first African-American man to play modern American major league baseball. In high school and college, he played many sports. He earned letters in track and field, basketball, football, and baseball. Unfortunately, Robinson had to quit college for financial reasons. It seemed his days of playing sports were over.

In 1942, Robinson was drafted into the army. He faced a lot of prejudice in the army. As an officer, he was asked to join the army football team. But when other teams objected to playing against a team with a black member, he turned to the army baseball team. There, he was rejected again because of his race.

After leaving the army in 1945, Robinson played shortstop for the Kansas City Monarchs, one of several teams in the Negro League. Professional baseball was still segregated at that time, but the Brooklyn Dodgers' president, Branch Rickey, recognized Robinson's athletic skills. Rickey was determined to make Robinson the first African-American player in major league baseball.

GO ON

Name ____________________

READING: COMPREHENSION

● Lesson 17: Nonfiction (cont.)

Robinson started playing with the Dodgers' farm team. Rickey advised Robinson not to fight back when people were unkind to him. Baseball players and fans alike thought he should not be allowed to play. But he played so well that in 1947, he joined the Brooklyn Dodgers.

At first his teammates didn't like playing with him; however, when other people screamed at him, they came to his defense. Because of his great performance at second base and his outstanding batting average, Robinson was selected Rookie of the Year. In 1949, he was named the Most Valuable Player in the National League. One of his greatest thrills was when he helped the Dodgers win the 1955 World Series.

Jackie Robinson paved the way for African-American men to play in the major leagues. In 1962, he was inducted into baseball's Hall of Fame. Ten years later, at the age of 53, Robinson died in Stamford, Connecticut.

1. What would be a good title for the passage?

- (A) Jackie Robinson: A Major League Success
- (B) Rickey and Robinson Make it to the Majors
- (C) How to Play Second Base
- (D) The Baseball Hall of Fame

2. Why was Robinson selected as Rookie of the Year?

- (F) for his batting average and his skills at second base
- (G) for his excellent attitude
- (H) for his skills as a shortstop
- (J) because he helped win the World Series

3. How do you think Jackie Robinson felt toward Branch Rickey?

- (A) hostile
- (B) disgusted
- (C) appreciative
- (D) embarrassed

4. What effect did segregation have on professional baseball?

- (F) White players were given the best positions.
- (G) Anyone with enough talent was invited to play.
- (H) People who did not graduate from college could not play professional baseball.
- (J) African Americans weren't allowed to play in the major leagues.

5. How do you think Robinson felt about his accomplishments?

- (A) disappointed
- (B) proud
- (C) dissatisfied
- (D) shy

6. Why did Robinson join the army?

- (F) He needed a job.
- (G) He wanted to travel.
- (H) He was drafted.
- (J) He didn't know what else to do after he left college.

STOP

Name ______________________________

READING: COMPREHENSION

SAMPLE TEST

● **Directions:** Read the passage. Choose the answer for each question that follows the passage.

Example

Cats were first kept as pets in 2500 B.C. by the Egyptians. These first house cats were probably a type of wildcat called a Caffre cat. The idea of keeping a cat as a pet spread to Europe. Caffre cats were brought to Europe and are the ancestors of many of the modern cat breeds.

A. Europeans probably thought that keeping cats as pets was—

- Ⓐ ridiculous.
- Ⓑ a health hazard.
- Ⓒ a good idea.
- Ⓓ dangerous.

Here is a story about two seabirds. Read the story and then answer questions 1 through 4.

The penguin is a seabird that is native to the waters of the Southern Hemisphere. Penguins cannot fly, but they are excellent swimmers. They spend most of their time out at sea but come to land to raise their young. Mother penguins lay one or two eggs each season.

Puffins are another kind of seabird, but they are native to the cold waters of the Northern Hemisphere. Puffins can fly, but not very well. Like penguins, they swim well and spend most of their time out at sea. Mother puffins lay only one egg each season and they raise their young on land.

1. This story mostly describes —

- Ⓐ how seabirds raise their young.
- Ⓑ how penguins and puffins are alike and different.
- Ⓒ how penguins and puffins swim.
- Ⓓ where penguins and puffins live.

2. Which of the following statements is true?

- Ⓕ Penguins live in the Northern Hemisphere.
- Ⓖ Puffins live in the Northern Hemisphere.
- Ⓗ Puffins lay more eggs than penguins.
- Ⓙ Both birds spend most of their time on land.

3. Given what you know from reading the passage, what do you think penguins most likely eat?

- Ⓐ fish
- Ⓑ other birds
- Ⓒ puffins
- Ⓓ eggs

4. Which of these is a true statement about how penguins and puffins are alike?

- Ⓕ The birds live in the Southern Hemisphere.
- Ⓖ The birds lay 17 eggs each season.
- Ⓗ The birds can fly for long distances.
- Ⓙ The birds are good swimmers.

GO ON

Name ______________________________

READING: COMPREHENSION

SAMPLE TEST (cont.)

Here is a story about the first battle of the Civil War. Read the story and then answer questions 5 through 10 on page 293.

The Flying Congressman

The first major battle of the Civil War was fought near the small town of Manassas Junction, Virginia. The Union army called the battle Bull Run, after the creek by that name. Inasmuch as this quaint little town lay just 30 miles southwest of Washington, D.C., a number of citizens from the nation's capital thought it might be fun to pack a picnic lunch, load up the family, and take a buggy ride out to watch the Confederates "get what was coming to them." They viewed the upcoming battle as nothing more than a sporting event. Even members of Congress were in attendance. No fewer than six senators and an undetermined number of congressmen showed up, as did pretty ladies in fancy gowns, all traveling in style in expensive buggies and carriages.

One particular congressman provided what turned out to be the only entertainment of the day for the spectators from the big city. What was predicted to be an easy victory for the Union forces turned into a rout. Federal troops retreated to the capital at a record pace, followed by carriages of Washington's elite—minus their picnic baskets. These were discarded when the rout began, and the Confederate soldiers had a feast when the battle was over.

Although those in flight were preoccupied with their safety, they could not help noticing a tall, long-legged congressman who, on foot, was leading the pack in its frantic race back to the capital. He was seen jumping ditches and gullies, and was said to have cleared a six-foot fence with a foot to spare. Many of the terror-stricken refugees howled with laughter, despite their fear.

History does not relate the name of the fleet and agile congressman. But there is a chance he might be the same legislator who, after reaching the safety of the capital, was confronted by President Lincoln. The President glared at the panting legislator and is supposed to have said dryly, "I congratulate you on winning the race!"

GO ON

Name ______________________________

READING: COMPREHENSION

SAMPLE TEST (cont.)

5. This story mostly shows that —

Ⓐ many people died at the Battle of Bull Run.

Ⓑ congressmen during the Civil War were quite athletic.

Ⓒ some people in Washington, D.C., did not take the beginning of the Civil War seriously.

Ⓓ the Confederates would win the war.

6. According to the story, who ended up eating the picnic lunches?

Ⓕ the Washington elite

Ⓖ President Lincoln

Ⓗ the Union soldiers

Ⓙ the Confederate soldiers

7. Reread the last sentence of the story. How do you suppose the President felt about the people who went to watch the battle?

Ⓐ He was angry with them.

Ⓑ He was worried about them.

Ⓒ He was proud of them.

Ⓓ He distrusted them.

8. Why did the spectators run away from the battle?

Ⓕ because the Union soldiers were winning the battle

Ⓖ because they had lost their picnic baskets

Ⓗ because they were in buggies

Ⓙ because the Union soldiers were losing the battle

9. This story tells us the most about —

Ⓐ Manassas Junction, Virginia.

Ⓑ why the Civil War took place.

Ⓒ the people who went to watch the battle.

Ⓓ President Lincoln's approach to the war.

10. Why was the battle named "Bull Run"?

Ⓕ because that was the name of the nearest town

Ⓖ because the people had to run away

Ⓗ because that was the name of a nearby creek

Ⓙ because the Confederates liked the name

GO ON

Name ___________________________

READING: COMPREHENSION

SAMPLE TEST (cont.)

Here is a story about a day at a baseball game. Read the story and answer questions 11 through 16 on page 295.

Bonkers for Baseball

I remember a special Mother's Day back in 1939. My mom was a big baseball fan so my father treated us to tickets for the Brainford Bisons game. We sat in box seats owned by my father's company. It was an exciting day.

Before the game began, we started talking to a woman sitting in a nearby box seat. We learned that she was the mother of the Beulah Blaze's pitcher. Her son, Brian Falls, had been pitching in the minor leagues for three years. This was the first time she had ever seen him pitch in a professional game.

For the special event, Brian Falls had treated his mother to a box seat. He had the box decorated in flowers. Mrs. Falls was so excited. She told us that she had always encouraged Brian to become a baseball player. Her dream for her son had come true.

My team wasn't doing very well in the early innings. With Brian Falls pitching, the Brainford Bisons' batters kept striking out. Then, Falls threw a fastball to the plate. The batter swung at it. He caught a piece of it and fouled it off. The foul ball flew into the crowd. It came straight toward us! My dad and I reached into the air to catch it, but the ball veered left and hit Mrs. Falls in the head. She was knocked unconscious. We couldn't believe it—out of all the people in the stands, the ball hit the pitcher's mother! Mrs. Falls was rushed to the hospital. For the rest of the game we wondered what had happened to her. Later we learned the rest of the story.

Brian Falls left the game to accompany his mom to the hospital. He was so upset that he told her he would quit the game. His mother, who was recovering nicely, convinced him to stay in baseball. It's a good thing, because three years later he joined the major leagues.

GO ON

Name ______________________________

READING: COMPREHENSION

SAMPLE TEST (cont.)

11. What would be another good title for this story?

Ⓐ Mother's Day at the Ballpark
Ⓑ Making It in the Majors
Ⓒ Brian Falls: His Career in Baseball
Ⓓ The Brainsford Bisons Steal Home

Here is a time line of what happens in the story.

The family goes to the baseball game for Mother's Day.
A foul ball is hit into the stands.
Brian Falls joins the major leagues.

12. Which of these events should go in the empty box?

Ⓕ Mrs. Falls convinces Brian not to quit baseball.
Ⓖ Mrs. Falls is taken to the hospital.
Ⓗ The family discovers that the woman they've been talking with is the mother of the Beulah Blaze's pitcher.
Ⓙ The ball is almost caught by the narrator.

13. Why do you suppose Brian Falls had his mother's box seat decorated with flowers?

Ⓐ because he wanted to impress his friends
Ⓑ because it was the first time she had seen him pitch professionally
Ⓒ because he was in the major leagues
Ⓓ because she told him not to quit

14. Why was Mrs. Falls taken to the hospital?

Ⓕ because she needed to tell Brian to stay in the game
Ⓖ because she was a nurse
Ⓗ because she was sick
Ⓙ because she was hit by a foul ball

15. Mrs. Falls probably taught Brian to —

Ⓐ follow his dreams.
Ⓑ give up when things got too hard.
Ⓒ play baseball.
Ⓓ fight against his opponents.

16. From reading the passage, how do you suppose the narrator feels about baseball?

Ⓕ He thinks it's a silly game.
Ⓖ He despises it.
Ⓗ He is bored with it.
Ⓙ He enjoys it.

GO ON

READING: COMPREHENSION

SAMPLE TEST (cont.)

Read this story about a special dinner. Then answer questions 17 through 22 on page 297.

A Delicious Dinner

Molly's family is Chinese-American. They serve a traditional Chinese meal once a week. Molly invited her friend Amy to join them this week.

Molly's family was busy preparing for dinner when Amy arrived. The house was filled with many good smells. "You can help me set the table," Molly told her friend. They laid the place settings on the table. They gave each person a pair of chopsticks, a soup bowl, a soup spoon, and a rice bowl on a saucer.

"Where are the forks and knives?" Amy asked

"Oh, you won't need those," Molly explained. "We use chopsticks. But don't worry. I'll show you how to use them."

The two girls went into the kitchen. Molly's father was slicing and chopping vegetables. He threw the vegetables into a large cooking pan coated with hot oil.

"That's a wok," Molly said.

Amy watched the vegetables sizzle. Then Molly's mother asked the girls to carry platters of food to the table. Amy carried the steamed rice. It was one of the few dishes she recognized. There were meat-filled bundles called won-tons, steamed noodles, stir-fried beef, sweet-and-sour chicken, and pork spareribs. The food was nutritious and seasoned with herbs, spices, and sauces.

Amy was a little nervous about eating with chopsticks. Molly gave her instructions on how to hold and pinch with the chopsticks.

Amy managed to pick up a piece of chicken in her chopsticks. Suddenly, her fingers slipped and the chicken flew across the table. It landed in Molly's soup with a splash. Everyone smiled. "We keep these on hand for emergencies," Molly's father said kindly. He brought out a knife and fork and handed them to Amy. Amy was relieved and ate her dinner. It was delicious!

At the end of the meal, Amy was given a fortune cookie. She broke it open and read the fortune inside. It said, "If you practice hard, you will learn many things." Amy laughed and said, "If you let me take home a pair of chopsticks, my fortune may come true!"

GO ON

Name ____________________

READING: COMPREHENSION

SAMPLE TEST (cont.)

17. This story is mostly about —

- (A) Chinese food.
- (B) a family's traditions.
- (C) a girl trying to use chopsticks.
- (D) what it takes to have friends.

18. What food was the most familiar to Amy?

- (F) sweet-and-sour chicken
- (G) rice
- (H) won-tons
- (J) steamed noodles

19. How do you think Molly's parents felt when Amy dropped her food?

- (A) They understood that Amy wasn't used to using chopsticks.
- (B) They felt Amy had insulted their culture.
- (C) They thought Amy had bad manners.
- (D) They wished Amy hadn't come to dinner.

20. Why did Amy's fortune make her laugh?

- (F) because she was trying to act brave
- (G) because she spilled her food
- (H) because she thought it was a joke
- (J) because she knew she needed to practice using chopsticks

21. In this story, we learn the most about —

- (A) Molly
- (B) Amy
- (C) Molly's mother
- (D) Molly's father

22. Molly's father said, "We keep these on hand for emergencies." What was he referring to?

- (F) platters of food
- (G) a wok
- (H) a knife and fork
- (J) chopsticks

STOP

ANSWER SHEET

STUDENT'S NAME			SCHOOL
LAST	FIRST	MI	TEACHER
			FEMALE ◯ MALE ◯

Name bubbles (each column of LAST, FIRST and MI): Ⓐ–Ⓩ (A B C D E F G H I J K L M N O P Q R S T U V W X Y Z)

BIRTH DATE

MONTH	DAY		YEAR	
JAN ◯	0	0		0
FEB ◯	1	1		1
MAR ◯	2	2		2
APR ◯	3	3		3
MAY ◯		4		4
JUN ◯		5	5	5
JUL ◯		6	6	6
AUG ◯		7	7	7
SEP ◯		8	8	8
OCT ◯		9	9	9
NOV ◯			0	
DEC ◯				

GRADE

④ ⑤ ⑥

Part 1: VOCABULARY

A	Ⓐ Ⓑ Ⓒ Ⓓ	6	Ⓕ Ⓖ Ⓗ Ⓙ	13	Ⓐ Ⓑ Ⓒ Ⓓ	20	Ⓕ Ⓖ Ⓗ Ⓙ
B	Ⓕ Ⓖ Ⓗ Ⓙ	7	Ⓐ Ⓑ Ⓒ Ⓓ	14	Ⓕ Ⓖ Ⓗ Ⓙ	21	Ⓐ Ⓑ Ⓒ Ⓓ
1	Ⓐ Ⓑ Ⓒ Ⓓ	8	Ⓕ Ⓖ Ⓗ Ⓙ	15	Ⓐ Ⓑ Ⓒ Ⓓ		
2	Ⓕ Ⓖ Ⓗ Ⓙ	9	Ⓐ Ⓑ Ⓒ Ⓓ	16	Ⓕ Ⓖ Ⓗ Ⓙ		
3	Ⓐ Ⓑ Ⓒ Ⓓ	10	Ⓕ Ⓖ Ⓗ Ⓙ	17	Ⓐ Ⓑ Ⓒ Ⓓ		
4	Ⓕ Ⓖ Ⓗ Ⓙ	11	Ⓐ Ⓑ Ⓒ Ⓓ	18	Ⓕ Ⓖ Ⓗ Ⓙ		
5	Ⓐ Ⓑ Ⓒ Ⓓ	12	Ⓕ Ⓖ Ⓗ Ⓙ	19	Ⓐ Ⓑ Ⓒ Ⓓ		

Part 2: COMPREHENSION

A	Ⓐ Ⓑ Ⓒ Ⓓ	7	Ⓐ Ⓑ Ⓒ Ⓓ	14	Ⓕ Ⓖ Ⓗ Ⓙ
1	Ⓐ Ⓑ Ⓒ Ⓓ	8	Ⓕ Ⓖ Ⓗ Ⓙ	15	Ⓐ Ⓑ Ⓒ Ⓓ
2	Ⓕ Ⓖ Ⓗ Ⓙ	9	Ⓐ Ⓑ Ⓒ Ⓓ	16	Ⓕ Ⓖ Ⓗ Ⓙ
3	Ⓐ Ⓑ Ⓒ Ⓓ	10	Ⓕ Ⓖ Ⓗ Ⓙ	17	Ⓐ Ⓑ Ⓒ Ⓓ
4	Ⓕ Ⓖ Ⓗ Ⓙ	11	Ⓐ Ⓑ Ⓒ Ⓓ	18	Ⓕ Ⓖ Ⓗ Ⓙ
5	Ⓐ Ⓑ Ⓒ Ⓓ	12	Ⓕ Ⓖ Ⓗ Ⓙ	19	Ⓐ Ⓑ Ⓒ Ⓓ
6	Ⓕ Ⓖ Ⓗ Ⓙ	13	Ⓐ Ⓑ Ⓒ Ⓓ	20	Ⓕ Ⓖ Ⓗ Ⓙ

Name ______________________________

READING PRACTICE TEST

● Part 1: Vocabulary

Directions: Read each item. Fill in the circle next to the correct answer.

Examples

Choose the word that means the same or about the same as the underlined word.

A. filled with grief

- (A) sorrow
- (B) cheer
- (C) admiration
- (D) worry

Choose the word that means the opposite of the underlined word.

B. determined attitude

- (F) difficult
- (G) wavering
- (H) courageous
- (J) enduring

For numbers 1–4, choose the word that means the same or about the same as the underlined word.

1. a bundle of goods

- (A) sweater
- (B) burden
- (C) rumble
- (D) package

2. restore the wood

- (F) repair
- (G) retread
- (H) relieve
- (J) reduce

3. The dishes clattered in the sink. Clattered means —

- (A) rattled.
- (B) broke.
- (C) jumped.
- (D) washed.

4. Max planted a sapling in the yard. A sapling is a —

- (F) type of vegetable.
- (G) flower.
- (H) shrub.
- (J) young tree.

For numbers 5–8, choose the word that means the opposite of the underlined word.

5. scamper away

- (A) run
- (B) jog
- (C) stroll
- (D) sprint

6. contemporary art

- (F) modern
- (G) ancient
- (H) imaginative
- (J) folksy

7. the collapse of the government

- (A) creation
- (B) structure
- (C) downfall
- (D) laws

8. reckless behavior

- (F) foolish
- (G) carefree
- (H) juvenile
- (J) thoughtful

GO ON

Name ____________________________

READING PRACTICE TEST

Part 1: Vocabulary (cont.)

For numbers 9 and 10, choose the word that best completes both sentences.

**9. Jennifer plays in a _______.
Use a rubber _______ to keep the papers together.**

- (A) group
- (B) ribbon
- (C) band
- (D) string

**10. What is the _______ of your birth?
His family has a _______ farm.**

- (F) date
- (G) month
- (H) citrus
- (J) year

For number 11, read the item. Fill in the circle next to the correct answer.

11. The ship sailed into the bay.

In which sentence does the word bay mean the same thing as in the sentence above?

- (A) The bay horse was my favorite.
- (B) Coyotes bay at the moon.
- (C) Johan sat in the bay window.
- (D) Marnie found buried treasure at the bottom of the bay.

For numbers 12 and 13, choose the answer that best defines the underlined part.

12. triathlon triangle

- (F) two
- (G) three
- (H) four
- (J) five

13. teacher waiter

- (A) the study of
- (B) small
- (C) art or skill of
- (D) one who

14. Which of these words probably comes from the Latin word *bini oculus* meaning "two eyes at a time"?

- (F) bindery
- (G) bingo
- (H) binoculars
- (J) binomial

15. Which of these words probably comes from the Italian word *ombra* meaning "shade"?

- (A) umbrella
- (B) omelette
- (C) omit
- (D) umpire

GO ON

Name ______________________________

READING PRACTICE TEST

Part 1: Vocabulary (cont.)

Read the paragraph. Choose the word that best fits in each numbered blank.

The armadillo is __(16)__ in several ways. First, the female gives birth to four babies, and they are always the same sex. Second, when an armadillo is __(17)__ and cannot escape to its __(18)__ or quickly dig itself into the ground, it rolls itself into a tight, protective ball. This is possible because of the joined, __(19)__ plates of its shell. The armadillo also tucks in its head and feet. If, by chance, it __(20)__ to reach the safety of its burrow, the armadillo can hold on so tightly with its strong claws that it is virtually __(21)__ to pull it out.

16.
- (F) honored
- (G) unusual
- (H) motivated
- (J) typical

17.
- (A) assisted
- (B) free
- (C) cornered
- (D) released

18.
- (F) burrow
- (G) vehicle
- (H) porch
- (J) dormitory

19.
- (A) overlapping
- (B) detached
- (C) soft
- (D) disconnected

20.
- (F) endeavors
- (G) insists
- (H) actually
- (J) manages

21.
- (A) simple
- (B) impossible
- (C) likely
- (D) difficult

STOP

Name ______________________________

READING PRACTICE TEST

● Part 2: Comprehension

Directions: Read the passage. Choose the answer for each question that follows the passage.

Example

When hunting, meerkats take turns at guard duty. Standing ramrod straight on its hind legs, the meerkat on duty scans the sky and horizon for predators. If an enemy is spotted, the alert sentry sounds a shrill alarm, and its fellow meerkats run for cover.

A. Why do meerkats take turns keeping guard?

- Ⓐ to prove that they can cooperate
- Ⓑ to allow the mother meerkats time to hunt
- Ⓒ to sound a warning when enemies are spotted
- Ⓓ because they can stand up straight and tall

Read this story about the changing of the seasons. Then, answer questions 1 through 4.

Autumn Dance

Every October, autumn bullies summer into letting go of the skies. The wind breathes a chill into the air. The sun gets tired and goes to bed earlier each night, and night sleeps in later each day. The trees dress in bright gowns for the last celebration of the season, and the leaves are skipping and dancing down the sidewalk. This is autumn, standing firm with hands on her hips, until winter peers over the edge of the world.

1. This passage mostly tells about —

- Ⓐ winter turning into spring.
- Ⓑ fall turning into winter.
- Ⓒ spring turning into summer.
- Ⓓ summer turning into fall.

2. How does the sun change during autumn?

- Ⓕ It rises and sets earlier than in the summer.
- Ⓖ It rises and sets later than in the summer.
- Ⓗ It rises later but sets earlier than in the summer.
- Ⓙ It rises earlier but sets later than in the summer.

3. What is the author referring to when she describes the trees dressed in "bright gowns"?

- Ⓐ leaves that have changed color but have not yet fallen from the trees
- Ⓑ green leaves
- Ⓒ formal dresses
- Ⓓ the trees' empty branches

4. Personification means "giving human qualities to animals or objects." Which sentence is not an example of personification?

- Ⓕ Every October, autumn bullies summer into letting go of the skies.
- Ⓖ A cold wind blows.
- Ⓗ The leaves skipped and danced down the sidewalk.
- Ⓙ The sun gets tired and goes to bed.

GO ON

Name ________________________________

READING PRACTICE TEST

Part 2: Comprehension (cont.)

Read this story about an interesting plant. Then, answer questions 5 through 10 on page 304.

Tough Tumbleweed

I'm a traveling tumbleweed, rolling along the dusty trails of the wild, wild West. Well, actually I'm blowing across somebody's backyard in suburban Texas. These days it's hard to find a large open space. Back in the good old days, my ancestors tumbled across miles and miles of deserts or plains. Today, it's hard to find a mile without a strip mall or housing complex. Life for tumbleweeds just isn't that exciting anymore.

My great-great-great grandfather was one of the first immigrants to America. He sneaked into the country with a load of wheat from Russia. He and the other tumbleweeds used to be called Russian thistle before they came to America. Tumbleweeds are able to live on very little water, so my ancestors were able to spread across dry western lands that previously couldn't support plants. When a tumbleweed matures, it becomes dry and brittle. A strong wind comes along and—snap!—off it goes, tumbling across the landscape. As it rolls, it drops seeds in new places.

My family has had many adventures over the years. My great-great uncle tumbled with Crazy Horse, the legendary American Indian. My great-grandmother tumbled with the covered wagons. My father even tumbled on the set of a Hollywood western movie.

But, modern times are not as kind to us tumbleweeds. We get caught in fences and ditches. Our worst enemy is the automobile. My cousin was trapped under a car and caught fire from the heat of the muffler. He became a tumbleweed torch! Some people hate us tumbleweeds and try to burn us up. They can burn all they want, because tumbleweeds are not in danger of becoming extinct. We will be around for a long, long time. Our species wouldn't have lasted this long if we weren't stubborn. We've learned to adapt to civilization and to deal with humans who have taken over our land.

Tumbleweeds aren't called tough for nothing!

GO ON

Name ____________________________

READING PRACTICE TEST

Part 2: Comprehension (cont.)

5. What is the main idea of this story?

- Ⓐ how tumbleweeds have been used throughout history
- Ⓑ how tumbleweeds survive and how modern times have affected them
- Ⓒ how people feel about tumbleweeds
- Ⓓ how tumbleweeds are used in Hollywood movies

6. Tumbleweeds came to America from —

- Ⓕ Russia.
- Ⓖ Texas.
- Ⓗ Hollywood.
- Ⓙ the West.

7. How does the narrator of this story feel?

- Ⓐ He is happy with modern inventions.
- Ⓑ He longs for the days when there were more wide-open spaces.
- Ⓒ He appreciates the need for housing complexes.
- Ⓓ He wishes he could be in a Hollywood movie.

8. Which of these sentences is an opinion?

- Ⓕ Tumbleweeds used to be called Russian thistle.
- Ⓖ Tumbleweeds are not in danger of becoming extinct.
- Ⓗ Tumbleweeds are able to live on very little water.
- Ⓙ Life for tumbleweeds just isn't that exciting anymore.

9. The narrator in this story is —

- Ⓐ a covered wagon.
- Ⓑ an American Indian.
- Ⓒ a tumbleweed.
- Ⓓ a Russian immigrant.

10. What would be a good word to describe tumbleweed?

- Ⓕ hardy
- Ⓖ fragile
- Ⓗ irritable
- Ⓙ delicate

GO ON

Name ____________________

READING PRACTICE TEST

Part 2: Comprehension (cont.)

Read the story. Then, answer questions 11 through 16 on page 306.

Pocahontas

There lived in Virginia in the early 1600s a beautiful girl named Pocahontas. Her name meant *Playful One*. She was the daughter of Powhatan, the chief of some 30 Indian tribes in Virginia.

Pocahontas is remembered for saving the life of Captain John Smith. Smith was the leader of the Jamestown colony founded by the English in 1607. In that same year, he was captured by the Indians and sentenced to death by Chief Powhatan. According to Smith's own account, he was ordered to lay his head on large stones in anticipation of being clubbed to death by several braves. At this point, Pocahontas is said to have knelt beside the Englishman and placed her head on his. Powhatan was apparently touched by this gesture, and he ordered that Smith be set free.

It is not certain if the above story is true. What casts doubt on its validity is that Smith later claimed to have been saved in the same manner by an Indian girl in New Hampshire.

Regardless, Pocahontas was a real person who did much to improve relations between her people and the English settlers. After the Smith incident, it was mostly peaceful between the two peoples until Powhatan's death in 1618.

In 1613, Pocahontas was captured and held hostage by the English. During her year of captivity, she met and married John Rolfe, a Virginia tobacco planter. In 1616, she accompanied Rolfe to England, where she was presented at the royal court. Pocahontas died there of smallpox in 1617, shortly before her planned return to America. She was buried at Gravesend, England.

John Rolfe returned to Virginia where he died in 1622. Thomas, the son of Rolfe and Pocahontas, later became a distinguished Virginian. Today, a number of Virginian families claim to be descendants of Pocahontas and John Rolfe.

GO ON

Name ______________________________

READING PRACTICE TEST

Part 2: Comprehension (cont.)

11. Which of the following would make a good title for this story?

Ⓐ Chief Powhatan and His Thirty Tribes

Ⓑ The Capture of John Smith

Ⓒ The Life of Pocahontas

Ⓓ Life on a Virginia Tobacco Farm

Here is a sequence of events that happened in the story.

Pocahontas improved relations between her tribe and the English.
The English captured Pocahontas.
Pocahontas traveled to England.

12. Which of these events should go in the empty box?

Ⓕ Chief Powhatan died.

Ⓖ Pocahontas married John Rolfe.

Ⓗ Pocahontas saved John Smith.

Ⓙ John Rolfe was killed.

13. Why do some people think John Smith's story about being saved by Pocahontas is not true?

Ⓐ because John Rolfe also claimed he was rescued by Pocahontas

Ⓑ because Pocahontas was not a real person

Ⓒ because there were no witnesses

Ⓓ because he said the same thing happened to him with another tribe

14. How did Pocahontas die?

Ⓕ She died of smallpox.

Ⓖ She was clubbed to death.

Ⓗ She was killed during an Indian uprising.

Ⓙ She drowned on her way to England.

15. In this story, you learn the most about —

Ⓐ Powhatan.

Ⓑ John Rolfe.

Ⓒ Pocahontas.

Ⓓ John Smith.

16. The people who claim to be descendants of Pocahontas and John Rolfe are probably —

Ⓕ members of an historical society.

Ⓖ proud of their heritage.

Ⓗ ashamed by their family history.

Ⓙ good storytellers.

GO ON

Name ______________________________

READING PRACTICE TEST

Part 2: Comprehension (cont.)

Here is a story about a very unusual animal. Read the story and then answer questions 17 through 20.

Mammal, Fish, or Fowl?

When scientists in England received reports from Australia about the duckbill platypus in the late 1700s, they thought they were the victims of a hoax. Surely, they must have reasoned, some jokester had sewn body parts from several different animals together in an attempt to trick them.

Indeed, the duckbill platypus is a strange animal. It has a bill resembling a duck; a flat, paddle-shaped tail like a beaver; and the shuffling gait of an alligator. Both its front and hind feet are webbed and have claws. Unlike most mammals, it has neither lips nor exterior ears. Although it nurses its young, it does not give birth to live babies. Instead it lays eggs—like a chicken! Small wonder that scientists were confused and not certain whether they were dealing with fish, fowl, or some kind of new species. They eventually classified the platypus with mammals.

17. This story mostly describes —

- (A) why scientists decided that the platypus was a mammal.
- (B) the unique features of the platypus.
- (C) where the platypus can be found.
- (D) a scientific hoax.

18. Which of the following statements is *false*?

- (F) The platypus has a tail that resembles a beaver's tail.
- (G) English scientists first learned about the platypus in the late 1700s.
- (H) The platypus does not have lips.
- (J) The platypus is a type of bird.

19. Which sentence is probably *true*?

- (A) One scientist probably made the decision on how the platypus would be classified.
- (B) Scientists were probably in complete agreement on how to classify the platypus.
- (C) Scientists probably debated over how the platypus should be classified.
- (D) Scientists probably let the people of England vote on how the platypus should be classified.

20. Which of these characteristics would have helped the scientists decide that the platypus was a mammal?

- (F) The platypus nurses its young.
- (G) The platypus lays eggs.
- (H) The platypus does not have external ears.
- (J) The platypus has a bill like a duck.

STOP

ANSWER KEY

READING: VOCABULARY
Lesson 1: Synonyms
• Page 264
A. B
B. J
1. A
2. H
3. C
4. F
5. B
6. J
7. A
8. H

READING: VOCABULARY
Lesson 2: Vocabulary Skills
• Page 265
A. D
B. G
1. A
2. J
3. B
4. F
5. D
6. H
7. C

READING: VOCABULARY
Lesson 3: Antonyms
• Page 266
A. C
B. F
1. A
2. J
3. A
4. H
5. B
6. J
7. A
8. G

READING: VOCABULARY
Lesson 4: Multi-Meaning Words
• Page 267
A. C
B. G
1. D
2. H
3. A

READING: VOCABULARY
Lesson 5: Words in Context
• Page 268
A. C
B. F
1. B
2. F
3. B
4. J
5. C
6. J

READING: VOCABULARY
Lesson 6: Word Study
• Page 269
A. A
B. H
1. B
2. J
3. A
4. F
5. C
6. G

READING: VOCABULARY SAMPLE TEST
• Pages 270–273
A. D
B. G
1. A
2. H
3. B
4. F
5. D
6. G
7. C
8. F
9. D
10. H
11. A
12. H
13. D
14. G
15. A
16. G
17. D
18. F
19. B
20. J
21. B
22. F
23. D
24. H
25. B
26. F
27. C
28. H
29. B
30. J
31. A
32. H
33. A
34. J
35. B

READING: COMPREHENSION
Lesson 7: Main Idea
• Page 274
A. A
1. B
2. H
3. D
4. F

READING: COMPREHENSION
Lesson 8: Recalling Details
• Page 275
A. B
1. A
2. J
3. C
4. J

READING: COMPREHENSION
Lesson 9: Inferencing and Drawing Conclusions
• Page 276
A. C
1. D
2. F
3. B
4. J

READING: COMPREHENSION
Lesson 10: Fact and Opinion/Cause and Effect
• Page 277
A. D
1. B
2. F
3. C

READING: COMPREHENSION
Lesson 11: Parts of a Story
• Page 278
A. A
1. A
2. H
3. A
4. J

READING: COMPREHENSION
Lesson 12: Fiction
• Pages 279–280
A. C
1. B
2. F
3. D
4. J
5. B
6. H

ANSWER KEY

READING: COMPREHENSION
Lesson 13: Fiction
• Pages 281–282
A. B
1. A
2. J
3. B
4. H
5. B
6. F

READING: COMPREHENSION
Lesson 14: Fiction
• Pages 283–284
A. D
1. B
2. H
3. A
4. J
5. C
6. F

READING: COMPREHENSION
Lesson 15: Nonfiction
• Pages 285–286
A. A
1. C
2. F
3. D
4. H
5. A
6. H

READING: COMPREHENSION
Lesson 16: Nonfiction
• Pages 287–288
A. D
1. D
2. G
3. D
4. H
5. A
6. G

READING: COMPREHENSION
Lesson 17: Nonfiction
• Pages 289–290
A. D
1. A
2. F
3. C
4. J
5. B
6. H

READING: COMPREHENSION SAMPLE TEST
• Pages 291–297
A. C
1. B
2. G
3. A
4. J
5. C
6. J
7. A
8. J
9. C
10. H
11. A
12. H
13. B
14. J
15. A
16. J
17. B
18. G
19. A
20. J
21. B
22. H

READING PRACTICE TEST
Part 1: Vocabulary
• Pages 299–301
A. A
B. G
1. D
2. F
3. A
4. J
5. C
6. G
7. A
8. J
9. C
10. F
11. D
12. G
13. D
14. H
15. A
16. G
17. C
18. F
19. A
20. J
21. B

READING PRACTICE TEST
Part 2: Comprehension
• Pages 302–307
A. C
1. D
2. H
3. A
4. G
5. B
6. F
7. B
8. J
9. C
10. F
11. C
12. G
13. D
14. F
15. C
16. G
17. B
18. J
19. C
20. F

Answer Key

Root and Base Words

A root, or base word, is the word that is left after you take off a prefix or suffix.

Directions: Divide the following words into parts so the root is separate.

	ato self
autobiography	the story of a person s life written by that person
autograph	a person s signature or handwriting
automatic	having a self-acting or self-regulating mechanism; done without thought or conscious effort
automobile	a passenger vehicle with its own engine
autonomous	self-governing

1. automobile
   auto mobile
2. autobiography
   auto biography
3. automatic
   auto matic
4. autograph
   auto graph
5. autonomous
   auto nomous

Directions: Complete each sentence using a word from the word box.

1. The writer finished the autobiography about her life.
2. Sally got an automatic camera for her birthday.
3. Joe was excited when he got the celebrity s autograph.
4. The people who lived on the island did not wish to be governed by a mother country any longer. They wanted to be autonomous.
5. Jack checked under the hood of his automobile.

5

Root and Base Words

	multi many
multicolored	having many colors
multimedia	combining more than two artistic techniques or means of communication or expression, such as acting, lighting effects, and music
multimillionaire	a person who has at least two million dollars
multiple	having many parts or elements
multitude	a large number of persons or things

Directions: Unscramble the word and write the definition.

Example: limptule multiple having many parts or elements

1. rollutimedoc multicolored having many colors
2. lemonlimitailiur multimillionaire a person who has at least two million dollars
3. demiitutu multitude a large number of persons or things
4. immediatul multimedia combining many art techniques

Directions: Complete each sentence using a

1. The unhappy result of John's skiing accident was a multiple fracture of the arm.
2. A kaleidoscope is constructed with multicolored glass.
3. The rock concert with television screens and a light show was a multimedia event.
4. A multimillionaire donated money for the starving children.
5. The multitude of people followed the celebrity into the theater.

6

Root and Base Words

	pre before
preamble	a statement that introduces a formal document, explaining its purpose
precede	to come or go before in rank, time, or order
prehistoric	of the period before written history
preoccupied	wholly occupied or absorbed in one's thoughts; absentminded
preschool	school before kindergarten; nursery school
prevent	to take action before an event to stop the event from happening

Directions: Write a short definition for each word.

Example: prehistoric of the period before written history.

1. precede
2. precedent
3. preoccupation
4. prevention
5. preventable

Answers will vary.

Directions: Complete each sentence using a word from the word box.

1. The four-year-old child will attend a preschool class.
2. The dinosaurs lived during prehistoric times.
3. The teacher said we had to memorize the preamble to the United States Constitution.
4. Roger couldn't enjoy the movie because he was preoccupied about the test the next day.
5. Seventh grade precedes (s) eighth grade.

7

Root and Base Words

	bi, di two
biceps	any muscle having two points of origin
bilingual	able to use two languages equally well
biped	a two-footed animal
bisect	divide into two (usually equal) parts
dichromatic	having two colors
dilemma	a situation requiring a choice between two equal alternatives
diploma	a certificate awarded when a student has successfully completed a particular course of study
dipterous	having two wings

Directions: Complete each sentence using a word from the word box.

1. A fly is a dipterous insect.
2. Lorenzo was taking a course in weight training, and would proudly flex his biceps when anyone asked how he was progressing.
3. Charlotte faced the dilemma of whether to go to the movie with her friends or take the babysitting job.
4. Silvia is bilingual because she speaks Spanish at home and English at school.
5. The geometry teacher told the students to bisect the circle.

Directions: Write a word with the prefix **bi** to complete each phrase.

1. *Annual* means once a year. Biannual means twice a year.
2. A *biennium* is a two-year period. Biennial means once every two years.
3. *Centum* is the Latin word for one hundred. Bicentennial means once every two hundred years.
4. A bimonthly event happens twice a month.
5. A biweekly event happens twice a week.

8

Root and Base Words

	ben, bene good, well
benediction	a blessing
benefactor	a person who gives help or support, especially financial aid
beneficial	having a good or helpful effect
beneficiary	a person who receives a benefit or advantage, such as an inheritance
benevolent	doing good things; being good-hearted, kind
benign	gentle and kind; not threatening life

Directions: Fill in each blank with a word from the word box.

1. The musician needed a benefactor to support him financially.
2. The priest said the benediction after the mass.
3. It is beneficial to study vocabulary before taking a standardized test.
4. The beneficiary of his life insurance policy would receive $25,000.
5. My grandmother was very relieved when the tests showed that the tumor was benign.

Directions: Circle each word below in which **ben** or **bene** is used as a prefix meaning *good, well.*

beneath	Benelux
Benedict	benighted
benefactor	benignant
benefit	benumb

Directions: List five things that are beneficial to your b...

1. 2.
3.

Answers will vary.

9

Root and Base Words

	cred to believe
accredit	to give credit for; to authorize or recognize officially
credence	acceptance or belief
credential	letter or document that proves or affirms a person's identity or right to hold a certain position
credo	a set of beliefs or opinions
credulous	inclined to believe anything, often without sufficient proof
discredit	to reject as untrue; to cast doubt on; to disgrace
incredible	unbelievable

Directions: Fill in each blank with a word from the word box.

1. His explanation for not having his homework was truly incredible.
2. The golden rule is an important part of my credo.
3. Five years of college study are usually required to obtain a teaching credential.
4. Because they knew that enrollment had been dropping, they gave credence to the rumor that the school would soon close.
5. Little Mikey was still credulous; he would believe anything his big brothers told him.
6. The candidate's staff was trying hard to find ways to discredit the opponent.

Directions: Look up the following words and phrases in a dictionary and write a brief definition for each.

1. on credit
2. to one's credit
3. creditor
4. incredulous
5. credibility

Answers will vary.

10

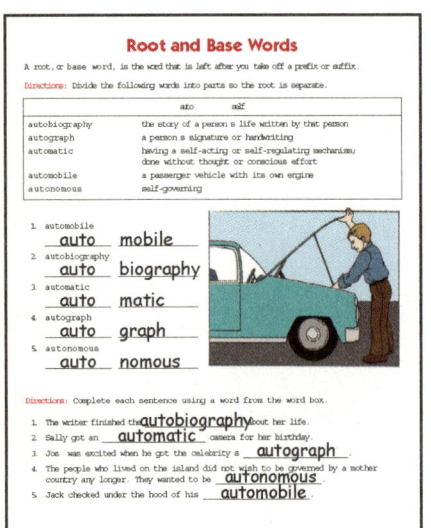

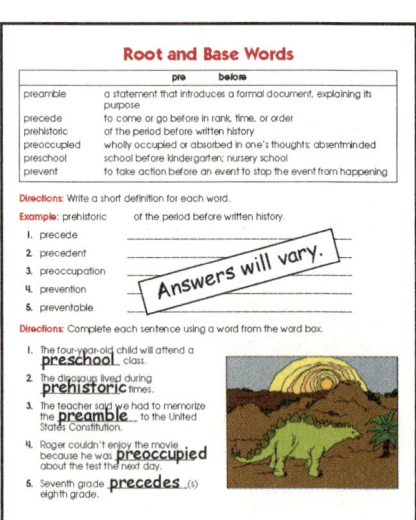

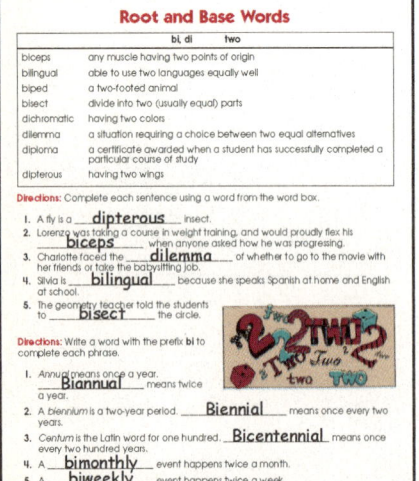

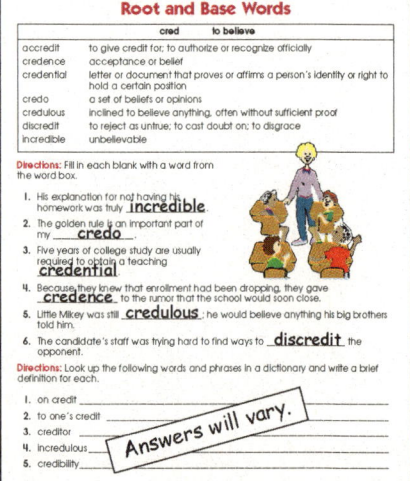

Prefixes

A **prefix** is a part **added to the beginning** of a word to change its meaning. The prefix **un** means *not* and the prefix **re** means *again*.

Directions: Add the correct prefix to each word in the word box. Write the new words in the correct column.

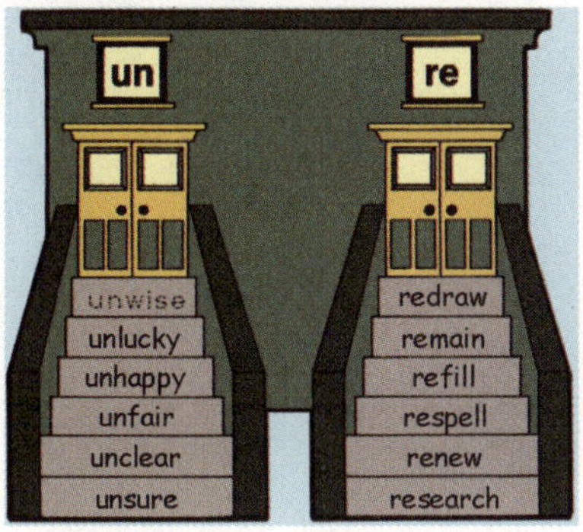

draw	lucky	new	clear
wise	fill	happy	safe
main	spell	fair	search

11

Prefixes

Directions: Read each definition. Complete each sentence using a word with the prefix **un** or **re**.

1. I **repainted** my sled. (painted again)
2. Did you **reconsider** your answer? (consider again)
3. Mei-Ling will **redraw** her poster. (draw again)
4. The treasure chest was **unlocked**. (not locked)
5. David's skates are **unlaced**. (not laced)
6. Grandfather likes to **retell** that story. (tell again)
7. The writing was **unclear** and hard to read. (not clear)
8. Watch the **replay** to see the touchdown. (play again)
9. How did she **redo** the book report? (do again)
10. It is best to avoid **unkind** words. (not kind)
11. Jan will **refinish** the bookcase. (finish again)
12. The **unsafe** stairway was marked with a sign. (not safe)

12

Prefixes

The prefix **mis** means *wrongly* and the prefix **non** means *not*.

Directions: Add the correct prefix to each word in the word box. Write the new words in the correct column.

stop	take	skid	fire	count
spell	fat	place	sense	human

13

Prefixes

The prefix **mis** means *wrongly* and the prefix **pre** means *before*.

Directions: Add the prefix to each word. Write the new word and then write its meaning.

Base Word	Prefix	New Word	Meaning
1. cook	pre	precook	cook beforehand
2. spell	mis	misspell	spell wrong
3. view	pre	preview	look at beforehand
4. school	pre	preschool	before kindergarten
5. pay	pre	prepay	pay ahead of time
6. place	mis	misplace	lose
7. use	mis	misuse	not use properly
8. treat	mis	mistreat	not treat properly

14

Suffixes

A **suffix** is a word part added to the **end of a word** to change its meaning.

-ist A noun-forming suffix, -ist means a person who makes, does, or practices.	**-ly** An adverb- or adjective-forming suffix, -ly means when, how, like, or in the manner of.
-less An adjective-forming suffix, -less means without or lacking.	**-fy** A verb-forming suffix, -fy means to make or cause to be or become.
-ness A noun-forming suffix, -ness means state or quality of being.	**-ize** A verb-forming suffix, -ize means to cause to be or to become.

Directions: From the following list, select the correct word to complete each sentence. Write the word on the line.

vaporize **naturalist** **harshly** **purify** **pitiless** **correctness**

1. Before drinking river water you should **purify** it because it may be polluted.
2. A person who practices the study of nature is a **naturalist**.
3. The **pitiless** football coach made the team run an extra mile.
4. Check your spelling for **correctness** when using new words.
5. The angry man spoke **harshly** to the telephone operator.
6. High temperatures will make water **vaporize**.

Directions: Use the suffixes in the word box to make new words that answer each phrase. Write the word on the line.

1. An adjective meaning without power. **powerless**
2. An adverb that tells how a brave person acts. **bravely**
3. A verb meaning to make simple. **simplify**
4. A noun meaning a person who makes works of art. **artist**
5. A verb meaning to form crystals. **crystallize**
6. A noun meaning the state of being dark. **darkness**

15

Suffixes

Directions: Use the word box to fill in the blanks with words containing suffixes. Put each boxed letter in the matching numbered blank below to find out the state you might visit to get something necessary for school.

invitation	penniless	wonderful	hopeless
careful	noisy	collection	peaceful
addition	followed	winning	

1. hopeless
2. addition
3. followed
4. winning
5. wonderful
6. careful
7. invitation
8. collection
9. noisy
10. peaceful
11. penniless

p (1) e (10) n (5) c (8) i (11) l (3) · v (7) a (2) n (9) i (4) a (6)

16

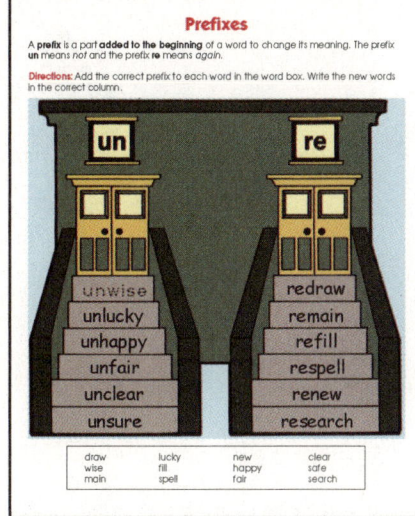

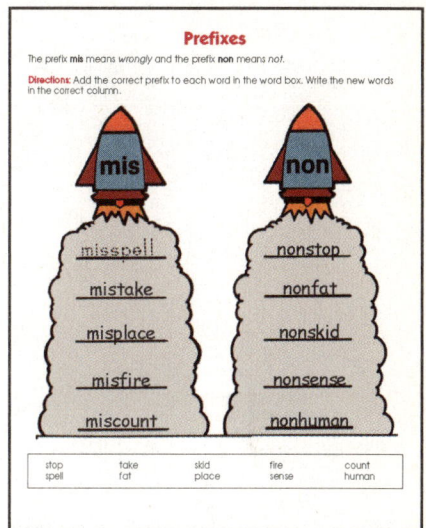

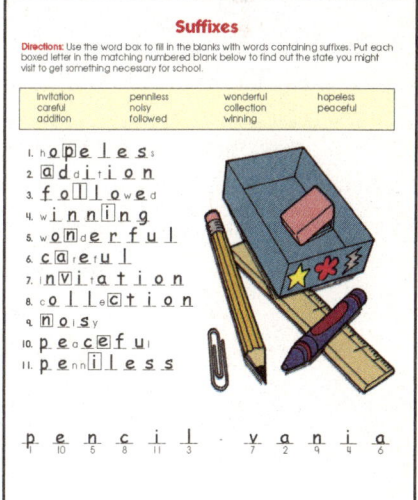

Suffixes

The suffix **able** means *capable of*. For example, a wire that is **bendable** can bend.

Directions: Add **able** to the words below. (If a word ends in a silent *e*, you may need to drop the *e* before adding a suffix beginning with a vowel.)

breakable — noticeable — reasonable

The suffixes **en** and **ize** mean to *make* or *cause to be*. Add **en** to the words below.

brighten — harden — sharpen

Add **ize** to the words below.

modernize — tenderize — steril~~e~~ize

The suffix **ist** means *one who does something*. Add **ist** to the words below.

typ~~e~~ist — violinist — perfectionist

The suffix **ous** means *having the quality of*. Add **ous** to the words below.

marvelous — nerv~~e~~ous — courageous

Directions: Use the words you wrote above to complete the sentences below.

1. Pat's answer was so reasonable everyone agreed she must be right.
2. The soldier received a medal for his courageous act in battle.
3. We went to the concert to listen to my favorite violinist.
4. In a hospital, someone must sterilize instruments that are used in operations.
5. My friends who read that novel said that it was marvelous!
6. Mrs. Grant wants to modernize her kitchen by replacing the old cupboard doors.
7. Painting this room white will help to brighten its appearance.
8. Mr. Burns is such a perfectionist that he will redo his work many times over.
9. Before a test, try to stay calm and not get nervous.
10. If you display the bulletin on this wall, it will be more noticeable
11. Clay will harden and be difficult to mold if you leave it out.
12. Try not to drop the vase because it is breakable.

17

Suffixes

Read the passage carefully.

"The treasure must be in here!" yelled Brad. He and his sister Lauren stood outside the **entrance** of a cave. As Brad took a step towards the **darkness**, Lauren touched his arm.

"Let's rest a bit," said Lauren, still **breathless** from running. "Besides, it might be **dangerous** in there."

Brad held up a tattered notebook that had *Abigail* etched faintly on its cover. "This diary we found says Abigail hid a treasure in here," he said. "I want to find it before anyone else does." Brad turned and stepped inside the cave with **determination**. Lauren sighed and **reluctantly** followed her brother.

Brad waved his flashlight impatiently around the cave. Moments later, he cried, "I see something!" Brad stooped down and started digging in the earth with a rock. Lauren came to help. Soon the two uncovered a small **wooden** box. Brad's hands shook with **excitement**. He took the box outside and opened it. Brad and Lauren gasped and looked at the contents in **astonishment**. Inside were letters addressed to Abigail.

"Nothing but letters!" moaned Brad with **disappointment**. "There's no treasure here at all." He sank to the ground feeling tired and a bit **foolish**.

Lauren stood with a **thoughtful** look on her face. "If it's any **consolation**," she said slowly, "we did find Abigail's treasure." Lauren fingered the letters **gently** and continued, "These letters were written by someone whose **friendship** Abigail felt very strongly about. She probably put the letters in the cave for safekeeping."

Directions: Write the **boldfaced** words beside their meanings below. Circle the suffix in each word.

1. place of entry entr(ance)
2. out of breath breath(less)
3. state of being exc excite(ment)
4. having little or no light dark(ness)
5. great surprise astonish(ment)
6. unwise fooli(sh)
7. deep in thought thought(ful)
8. state of being friends friend(ship)
9. with unwillingness reluctant(ly)
10. act of being co consol(ation)
11. feeling let disappoint(ment)
12. quality of b determin(ation)
13. in a gentle manner gent(ly)
14. made of wood wood(en)
15. involving something that can cause harm danger(ous)

18

Synonyms

Synonyms are words that mean the **same** thing. *Cute* and *adorable* are synonyms.

Directions: Circle the synonyms for the first word in each row.

1. fast (quick) hard (swift) (speedy) small
2. bright (dazzling) dull (glittering) (sparkling)
3. friend stranger (companion) (chum) (pal) (buddy)
4. scary scream (frightening) rough (terrifying)
5. throw (fling) carry (hurl) (toss) catch

Directions: Look at the pictures below. Using the words you circled, write a list of synonyms to describe each picture.

1. fast: quick, swift, speedy
2. bright: dazzling, glittering, sparkling
3. friend: companion, chum, pal, buddy
4. scary: frightening, terrifying
5. throw: fling, hurl, toss

19

Synonyms

Directions: Choose the word from the word box that could replace the **boldfaced** word in each sentence. Write the word on the line.

fortunate	discovered	grimy	ancient
sizzling	entire	select	chuckle

1. The dinosaur bones were **old**. ancient
2. We were **lucky** that it didn't rain. fortunate
3. After playing football, my clothes were **dirty**. grimy
4. That joke made me **laugh**. chuckle
5. I rode my bike the **whole** way home. entire
6. I had to **choose** a book for my report. select
7. It was a **hot** day in the desert. sizzling
8. I **found** the missing puzzle piece on the floor. discovered

20

Synonyms

Directions: Use the words from the word box to write a synonym for each underlined word.

enjoyable
receive
also
scorching
most
friend
tease
like
happy
watching

Dear Pen Pal,

I was <u>glad</u> happy to <u>get</u> receive your letter. Soccer is my favorite sport <u>too</u> also. And I have three brothers who always <u>bother</u> tease me, too! Seattle sounds like a <u>great</u> enjoyable place to live, but I wouldn't <u>enjoy</u> like all the rain. It's always sunny and <u>hot</u> scorching in Houston. My friends and I like <u>viewing</u> watching movies and going out for ice cream afterwards. I like chocolate <u>best</u> most.

Your <u>pal</u> friend.

21

Synonyms

Directions: Circle the two words in each row that are synonyms.

1. (mistake) (error) repair
2. (rich) money (wealthy)
3. (frighten) (startle) secret
4. song (noisy) (loud)
5. (imitate) (copy) return
6. (hasty) funny (speedy)
7. (cheap) expensive (inexpensive)
8. break (repair) (fix)
9. (travel) (vacation) work
10. (gift) (present) watch
11. (friend) enemy (pal)
12. (watch) (see) mean

22

Synonyms

Directions: Answer the clues using words from the word box to complete the puzzle.

	1 b		2 e	v	3 e	n						4 l		
	u		x		l		5 c					e		
6 a	r	r	i	v	e		h		7 h			s		
	r		t		8 c	a	u	t	i	o	u	s		
	o				t		c		n					
	w						k		9 d	r	e	a	d	
				10 f	u	l	l		e					
							e		11 r	e	p	a	i	r

chuckle	elect	full	arrive
cautious	burrow	dread	hinder
repair	exit	less	even

Across

2. synonym for *same*
6. synonym for *come*
8. synonym for *careful*
9. synonym for *fear*
10. synonym for *crowded*
11. synonym for *fix*

Down

1. synonym for *dig*
2. synonym for *leave*
3. synonym for *choose*
4. synonym for *fewer*
5. synonym for *laugh*
7. synonym for *obstruct*

23

Locating Synonyms

Directions: Read each sentence. Find a word in each sentence that is a synonym for the word in the parentheses. Write the synonym on the line.

1. Leslie and Mike enjoy soccer. (like) enjoy
2. Today, they will begin practicing for the upcoming season. (start) begin
3. They bought new shin guards and cleats and were ready for practice. (purchased) bought
4. Leslie and Mike are strong competitors. (tough) strong
5. While they are cautious about avoiding injury, they show no fear. (careful) cautious
6. As Mike dribbles the ball down the field, he manages it with remarkable control. (fantastic) remarkable
7. Leslie heads the ball into the goal. Her aim is exact. (accurate) exact
8. Leslie and Mike are clever players who can execute the complex strategies needed to win games. (complicated) complex
9. The fans are appreciative for an exciting season. (grateful) appreciative
10. The number of wins this year has surpassed all other years. (exceeded) surpassed

24

Antonyms

An **antonym** is a word that means the **opposite**.

Directions: Answer the clues using words from the word box to complete the puzzle.

	1 b		2 e	v	3 e	n						4 l		
	o		x		l		5 c					e		
6 a	r	r	i	v	e		h		7 h			s		
	r		t		8 c	a	u	t	i	o	u	s		
	o				t		c		n					
	w						k		9 d	r	e	s	s	
				10 f	u	l	l		e					
							e		11 r	e	p	a	i	r

chuckle	elect	full	arrive
cautious	borrow	dress	hinder
repair	exit	less	even

Across

2. antonym for *odd*
6. antonym for *depart*
8. antonym for *careless*
9. antonym for *undress*
10. antonym for *empty*
11. antonym for *break*

Down

1. antonym for *lend*
2. antonym for *enter*
3. antonym for *impeach*
4. antonym for *more*
5. antonym for *cry*
7. antonym for *help*

25

Antonyms

Directions: Write an antonym on the line to complete each sentence.

old	select
big	cute
play	wild
female	hard
tell	loves
baby	friend
found	long

Dear Pen Pal,

I have something exciting to tell (ask) you! Yesterday we went to the animal shelter. I found (lost) three kittens that were cute (ugly). It was hard (easy) to decide which one to select (refuse). I chose a female (male) kitten. She is six weeks old (young). She has long (short) white fur with a big (small) black spot on her face. She loves (hates) to play (work) with a tissue on a string. She acts like a wild (tame) tiger. We made a cozy bed for her in a box. My baby (adult) sister gave her a warm blanket for her box. I'll send you a picture of my cat soon. Do you have any pets?

Your friend (enemy),

26

Antonyms

Directions: Circle the two words in each row that have opposite meanings.

1. return (break) (fix)
2. (rich) (poor) wealthy
3. (light) sun (dark)
4. (loud) nosy (quiet)
5. (borrow) (lend) reduce
6. haste (slow) (speedy)
7. (cheap) (expensive) silly
8. watch (break) (repair)
9. travel (play) (work)
10. (lost) (found) cook
11. write (buy) (sell)
12. (kind) friendly (mean)

27

Antonyms

Directions: Write an antonym for each word.

1. son daughter
2. lost found
3. chilly warm
4. whole part
5. speak listen
6. sent receive
7. bare covered
8. won lost
9. male female
10. high low
11. sell buy
12. girl boy
13. dark light
14. empty full
15. inside outside

28

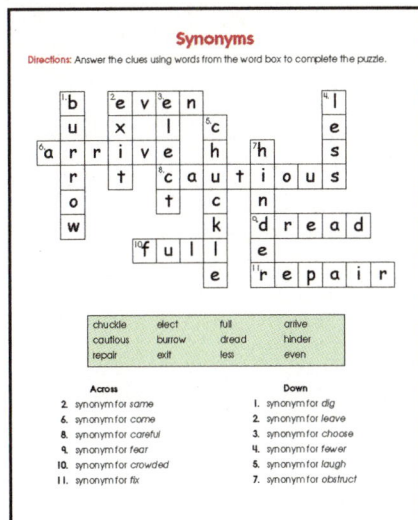

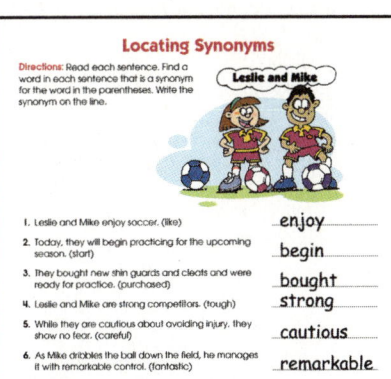

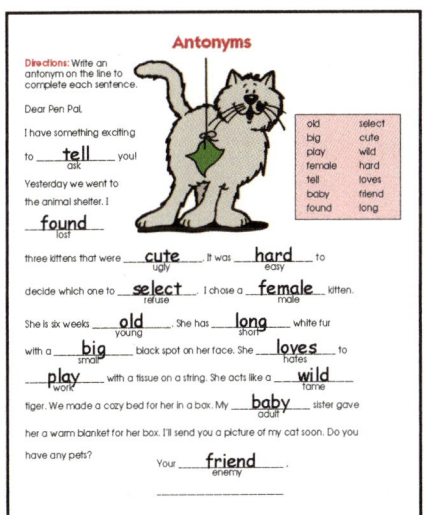

Antonyms

Directions: Each sentence below was meant to say the opposite. Circle the incorrect word in each sentence. Choose a word from the word box to replace it. Rewrite each sentence using the new word.

Whoops!

sad	after	hard	odd	apart	borrow

1. I chipped a tooth on the (soft) candy.
   I chipped a tooth on the hard candy.
2. Three and five are (even) numbers.
   Three and five are odd numbers.
3. My puzzle pieces fell (together).
   My puzzle pieces fell apart.
4. June comes (before) May.
   June comes after May.
5. I was (happy) when my friend moved.
   I was sad when my friend moved.
6. May I (lend) your eraser?
   May I borrow your eraser?

29

Can You Match This?

Antonyms are words that have opposite or nearly opposite meanings.

Directions: Can you identify the antonyms below? Draw a line to match each pair. Then, write the antonym pair that best completes each sentence.

dishonest	prevent
start	problem
calm	different
change	preceding
alike	apart
allow	discourteous
together	finish
solution	remain
polite	truthful
following	violent

1. They will not allow us to board the plane because the severe weather conditions prevent a safe take-off.
2. My twin sisters may look exactly alike but you will soon discover how different they are.
3. It took weeks to put this jigsaw puzzle together and just minutes to take it apart.
4. If you are dishonest instead of truthful, you will lose the respect of your friends.
5. Seas that were calm grew violent as an unexpected storm hit full force.
6. We used all the clues to find the solution to the problem.
7. You can change seats with me or remain where you are.
8. If we start on time, we will finish this project in three hours.
9. If this is June, then the following month is July and the preceding month was May.
10. An operator must always be patient and polite, even though callers are sometimes rude and discourteous

30

Homophones

Homophones are words that sound alike but have different spellings and meanings.

Directions: Write the correct homophone in each blank.

Examples: rein, rain ewe, you to, two, too

1. We couldn't decide whether to visit Boston or St. Louis. (weather, whether)
2. We chose to visit Boston, the capital of Massachusetts. (capital, capitol)
3. We drove to the city in two days. (to, too, two)
4. Our route was over interstate highways. (route, root)
5. We read many signs along the way. (read, red)
6. My brothers couldn't hide their excitement. (their, there)
7. We found that it's an exciting city. (its, it's)
8. It was interesting to hear the accent of the people. (hear, here)
9. Many people related interesting tales to us about the city's history. (tales, tails)
10. We appreciated the peace and quiet of the parks. (peace, piece)
11. We walked up and down rows of houses in the historic district. (rows, rose)
12. I wore a hole in one of my shoes from so much walking. (whole, hole) (so, sew)
13. Luckily, this caused me no pain. (know, no) (pain, pane)
14. I had to have the sole of the shoe repaired. (soul, sole)
15. My family did little sightseeing at night. (night, knight)

31

Definitely Daffy Definitions

Directions: Write a pair of homophones to complete each definition. The homophones are spelled phonetically in the box.

plane	horss	strayt	dihr
fair	payl	sent	reel
mye-nur	flou-ur	beet	stay-shuh-ner-ee
wale	hayl	foul	bair

1. A very tired reddish-purple vegetable is a beat beet
2. The forest animal with antlers that everyone likes is a dear deer
3. A large animal that's missing its thick, coarse fur is a bare bear
4. A nasty farm bird is a foul fowl
5. A four-legged animal with hoofs that has a sore throat is a hoarse horse
6. A young coal digger is a minor miner
7. A water channel that is not crooked is a straight strait
8. The cry of the world's largest sea mammal is a whale wail
9. A very simple, no-frills flying machine is a plain plane
10. An old, faded bucket is a pale pail
11. A mailed bottle of perfume is a sent scent
12. A genuine spool for holding fish line is a real reel
13. Writing paper that has been weighted down is stationary stationery
14. The reasonable cost for riding a bus or cab is a fair fare
15. Dried and finely ground blossoms used for baking make flower flour
16. Hardy pellets of ice falling from the clouds are hale hail

32

What's the Meaning of This?

Directions: Underline the pair of homophones in each sentence. Then, write each word next to its meaning.

1. Will you help me haul this trunk down the hall to my room?
   hall passageway haul carry
2. No one guessed the identity of the mystery guest until he removed his mask.
   guest company guessed surmised
3. We do not think it is fair that the bus has doubled the fare.
   fair just fare cost of a ride
4. My brother accidentally threw a baseball through our neighbor's window.
   through in one side and out the other threw past tense of "to throw"
5. Luxury cruise ships require large crews of men and women to meet the needs of the passengers.
   crews groups of workers cruise sail
6. If you heed the lesson in this chapter, you will lessen your risk of injury.
   lessen reduce; make less lesson something taught
7. You should have seen the final scene of the play!
   seen viewed scene part of an act
8. A principal must be a person of very high principle to set a good example for students.
   principle rule of behavior principal head of a school
9. Do you know whether tomorrow's weather will be clear and mild?
   weather climate whether if
10. We are going to see the newly built capitol at our state's capital.
    capital city capitol building where state legislature meets

33

What's the Difference?

Directions: Write the correct homophone from the box next to each definition. Then, write the boxed letters in order to discover the answer to the riddle below.

threw/through
peace/piece
base/bass
colonel/ kernel
scents/cents
brood/brewed
caret/carrot
herd/heard
threw/through
creek/creak
right/rite
vise/vice
hanger/hangar
berry/bury
slay/sleigh
stationery/stationary
wade/weighed
suite/sweet
heir/air
missed/mist

1. military rank colonel
2. odors scents
3. tossed threw
4. flock brood
5. grating noise creak
6. sled sleigh
7. writing paper stationery
8. walk in water wade
9. sugary sweet
10. successor heir
11. an orange, edible root carrot
12. group of animals herd
13. put underground bury
14. tranquility peace
15. grain of corn kernel
16. fog mist
17. used for hanging things hanger
18. clamp vise
19. correct right
20. deep voice bass

What's the difference between someone who parks a car and someone who is smashing dishes?

One sets the brakes and the other breaks the sets.

34

Watch for Grandpa's Watch

Directions: Each "watch" in the title of this activity sheet has a different meaning. One means "to look for," and the other means "timepiece." Write two meanings for each of the words below.

Answers may include:

	Meaning 1	Meaning 2
1. spring	a season	a coil of metal
2. run	operate	move quickly
3. ruler	monarch	measuring device
4. duck	a feathered animal	bend down
5. suit	a man's clothes	agree
6. cold	illness	low temperature
7. fall	season	topple over
8. tire	wheel	become exhausted
9. rose	a flower	get up
10. face	body part	look straight at
11. train	instruct	line of boxcars on a track
12. play	stage production	to have fun
13. foot	12 inches	body part
14. pen	writing instrument	fenced in area
15. box	carton	hit with fists
16. dice	cut up	small cubes with numbers
17. fly	an insect	move through the air
18. seal	close	an animal
19. bowl	game using 10 pins, 1 ball	container for soup
20. ride	carried on an animal	pester someone

Choose some of the above words and illustrate both meanings on another sheet of paper.

35

Which Is It?

Some words with more than one meaning are spelled the same but pronounced differently. Phonetic spellings can help you figure out how to pronounce the words.

Directions: Two words written with phonetic spellings appear above each pair of sentences. Write the regular spelling for the two words in the sentences. Then, write the letter that tells the correct phonetic spelling of the word in each sentence.

1. (a) kon′ •tent (b) kuhn•tent′
   Does this cereal have a high sugar content? a
   We are content to stay inside and read. b
2. (a) dez′ •urt (b) di•zurt′
   Why did the soldier desert his platoon? b
   It took weeks to cross the desert. a
3. (a) meye•noot′ (b) min′ •it
   We will be there in just one minute. b
   There is a minute speck of dust on the telescope lens. a
4. (a) ri•fyooz′ (b) ref′ •yoos
   Volunteers picked up refuse the along the road. b
   The children refuse to do what they were asked. a
5. (a) prez′ •uhnt (b) pri•zent′
   Everyone was present in class today. a
   The mayor will present us with a special award. b
6. (a) bays (b) bas
   I caught one bass the last time we went fishing. b
   My older brother sings bass in the choir. a
7. (a) leed (b) led
   Are these pipes made of copper or lead? b
   Our coach will lead our team to victory this year. a

36

Look Alikes

Some words have more than one meaning.

Example: ear and ear

Directions: Find each word in the puzzle that correctly completes two sentences below. Circle the word in the puzzle. Then, write it correctly in the sentences.

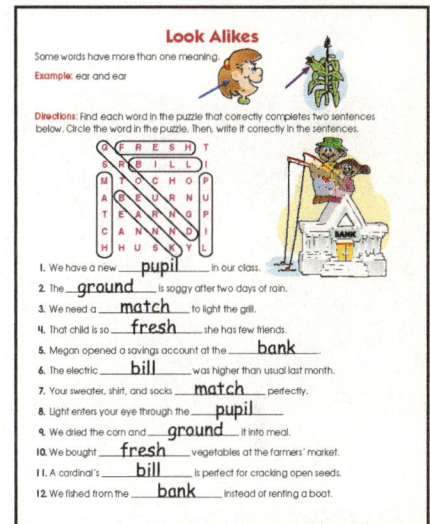

1. We have a new pupil in our class.
2. The ground is soggy after two days of rain.
3. We need a match to light the grill.
4. That child is so fresh she has few friends.
5. Megan opened a savings account at the bank.
6. The electric bill was higher than usual last month.
7. Your sweater, shirt, and socks match perfectly.
8. Light enters your eye through the pupil.
9. We dried the corn and ground it into meal.
10. We bought fresh vegetables at the farmers' market.
11. A cardinal's bill is perfect for cracking open seeds.
12. We fished from the bank instead of renting a boat.

37

What's the Word?

Directions: Each rebus below makes a word with more than one meaning. Follow the clues and write the word.

1. + 10 - n +r = batter
2. -x + -d = bore
3. + -n +r = hamper
4. -p + -i = mold
5. + -ry = pitcher
6. -t + -s +d = pound
7. -t + -n = racket
8. -r + -g = scale
9. -a + -b -c = swallow
10. -rn + -o = yard

Directions: Read the meanings below. Then, write the number of the rebus next to the matching definition.

1 a. flour, egg, and milk mixture; player who hits the ball
4 b. fungus; a form or shape
10 c. 36 inches; enclosed space around a house
2 d. make a hole; make weary
5 e. player who throws the ball; container for pouring liquid
7 f. noise; a tennis paddle
8 g. balance; series of notes
3 h. large basket; hold back
6 i. unit of weight; hit hard repeatedly
9 j. kind of bird; gulp

38

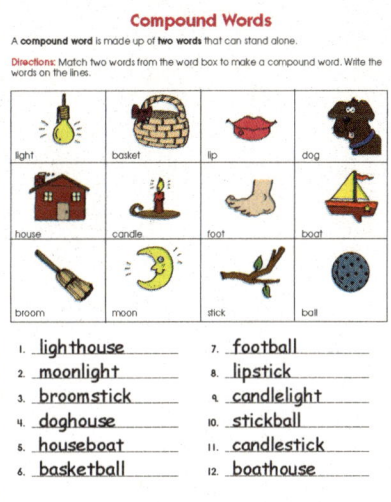

Compound Words

A **compound word** is made up of **two words** that can stand alone.

Directions: Match two words from the word box to make a compound word. Write the words on the lines.

light	basket	lip	dog
house	candle	foot	boat
broom	moon	stick	ball

1. lighthouse
2. moonlight
3. broomstick
4. doghouse
5. houseboat
6. basketball
7. football
8. lipstick
9. candlelight
10. stickball
11. candlestick
12. boathouse

39

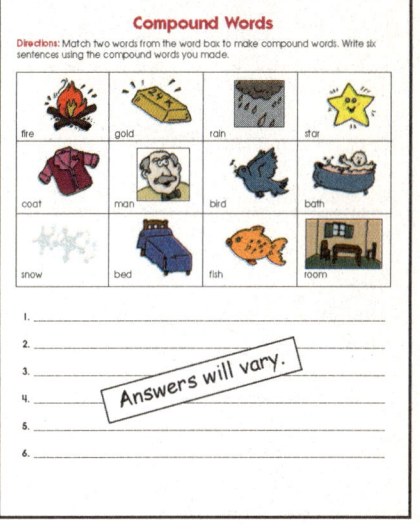

Compound Words

Directions: Match two words from the word box to make compound words. Write six sentences using the compound words you made.

fire	gold	rain	star
coat	man	bird	bath
snow	bed	fish	room

1.
2.
3.
4.
5.
6.

Answers will vary.

40

Compound Words

Directions: Match two words from the word box to make compound words. Write definitions for six of the compound words you made.

night	down	bed	hand
town	hill	boy	up
back	stairs	time	paper

1. ______
2. ______
3. ______
4. ______
5. ______
6. ______

Answers will vary.

41

Compound Words

Directions: Write a sentence using each compound word from the word box.

classmate	tiptoe
starfish	somebody
woodland	airport
popcorn	hardware

1. ______
2. ______
3. ______
4. ______
5. ______
6. ______
7. ______
8. ______

Answers will vary.

42

Conquering Compounds

There are three types of compound words:
(1) **closed compound**—two separate words joined together, that create a new meaning and are written as one word
(2) **open compound**—two separate words that create a new meaning, but the two words are not joined together
(3) **hyphenated compound**—two or more words, written separately but connected by a hyphen, that create a new meaning

barnyard
blastoff
brand-new
chairperson
cupboard
hide-and-seek
homesick
ice skate
jack-o'-lantern
peanut butter
polar bear
post office
seagull
snowstorm
topsy-turvy
town crier
yardstick
zip code

Directions: Add a word or words to each word below to form a compound word from the spelling list.

1. cup cupboard
2. snow snowstorm
3. home homesick
4. barn barnyard
5. chair chairperson
6. yard yardstick
7. sea seagull
8. hide- hide-and-seek
9. brand- brand-new
10. polar polar bear
11. ice ice skate
12. pean peanut butter
13. blast blastoff
14. post post office
15. topsy- topsy-turvy
16. town town crier
17. zip zip code
18. jack- jack-o'-lantern

43

Puzzling Compounds

baseball	basketball	breakfast	classroom	driftwood	firefly
flagpole	harmless	knickknack	lifetime	motorcycle	paperback
playhouse	railway	switchboard	taxicab	textbook	tiptoe

Directions: Write a spelling word that matches each clue. Then, read down the boxed letters to solve the riddle.

1. a place to learn — classroom
2. the morning meal — breakfast
3. not capable of hurting — harmless
4. game played with a bat and a ball — baseball
5. to walk softly — tiptoe
6. sometimes called a lightning bug — firefly
7. one's entire period of existence — lifetime
8. It supports Old Glory — flagpole

Riddle: *Which tree is the most difficult to get along with?*

Answer: crabtree

Directions: Write a compound word that belongs in each group.

1. hoop, whistle, basketball
2. tracks, railroad, railway
3. school, subjects, textbook
4. toys, games, playhouse
5. wood, ashore, driftwood
6. circuit, panel, switchboard
7. read, novel, paperback
8. 2-wheeled, hel motorcycle
9. fare, driver, taxicab
10. trinket, decorati knickknack

44

Following Directions

Directions: Read and follow the directions.

1. Draw a vertical line from the top midpoint of the square to the bottom midpoint of the square.
2. Draw a diagonal line from top left to bottom right of the square.
3. In each of the two triangles, draw a heart.
4. Draw a picture of a cat's face below the square.
5. Draw a horizontal line from the left midpoint to the right midpoint of the square.
6. Draw two intersecting lines in each of the two smaller squares so they are equally divided into four quadrants.
7. Draw a triangle-shaped roof on the square.
8. Draw a circle next to each heart.
9. Write your name in the roof section of your drawing.

45

Following Directions: Continents

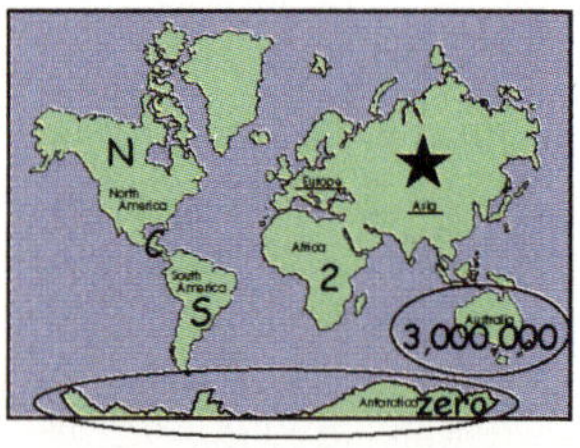

Directions: Read the facts about the seven continents and follow the directions.

1. Asia is the largest continent. It has the largest land mass and the largest population. Draw a star on Asia.
2. Africa is the second largest continent. Write a **2** on Africa.
3. Australia is the smallest continent in area: 3 million square miles, compared to 17 million square miles for Asia. Write **3,000,000** on Australia.
4. Australia is not a very crowded continent, but it does not rank lowest in population. That honor goes to Antarctica, which has no permanent population at all! This ice-covered continent is too cold for life. Write **zero** on Antarctica.
5. Australia and Antarctica are the only continents entirely separated by water. Draw circles around Australia and Antarctica.
6. North America and South America are joined together by a narrow strip of land. It is called Central America. Write an **N** on North America, an **S** on South America and a **C** on Central America.
7. Asia and Europe are joined together over such a great distance that they are sometimes called one continent. The name given to it is Eurasia. Draw lines under the names of the two continents in Eurasia.

46

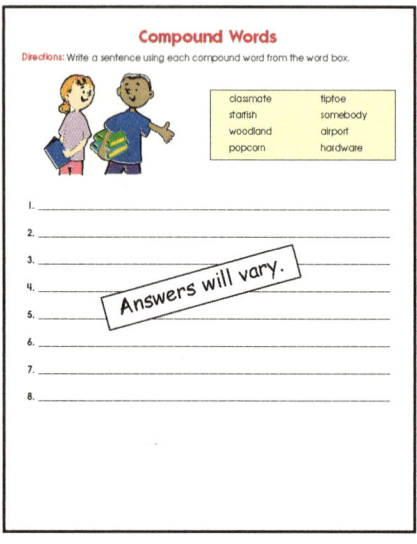

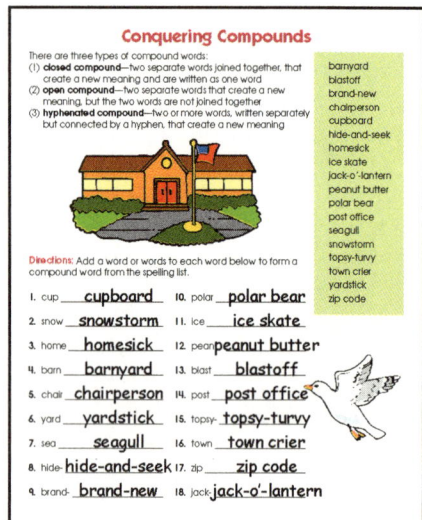

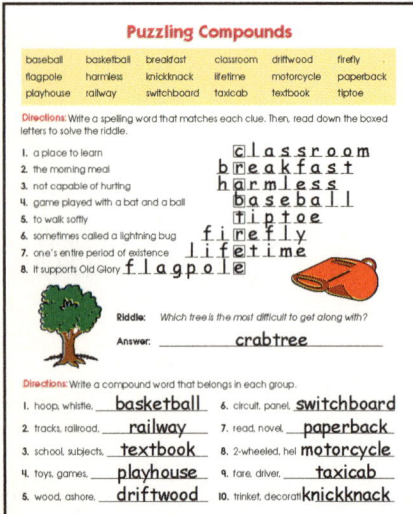

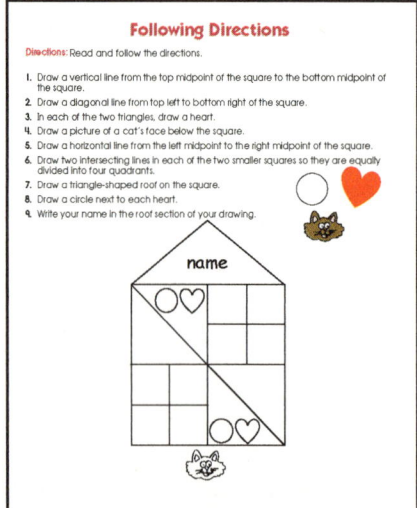

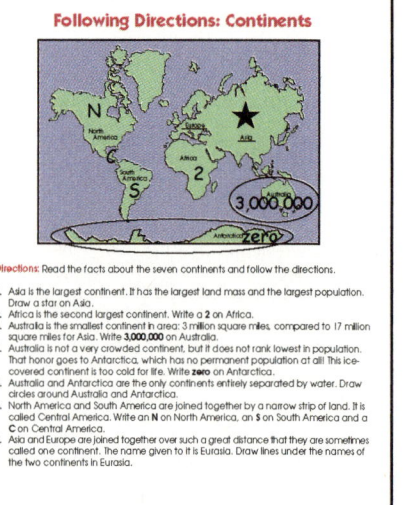

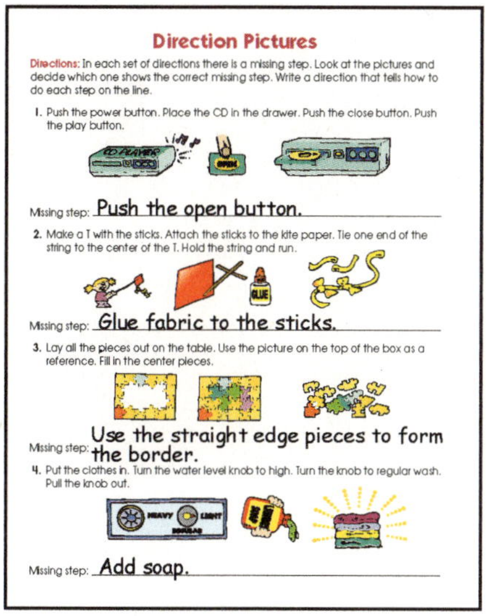

Direction Pictures

Directions: In each set of directions there is a missing step. Look at the pictures and decide which one shows the correct missing step. Write a direction that tells how to do each step on the line.

1. Push the power button. Place the CD in the drawer. Push the close button. Push the play button.

Missing step: Push the open button.

2. Make a T with the sticks. Attach the sticks to the kite paper. Tie one end of the string to the center of the T. Hold the string and run.

Missing step: Glue fabric to the sticks.

3. Lay all the pieces out on the table. Use the picture on the top of the box as a reference. Fill in the center pieces.

Missing step: Use the straight edge pieces to form the border.

4. Put the clothes in. Turn the water level knob to high. Turn the knob to regular wash. Pull the knob out.

Missing step: Add soap.

47

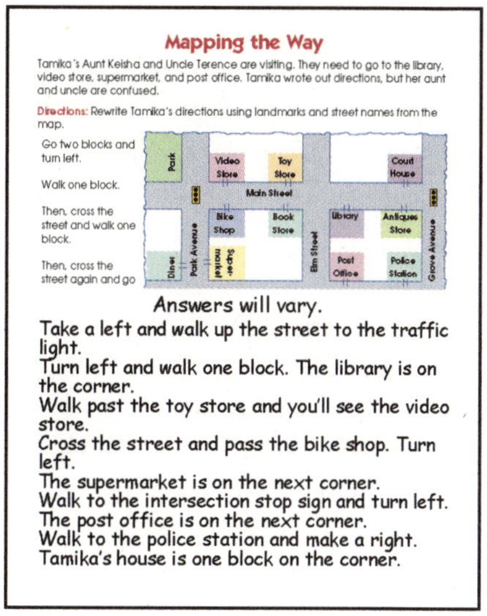

Mapping the Way

Tamika's Aunt Keisha and Uncle Terence are visiting. They need to go to the library, video store, supermarket, and post office. Tamika wrote out directions, but her aunt and uncle are confused.

Directions: Rewrite Tamika's directions using landmarks and street names from the map.

Go two blocks and turn left.

Walk one block.

Then, cross the street and walk one block.

Then, cross the street again and go

Answers will vary.

Take a left and walk up the street to the traffic light.
Turn left and walk one block. The library is on the corner.
Walk past the toy store and you'll see the video store.
Cross the street and pass the bike shop. Turn left.
The supermarket is on the next corner.
Walk to the intersection stop sign and turn left.
The post office is on the next corner.
Walk to the police station and make a right.
Tamika's house is one block on the corner.

48

Following Directions: Chunky Tomato and Green Onion Sauce

Following directions means to do what the directions say to do, step by step, in the correct order.

Directions: Read the recipe for chunky tomato and green onion sauce. Answer the questions below.

Ingredients:
- 2 tablespoons corn oil
- 2 cloves of garlic, finely chopped
- $1\frac{1}{2}$ pounds plum tomatoes, cored, peeled, seeded, then coarsely chopped
- 3 green onions, cut in half lengthwise, then thinly sliced
- salt
- freshly ground pepper

Heat oil in a heavy skillet over medium heat. Add garlic and cook until yellow, about 1 minute. Stir in tomatoes. Season with salt and pepper. Cook until thickened, about 10 minutes. Stir in green onions and serve.

1. What is the last thing the cook does to prepare the tomatoes before cooking them? chops them
2. What kind of oil does the cook heat in the heavy skillet? corn oil
3. How long should the garlic be cooked? about 1 minute
4. What does the cook do to the tomatoes right before removing the seeds? peels them
5. Is the sauce served hot or cold? hot

49

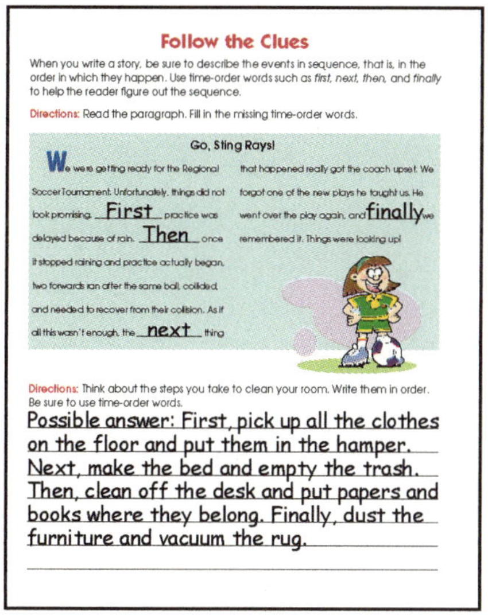

Follow the Clues

When you write a story, be sure to describe the events in sequence, that is, in the order in which they happen. Use time-order words such as *first, next, then,* and *finally* to help the reader figure out the sequence.

Directions: Read the paragraph. Fill in the missing time-order words.

Go, Sting Rays!

We were getting ready for the Regional Soccer Tournament. Unfortunately, things did not look promising. First practice was delayed because of rain. Then once it stopped raining and practice actually began, two forwards ran after the same ball, collided, and needed to recover from their collision. As if all this wasn't enough, the next thing that happened really got the coach upset. We forgot one of the new plays he taught us. He went over the play again, and finally we remembered it. Things were looking up!

Directions: Think about the steps you take to clean your room. Write them in order. Be sure to use time-order words.

Possible answer: First, pick up all the clothes on the floor and put them in the hamper. Next, make the bed and empty the trash. Then, clean off the desk and put papers and books where they belong. Finally, dust the furniture and vacuum the rug.

50

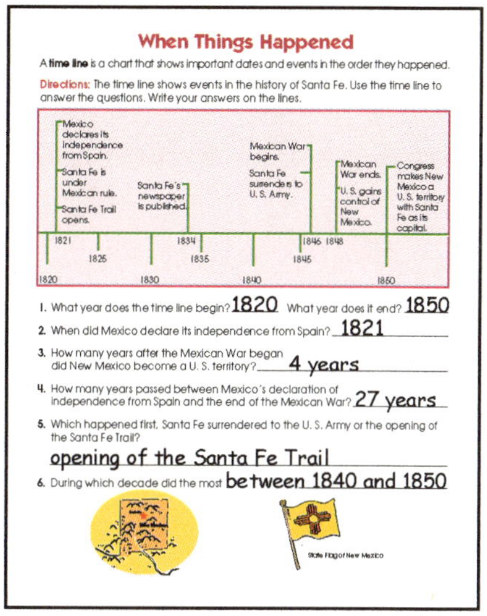

When Things Happened

A **time line** is a chart that shows important dates and events in the order they happened.

Directions: The time line shows events in the history of Santa Fe. Use the time line to answer the questions. Write your answers on the lines.

1. What year does the time line begin? 1820 What year does it end? 1850
2. When did Mexico declare its independence from Spain? 1821
3. How many years after the Mexican War began did New Mexico become a U. S. territory? 4 years
4. How many years passed between Mexico's declaration of independence from Spain and the end of the Mexican War? 27 years
5. Which happened first, Santa Fe surrendered to the U. S. Army or the opening of the Santa Fe Trail? opening of the Santa Fe Trail
6. During which decade did the most between 1840 and 1850

State Flag of New Mexico

51

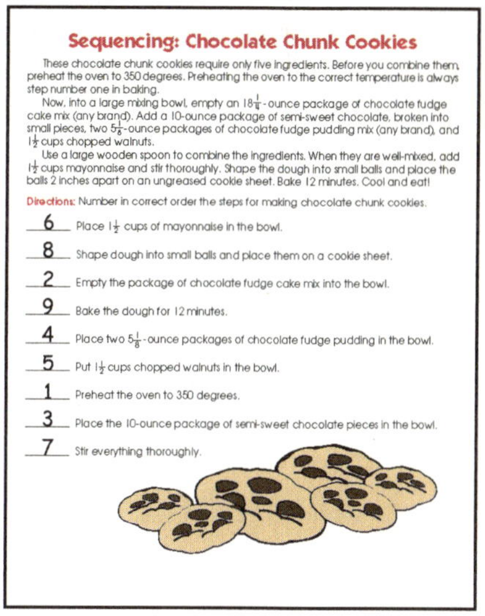

Sequencing: Chocolate Chunk Cookies

These chocolate chunk cookies require only five ingredients. Before you combine them, preheat the oven to 350 degrees. Preheating the oven to the correct temperature is always step number one in baking.

Now, into a large mixing bowl, empty an $18\frac{1}{4}$-ounce package of chocolate fudge cake mix (any brand). Add a 10-ounce package of semi-sweet chocolate, broken into small pieces, two $5\frac{1}{8}$-ounce packages of chocolate fudge pudding mix (any brand), and $1\frac{1}{2}$ cups chopped walnuts.

Use a large wooden spoon to combine the ingredients. When they are well-mixed, add $1\frac{1}{2}$ cups mayonnaise and stir thoroughly. Shape the dough into small balls and place the balls 2 inches apart on an ungreased cookie sheet. Bake 12 minutes. Cool and eat!

Directions: Number in correct order the steps for making chocolate chunk cookies.

6 Place $1\frac{1}{2}$ cups of mayonnaise in the bowl.
8 Shape dough into small balls and place them on a cookie sheet.
2 Empty the package of chocolate fudge cake mix into the bowl.
9 Bake the dough for 12 minutes.
4 Place two $5\frac{1}{8}$-ounce packages of chocolate fudge pudding in the bowl.
5 Put $1\frac{1}{2}$ cups chopped walnuts in the bowl.
1 Preheat the oven to 350 degrees.
3 Place the 10-ounce package of semi-sweet chocolate pieces in the bowl.
7 Stir everything thoroughly.

52

Delivery Dilemma

Dilly's Deliveries is under new management, and the new boss just instructed his top driver to follow a most peculiar route. The driver is to deliver packages to each of the eight businesses shown below, but she is not necessarily meant to visit them in a logical order.

3 3 8 26 2 2 5 3

6 5 7 4 1 3 4 6

Directions: Help the confused driver plan her route. Number the businesses above in the order in which they should be visited in the first blank. Write the number of packages to be delivered in the second blank.

1. The second delivery is directly north of the first delivery and has one fewer package than the first.
2. Melody's Music needs all five packages delivered before 11:00 A.M.
3. By the time the paperwork is completed, the packages are verified and greetings are exchanged between the driver and the recipient, each delivery takes fifteen minutes.
4. The bank is never the last delivery. It always receives four packages.
5. Troy's Toys has the most packages of all. His delivery will contain as many packages as all the others combined.
6. Pete's deliveries are live animals, which need to be unloaded first when the store opens at 9:30 A.M.
7. The fourth delivery is directly east of the first delivery and contains twice the number of packages.
8. The travel agency and the pet store combined are to receive the same number of packages as the music store.
9. The fifth delivery contains three boxes.
10. The third delivery is two stores west of the second.
11. The tire store, the grocery store, and the pet store will all receive the same number of packages. They are the only ones to receive this exact amount.

53

Sequencing: Maps

Directions: Read the information about planning a map.

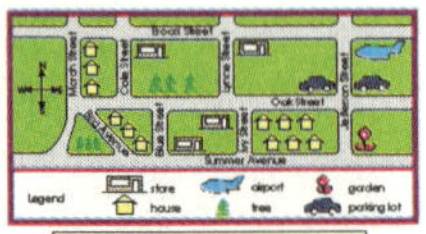

1 inch = 1 mile
0 1

Maps have certain features that help you to read them. A **compass rose** points out directions. Color is often used so you can easily see where one area (such as a county, state, or country) stops and the next starts.

To be accurate, a map must be drawn to scale. The **scale** of a map shows how much area is represented by a given measurement. The scale can be small: one inch = one mile; or large: one inch = 1,000 miles.

Symbols are another map tool. An airplane may represent an airport. Sometimes a symbol does not look like what it represents. Cities are often represented by dots. A map **legend** tells what each symbol means.

One of the best ways to learn about maps is to make one of your own. You may be surprised at how much you learn about your neighborhood, too. You will need a large piece of paper, a ruler, a pencil, and colored pencils.

You will need to choose the area you want to map out. It is important to decide on the scale for your map. It could be small: one inch = three feet, if you are mapping out your own backyard. Be sure to include symbols, like a picnic table to represent a park or a flag to represent a school. Don't forget to include the symbols and other important information in your legend.

Directions: Number in order the steps to making your own map.

3 Figure out the scale that will work best for your map.
1 Obtain a large piece of paper, ruler, pencil, and colored pencils.
5 Make a legend explaining the symbols you used.
6 Draw your map!
4 Draw symbols to represent features of the area you are mapping.
2 Decide on the area you want to map out.

54

Main Idea

The **main idea** is the most important idea, or main point, in a sentence, paragraph, or story.

Directions: Read the paragraphs below. For each paragraph, underline the sentence that tells the main idea.

Sometimes people think they have to choose between exercise and fun. For many people, it is more fun to watch television than to run 5 miles. Yet, if you don't exercise, your body gets soft and out of shape. You move more slowly. You may even think more slowly. But why do something that isn't fun? Well, there are many ways to exercise and have fun.

One family solved the exercise problem by using their TV. They hooked up the television to an electric generator. The generator was operated by an exercise bike. Anyone who wanted to watch TV had to ride the bike. The room with their television in it must have been quite a sight!

Think of the times when you are just "hanging out" with your friends. You go outside and jump rope, play ball, run races, and so on. Soon you are all laughing and having a good time. Many group activities can provide you with exercise and be fun, too.

Maybe there aren't enough kids around after school for group games. Perhaps you are by yourself. Then what? You can get plenty of exercise just by walking, biking, or even dancing. In the morning, walk the long way to the bus. Ride your bike to and from school. Practice the newest dance by yourself. Before you know it, you will be the fittest dancer of all your friends!

Directions: Write other ideas you have for combining fun and exercise below.

Answers will vary.

55

Topics and Main Ideas

To find the **topic** of a paragraph, ask yourself what the paragraph is about. To find the **main idea**, look for the sentence that best tells about the topic.

Directions: Read each paragraph. Then, identify the topic and the main idea of each of the paragraphs.

"Be a Bazillionaire" is a popular television game show. In the game, contestants answer questions on different topics. As they answer correctly, contestants reach different money levels and can use one of three lifelines to get help in answering questions. The chance to win a bazillion dollars and Reggie Binphil, the engaging host, have made the show popular.

1. What is the topic of this paragraph? "Be a Bazillionaire"
2. Which sentence states the most important idea about the topic? "Be a Bazillionaire" is a popular television game show.

Everyone has seen "Celestial Wars," a classic movie loved by many generations. There are tons of exciting special effects used to create realistic space battles between the forces of good and evil. The story, about a father and son who battle against each other, is also memorable. "Celestial Wars" is one of the greatest and most well-known movies of all time.

1. What is the topic of this paragraph? "Celestial Wars"
2. Which sentence states the most important idea about the topic? "Celestial Wars" is one of the greatest and most well-known movies of all time.

56

Main Idea Multiple Choice

Directions: Read each science report. Circle the sentence that states the main idea of each report.

Isaac Newton lived during the 1600s. He was known for his scientific accomplishments. Among these accomplishments are a new form of math, the invention of the reflecting telescope, the discovery of the range of colors in visible light, the formulation of the laws of motion, and most importantly, the discovery of the laws of gravity. Isaac Newton is one of the greatest scientists of all time.

1. Which of the following is the main idea sentence?
   A. Isaac Newton lived during the 1600s.
   B. Isaac Newton was known for his scientific accomplishments.
   C. Isaac Newton is one of the greatest scientists of all time.

Clouds can be used to predict weather. This is because different types of clouds bring different kinds of weather. Cirrus clouds, which are made of ice crystals, usually appear before a storm. Stratus clouds, which are low, dark clouds, may indicate snow or rain. Cumulus clouds are white and may appear during good weather or during heavy rain showers. So, watch the clouds to figure out tomorrow's weather!

2. Which of the following is the main idea sentence?
   A. Clouds can be used to predict weather.
   B. So, watch the clouds to figure out tomorrow's weather!
   C. This is because different types of clouds bring different kinds of weather.

Water can appear in three forms: solid, liquid, or gas. These are all in the Earth's atmosphere. Solid and liquid water are seen in clouds, snowflakes, and raindrops. But water as a gas is invisible. It is found in the atmosphere in the form of water vapor.

3. Which of the following is the main idea sentence?
   A. These are all in the Earth's atmosphere.
   B. Solids and liquids are found in clouds, snowflakes, and raindrops.
   C. Water can appear in three forms: solid, liquid, or gas.

57

Main Idea Match

Directions: Look at the illustrations for six different social studies topics. Circle the sentence that best tells the main idea of the illustration.

1. Women worked to get the right to vote.
   Women liked to protest.
   It is important to vote.

2. The Capitol is a large, white building.
   Washington D.C. has many important monuments.
   Congress is the branch of government that makes new laws.

3. Flags are pretty.
   The American flag is a symbol of the United States.
   Every country has a flag.

4. People traveled to California during the Gold Rush.
   In 1849, people known as Forty-niners panned for gold.
   Gold is an important metal.

5. There are lots of things to see in space.
   Becoming an astronaut takes a lot of time and effort.
   The United States was the first nation to land a person on the moon.

6. Thomas Edison invented the electric light bulb.
   Thomas Edison made many important discoveries.
   Thomas Edison lived in New Jersey.

58

Main Idea: Where Did Songs Come From?

Historians say the earliest music was probably connected to religion. Long ago, people believed the world was controlled by a variety of gods. Singing was among the first things humans did to show respect to the gods.

Singing is still an important part of most religions. Buddhists (bood-ists), Christians, and Jews all use chants and/or songs in their religious ceremonies. If you have ever sung a song—religious or otherwise—you know that singing is fun. The feeling of joy that comes from singing must also have made ancient people feel happy.

Another time people sang was when they worked. Egyptian slaves sang as they carried the heavy stones to build the pyramids. Soldiers sang as they marched into battle. Farmers sang one song as they planted and another when they harvested. Singing made the work less burdensome. People used the tunes to pace themselves. Sometimes they followed instructions through songs. For example, "Yo-oh, heave ho!/Yo-oh, heave ho!" was sung when sailors pulled on a ship's ropes to lift the sails. *Heave* means "to lift," and that is what they did as they sang the song. The song helped sailors work together and pull at the same time. This made the task easier.

Directions: Answer these questions about music.

1. Circle the main idea:

   Singing is fun, and that is why early people liked it so much.

   Singing began as a way to show respect to the gods and is still an important part of most religious ceremonies.

   Traditionally, singing has been important as a part of religious ceremonies and as inspiration to workers. (circled)

Sample answers:

2. Besides religious ceremonies, what other activity foste[red singing?] working, marching into battle, planting, harvesting
3. When did farmers sing two different songs? planting and harvesting
4. How did singing "Yo-oh, heave ho!" help sailors work? The song helped them work together to pull the ropes at the same time.

59

Main Idea: Penguins

Directions: Read the information about penguins.

People are amused by the funny, duck-like waddle of penguins and by their appearance because they seem to be wearing little tuxedos. Penguins are among the best-liked animals on Earth, but are also a most misunderstood animal. People may have more wrong ideas about penguins than any other animal.

For example, many people are surprised to learn that penguins are really birds, not mammals. Penguins do not fly, but they do have feathers, and only birds have feathers. Also, like other birds, penguins build nests and their young hatch from eggs. Because of their unusual looks, though, you would never confuse them with any other bird!

Penguins are also thought of as symbols of the polar regions, but penguins do not live north of the equator, so you would not find a penguin on the North Pole. Penguins don't live at the South Pole, either. Only two of the seventeen *species* of penguins spend all of their lives on the frozen continent of Antarctica. You would be just as likely to see a penguin living on an island in a warm climate as in a cold area.

Directions: Draw an **X** on the blank for the correct answer.

1. The main idea is:
   ___ Penguins are among the best-liked animals on Earth.
   X The penguin is a much misunderstood animal.
2. Penguins live
   ___ only at the North Pole.
   ___ only at the South Pole.
   X only south of the equator.
3. Based on the other words in the sentence, what is the correct definition of the word *species*?
   ___ number
   ___ bird
   X a distinct kind

Directions: List three ways penguins are like other birds.

have feathers, lay eggs, build nests

60

Recognizing Details: The Coldest Continent

Directions: Read the information about Antarctica. Then, answer the questions.

Antarctica lies at the South Pole and is the coldest continent. It is without sunlight for months at a time. Even when the sun does shine, its angle is so slanted that the land receives little warmth. Temperatures often drop to 100 degrees below zero, and a fierce wind blows almost endlessly. Most of the land is covered by snow heaped thousands of feet deep. The snow is so heavy and tightly packed that it forms a great ice cap covering more than 95 percent of the continent.

Considering the conditions, it is no wonder there are no towns or cities in Antarctica. There is no permanent population at all, only small scientific research stations. Many teams of explorers and scientists have braved the freezing cold since Antarctica was sighted in 1820. Some have died in their effort, but a great deal of information has been learned about the continent.

From fossils, pieces of coal, and bone samples, we know that Antarctica was not always an ice-covered land. Scientists believe that 200 million years ago it was connected to southern Africa, South America, Australia, and India. Forests grew in warm swamps, and insects and reptiles thrived there. Today, there are animals that live in and around the waters that border the continent. In fact, the waters surrounding Antarctica contain more life than oceans in warmer areas of the world.

1. Where is Antarctica? at the South Pole
2. How much of the continent is covered by an ice cap? more than 95%
3. When was Antarctica first sighted by explorers? 1820
4. What clues indicate that Antarctica was not always an ice-covered land? fossils, pieces of coal, bone samples
5. Is Antarctica another name for the North Pole? Yes (No) — No circled

61

Recognizing Details: The Frozen Continent

Directions: Read the information about explorers. Then, answer the questions.

By the mid-1800s, most of the seals of Antarctica had been killed. The seal hunters no longer sailed the icy waters. The next group of explorers who took an interest in Antarctica were scientists. Of these, the man who took the most daring chances and made the most amazing discoveries was British Captain James Clark Ross.

Ross first made a name for himself sailing to the north. In 1831, he discovered the North Magnetic Pole—one of two places on Earth toward which a compass needle points. In 1840, Ross set out to find the South Magnetic Pole. He made many marvelous discoveries, including the Ross Sea, a great open sea beyond the ice packs that stopped other explorers, and the Ross Ice Shelf, a great floating sheet of ice bigger than all of France!

The next man to make his mark exploring Antarctica was British explorer Robert Falcon Scott. Scott set out in 1902 to find the South Pole. He and his team suffered greatly, but they were able to make it a third of the way to the pole. Back in England, Scott was a great hero. In 1910, he again attempted to become the first man to reach the South Pole. But this time he had competition: an explorer from Norway, Roald Amundsen, was also leading a team to the South Pole.

It was a brutal race. Both teams faced many hardships, but they pressed on. Finally, on December 14, 1911, Amundsen became the first man to reach the South Pole. Scott arrived on January 17, 1912. He was bitterly disappointed at not being first. The trip back was even more horrible. None of the five men in the Scott expedition survived.

1. After the seal hunters, who were the next group of explorers interested in Antarctica? scientists
2. What great discovery did James Ross make before ever sailing to Antarctica? He discovered the North Magnetic Pole.
3. What were two other great discoveries made by James Ross? Ross Sea; Ross Ice Shelf
4. How close did Scott and his team come to the South Pole in 1902? one-third of the way
5. Who was the first person to reach the South Pole? Roald Amundsen

62

Recognizing Details: The Cactus Family

Directions: Read the information about cacti. Pay close attention to details. Answer the questions.

Although cacti are the best-known desert plants, they don't live only in hot, dry places. While cacti are most likely to be found in the desert areas of Mexico and the southwestern United States, they can be seen as far north as Nova Scotia, Canada. Certain types of cacti can live even in the snow!

Desert cacti are particularly good at surviving very long dry spells. Most cacti have a very long root system so they can absorb as much water as possible. Every available drop of water is taken into the cactus and held in its fleshy stem. A cactus stem can hold enough water to last for 2 years or longer.

A cactus may be best known for its spines. Although a few kinds of cacti don't have spines, the stems of most types are covered with these sharp needles. The spines have many uses for a cactus. They keep animals from eating the cactus. They collect raindrops and dew. The spines also help keep the plant cool by forming shadows in the sun and by trapping a layer of air close to the plant. They break up the desert winds that dry out the cactus.

Cacti come in all sizes and shapes. The biggest type in North America is the saguaro. It can weigh 12,000 to 14,000 pounds and grow to be 50 feet tall! A saguaro can last several years without water, but it will grow only after summer rains. In May and June, white blossoms appear. Many kinds of birds nest in these enormous cacti: white-winged doves, woodpeckers, small owls, thrashers, and wrens all build nests in the saguaro.

1. Where are you most likely to find a cactus growing? in deserts
2. How long can most cacti survive without water? 2 years or longer
3. What are two ways the spines help a cactus? collect moisture, form cooling shadows, keep animals from eating the plant
4. What is the biggest cactus in North America? saguaro
5. What animals live in a saguaro cactus? doves, woodpeckers, owls, thrashers, wrens

63

Sort 'Em Out

Vertebrates are animals with backbones. Animals without backbones are called **invertebrates**. At the bottom of the page are pictures of both kinds of animals. Write the name of each animal under the correct heading below.

	Vertebrates		Invertebrates
1.	dog	1.	octopus
2.	boy	2.	snail
3.	turtle	3.	starfish
4.	frog	4.	lobster
5.	lizard	5.	oyster

64

Sorting Word Pairs

Directions: Look at the pairs of words in the box. Classify the pairs as **synonyms** or **antonyms**. Remember, synonyms are words with almost the same meaning and antonyms are words with the opposite meaning.

smooth, rough
terrific, great
started, began
relieved, worried
ran, jogged
forget, remember
simple, complex
delicate, frail

Synonym Pairs		Antonym Pairs	
started	began	smooth	rough
delicate	frail	forget	remember
terrific	great	relieved	worried
ran	jogged	simple	complex

Directions: Classify each word from the box as an action, a feeling, or a characteristic. Write the words correctly on the lines.

Action	Feeling	Characteristic
started	terrific	delicate
began	great	frail
ran	relieved	smooth
jogged	worried	rough
forget		simple
remember		complex

65

Categories Galore

Directions: In the box below are names of sports. Write the names of the sports that best fit in each category.

baseball, soccer, tennis, football, surfing, golf, volleyball, basketball, fishing, swimming

Team Sport	Individual Sport
baseball	golf
football	tennis
soccer	fishing
basketball	swimming
volleyball	surfing

Directions: In the box below are names of musical instruments. Classify them into four groups.

violin, string bass, bassoon, flute, trumpet, cymbals, cello, triangle, xylophone, trombone, viola, French horn, tuba, snare drum, clarinet, oboe

Strings	Brass
violin	trumpet
viola	trombone
cello	French horn
string bass	tuba

Woodwinds	Percussion
flute	triangle
clarinet	snare drum
oboe	cymbals
bassoon	xylophone

66

Classifying

Classifying means putting items into categories based on similar characteristics.

Example: Apple pie, cookies, and ice cream could be classified as desserts.

Directions: Cross out the word in each group that does not belong. Then, add a word of your own that does belong. The first one has been done for you.

1. wren, robin, ~~feather~~, sparrow, eagle — bluebird
2. sofa, stool, chair, carpet, bench
3. lettuce, salad, corn, broccoli, spinach
4. pencil, chalk, pen
5. perch, penguin, bass
6. rapid, quick, unhurried, swift, speedy
7. lemon, daisy, melon, lime, grapefruit

Answers will vary.

Directions: Sample answers: group of words. Then, write a word of your own

Weather blizzard hurricane thunder tornado	**Parts of a Leg** ankle shin thigh knee
Radio Parts antenna speaker battery knob	**Winter Sports** hockey ice skating bobsledding skiing

67

Classifying

Sample answers: could belong in each category.

1. whales	humpback	blue	killer
2. songs	Happy Birthday	Blue Suede Shoes	Are You Sleeping?
3. sports	Michael Jordan	Steffi Graf	Mark Martin
4. fruit	apple	lemon	banana
5. schools	Lincoln High	Harvard	UCLA
6. teachers	Ms. McCall	Mr. Springer	Dr. Burns
7. tools	hammer	broom	ax
8. friends	Mary	Sue	Jon
9. books	Huckleberry Finn	Wrinkle in Time	Watership Down
10. mammals	bear	bat	people
11. fish	bass	cod	shark
12. desserts	cookies	cake	pie
13. cars	Ford	Chevy	VW
14. hobbies	collect stamps	painting	gardening
15. vegetables	potatoes	spinach	eggplant
16. insects	bee	wasp	hornet

68

Classifying: Regional Forecast

Directions: Read the forecast. Then, write words in the correct categories.

The very warm, early spring weather will continue to spread along the East Coast today. With some sunshine, afternoon temperatures will climb to 90 degrees in many places. Columbia, South Carolina, and neighboring areas could reach 100 degrees. Showers are expected from Washington, D.C., to New York City. Severe thunderstorms are likely in Virginia and North Carolina. Central South Carolina will be under a tornado watch during the afternoon.

Cities
Columbia
Washington, D.C.
New York City

States
South Carolina
Virginia
North Carolina

Weather Conditions
sunshine
showers
thunderstorms
tornado watch

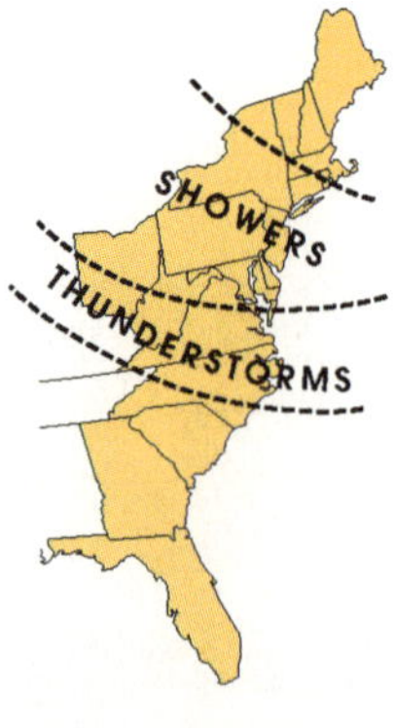

69

Clue Search

When you come to a word you do not know, you can look at its **context**, or the words and phrases around it, to try to figure out its meaning. Context clues within a sentence can include synonyms, antonyms, and explanations.

Directions: As you read each of the following sentences, look for context clues to help determine the meaning of each underlined word. Circle the clues. Write what you think each word means. You can use a dictionary **Possible answers:**

1. Two flood victims clung tenaciously to a branch, refusing to let go or give up hope.
   hold firmly; cling to; not giving up
2. The man will be incarcerated for breaking the law and will not be paroled until 2015.
   locked up in prison or jail; kept in prison or jail
3. The doctor waited until the hysterical child had calmed down enough to be examined.
   out of control; to be very upset
4. So many wild animals live in our backyard that it is like a menagerie, only without the cages.
   a collection of animals
5. After exploring cartography as a possible career, I've decided that map making would be quite interesting.
   a job in which you make maps
6. The man was so frugal in his spending for meals that they were barely enough to satisfy his hunger.
   cheap, thrifty
7. As a philatelist, I subscribe to *Stamp Collectors' Digest*. a stamp collector
8. Thomas Edison and Alexander Graham Bell were not only contemporaries but were even born in the same year of 1847.
   people who lived at the same time
9. Try to make your definitions concise by using as few words as possible.
   brief; short
10. John is a conscientious student whose work shows great care and concern for detail.
    very thorough and carefully done

70

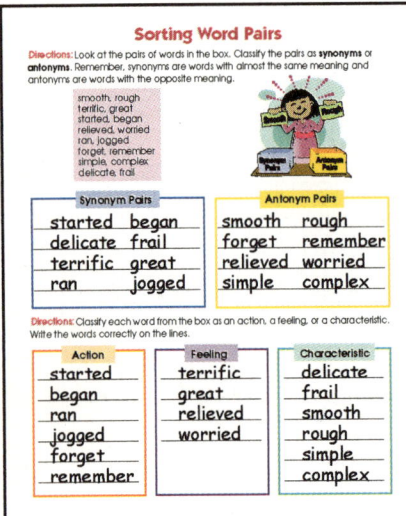

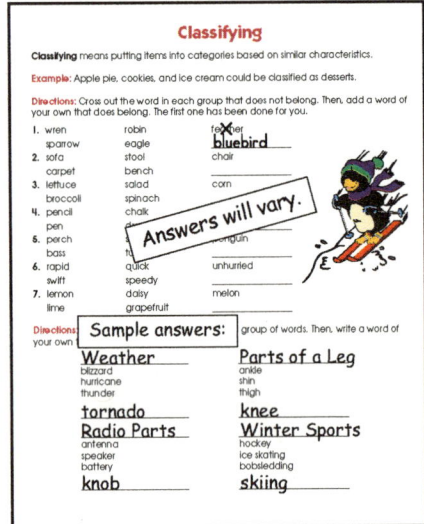

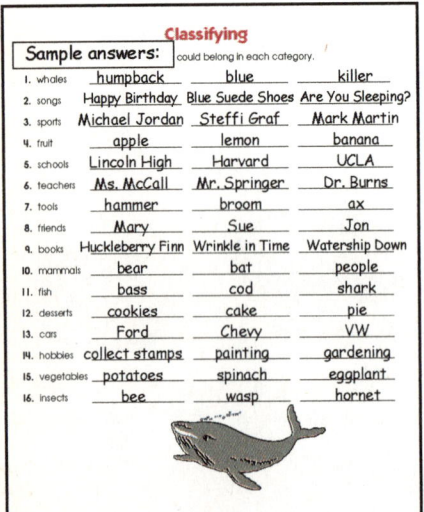

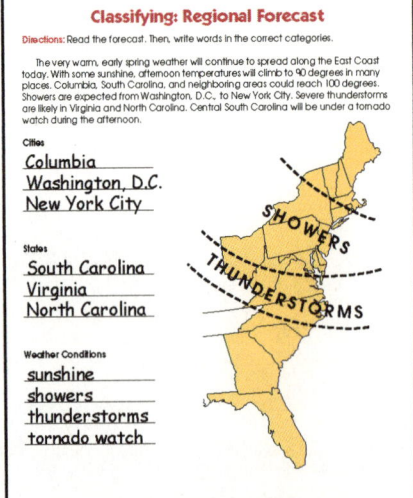

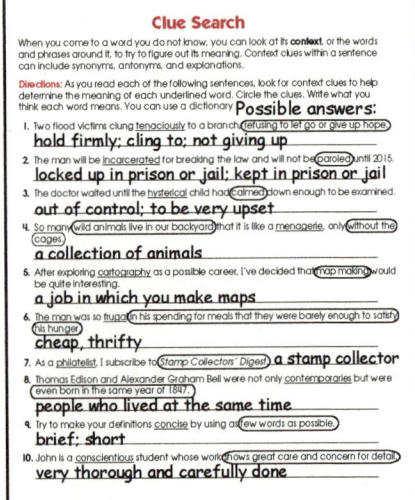

A Fitting Choice

Directions: Read each sentence. Look at the three word choices. Use context clues to help you choose the correct word to complete the sentence. Write it on the line.

1. The chef prepared a s**scrumptious**s meal that absolutely everyone enjoyed.
   scrumptious scrunches sponges

2. The text was extremely difficult to read and beyond my c**comprehension**n.
   communication complain comprehension
3. High-wire performers have a rather p**precarious**s job when you consider what could happen if they should fall.
   previous princess precarious
4. It was with great r**reluctance**e that John agreed to take on such a dangerous job.
   responsible reluctance receive
5. The v**velocity**y of light is approximately 186,000 miles per second.
   velocity velvety victory
6. The judge issued a w**warrant**t allowing the police to search the building.
   wrist wallet warrant
7. It is an a**absurd**d idea and obviously untrue.
   absurd award aboard
8. Maria's tale of her journey through South America made an interesting n**narrative**e for her readers.
   native nature narrative
9. The wolves attacked their prey with such f**ferocity**y that it was difficult for some of us to observe.
   family ferocity fiery
10. Unearthing fossil remains of dinosaurs is l**laborious**s work requiring time, skill, and patience.
    laborious laboratories labors

71

Comprehension and Context

Comprehension is understanding what is seen, heard, or read.

Context is the rest of the words in a sentence or the sentences before or after a word. Context can help with comprehension.

Context clues help you figure out the meaning of a word by relating it to other words in the sentence.

Directions: Use the context clues in the sentences to find the meanings of the bold words.

1. Jane was a **wizard** at games. She mastered them in no time and seldom lost.
   [ ] evil magician [X] gifted person [ ] average player
2. The holiday was so special that she was sure she'd never forget it. The memory would be **imprinted** forever on her mind.
   [ ] found [ ] weighed [X] fixed
3. "John will believe anything anyone tells him," his teacher said. "He's a very **impressionable** young man."
   [X] easily influenced [ ] unhappy [ ] unintelligent
4. "Do you really think it's **prudent** to spend all your money on clothes?" his mother asked crossly.
   [ ] foolish [X] wise [ ] funny
5. "Your plan has **merit**," Elizabeth's father said. "Let me give it some thought."
   [X] value [ ] awards [ ] kindness
6. John was very **gregarious** and loved being around people.
   [ ] shy [X] outgoing [ ] unfriendly

72

Context Clues: Remember Who You Are

Directions: Read each paragraph. Then, use context clues to figure out the meanings of the bold words.

During the 1940s, Esther Hautzig lived in the town of Vilna, which was then part of Poland. Shortly after the **outbreak** of World War II, she and her family were **deported** to Siberia by Russian communists, who hated Jews. She told what happened to her and other Polish Jews in a book. The book is called *Remember Who You Are: Stories About Being Jewish*.

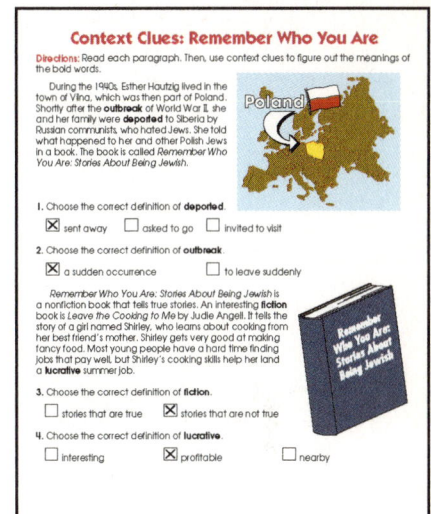

1. Choose the correct definition of **deported**.
   [X] sent away [ ] asked to go [ ] invited to visit
2. Choose the correct definition of **outbreak**.
   [X] a sudden occurrence [ ] to leave suddenly

Remember Who You Are: Stories About Being Jewish is a nonfiction book that tells true stories. An interesting **fiction** book is *Leave the Cooking to Me* by Judie Angell. It tells the story of a girl named Shirley, who learns about cooking from her best friend's mother. Shirley gets very good at making fancy food. Most young people have a hard time finding jobs that pay well, but Shirley's cooking skills help her land a **lucrative** summer job.

3. Choose the correct definition of **fiction**.
   [ ] stories that are true [X] stories that are not true
4. Choose the correct definition of **lucrative**.
   [ ] interesting [X] profitable [ ] nearby

73

Context Clues: Kids' Books Are Big Business

Between 1978 and 1988, the number of children's books published in the United States doubled. The publishing **industry**, which prints, promotes, and sells books, does not usually move this fast. Why? Because if publishers print too many books that don't sell, they lose money. They like to wait, if they can, to see what the "public demand" is for certain types of books. Then, they accept manuscripts from writers who have written the types of books the public seems to want. More than 4,600 children's books were published in 1988, because publishers thought they could sell that many titles. Many copies of each title were printed and sold to bookstores and libraries. The publishers made good profits and, since then, the number of children's books published each year has continued to grow.

The title of a recent new book for children is *The Wild Horses of Sweetbriar* by Natalie Kinsey-Warnock. It is the story of a girl and a band of wild horses that lived on an island off the coast of Massachusetts in 1903. The story sounds very exciting! Wild horses can be quite dangerous. The plot of *The Wild Horses of Sweetbriar* is probably filled with danger and suspense.

Directions: Answer these questions about how interest in writing, reading, and selling children's books has grown.

1. Use context clues to choose the correct definition of **industry**.
   [ ] booksellers [ ] writers [X] entire business
2. If 4,600 books were sold in 1988, how many books were sold in 1978? **2,300**
3. The number of children's books published in the United States doubled between 1978 and 1988. (Fact) Opinion
4. *The Wild Horses of Sweetbriar* is the story of a girl and a band of wild horses that lived on an island in 1903. (Fact) Opinion
5. The story sounds very exciting! Fact (Opinion)
6. The plot of *The Wild Horses of Sweetbriar* is probably filled with danger and suspense. Fact (Opinion)

74

Context Clues: Leonardo da Vinci

Directions: Read the sentences below. Use context clues to figure out the meaning of the bold words.

1. Some people are **perplexed** when they look at *The Last Supper*, but others understand it immediately.
   [ ] unhappy [ ] happy [X] puzzled
2. Because his model felt **melancholy** about the death of her child, da Vinci had music played to lift her spirits as he painted the *Mona Lisa*.
   [X] sad [ ] unfriendly [ ] hostile
3. Because da Vinci's work is so famous, many people **erroneously** assume that he left behind many paintings. In fact, he left only 20.
   [ ] rightly [ ] correctly [X] wrongly
4. Leonardo da Vinci was not like most other people. He didn't care what others thought of him—he led an interesting and **unconventional** life.
   [ ] dull [X] not ordinary [ ] ordinary
5. The **composition** of *The Last Supper* is superb. All the parts of the painting seem to fit together beautifully.
   [ ] the picture frame [X] parts of the picture
6. Leonardo's **genius** set him apart from people with ordinary minds. He never married, he had few friends, and he spent much of his time alone.
   [X] great mental abilities [ ] great physical abilities
   [ ] improper way to do things [ ] proper way to do things
7. Because he was a loner, da Vinci worried no one would come to his funeral when he died. In his will, he set aside 70 cents each to hire 60 **mourners** to accompany his body to his grave.
   [ ] friends [X] people who grieve [ ] people who smile

75

Facts and Opinions

A **fact** is information that can be proved.

Example: Hawaii is a state.

An **opinion** is a belief. It tells what someone thinks. It cannot be proved.

Example: Hawaii is the prettiest state.

Directions: Write **F** (fact) or **O** (opinion) on the line by each sentence. The first one has been done for you.

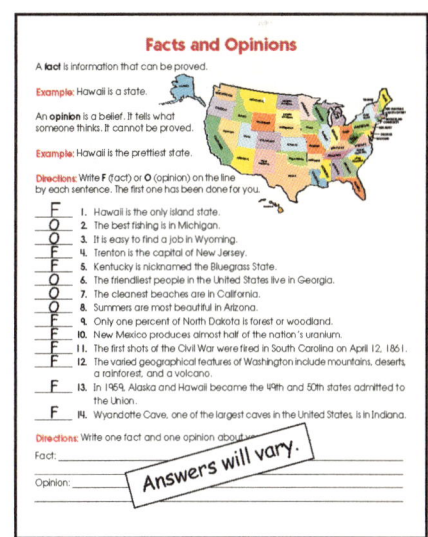

F 1. Hawaii is the only island state.
O 2. The best fishing is in Michigan.
O 3. It is easy to find a job in Wyoming.
F 4. Trenton is the capital of New Jersey.
F 5. Kentucky is nicknamed the Bluegrass State.
O 6. The friendliest people in the United States live in Georgia.
O 7. The cleanest beaches are in California.
O 8. Summers are most beautiful in Arizona.
F 9. Only one percent of North Dakota is forest or woodland.
F 10. New Mexico produces almost half of the nation's uranium.
F 11. The first shots of the Civil War were fired in South Carolina on April 12, 1861.
F 12. The varied geographical features of Washington include mountains, deserts, a rainforest, and a volcano.
F 13. In 1959, Alaska and Hawaii became the 49th and 50th states admitted to the Union.
F 14. Wyandotte Cave, one of the largest caves in the United States, is in Indiana.

Directions: Write one fact and one opinion about y…

Fact: ____________

Opinion: ____________

Answers will vary.

76

GRADE 5

I. Reading
A. Directions
B. Sequencing
C. Main Idea
II. Writing
A. Capitalization
B. Proofreading

More Facts and Opinions

Directions: Write **F** if the statement is a fact. Write **O** if the statement is an opinion.

1. O The Grand Canyon is the most scenic site in the United States.
2. F Dinosaurs roamed Earth millions of years ago.
3. F Scientists have discovered how to clone sheep.
4. O All people should attend this fair.
5. O Purebreds are the best dogs to own because they are intelligent.
6. O Nobody likes being bald.
7. O Students should be required to get straight A's to participate in extracurricular activities.
8. F Reading is an important skill that is vital in many careers.
9. O Snakes do not make good pets.
10. F Many books have been written about animals.
11. F Thomas Edison invented the lightbulb.
12. O Most people like to read science fiction.
13. F Insects have three body parts.

77

Wolfways

Directions: The following sentences are either facts stating that something is true or opinions stating how someone may feel about something. Write **F** beside a statement if it is a fact, and **O** if it is an opinion.

1. O Wolves are big, bad, and ferocious.
2. F Wolves live in packs.
3. O I'd like to find a wolf in my yard.
4. O A wolf pack is very large.
5. F Members of wolf packs usually cooperate with one another.
6. O Wolves like to howl at the moon.
7. F A wolf's howl communicates a message to other wolves.
8. F Wolves have a strong sense of smell.
9. F Wolves hunt large animals.
10. O Elk tastes better to a wolf than other animals.
11. F When a wolf has its tail down, it is communicating a message to other wolves.
12. O Wolves are scary animals.

Directions: What is your opinion about the following statement: Wolves are ferocious animals that should be hunted and killed. Defend your opinion … facts from the article.

Answers will vary.

79

Scrambled Sentences

Directions: Unscramble each sentence below. Write it correctly on the lines. Then, if the sentence is a fact, write **F**. If it is an opinion, write **O**.

1. F U.S. Presidents Virginia eight in were born Eight U.S. Presidents were born in Virginia.
2. O Mount Rushmore everyone should to see South Dakota to go Everyone should go to South Dakota to see Mount Rushmore.
3. O can get sandwiches cheese steak great only you in Philadelphia You can get great cheese steak sandwiches only in Philadelphia.
4. O vacation winter your best the Colorado place is to spend Colorado is the best place to spend your winter vacation.
5. F Mt. McKinley is the Alaska's United States point highest in the Alaska's Mt. McKinley is the highest point in the United States.
6. O parks enjoy Utah's awesome all visitors really All visitors really enjoy Utah's awesome parks.
7. F is state area in Rhode Island the smallest Rhode Island is the smallest state in area.
8. O thinks is everyone that spectacular Yellowstone Park Everyone thinks that Yellowstone Park is spectacular.
9. F North America is only state on the Hawaii not the mainland Hawaii is the only state not on the mainland of North America.
10. F Union the first join to state the Delaware was Delaware was the first state to join the Union.
11. O beaches nicest the states coastal of all the has Florida Florida has the nicest beaches of all the coastal states.

80

Then and Now

You **compare** to show how things are alike. You **contrast** to show how they are different. You can compare and contrast things, ideas, facts, people, or stories. Here are some clue words you can use to show readers that you are comparing or contrasting things.

similarly	in the same way	however	opposite
likewise	and	in contrast	different from
too	also	but	on the other hand
in addition	or	rather	

Directions: Read the following passage. Then, write three sentences that compare and three sentences that contrast the one-room school of the 1800s and your school today. Use clue words from the box.

Imagine that you live in a rural American town during the 1800s. Chances are you attend a one-room school with your brothers, sisters, and friends. There is only one teacher and she teaches all the grades. Your teacher doesn't stand for any nonsense either; she is a very strict disciplinarian. She has to be with 60 children in one room. Reading, writing, and arithmetic are the main subjects. You spend a lot of time memorizing because that is the method of learning. Everyone learns to read using William H. McGuffey's *Eclectic Reader*. These readers emphasize patriotism. Your teacher also stresses that to be a good American, you must work hard and be honest, thrifty, and courageous.

Compare Possible answers: We learn reading, writing, and arithmetic which is similar to the past; my teacher doesn't stand for much nonsense like teachers in the past; I'm in a class with friends like children in the past.

Possible answers: Unlike the past, where all grades

Contrast were in one class, my school has different classes for each grade; In the past, there were 60 children in a class but in my class there are only 25 children; In the past they read the Eclectic Reader. That's different from today because we read all kinds of books about many subjects.

81

Compare! Contrast! Choose!

Directions: Kobe wants to buy a bike and has saved $125. He found some information about one bike from a company online. He also cut out an ad from the newspaper for a similar bike. Help Kobe compare and contrast the two bikes. Complete the chart.

Rally Boy's Mountain Master

When it comes to bicycles for active, hard-playing boys, ages 10-14, sturdiness and safety are essential. This yellow and black 24"-wheel Mountain Master offers both and is sure to please both parents and kids. It features a unique oversized frame that makes getting on and off a snap, a large derailleur guard, alloy hubs and rims, and many other dependable components. A 21-speed drive train makes riding effortless. The twist shifters come equipped with an easy-to-read gear display to let you know what gear you're in. Top-notch linear pull brakes allow young riders to stop when they need to. The 1.95-inch all-terrain tires perform well on any surface. Your cost is only $229.99.*

*Price does not include shipping. Delivery 4-5 working days. Assembly required.

FOR SALE

Used boy's 24" blue Rally Mountain King bike 21-speed, easy-to-read gear shift display, pull brakes, large derailleur guard, and an extra set of 1.95 all-terrain tires. Just a year old, still like new. Perfect for a 10- to 14-year-old boy. Come and check it out. Take it for a spin around the block. Asking only $100. Call 555-1234 for more details.

Compare

Rally bikes	same size
Similar features	for riders 10-14

Contrast

black and yellow	blue
$229.99 + shipping	$100
new	used
assembly required	ready to ride
can't test ride	can test ride
doesn't come with an extra set of tires	comes with an extra set of tires

If you were Kobe, which bike would you buy? Why?

Answers will vary.

82

Mandy Muffet's Maze

Directions: Sometimes one cause can have many effects and lead to a series of events. Complete the maze to find out everything that happened to Mandy Muffet. Start at BEGIN and read the sentence in the first square. Then, read the sentence in a square that's above, below, or next to the one you're on. Decide which one has the correct effect and draw a line to connect the boxes. Continue to identify each effect in sequential order until you get to the end of the maze.

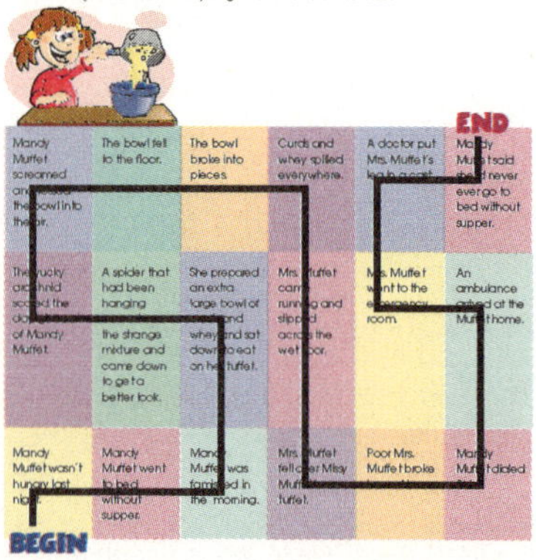

END
The bowl fell to the floor.
The bowl broke into pieces.
Curds and whey spilled everywhere.
A spider that had been hanging
the strange mixture and came down to get a better look.
An ambulance
Poor Mrs. Muffet broke
BEGIN

83

Niagara Falls

Directions: Answer the following questions about Niagara Falls.

1. The surface of the land was changed by the ice. When the ice withdrew, it caused waterways and streams to develop new paths. Lake Erie overflowed, and this produced Niagara Falls.

2. To make the Falls more attractive for tourists, observation towers are accessible, the Falls are lit up at night, and a steamer takes visitors for rides around the base of the Falls.

3. The shale underneath the dolomitic limestone is worn away more quickly, causing an overhang of limestone. This allows the Falls to drop at a sharp angle. When the layer of limestone breaks off, the Falls gradually move back up the river.

4. Security around the Falls may have been tightened as a result of so many daredevils attempting to ride over the Falls.

Directions: The **cause** is the reason for the action or **why** something happened. The **effect** is the result of the action or **what** actually happened. Match each effect to its correct cause.

Effect	Cause
1. remarkable views of the Falls from above	erosion
2. Niagara Falls was created	limestone overhanging edge
3. Niagara Falls drops down at a sharp angle	Maid of the Mist
4. waterways and streams developed new paths	overflow of Lake Erie
5. Horseshoe Falls is worn back three feet a year	ice sheets changed the land
6. visitors ride near base of the Falls	observation towers

85

Cause and Effect

A **cause** is an event or reason which has an effect on something else.

Example:
The heavy rains produced flooding in Chicago.
Heavy rains were the **cause** of the flooding in Chicago.

An **effect** is an event that results from a cause.

Example:
Flooding in Chicago was due to the heavy rains.
Flooding was the **effect** caused by the heavy rains.

Directions: Read the paragraphs. Complete the charts by writing the missing cause (reason) or effect (result).

Club-footed toads are small toads that live in the rainforests of Central and South America. Because they give off a poisonous substance on their skins, other animals cannot eat them.

Cause: They give off a poisonous substance.
Effect: Other animals cannot eat them.

Civets (siv its) are weasel-like animals. The best known of the civets is the mongoose, which eats rats and snakes. For this reason, it is welcome around homes in its native India.

Cause: It eats rats and snakes.
Effect: It is welcome around homes in its native India.

Bluebirds can be found in most areas of the United States. Like other members of the thrush family of birds, young bluebirds have speckled breasts. This makes them difficult to see and helps them hide from their enemies. The Pilgrims called them "blue robins" because they are much like the English robin. They are the same size and have the same red breast and friendly song as the English robin.

Cause: Young bluebirds have speckled breasts.
Effect: It helps them hide from enemies.

Cause: They are much like English robins.
Effect: The Pilgrims called them "blue robins."

86

The New Outfit

When you **predict**, you tell what you think will happen next. Predictions are based on things that have already happened.

Directions: Read each paragraph. Answer each set of questions. Then, write your own ending to the story.

Millie and her mother are shopping for a new outfit for a party at her father's office. Her father's boss will be there so it's important that Millie look nice. At the first store, Millie's mom chooses a dress with big flowers all over it and a frilly white collar. The dress Millie picks is simple, black, and very sh dress and raises h Answers will vary, but

1. What will happen next? should indicate that Millie's mom does not like the dress that Millie picked.
2. What makes you think so? Millie's mom raised her eyebrow.

Millie and her mom disagree. Millie says she will not wear the flowered dress. Millie's mom says she can't wear the black Answers will vary, but

3. it's likely that Millie's mom will suggest that they keep looking and/or go to another store.
4. If they can't agree on the black dress or the flowered dress, then they must keep looking.

Millie's mom suggests that they go to another store and try to find an outfit they can agree on. At the next store, Millie looks for a dress that isn't so short. Millie's mom looks for a dress that doesn't have a frilly white collar. When they meet at the dressing room, they are both holding the same dress!

5. What will happen next? Millie and her Mom will probably agree to get the new dress.

87

To Your Health!

Directions: Read the following passage about the food pyramid. Then, answer the questions at the bottom of the page.

Have you ever skipped a meal and regretted it later? Have you ever felt tired or sluggish after eating junk food? Most of us can say "yes" to at least one of these questions. That's why it's so important that we use the food pyramid to help us eat properly.

The group at the bottom of the food pyramid is called the Bread, Cereal, Rice, and Pasta Group. Foods in this group contain **carbohydrates**, which give us energy. Foods high in carbohydrates and low in sugar, such as rice, wheat bread, pasta, and low-sugar cereals, provide lasting energy for school, play, and other activities.

The Vegetable Group is also important: vegetables contain **vitamins** and **minerals** to keep your body running smoothly and **fiber** to help digest your food properly. If you don't get the correct amount of vitamins, minerals, and fiber, it's hard for your body to process the other foods you eat. You might even get sick.

The Fruit Group provides more vitamins, as well as natural **sugar** (different from the sugar found in sweets). Natural sugar gives you concentrated bursts of energy—perfect for running in a short race, getting through that extra-long homework assignment, or keeping you from being hungry until dinnertime.

The Meat, Beans, Eggs, and Nuts Group is important because foods from this group give you the vitamins and minerals you need, as well as **protein**. Proteins are called the "building blocks" of life: they help build strong muscles and organs, as well as keep your body strong to fight off diseases. Even if you ate lots of carbohydrates and natural sugars, you would still get tired quickly if you weren't getting enough protein.

The Milk, Yogurt, and Cheese Group provides proteins and **calcium** for strong bones and teeth. Your bones and teeth have to last your entire life, so you need to get enough calcium to keep them healthy into your old age.

The Fats, Oils, and Sweets Group is at the top of the pyramid; that's because it contains foods with refined (not natural) sugar, **fats**, and artificial ingredients. You need some fat and sugar in your diet. However, you can get all the fats and sugar you need from foods in the other five food groups. So try not to eat too much from the Fats, Oils, and Sweets Group.

1. Predict what might happen to someone who ate lots of fruit and sugary foods but not enough foods from the Bread, Cereal, Rice, and Pasta Group.
   They would have bursts of energy but get tired very quickly.
2. Predict what might happen to someone who ate foods from the Fats, Oils, and Sweets
   He or she would probably be tired all the time and his or her body might not run smoothly. He or she might get sick.

88

In Conclusion . . .

A **conclusion** is a sensible decision you make from the information you have been given.

Directions: Read the following paragraphs and circle the sentences that are the best possible conclusions to each paragraph. Underline the information in each paragraph that helped you draw your conclusions.

1. Dale and his friends want to make a music video. They each want to play an instrument. No one wants to sing except Dale, but he doesn't have a good singing voice. Dale sings the song anyway.
   - Dale is a good piano player.
   - The song does not sound as good as it could.
   - Dale's friends are no good at playing their instruments.
   - They should get someone else to sing the song.
2. Carlos's class wants to act out a scene from the Civil War. All the actors must bring props and costumes to go with their characters. On Thursday, Carlos brings a suit, a fake beard, and a tall black top hat.
   - Carlos will be acting in the play.
   - Carlos will be a soldier in the play.
   - Carlos will be George Washington in the play.
   - Carlos will be Abraham Lincoln in the play.
3. Janice's friends stop by unexpectedly. They have been playing basketball all afternoon. They are very thirsty. Janice looks around her kitchen for something to drink, but there's no soda or juice. All she can find is sugar, bread, cereal, and some lemons. Then, she has an idea.
   - Janice eats some cereal.
   - Janice makes some lemonade.
   - Janice tells her friends not to stop by unexpectedly anymore.
   - Janice gives her friends some soda.
4. Michelle hasn't been to school all week. Her mother sent the teacher a note at the beginning of the week explaining that Michelle had a fever. The next day, Michelle's brother told the whole class that she was covered with itchy spots and that the doctor didn't want her around other children.
   - Michelle might have chicken pox.
   - Michelle is having a tooth removed.
   - Michelle can have her brother bring home her assignments.
   - Michelle can't come to school because she might make other children sick.

89

The Lady With the Lamp

Directions: Read the article below. Then, answer the questions.

Do you recognize the famous lady shown here? She is the Statue of Liberty, one of the most famous statues in the world. She has been an important symbol for immigrants to the United States for over 100 years.

France gave the statue to the United States as a gift in the late 19th century. It was designed by French artist Frederic Auguste Bartholdi and was constructed from tons of copper and iron. The statue was erected in New York Harbor in 1886, and, with its pedestal, it stands over 306 feet tall—making it also one of the largest statues in the world.

Millions of immigrants have passed the Statue of Liberty on their way to new lives in the United States. More than 12 million people were greeted by "The Lady With the Lamp" between the years of 1892 and 1924 alone!

Many of these people stopped at Ellis Island, a large immigration center near the statue. Important information was recorded there such as the names, occupations, and original nationalities of the immigrants. The immigration center was closed in 1954, but now there is a museum there. And people from all over the world are still greeted by the Statue of Liberty when they enter New York Harbor.

In 1903, Emma Lazarus wrote a poem to describe the Statue of Liberty and what it meant to the people who had passed it on their way to America. In the poem, the statue says, "with silent lips":

Give me your tired, your poor,
Your huddled masses yearning to breathe free,
The wretched refuse of your teeming shore.
Send these, the homeless, the tempest-tossed, to me:
I lift my lamp beside the golden door.
—from "The New Colossus"

1. What do you think the Statue of Liberty is a symbol of? Use examples from the article to support your argument.
   Answers will vary.
2. Answers will vary, but may include: "Golden door" referred to Ellis Island, New York Harbor, or New York in general as the entrance to the United States for millions of people. This entrance was considered "golden" because it was the final passage into a country that promised a better life.

90

Bestseller Summaries

When you **summarize** something, you restate the important ideas from a piece of writing. A summary gives the most important information from a selection. It includes the topic, main idea, and details about the plot or information provided such as "who" or "what" the selection is about.

Directions: Read the short summaries below. Make a check mark next to each one that includes the topic, main idea, and important supporting details. If you think a summary is not complete, explain why on the lines below it.

✔ ***Cowboys of the Wild West*** by Russell Freedman

This book contains everything you ever wanted to know about the cowboy way of life: the equipment cowboys used, the clothing they wore, and the work they did. It also contains many exciting photographs to illustrate this adventurous and sometimes difficult profession.

Little House on the Prairie by Laura Ingalls Wilder

In the 1800s, many families moved to the

This summary is missing the topic of the book and details about the plot, such as who the important characters are.

✔ ***Galileo*** by Leonard Everett Fisher

This book is a biography of Galileo, one of the most famous astronomers of all time. It includes information about Galileo's life, scientific studies, and theories. It also explains why many people disagreed with his ideas.

The Impressionists by Yolanda Baillet

This book is about Impressionism. Edgar Degas, Eduard Manet, Claude Monet, and Berthe Morisot were all important Impressionist painters.

This summary is missing the main idea of the book and also important supporting details.

This exciting book includes tales of pirates and treasure. It has many chapters, but you will enjoy reading it if you like adventure.

This summary is missing the topic of the book, its main idea, and important plot details.

91

Get Organized

When writing summaries, it is sometimes helpful to make a graphic organizer, such as a story web, to help organize your ideas.

Directions: Read the article below. Then, fill in the story web, putting the main point in the middle and important details in the outer circles. Use the web to write a summary of the article on a separate sheet of paper.

When it comes to the best athletes in the world, animals have us beat. The strongest human weightlifter can lift about four times his or her own weight. An ant can pick up and carry 50 times its own weight.

When it comes to swimming, people definitely don't come in first. Olympic swimmers can reach speeds around 5 miles per hour. A tiny shrimp swims at around 2 miles per hour. But the fastest swimmer is the sailfish. It has been recorded going as fast as 68 miles per hour!

The fastest runner is the cheetah. It can run at speeds of up to 70 miles per hour. The fastest a person can run is about 27 miles an hour.

Compared to other animals, people do the best in the long jump. A person can jump about 30 feet. The kangaroo still wins, though. A kangaroo can jump about 43 feet!

Center: Animals are better athletes than people.

- Ants can carry more times their own weight than people.
- Sailfish can swim faster than people.
- Cheetahs can run faster than people.
- Kangaroos can jump farther than people.

92

One Wild Ride

You can use details from your reading to make **judgments**, or educated opinions, about what you have read.

Directions: Callie and Ryan are having an argument about amusement park rides. Use details from the argument to make your own judgment about which ride is better.

Callie and Ryan went to the park together. They agreed to go on the best ride first. But they had a decision to make. They could go to the Ultimate Scream Machine roller coaster or to the Wild Rapids water slide.

"Oh, let's go on the roller coaster first," said Callie.

"No way. Let's go on the best ride here, the water slide," said Ryan.

"How can you possibly think the water slide is the best ride? The roller coaster not only goes higher than the trees, but you also flip upside down twice," Callie said.

"The water slide is just as cool. It takes almost three minutes to climb the stairs up to the very top. The best part is there's no turning around once you get up there," Ryan explained.

"Well, once you think the roller coaster has stopped, you have to do the entire ride backwards. Besides, while you wait in line, you get to listen to everyone screaming while they are on the ride," Callie said.

"I've never done anything more exciting than jumping down a slide and flying through a huge tube into a pool," Ryan said.

1. It goes higher than the trees. You flip upside down twice. You do the ride backwards. You get to listen to everyone scream.
2. It takes three minutes to climb to the top. There's no turning around when you get there. It's very exciting to push off and go down the slide.
3. Whose argument is stronger? What makes you think so? Answers will vary.
4. What is your own favorite ride? Why? Answers will vary.

93

A New Movie Theater

Because each person has different experiences, feelings, and opinions, everyone has his or her own **perspective**. In writing, perspective is the point of view from which something is written.

Directions: Residents of Oakdale are concerned about a new movie theater that is being built. Match each letter with the correct author. Use details from the letter to guess the perspective of each one.

- Theodore T. Theobus, Mayor
- Mrs. Lillian Tataki, a concerned mother
- Walter Little, President of the Oakdale Historical Society
- Angela Ardsley, a resident of Park Street

Dear Editor,

The children of this town don't need to spend more time inside watching movies and eating junk food. What they need is a new park where they can breathe fresh air and get exercise! I propose that, instead of building a movie theater at 199 Park Street, we turn the lot into a park for the families of Oakdale.

Signed,

Mrs. Lillian Tataki, a concerned mother

Dear Editor,

I am opposed to building the movie theater on Park Street. Park Street is the town's oldest street and has many beautiful buildings dating back over 100 years. It was the site of the first house built in Oakdale and the original town hall. The new movie theater will be an eyesore and an insult to our town's heritage!

Yours truly,

Walter Little, President of the Oakdale Historical Society

Dear Editor,

We do not need a movie theater. If a movie theater is built on Park Street, traffic will get out of control and it will be dangerous to cross the street. It will also produce litter and noise which is totally unfair to people who live in the neighborhood!

Thank you,

Angela Ardsley, a resident of Park Street

Dear Editor,

The majority of the people in Oakdale have told me they want the movie theater. It will provide jobs and entertainment for the people of this town, and I want to provide them with what they want.

Sincerely,

Theodore T. Theobus, Mayor

94

Judging a Book by Its Cover

The **setting** of a story is the time and location in which it takes place.

Directions: The following is a collection of books for Mrs. Smith's class to read over the summer. But these books are missing their titles! First, look at each cover and identify the book's setting. Write the setting on the line underneath. Then, use this information to choose the correct book title from the choices in the box. Write the number in the small box.

1. Dr. Wizmo's Strange Experiment
2. Our Fantastic Journey
3. Big City Budget Tours
4. Exercising to Stay Healthy
5. Rover's Trip
6. Steve's Stupendous Shopping Spree
7. Growing Vegetables the Easy Way
8. Cooking With Grandpa

dog kennel | garden | kitchen | laboratory

hot air balloon the sky | New York City | department store | roller rink

95

Story Theme Match-Up

The main idea or subject of a piece of writing is called its **theme**. You can usually figure out the theme of a work by reading it closely.

Directions: Below are examples of some common story themes. Read the six story excerpts and choose the theme that goes with each one. Write your choice on the line beneath each one. Each theme is used twice.

- sportsmanship
- perseverance
- practice makes perfect

The events at field day were almost over and the students in Mr. Amato's class were feeling discouraged. Their class had won First Place only once. But they had received Second and Third places several times. When the scores were added up, they couldn't believe it—theirs was the winning class! All the students congratulated each other.

sportsmanship

Andy felt tired. He didn't think he would be able to finish the run. People were clapping on the sidelines, but still he wanted to give up. He looked ahead and saw a stop sign at an intersection. He kept his eyes on the sign. In his mind, he said to himself over and over "Just get to the stop sign! Just get to the stop sign!" But right after he passed it, people started cheering wildly. The stop sign marked the end of the course, and he had finished!

perseverance

Ginny followed the directions exactly. She measured all the ingredients as it said in the book. But the pie just didn't taste right. She knew it had something to do with either how she handled the dough or how she mixed the ingredients. To practice, she made pie every day for a week. Finally, on Friday, she made a perfect pie.

practice makes perfect

If Jessica's mom nagged her one more time about practicing the piano, she was going to scream. It was tedious and boring. Saturday finally arrived and she played her song for the director of the music school. While Jessica was waiting in the hallway, her mom came to tell her that she had played so well she had qualified for a scholarship to a performing arts camp.

practice makes perfect

The mathletes of Maywood School were on stage smiling, hooting, and accepting a huge trophy. Sitting in the audience with his team from Wayside, Justin knew that Maywood's team deserved the award. While his own team had also known the answers, Maywood's team had been quicker to respond to every question. Justin stood up and clapped for them.

sportsmanship

RJ knew he needed to find a summer job. Each day, he looked in the classifieds and called every listing for restaurant help. On his eighth interview, he finally got a job at Rick's Raft House. He'd have to start as a dishwasher, but he would show them he could also be a great waiter.

perseverance

96

Plot Out the Action

The **plot** is the main storyline in any work of fiction. The most important parts of a plot are:

background: the introduction; what the reader needs to know about the characters and the general situation	**conflict:** the problem that the main character/characters must solve or the goal that he/she/they want to achieve	**rising action:** what the characters do to overcome the conflict; this may include encountering more problems	**climax:** usually the most exciting part of the story, often when character(s) must resolve the conflict	**falling action:** events that occur after the conflict has been resolved

Directions: Read this story about Luis. Then, answer the questions at the bottom of the page. Make sure to use complete sentences.

Luis's mom needed his help. She was planning a backyard party for his grandmother. She was so busy getting the house ready, she needed someone to help her do the shopping. She gave Luis her shopping list and $40.

Luis had been to the store many times before but never by himself. He got a cart and walked up the first aisle. As he put each item in the cart, he crossed it off the list.

told him that the total was $47.25. But Luis had only $40. He couldn't believe his mother hadn't given him enough money! Then, he remembered that he had put extra things in the cart. He asked the cashier if he could put some of his items back. When she told him yes, he gave back the extra snacks and drinks. By doing this, he brought the total down to $38.

When Luis arrived home with the

1. Luis' mom is too busy to go to the store.
2. Luis must go to the store by himself for the first time.
3. Luis decides on a plan when in the store. He picks up more food than is on his list. He doesn't have enough money to pay for all the items in his cart. He puts the extra food back so he can pay for the items on his mother's list.

97

Doing Your Chores

Directions: Read the story. Then, fill in the story web with what you know about setting, plot, theme, and story elements.

Ellie and Allen were in the backyard playing basketball when Ellie's mother came out and reminded her to give her dog, Marley, a bath. Ellie hated this job because Marley hated his bath. Allen told Ellie he would help her. They came inside, picked up Marley, and took him down to the basement.

"I'll get the tub and fill it with water while you get the towels and shampoo," said Ellie.

"No problem," said Allen. When he put Marley down, the dog ran back up the stairs. So when Ellie and Allen had everything ready for the bath, they couldn't find Marley.

"He must have gone back upstairs," said Allen.

"Let's go find him," said Ellie.

They looked everywhere but couldn't find the dog. Ellie finally found him under the bed in her bedroom. But he wouldn't come out. He knew what was going to happen. Neither Ellie nor Allen could reach the dog because he was too far under the bed.

"I know!" said Ellie. She ran into the kitchen and put peanut butter on a small dog biscuit and brought it up to the bedroom.

She held it under the bed for Marley to smell. The lure of peanuts was too great for the dog. He came out from under the bed, and, as he took the cracker from Ellie, Allen grabbed him. They took him downstairs and finally gave him a bath.

Characters: Ellie; Allen; Ellie's mom; Marley, the dog

Setting: Ellie's house

Background: Ellie and Allen are playing outside. Ellie's mom reminds her to wash Marley.

Theme: perserverance (or) taking care of a pet

Title: *Doing Your Chores*

Conflict: Ellie must find Marley because he runs away.

Solution: Ellie puts peanut butter on a dog biscuit and lures Marley from under the bed.

98

Half Empty?

Directions: Read what happens while Tim and Tom are in the park. Then, answer the questions at the bottom of the page. Use complete sentences.

On the way to the park, Tim stopped to see if Tom wanted to hang out at the park.

"It's such a sunny day, we should go to the park and see who is around," said Tim.

"It's too hot to be out in the sun," said Tom.

Riding to the park was easy since the road to the entrance was blocked off. There were no cars allowed on the street. The bike path started at the entrance to the park. They rode past the tennis courts, the picnic area, and the duck pond. Tim was smiling and cracking jokes the whole time. But Tom never smiled once. All of a sudden, it started to rain.

"This is great," said Tim. "The rain will cool things down."

"This isn't great," said Tom. "I'm going to get soaked. Let's just hurry up and get out of here."

As they curved around a bank of trees, there was a police barricade blocking off the bike path.

"I knew this wasn't going to be easy. Why did you talk me into this?" asked Tom.

Tim said, "Tom, my grandfather once put a glass of water on the table and asked me how much water was in it. I told him it was half full. He liked my answer. He said there are two kinds of people: the 'half-full' people and the 'half-empty' people. Tom, I think you should try to be a 'half-full' person."

"Yeah, well, why don't you just go and fill the glass with all the rain that's falling on us right now!" Tom said angrily.

1. Tom, Tim, and Tim's grandfather
2. Tim: thinks it's a good day to ride his bike, smiles, thinks rain will cool things down, happy; Tom: thinks it's too hot to ride, doesn't smile, thinks rain will get him wet, crabby; Tim's grandfather: thinks there are two kinds of people in the world
3. If you look at a glass and think that it's half-full, that means you have a positive attitude. Tom should try to be a "half-full" person because right now, he has a bad attitude and he isn't having any fun.

99

The Amusement Park

Directions: Arrowhead Camp is spending a day at Six Banners Amusement Park. Read the story. Then, answer the questions at the bottom of the page. Circle your answers.

When the kids arrived at the park, Joe—the head counselor—gave them permission to go explore the park on their own. They would all meet back at the big water fountain at 4:00. Cindy and Katie started looking at their map. Roberto and Bucky took off running down the path towards the roller coaster.

"See you later," Roberto yelled to the rest of the group as he sped off. He and Bucky didn't want to waste one second standing around talking! They planned to go on as many rides as possible in their short time at the park.

Cindy and Katie started walking and saw a hot dog stand.

"I'm a little hungry," Cindy said.

"I could go for something to eat, too," said Katie.

"I think I'll sit here in the shade while I eat," Cindy said after she got her lunch and drink.

"I'm going into the arcade to play some games," said Katie.

"Don't forget to be back in time for the dolphin show! It starts in twenty minutes," Cindy said.

By the time Cindy and Katie arrived at the dolphin show, Bucky and Roberto were already on their fourth ride. They had ridden the Scream Machine twice, the Dare Devil twice, and were waiting for their turn on the Big Splash.

"I can't wait to get soaked," said Bucky.

"How wet do you think we'll get?" asked Roberto.

"We'll have to wait and see," said Bucky.

When they got off the Big Splash, both boys were drenched. Six rides later, their clothes were still wet!

At quarter to four, Cindy and Katie got on the Ferris wheel. They knew they had plenty of time to ride the Ferris wheel before they had to be at the water fountain. But Bucky and Roberto were still waiting in line at the bumper cars. When they finally got into the ride, they were so excited they lost track of time. They didn't get back to the fountain until twenty after four!

"I'm glad I asked you to meet back here at 4:00. The bus isn't supposed to leave for another half an hour," said Joe as they arrived. "We'll still be on time getting home—even though Bucky and Roberto were late to meet the group!"

1. What is the best adjective to describe Joe?
   a. older
   b. counselor
   c. in charge
   d. practical (circled)
2. What is the reason that Bucky and Roberto were late to meet the group?
   a. They decided to ride the bumper cars.
   b. They wanted to go on as many rides as possible.
   c. They were already running toward the roller coaster when Joe told them to meet at 4:00.
   d. They lost track of time. (circled)
3. What is a good adjective to describe Bucky and Roberto?
   a. adventurous (circled)
   b. helpful
   c. friends
   d. fast
4. What is the reason Cindy and Katie were on time to meet the group?
   a. They were sure to leave enough time to ride the Ferris wheel before they had to meet the group at the water fountain. (circled)
   b. They read their map before entering the park.

100

What a Character!

Directions: Who is your favorite TV character? List words to describe the character on the left side of the Venn diagram. Do the same for your favorite character from a book, listing his or her traits on the right. Make sure that any traits the two share are listed in the middle. Then, answer the questions at the bottom of the page.

Favorite TV Character ________ Favorite Book Character ________

Show: ________ Book Title: ________

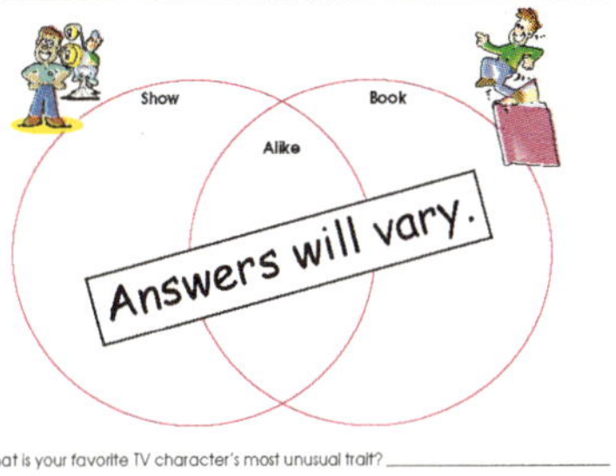

1. What is your favorite TV character's most unusual trait? ________
2. What is your favorite book character's most unusual trait? ________

101

Have It Your Way!

Directions: Here's your chance to create some crazy characters for a short story of your own! But there's a catch—each character must have certain traits, as shown on the chart below. Complete the chart with more ideas for each character. Then, use the chart to write a short story, at least four paragraphs long, on a separate sheet of paper.

	Physical Traits	Personality Traits	Other
Character #1	5 years old; brown hair and brown eyes		lives in the same house as character #3
Character #2 Louis		loves to play baseball	
Character	oy; very tall; glasses		wants to go to the movies; fights a lot with little sister
Character #4	11 years old; girl	friendly; has known Louis for a long time	

Answers will vary.

102

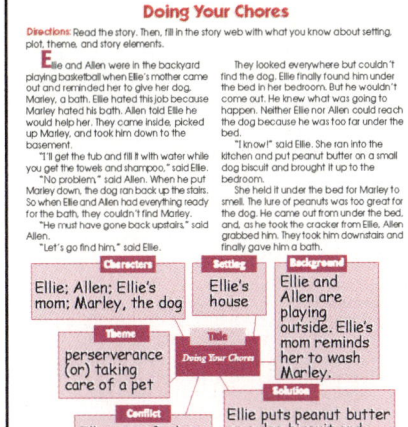

Comprehension: Jaguars

The jaguar is a large cat, standing up to 2 feet tall at the shoulder. Its body can reach 73 inches long, and the tail can be another 30 inches long. The jaguar is characterized by its yellowish-red coat covered with black spots. The spots themselves are made up of a central spot surrounded by a circle of spots.

Jaguars are not known to attack humans, but some ranchers claim that jaguars attack their cattle. This claim has given jaguars a bad **reputation**.

The jaguar can be found in southern North America, but is most **populous** in Central and South America. Jaguars are capable climbers and swimmers, and they eat a wide range of animals.

Female jaguars have between one and four cubs after a **gestation** of 93 to 105 days. Cubs stay with the mother for 2 years. Jaguars are known to have a life expectancy of at least 22 years.

Directions: Use context clues for these definitions.

1. populous: ______
2. reputation: ______
3. gestation: ______

Answers will vary.

Directions: Answer these questions about jaguars.

1. Describe the spots on a jaguar's coat.
a central spot surrounded by a circle of spots

2. Why would it be to a jaguar's advantag... oat?
Answers will vary.

103

Comprehension: Leopards

The leopard is a talented **nocturnal** hunter and can see very well in the dark. Because of its excellent climbing **ability**, the leopard is able to stalk and kill monkeys and baboons. Leopards are also known to **consume** mice, porcupines, and fruit.

Although the true leopard is characterized by a light beige coat with black spots, some leopards can be entirely black. These leopards are called *black panthers*. Many people refer to other cat species as leopards. Cheetahs are sometimes referred to as *hunting leopards*. The clouded leopard lives in southeastern Asia and has a grayish spotted coat. The snow leopard, which has a white coat, lives in Central Asia. A leopard's spots help to camouflage (cam-o-flo) it as it hunts.

True leopards can grow to over 6 feet long, not including their 3-foot-long tail. Leopards can be found in Africa and Asia.

Directions: Use context clues for these definitions.

1. consume: ______
2. ability: ______
3. nocturnal: ______

Answers will vary.

Directions: Answer these questions about leopards.

1. List three differences between the leopard and the jaguar.
1. Leopards live in Africa and Asia, while jaguars live in Central and South America.
2. Leopards are light beige with black spots; jaguars are yellowish-red with black spots.
3. Leopards have black spots; jaguars have a central spot surrounded by a circle of spots.

2. What makes a leopard able to hunt monkeys and baboons?
It has excellent climbing ability.

104

Comprehension: Lynxes

Lynxes are strange-looking cats with very long legs and large paws. Their bodies are a mere 51 inches in length, and they have short tails. Most lynxes have a clump of hair that extends past the tip of their ears.

Lynxes not only are known to chase down their **prey**, but also to leap on them from a **perch** above the ground. They eat small mammals and birds, as well as an occasional deer.

There are four types of lynxes. Bobcats can be found in all areas of the United States except the Midwest. The Spanish lynx is an endangered species. The Eurasian lynx, also known as the northern lynx, and the Canadian lynx are two other kinds of lynxes.

Directions: Use context clues for these defini...

1. prey: ______
2. perch: ______

Answers will vary.

Directions: Answer these questions about lynxes.

1. What are the four types of lynxes? bobcats, Spanish lynx, Eurasian lynx, Canadian lynx

2. Use the following words in a sentence of your own.
mammal ______
endangered ______
Answers will vary.

3. Do you believe it is im...nt to classify animals as "endangered" to protect a species that is low in population? Explain your answer.
Answers will vary.

105

Comprehension: Pumas

The puma is a cat most recognized by the more popular names of "cougar" or "mountain lion." Just like other large cats, the puma is a carnivore. It feeds on deer, elk, and other mammals. It can be found in both North and South America.

Pumas have small heads with a single black spot above each eye. The coat color ranges from bluish-gray (North America) to reddish-brown (South America). The underside of the body, as well as the throat and muzzle, are white. The puma's body can be almost 6 feet long, not including the tail.

Female pumas give birth to two to four young. When first born, pumas have brown spots on their backs, and their tails are lined with dark brown rings.

As with the jaguar, pumas are blamed for killing cattle. Because of this, pumas are either nonexistent in some are... endangered.

Directions: Answer these questions about...

1. What is a muzzle? ______
Answers will vary.

2. As the population inc... America, predict wh... ht happen to pumas.
Answers will vary.

3. What are two other popular names for the puma? cougar, mountain lion

4. What other cat besides the puma is blamed for killing cattle? jaguar

5. Reviewing the sizes of cats discussed so far, write their names in order, from smallest to largest.
1) lynx 2) puma
3) leopard 4) jaguar

106

Comprehension: Tigers

Tigers live on the continent of Asia. The tiger is the largest cat, often weighing over 500 pounds. Its body can grow to be 9 feet long and the tail up to 36 inches in length.

There are three types of tigers. The Siberian tiger is very **rare** and has a yellow coat with dark stripes. The Bengal tiger can be found in southeastern Asia and central India. Its coat is more orange and its stripes are darker. There is a tiger that lives on the island of Sumatra as well. It is smaller and darker in color than the Bengal tiger.

Tigers lead **solitary** lives. They meet with other tigers only to mate and share food or water. Tigers feed primarily on deer and cattle but are also known to eat fish and frogs. If necessary, tigers will also eat dead animals.

Female tigers bear one to six cubs at a time. The cubs stay with their mother for almost 2 years before going out on their own.

Because tiger parts are in high demand for use in Chinese medicine and recipes, tigers have been hunted almost to ***extinction***. All tigers are currently listed as endangered.

Directions: Use context clues for these definitions.

1. rare: ______
2. solitary: ______
3. extinction: ______

Answers will vary.

Directions: Answer these questions about tigers.

1. Why have tigers been hunted almost to extinction?
Their body parts are used in Chinese medicine and recipes.

2. Name the three types of tigers.
Siberian, Bengal, and Sumatran

107

Comprehension: Lions

The lion, often referred to as the king of beasts, once commanded a large **territory**. Today, their territory is very limited. Lions are **savanna**-dwelling animals, which has made them easy targets for hunters. The increasing population of humans and their livestock has also contributed to the lion's decreased population.

Lions are heavy cats. Males weigh over 500 pounds and can grow to be over 8 feet in length, with a tail more than 36 inches long. Males are characterized by a long, full mane that covers the neck and most of the head and shoulders. Females do not have a mane and are slightly smaller in size. Both males and females have beige coats, hooked claws, and powerful jaws. Their roars can be heard up to 5 miles away!

Lions tend to hunt in the evening and spend the day sleeping. They prefer hunting zebra or giraffe but will eat almost anything. A lion is **capable** of eating more than 75 pounds of meat at a single kill and then going a week without eating again. Generally, female lions do the hunting, and the males come to share the kill.

Lions live in groups called **prides**. Each pride has between 4 and 37 lions. Females bear one to four cubs approximately every 2 years.

Directions: Answer these questions about lions.

1. What are the differences between male and female lions? Male lions have a mane of hair and are larger in size.

2. Why would living on a savanna make the lion an "easy target"? ______

Directions: Use context clues fo...

1. pride: ______
2. territory: ______
3. savanna: ______
4. capable: ______

Answers will vary.

108

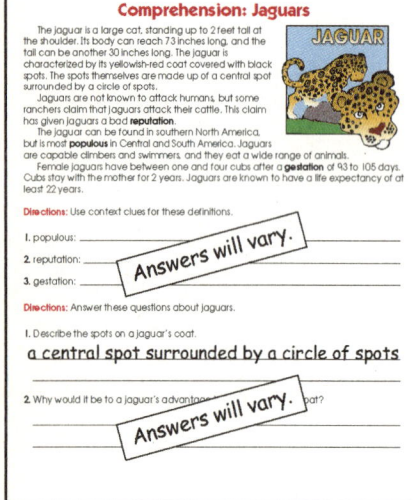

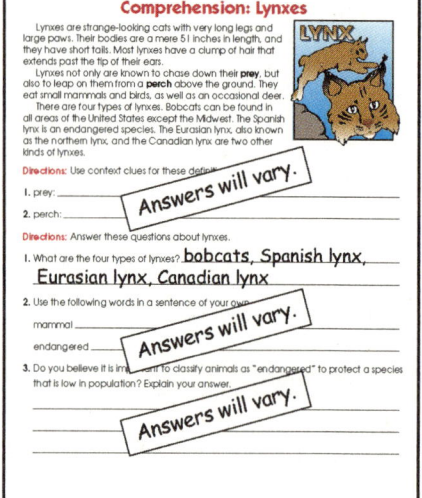

Comprehension: All About Sheep

Did you ever wonder what really happened to the tails of Little Bo-Peep's sheep? Here's the real story.

When sheep are born, they are called *lambs*. Lambs are born with long tails. A few days after lambs are born, the shepherd cuts off their tails. Because they get dirty, the lambs' long tails can pick up lots of germs. Cutting them off helps to prevent disease. The procedure is called **docking**. This is probably what happened to Bo-Peep's sheep! Another shepherd must have cut off their tails without telling her.

Little lambs are cute. A lamb grows inside its mother for 150 days before it is born. This is called the *gestation period*. Some types of sheep, such as hill sheep, give birth to one lamb at a time. Other types of sheep, such as lowland sheep, give birth to two or three lambs at a time.

After it is born, it takes a lamb 3 or 4 days to recognize its mother. Once it does, it stays close to her until it is about 3 weeks old. After that, the lamb becomes friendly toward other lambs.

Young lambs then form play groups. They chase each other in circles. They butt into each other. Like children, they pretend to fight. When play gets too rough, the lambs run back to their mothers for protection.

Lambs follow their mothers as they graze on grass. Usually, sheep move in single file behind an older female sheep. Female sheep are called *ewes*. The ewes teach their lambs how to keep themselves clean. This is called *grooming*. Sheep groom only their faces. Here is how they do it: They lick one of their front legs, then they rub their faces against the spot they have licked.

Directions: Follow the instructions below.

1. Define the word **docking**. to cut off the lamb's tail
2. Name a type of sheep that gives birth to one lamb at a time. hill sheep
3. Name a type of sheep that gives birth to two or three lambs at a time.
lowland sheep
4. Female sheep are called
☐ grazers. ☒ ewes. ☐ dockers.
5. Lambs begin playing in groups when they are
☐ 2 weeks old. ☒ 3 weeks old. ☐ 4 weeks old.

109

Comprehension: Pigs Are Particular

Have you ever wondered why pigs wallow in the mud? It's not because they are dirty animals. Pigs have no sweat glands. They can't sweat, so they roll in the mud to cool themselves. The next time you hear anyone who's hot say, "I'm sweating like a pig!" be sure to correct him or her. Humans can sweat but pigs cannot.

Actually, pigs are particular about their pens. They are very clean animals. They prefer to sleep in clean, dry places. They move their bowels and empty their bladders in another area. They do not want to get their homes dirty.

Another misconception about pigs is that they are smooth. Only cartoon pigs are pink, smooth, and shiny-looking. The skin of real pigs is covered with bristles—small, stiff hairs. Their bristles protect their tender skin. When pigs are slaughtered, their bristles are sometimes made into hair brushes or clothes brushes.

Female pigs are called *sows*. Sows have babies twice a year and give birth to 10 to 14 piglets at a time. The babies have a gestation period of 16 weeks before they are born.

All the piglets together are called a *litter*. Newborn piglets are on their tiny feet within a few minutes after birth. Can you guess why? They are hungrily looking for their mother's teats so they can get milk. As they nurse, piglets snuggle in close to their mother's belly to keep warm.

Directions: Answer these questions about pigs.

1. Why do pigs wallow in mud? to cool off
2. How long is the gestation period for pigs? 16 weeks
3. What are pig bristles used for? hairbrushes or clothes brushes
4. Tell two reasons pigs are on their feet soon after they are born.
1) to get milk 2) to get warm
5. A female pig is called a
☐ bristle. ☐ piglet. ☒ sow.
6. Together, the newborn piglets are called a
☐ group. ☐ family. ☒ litter.

110

Context Clues: No Kidding About Goats

Goats are independent creatures. Unlike sheep, which move easily in herds, goats cannot be driven along by a **goatherd**. They must be moved one or two at a time. Moving a big herd of goats can take a long time, so goatherds must be patient people.

Both male and female goats can have horns, but some goats don't have them at all. Male goats have beards but females do not. Male goats also have thicker and shaggier coats than females. During breeding season, when goats mate to produce babies, male goats have a very strong smell.

Goats are kept in **paddocks** with high fences. The fences are high because goats are good jumpers. They like to **nibble** on hedges and on the tips of young trees. They can cause a lot of damage this way! That is why many farmers keep their goats in a paddock.

Baby goats are called *kids*, and two or three at a time are born to the mother goat. Farmers usually begin to bottle-feed kids when they are a few days old. They milk the mother goat and keep the milk. Goat's milk is much easier to digest than cow's milk, and many people think it tastes **delicious**.

Directions: Answer these questions about goats.

1. Use context clues to choose the correct definition of **goatherd**.
☒ person who herds goats ☐ goats in a herd ☐ person who has heard of goats
2. Use context clues to choose the correct definition of **paddock**.
☐ pad ☐ fence ☒ pen
3. Use context clues to choose the correct definition of **nibble**.
☒ take small bites ☐ take small drinks ☐ take little sniffs
4. Use context clues to choose the correct definition of **delicious**.
☐ delicate ☒ tasty ☐ terrible

111

Comprehension: Cows Are Complicated

If you believe cows have four stomachs, you're right! It sounds incredible, but it's true.

Here are the "hows" and "whys" of a cow's digestive system. First, it's important to know that cows do not have front teeth. They eat grass by wrapping their tongues around it and pulling it from the ground. They do have back teeth, but still they cannot properly chew the grass.

Cows swallow grass without chewing it. When it's swallowed, the grass goes into the cow's first stomach, called a *rumen* (roo-mun). There, it is broken up by the digestive juices and forms into a ball of grass. This ball is called a *cud*. The cow is able to bring the cud back up into its mouth. Then, the cow chews the cud into a pulp with its back teeth and re-swallows it.

After it is swallowed the second time, the cud goes into the cow's second stomach. This second stomach is called the *reticulum* (re-tick-u-lum). The reticulum filters the food to sort out any small stones or other non-food matter. Then it passes the food onto the cow's third stomach. The third stomach is called the *omasum* (oh-mass-um).

From there, any food that is still undigested is sent back to the first stomach so the cow can bring it back up into her mouth and chew it some more. The rest goes into the cow's fourth stomach. The fourth stomach is called the *abomasum* (ab-oh-ma-sum). Digesting food that can be turned into milk is a full-time job for cows!

Directions: Answer these questions about cows.

1. List in order the names of a cow's four stomachs.
1) rumen 2) reticulum 3) omasum 4) abomasum
2. What is the name of the ball of grass a cow chews on? cud
3. A cow has no
☒ front teeth. ☐ back teeth. ☐ fourth stomach.
4. Which stomach acts as a filter for digestion?
☒ reticulum ☐ rumen ☐ abomasum

112

Context Clues: Dairy Cows

Some cows are raised for beef. Other cows, called *dairy cows*, are raised for milk. A dairy cow cannot produce any milk until after its first calf is born. Cows are not mature enough to give birth until they are 2 years old. A cow's gestation period is 40 weeks long, and she usually gives birth to one calf. Then she produces a lot of milk to feed it. When the calf is 2 days old, the dairy farmer takes the calf away from its mother. After that, the cow is milked twice a day.

The dairy cow's milk comes from the large, smooth udder beneath her body. The udder has four openings called *teats*. To milk the cow, the farmer **grasps** a teat and squeezes it with his thumb and forefinger. Then he gently but firmly pulls his hand down the teat to squeeze the milk out. Milking machines that are hooked to the cow's teats **duplicate** this action and can milk many cows quickly.

A dairy cow's milk production is not at the same level all the time. When the cow is pregnant, milk production gradually **decreases**. For 2 months before her calf is born, a cow is said to be "dry" and is not milked. This happens because, like humans, much of the cow's food is actually being used to nourish the unborn calf.

Farmers give the cow extra food at this time to make sure the mother and unborn calf are **well-nourished**. Again, like humans, well-nourished mother cows are more likely to produce healthy babies.

Directions: Answer these questions about dairy cows.

1. Use context clues to choose the correct definition of **grasp**.
☐ pull firmly ☒ hold firmly ☐ hold gently
2. Use context clues to choose the correct definition of **duplicate**.
☐ correct ☐ make ☒ copy
3. Use context clues to choose the correct definition of **decrease**.
☐ become more ☒ become less ☐ become quicker
4. Use context clues to choose the correct definition of **nourish**.
☐ to be happy ☐ to be friendly ☒ to feed

113

Comprehension: Chickens

Have you ever heard the expression "pecking order"? In the pecking order of a school, the principal is at the top of the order. Next comes the assistant principal, then the teachers and students.

In the pecking order of chickens, the most **aggressive** chicken is the leader. The leader is the hen that uses her beak most often to peck the chickens she bosses. These chickens, in turn, boss other chickens by pecking them, and so on. Chickens can peck all others who are "below" them in the pecking order. They never peck "above" themselves by pecking their bosses.

Directions: Answer these questions about chickens.

1. Put this pecking order of four chickens in order.
2 This chicken pecks numbers 3 and 4 but never 1.
1 No one pecks this chicken. She's the top boss.
4 This chicken can't peck anyone.
3 This chicken pecks chicken number 4.
2. Use context clues to figure out the definiti[...]
Answers will vary.
3. Who is at the top of the pecking order in a[...]
Answers may include:
principal

114

Comprehension: Cooking With Care

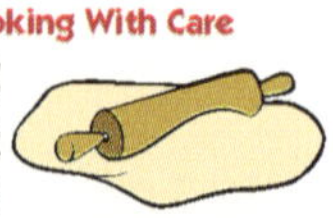

People are so busy these days that many have no time to cook. This creates a problem, because most families love home cooking! The food tastes good and warm, and a family meal brings everyone together. In some families, meals are often the only times everyone sees one another at the same time.

Another reason people enjoy home cooking is that it is often a way of showing love. A parent who bakes a batch of chocolate chip cookies isn't just satisfying a child's sweet tooth. He or she is sending a message. The message says, "I care about you enough to spend an hour making cookies that you will eat up in 15 minutes if I let you!"

There's also something about the smell of good cooking that appeals to people of all ages. It makes most of us feel secure and loved—even if we are the ones doing the cooking! Next time you smell a cake baking, stop for a moment and pay attention to your mood. Chances are, the good smell is making you feel happy.

Real estate agents know that good cooking smells are important. They sometimes advise people whose homes are for sale to bake cookies or bread if prospective buyers are coming to see the house. The good smells make the place "feel like home." These pleasant smells help convince potential buyers that the house would make a good home for their family, too!

Directions: Answer these questions about good cooking.

1. Why do fewer people cook nowadays? They are too busy.
2. Why are family meals important? They bring everyone together.
3. What do homemade cookies do besides satisfy a child's sweet tooth?
Someone cared enough to spend his/her time making them.
4. Real estate agents often advise home sellers holding open houses to
☐ clean the garage. ☒ bake cookies or bread.
5. The smell of baking at open houses may encourage buyers to
☐ bake cookies. ☒ buy the house. ☐ bake bread.

115

Comprehension: Eating High-Fiber Foods

Have you heard your parents or other adults talk about "high-fiber" diets? Foods that are high in fiber, like oats and other grains, are believed to be very healthy. Here's why: The fiber adds bulk to the food the body digests and helps keep the large intestines working properly. Corn, apples, celery, nuts, and other chewy foods also contain fiber that helps keep the body's systems for digesting and eliminating food working properly.

Researchers at the University of Minnesota have found another good reason to eat high-fiber food, especially at breakfast. Because fiber is bulky, it absorbs a lot of liquid in the stomach. As it absorbs the liquid, it swells. This "fools" the stomach into thinking it's full. As a result, when lunchtime comes, those who have eaten a high-fiber breakfast are not as hungry. They eat less food at lunch. Without much effort on their parts, dieters eating a high-fiber breakfast can lose weight.

The university researchers say a person could lose 10 pounds in a year just by eating a high-fiber breakfast! This is good news to people who are only slightly overweight and want an easy method for losing that extra 10 pounds.

Directions: Answer these questions about eating high-fiber foods.

1. Why is fiber healthy? It adds bulk and helps the large intestine work properly.
2. How does fiber "fool" the stomach? It absorbs liquid and swells.
3. How does "fooling" the stomach help people lose weight? People feel full and aren't as hungry.
4. How many pounds could a dieter eating a high-fiber breakfast lose in a year?
☐ 20 pounds ☐ 30 pounds ☒ 10 pounds
5. The university that did the research is in which state?
☐ Michigan ☒ Minnesota ☐ Montana

116

Comprehension: The French Eat Differently

Many people believe that French people are very different from Americans. This is certainly true where eating habits are concerned! According to a report by the World Health Organization, each year the French people eat four times more butter than Americans. The French also eat twice as much cheese! In addition, they eat more vegetables, potatoes, grain, and fish.

Yet, despite the fact that they eat larger amounts of these foods, the French take in about the same number of calories each day as Americans. (French and American men consume about 2,500 calories daily. French and American women take in about 1,600 calories daily.)

How can this be? If the French are eating more of certain types of foods, shouldn't this add up to more calories? And why are so few French people overweight compared to Americans? The answer—Americans consume 18 times more refined sugar than the French and drink twice as much whole milk!

Although many Americans believe the French end each meal with grand and gooey desserts, this just isn't so. Except for special occasions, dessert in a typical French home consists of fresh fruit or cheese. Many American families, on the other hand, like to end their meals with a bowl or two of ice cream or another sweet treat.

It's believed that this difference in the kind of calories consumed—rather than in the total number of calories taken in—is what causes many Americans to be chubby and most French people to be thin.

Directions: Answer these questions about the eating habits of French and American people.

1. How many calories does the average French man eat each day? 2,500
2. How much whole milk does the average French person drink compared to the average American? half as much
3. How much more refined sugar do Americans eat than the French?
☐ 2 times more ☒ 18 times more ☐ 15 times more
4. What do French families usually eat for dessert?
☐ refined sugar ☐ ice cream ☒ fruit and cheese

117

Comprehension: Chinese Cabbage

Many Americans enjoy Chinese food. In big cities, like New York and Chicago, many Chinese restaurants deliver their food in small boxes to homes. It's just like ordering a pizza! Then, the people who ordered the "take-out" food simply open it, put it on their plates, and eat it while it's hot.

Because it tastes so good, many people are curious about the ingredients in Chinese food. Siu choy and choy sum are two types of Chinese cabbage that many people enjoy eating. Siu choy grows to be 2 to 3 feet! Of course, it is chopped into small pieces before it is cooked and served. Its leaves are light green and soft. It is not crunchy like American cabbage. Siu choy is used in soups and stews. Sometimes it is pickled with vinegar and other ingredients and served as a side dish to other courses.

Choy sum looks and tastes different from siu choy. Choy sum grows to be only 8 to 10 inches. It is a flowering cabbage that grows small yellow flowers. The flowers are "edible," which means they can be eaten. Its leaves are long and bright green. After its leaves are boiled for 4 minutes, choy sum is often served as a salad. Oil and oyster sauce are mixed together and poured over choy sum as a salad dressing.

Directions: Answer these questions about Chinese cabbage.

1. Which Chinese cabbage grows small yellow flowers? choy sum
2. Which Chinese cabbage is served as a salad? choy sum
3. Is siu choy crunchy? no
4. What ingredients are in the salad dressing used on choy sum?
oil and oyster sauce
5. To what size does siu choy grow? 2 to 3 feet
6. Name two main dishes in which siu choy is used. soups and stews

118

Comprehension: Roman Legends

Long ago, people did not know as much about science and astronomy as they do today. When they did not understand something, they thought the "gods" were responsible. The ancient Romans believed there were many gods and that each god or goddess (a female god) was responsible for certain things.

For example, the Romans believed Ceres (Sir-eez) was the goddess who made flowers, plants, trees, and other things grow. She was a lot like what people today refer to as Mother Nature. Ceres was also responsible for the good weather that made crops grow. You can see why Ceres was such an important goddess to the ancient Romans.

Apollo was the god of the sun. People believed he used his chariot to pull the sun up each day and take it down at night. Apollo was extremely good-looking. His home was a golden palace near the sun surrounded by fluffy white clouds. Apollo had to work every single day, but he lived a wonderful life.

Jupiter was the most important god of all. He was the god who ruled all of the other gods, as well as the people. Jupiter was also called Jove. Maybe you have heard someone use the exclamation, "By Jove!" That person is talking about Jupiter! The word **father** is derived from the word "Jupiter". Although he did not really exist, Jupiter influenced our language.

Directions: Answer these questions about Roman legends.

1. What imaginary figure is Ceres compared to today? Mother Nature
2. Where did Apollo live? a golden palace near the sun
3. The word **father** is derived from the name of this god:
☐ Ceres ☐ Apollo ☒ Jupiter
4. Which is not true of Apollo?
☐ He had to work every day.
☒ He lived in a mountain cave.
☐ He was very handsome.

119

Comprehension: Apollo and Phaethon

Apollo, the sun god, had a son named Phaethon (Fay-a-thun). Like most boys, Phaethon was proud of his father. He liked to brag to his friends about Apollo's important job, but no one believed that the great Apollo was his father.

Phaethon thought of a way to prove to his friends that he was telling the truth. He went to Apollo and asked if he could drive the chariot of the sun. If his friends saw him making the sun rise and set, they would be awestruck!

Apollo did not want to let Phaethon drive the chariot. He was afraid Phaethon was not strong enough to control the horses. But Phaethon begged until Apollo gave in. "Stay on the path," Apollo said. "If you dip too low, the sun will catch the earth on fire. If you go too high, people will freeze."

Unfortunately, Apollo's worst fears came true. Phaethon could not control the horses. He let them pull the chariot of the sun too close to the earth. To keep the earth from burning, Jupiter, father of the gods, sent a thunderbolt that hit Phaethon and knocked him from the driver's seat. When Phaethon let go of the reins, the horses pulled the chariot back up onto the proper path. Phaethon was killed as he fell to earth. His body caught fire and became a shooting star.

Directions: Answer these questions about the Roman legend of Apollo and his son.

1. Who did not believe Apollo was Phaethon's father? Phaethon's friends
2. What did Phaethon do to prove Apollo was his father? drove the chariot of the sun
3. Why did Jupiter send a lightning bolt? to keep the earth from burning by knocking Phaethon from the driver's seat
4. Which was not a warning from Apollo to Phaethon?
☐ Don't go too close to the earth. It will burn up.
☒ Don't pet the horses. They will run wild.
☐ Don't go too far from the earth. It will freeze.

120

Context Clues: Mighty Hercules

Some people lift weights to build their strength. But Hercules (Her-cu-lees) had a different idea. He carried a calf on his shoulders every day. As the calf grew, it got heavier, and Hercules got stronger. Eventually, Hercules could carry a full-grown bull!

Hercules used his **enormous** strength to do many kind things. He became famous. Even the king had heard of Hercules! He called for Hercules to kill a lion that had killed many people in his kingdom. Hercules tracked the lion to its **den** and **strangled** it. Then, Hercules made clothes for himself from the lion's skin. This kind of **apparel** was unusual, and soon Hercules was recognized everywhere he went. Hercules was big and his clothes made it easy to pick him out in a crowd!

The king asked Hercules to stay in his kingdom and help protect the people who lived there. Hercules performed many **feats** of strength and bravery. He caught a golden deer for the king. The deer had outrun everyone else. Then Hercules killed a giant, a dragon and other dangerous creatures. Hercules became a hero and was known throughout the kingdom.

Directions: Answer these questions about Hercules.

1. Use context clues to choose the correct definition of **enormous**.
   ☒ huge ☐ tiny ☐ smart
2. Use context clues to choose the correct definition of **strangle**.
   ☐ beat ☒ choke ☐ tickle
3. Use context clues to choose the correct definition of **den**.
   ☐ pond ☐ hutch ☒ home
4. Use context clues to choose the correct definition of **apparel**.
   ☐ appearance ☒ clothing ☐ personality
5. Use context clues to choose the correct definition of **feat**.
   ☐ trick ☐ treat ☒ act

121

Comprehension: Ceres and Venus

Remember Ceres? She was like Mother Nature to the ancient Romans.

Ceres made the flowers, plants, and trees grow. She made crops come up and rain fall. Ceres was a very important goddess. The ancient Romans depended on her for many things.

Although the gods and goddesses were important, they had faults like ordinary people. They argued with one another. Sometimes they got mad and lost their tempers. This is what happened to Ceres and another goddess named Venus (Veen-us). Venus, who was the goddess of love and beauty, got mad at Ceres. She decided to hurt Ceres by causing Pluto, gloomy god of the underworld, to fall in love with Ceres' daughter, Proserpine (Pro-sur-pin-ay).

To accomplish this, Venus sent her son Cupid to shoot Pluto with his bow and arrow. Venus told Cupid that the man shot by this arrow would then fall in love with the first woman he saw. Venus instructed Cupid to make sure that woman was Ceres' daughter. Cupid waited with his bow and arrow until Pluto drove by Ceres' garden in his chariot. In the garden was Proserpine. Just as Pluto's chariot got near her, Cupid shot his arrow.

Ping! The arrow hit Pluto. It did not hurt, but it did its job well. Pluto fell instantly in love with poor Proserpine, who was quietly planting flowers. Pluto was not a gentleman. He did not even introduce himself! Pluto swooped down and carried Proserpine off in his chariot before she could call for help.

Directions: Answer these questions about Ceres and Venus.

1. With whom was Venus angry? Ceres
2. How did Venus decide to get even? She made Pluto fall in love with Ceres' daughter.
3. Ceres' daughter's name was
   ☐ Persperpine. ☐ Prosperline. ☒ Proserpine.
4. Venus' son's name was
   ☐ Apollo. ☒ Cupid. ☐ Persperpine.

122

Comprehension: Proserpine and Pluto

Proserpine was terrified in Pluto's palace in the underworld. She missed her mother, Ceres, and would not stop crying.

When Ceres discovered her daughter was missing, she searched the whole earth looking for her. Of course, she did not find her. Ceres was so unhappy about Proserpine's disappearance that she refused to do her job, which was to make things grow. When Ceres did not work, rain could not fall and crops could not grow. Finally, Ceres went to Jupiter for help.

Jupiter was powerful, but so was Pluto. Jupiter told Ceres he could get Proserpine back from Pluto if she had not eaten any of Pluto's food. As it turned out, Proserpine had eaten something. She had swallowed six seeds from a piece of fruit. Because he felt sorry for the people on earth who were suffering, Pluto told Jupiter that Proserpine could return temporarily to Ceres so she would cheer up and make crops grow again. But Pluto later came back for Proserpine and forced her to spend six months each year with him in the underworld—one month for each seed she had eaten. Every time she returned to the underworld, Ceres mourned and refused to do her job. This is how the Romans explained the seasons—when Proserpine is on earth with Ceres, it is spring and summer; when Proserpine goes to the underworld, it is fall and winter.

Directions: Answer these questions about Proserpine and Pluto.

1. What happened to Ceres when Pluto took her daughter? She was very unhappy and refused to do her job.
2. Whom did Ceres ask for help to get her daughter back? Jupiter
3. Why did Proserpine have to return to Pluto's underworld? She had to spend one month there for each seed she had eaten.
4. How long did Proserpine have to stay in the underworld each time she returned? six months

123

Comprehension: Orpheus Saves the Day

Orpheus (Or-fee-us) was a talented Greek musician. Once, by playing beautiful music on his lyre (ly-er), he caused a ship that was stuck in the sand to move into the water. (A lyre is a stringed instrument that looks like a small harp and fits in the musician's lap.) The song was about how wonderful it was to sail upon the sea. The ship itself must have thought the song was wonderful, too, because it slipped into the water and sailed away!

There was a reason the ship understood Orpheus' song. Inside the ship was a piece of wood that a goddess had given to the captain of the ship. The captain's name was Jason. Once, Jason had helped an old woman across a deep river. He later learned that the old woman was a goddess. To thank him, the goddess gave Jason a piece of wood that could talk. She told him to use the wood when he built a new ship. If he ever got stuck while building the ship and did not know what to do, the goddess told Jason to ask the wood.

Several times, Jason and his crew got instructions from the wood. Finally, the ship was finished. It was beautiful and very large. Because it was so big, Jason and his men were unable to move it into the water. They called on Hercules for help, and even he could not make it budge. That's when Orpheus saved the day with his lyre.

Directions: Answer these questions about Orpheus' amazing talent.

1. Who owned the ship that was stuck? Jason
2. Where was the ship stuck? in the sand
3. Why did the ship get stuck? It was too large to move.
4. A lyre looks like what other instrument?
   ☐ harmonica ☐ guitar ☒ harp
5. Who did Jason first ask for help to move the ship?
   ☐ Orpheus ☒ Hercules ☐ Jupiter

124

Comprehension: The *Constitution*

The *Constitution*, or "Old Ironsides," was built by the United States Navy in 1798. Its success in battle made it one of the most famous vessels in the United States.

The *Constitution's* naval career began with the war with Tripoli from 1803 to 1804. Later, it was also used in the War of 1812. During this war, it was commanded by Isaac Hull. The *Constitution* won a 30-minute battle with the British ship, *Guerriere*, in August of 1812. The *Guerriere* was nearly demolished. Later that same year, the *Constitution* was used to capture a British frigate near Brazil.

The *Constitution* was taken out of service in 1829 and was rebuilt many times over the years. Today, it is on display at the Boston Navy Yard.

Directions: Answer these questions about ...

1. What is the main idea ...

Answers will vary.

2. Which ship was almost demolished by the *Constitution*? Guerriere
3. In which two wars was the war with Tripoli, War of 1812
4. Where is the *Constitution* now on display? Boston Navy Yard
5. Complete the following time line with dates and events described above.

Constitution was built	War with Tripoli	War of 1812 Battle-Guerriere	Taken out of service	on display at Boston Navy Yard
1798	1803-1804	1812	1829	Today (2005)

125

Comprehension: The *Santa Maria, Niña,* and *Pinta*

When Christopher Columbus decided to attempt a voyage across the ocean, the ships he depended upon to take him there were called *caravels*. A caravel is a small sailing ship built by Spain and Portugal in the 15th and 16th centuries. The caravels Columbus used to sail to the New World were named the *Santa Maria, Niña,* and *Pinta*.

The ships were not very large. It is believed the *Santa Maria* was only 75 to 90 feet long, and the *Niña* and *Pinta* were only about 70 feet long. Caravels typically had three to four masts with sails attached. The foremast carried a square sail, while the others were more triangular in shape. These triangular-shaped sails were called *lateen sails*.

These three small ships were quite seaworthy and proved excellent ships for Columbus. They got him where he wanted to go.

Directions: Answer these questions about the *Santa Maria, Niña,* and *Pinta*.

1. What is a lateen sail? triangular-shaped sail
2. What is the main idea of the selection?

Answers will vary.

3. small sailing ship built by Portugal and Spain
4. Where did Columbus sail in his caravels? to the New World
5. Do some research and compare a 15th-century caravel with a ship built in the 20th century.

Answers will vary.

126

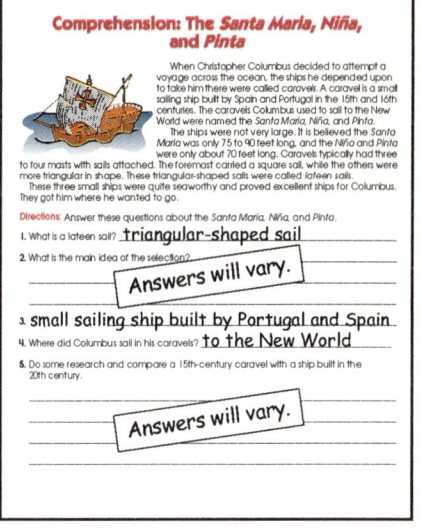

Comprehension: The *Lusitania*

The *Lusitania* was a British passenger steamship. It became famous when it was torpedoed and sunk by the Germans during World War I. On May 7, 1915, the *Lusitania* was traveling off the coast of Ireland when a German submarine fired on it without warning. The ship stood no chance of surviving the attack and sunk in an astonishing 20 minutes. 1,198 people **perished**, of whom 128 were American citizens. At the time the ship was torpedoed, the United States was not yet involved in the war. Public opinion over the attack put pressure on President Woodrow Wilson to declare war on Germany. The Germans **proclaimed** that the *Lusitania* was carrying weapons for the use of the **allies**.

This claim was later proven to be true. President Wilson demanded that the German government apologize for the sinking and make **amends**. Germany did not accept responsibility but did promise to avoid sinking any more passenger ships without first giving a warning.

Directions: Answer these questions about the *Lusitania*.

1. What does **proclaimed** mean?
2. What does **perished** mean?
3. What does **amends** mean?
4. What does **allies** me...
5. If the *Lusitania* was c... ...o you think the Germans had a right to sink it? Why or why not?

Answers will vary.

127

Comprehension: The *Titanic*

The British passenger ship, the *Titanic*, debuted in the spring of 1912. It was billed as an unsinkable ship due to its construction. It had 16 watertight compartments that would hold the ship afloat even in the event that four of the compartments were damaged.

But on the evening of April 14, 1912, during the *Titanic's* first voyage, its design proved unworthy. Just before midnight, the *Titanic* struck an iceberg, which punctured 5 of the 16 compartments. The ship sunk in a little under 3 hours. Approximately 1,513 of more than 2,220 people onboard died. Most of these people died because there weren't enough lifeboats to accommodate everyone onboard. These people were left floating in the water. Many died from exposure, since the Atlantic Ocean was near freezing in temperature. It was one of the worst ocean disasters in history.

Because of the investigations that followed the *Titanic* disaster, the passenger ship industry instituted many reforms. It is now required that there is ample lifeboat space for all passengers and crew. An international ice patrol and full-time radio coverage were also instituted to prevent such disasters in the future.

Directions: Answer these questions about the *Titanic*.

1. How did most of the 1,513 people onboard the *Titanic* exposure to cold
2. Why did this "unsinkable" ship sink? an iceberg punctured too many of its compartments
3. What changes have been made in ship safety as a result of the *Titanic* tragedy? They must have enough lifeboats, international ice patrol, full-time radio coverage.
4. There have been many attempts to rescue artifacts from the *Titanic*. But many families of the dead wish the site to be left alone, as it is the fi... ...place of their relatives. They feel burial sites should not be disrupted... ...sagree? Why?

Answers will vary.

128

Comprehension: The *Monitor* and the *Virginia*

During the Civil War, it became **customary** to cover wooden warships with iron. This increased their **durability** and made them more difficult to sink. Two such ships were built using iron. They were the *Monitor* and the *Virginia*.

Most people are more familiar with the name the *Merrimack*. The *Merrimack* was a U.S. steam frigate that had been burnt and sunk by Union forces when the Confederates were forced to abandon their navy yard. The Confederate Navy raised the hull of the *Merrimack* and rebuilt her as the **ironclad** *Virginia*.

Both the *Monitor* and the *Virginia* engaged in battle on March 9, 1862. After several hours of battle, the bulky *Virginia* had no choice but to withdraw in order to avoid the lowering tides. This battle, called *Hampton Roads*, was considered to be a tie between the two ships.

Although both ships survived the battle, they were later destroyed. Two months later, the *Virginia* was sunk by her crew to avoid capture. The *Monitor* sunk on December 31, 1862, during a storm off the coast of North Carolina.

Directions: Use context clues for these definitions.

1. **customary:**
2. **durability:**
3. **ironclad:**

Answers will vary.

Directions: Answer these questions about the *Monitor* and the *Virginia*.

1. Who won the battle between the *Virginia* and the *Monitor*? It was a tie.
2. Why would lowering tides pr... Answers will vary.
3. Describe how each ship was finally destroyed. The *Virginia* was sunk by its crew to avoid capture. The *Monitor* sunk in a storm.

129

Comprehension: Railroads

Directions: Read the information about railroads. Then, answer the questions.

As early as the 1550s, a rough form of railroad was already being used in parts of Europe. Miners in England and other areas of western Europe used horse- or mule-drawn wagons on wooden tracks to pull loads out of mines. With these tracks, the horses could pull twice as much weight as they could without them. No one could have known then that one day this simple idea would change the world.

There were many developments along the way that helped make railroads a practical and valuable form of transportation. Two of the most important were the iron track and the "flanged" wheel, which has a rim around it to hold it onto the track. The most important invention was the steam engine by James Watt in 1765.

The first railroads in the United States were built during the late 1820s and caused a lot of excitement. They were faster than other forms of travel, and they could provide service year-round, unlike boats and stagecoaches. Trains were soon the main means of travel in the U.S.

Railroads played a major part in the Industrial Revolution—the years of change when machines were first used to do work that had been done by hand for many centuries. Trains provided cheaper rates and quicker service for transporting goods. Because manufacturers could ship their goods over long distances, they could sell their products all over the nation instead of only in the surrounding cities and towns. This meant greater profits for the companies. Trains also brought people into the cities to work in factories.

1. What was the source of power for the earliest railroads? horses or mules
2. What were three important developments that made railroads a practical means of transportation? iron track / "flanged" wheels / steam engine

3. What is meant by the Industrial Revolution? the years of change from people-made to machine-made products
4. What were two ways that railroads They provided more reliable and faster transportation for people and products.

130

Main Idea: Locomotives

Directions: Read the information about locomotives. Then, answer the questions.

In the 1800s, the steam locomotive was considered by many to be a symbol of the new Industrial Age. It was, indeed, one of the most important inventions of the time. Over the years, there have been many changes to the locomotive. One of the most important has been its source of power. During its history, the locomotive has gone from steam to electric to diesel power.

The first railroads used horses or mules for power, but the development of the steam locomotive made railroads a practical means of transportation. The first steam locomotive was built in 1804 in Great Britain by Richard Trevithick. It could haul 50,000 pounds, but it was not very successful because it was so heavy it caused the tracks to fall apart. However, it encouraged other engineers to try to build steam locomotives. Two of the most important men to accept the challenge were George Stephenson and his son, Robert. Robert once won a contest to build the best locomotive. *The Rocket*, as he called it, had a top speed of 29 miles per hour.

In America, developments in steam engines were close behind those of the British. In 1830, Peter Cooper's tiny locomotive, called *Tom Thumb*, lost a famous race against a horse-drawn coach. In spite of the loss, it still convinced railroad officials that steam power was more practical than horsepower.

Just before the turn of the century, the electric locomotive was widely used. At its peak in the 1940s, U.S. railroads had 2,400 miles of electric routes.

The diesel locomotive was invented in the 1890s by Rudolf Diesel, a German engineer. The power of this locomotive was supplied by a diesel fuel engine. The diesel locomotive is still used today. It costs about twice as much as a steam locomotive to build, but it is much cheaper to operate.

1. What is the main idea of this selection?
   ___ The steam locomotive was considered a symbol of the Industrial Age.
   X Over the years, there have been many changes to the locomotive.
2. Who built the first steam locomotive in 1804? Richard Trevithick
3. How fast could *The Rocket* travel? 29 miles per hour
4. Who built the locomotive called *Tom Thumb*? Peter Cooper
5. *Tom Thumb* was in a race against a horse-drawn coach. Which won? the horse-drawn coach
6. What kind of fuel does a diesel engine use? diesel fuel

131

Comprehension: Railroad Pioneer

Directions: Read the information about railroad pioneers. Then, respond to the statements by circling **True** or **False**.

George Stephenson was born in Wylam, England, in 1781. His family was extremely poor. When he was young, he didn't go to school but worked in the coal mines. In his spare time, he taught himself to read and write. After a series of explosions in the coal pits, Stephenson built a miner's safety lamp. This helped bring him to the attention of the owners of the coal mines. They put him in charge of all the machinery.

In 1812, Stephenson became an engine builder for the mines. The owners were interested in locomotives because the cost of horse feed was so high. They wanted Stephenson to build a locomotive to pull the coal cars from the mines. His first locomotive, The *Blucher*, was put on the rails in 1814.

Stephenson was a good engineer, and he was fortunate to work for a rich employer. Between 1814 and 1826, Stephenson was the only man in Great Britain building locomotives.

When the Stockholm and Darlington Railway, the first public railroad system, was planned, Stephenson was named company engineer. He convinced the owners to use steam power instead of horses. He built the first locomotive on the line. *The Locomotion*, as it was called, was the best locomotive that had been built anywhere in the world up to that time. Over the years, Stephenson was responsible for many other important developments in locomotive design, such as improved cast-iron rails and wheels, and the first steel springs strong enough to carry several tons.

Stephenson was convinced that the future of railroads lay in steam power. His great vision of what the railroad system could become was a driving force in the early years of its development.

1. George Stephenson was an excellent student in school.	True	(False)
2. Stephenson's first invention was a miner's safety lamp.	(True)	False
3. Between 1814 and 1826, Stephenson was one of many engineers building locomotives in Great Britain.	True	(False)
4. The Stockholm and Darlington Railway was the first public railroad system.	(True)	False
5. The first locomotive on the Stockholm and Darlington line was *The Locomotion*, built by Stephenson.	(True)	False
6. Stephenson's ideas did not influence the development of the railroad system.	True	(False)

132

Tall Tales

A **tall tale** is a fictional story with exaggerated details and a "super" hero. The main character in a tall tale is much larger, stronger, smarter or better than a real person. Tall tales may be unbelievable, but they are fun to hear.

America had nearly 200,000 miles of railroad track by 1900. Because of the rapid growth and the excitement over the railroads, many colorful tall tales about railroad heroes and their adventures were told.

Directions: Read the story about John Henry. Then, answer the questions.

A Steel-Driving Man

On the night John Henry was born, forked lightning split the air and the earth shook. He weighed 44 pounds at birth, and the first thing he did was reach for a hammer hanging on the wall. "He's going to be a steel-driving man," his father told his mother.

One night, John Henry dreamed he was working on a railroad. Every time his hammer hit a spike, the sky lit up with the sparks. "I dreamed that the railroad was going to be the end of me, and I'd die with a hammer in my hand," he said. When John Henry grew up, he did work for the railroad. He was the fastest, most powerful steel-driving man in the world.

In about 1870, the steam drill was invented. One day, the company at the far end of a tunnel tried it out. John Henry's company, working at the other end, continued to use men to do the drilling. There was much bragging from both companies as to which was faster. Finally, they decided to have a contest. John Henry was matched against the best man with a steam drill.

1. 44 pounds
2. He reached for a hammer first.
3. steam drill
4. to see which was faster
5. two 20-pound hammers
6. John Henry
7. He died.

133

Context Clues: Passenger Cars

Directions: Read the information about passenger cars. Use context clues to determine the meaning of words in bold. Check the correct answers.

Early railroad passenger cars were little more than stagecoaches fitted with special wheels to help them stay on the tracks. They didn't hold many passengers, and because they were made out of wood, they were fire **hazards**. They also did not hold up very well if the train came off the track or had a **collision** with another train.

In the United States, it wasn't long before passenger cars were lengthened to hold more people. Late in the 1830s, Americans were riding in **elongated** cars with double seats on either side of a center aisle. By the early 1900s, most cars were made of metal instead of wood.

Sleeping and dining cars were introduced in the United States by the early 1860s. Over the next 25 years other improvements were made, including electric lighting, steam heat and covered **vestibules** that allowed passengers to walk between cars. All of these **luxuries** helped make railroad travel much more comfortable.

1. Based on the other words in the sentence, what is the correct definition of **hazards**?
   ___ engines X risks ___ stations
2. Based on the other words in the sentence, what is the correct definition of **collision**?
   X crash ___ race ___ track
3. Based on the other words in the sentence, what is the correct definition of **elongated**?
   ___ wooden ___ new X lengthened
4. Based on the other words in the sentence, what is the correct definition of **vestibules**?
   X passageways ___ cars ___ depots
5. Based on the other words in the sentence, what is the correct definition of **luxuries**?
   ___ additions X things offering the greatest comfort ___ inventions

134

Reading Skills: Railroads

Directions: Read the information about railroads. Then, answer the questions.

When railroads became the major means of transportation, they replaced earlier forms of travel, like the stagecoach. Railroads remained the unchallenged leader for a hundred years. Beginning in the early 1900s, railroads faced **competition** from newer forms of transportation.

Today, millions of people have their own automobiles. Buses offer inexpensive travel between cities. Large trucks haul goods across the country. Airplanes provide quick transportation over long distances. The result has been a sharp drop in the use of trains.

Today, nearly all railroads face serious problems that threaten to drive them out of business. But railroads still provide low-cost, fuel-saving transportation that will remain important. One gallon of diesel fuel will haul about four times as much by railroad as by truck. In a time when the world is concerned about saving fuel, this is but one area in which the railroads still have much to offer.

1. What is the main idea of this selection?
   ___ When railroads became the major means of transportation, they replaced earlier forms of travel.
   X Beginning in the early 1900s, railroads have faced competition from newer forms of transportation.
2. Based on the other words in the sentence, what is the correct definition of **competition**?
   X businesses trying to get the same customers
   ___ problems
   ___ support
3. What are four newer forms of transportation that have challenged railroads?
   cars, trucks, buses, airplanes
4. One gallon of diesel fuel will haul about twice as much by railroad as by truck. True (False)

135

Comprehension: Printing

Directions: Read the information about printing. Then, answer the questions.

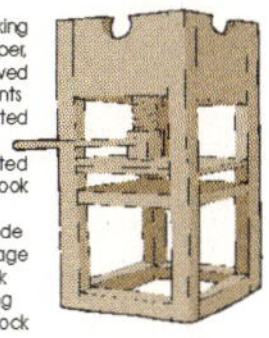

When people talk about printing, they usually mean making exact copies of an original document, such as a newspaper, magazine, or an entire book. The inventions that have allowed us to do this are some of the most important developments in history. Look around you at the many examples of printed materials. Can you imagine life without them?

Until the thirteenth century, all material had to be printed by hand, one copy at a time. To make a copy of a book took much time and effort.

The oldest known example of a printed book was made in China in 848 A.D. by Wang Chieh, who carved each page of a book by hand onto a block of wood. He then put ink on the wood and pressed it on paper. The idea of printing with wood blocks spread to Europe. The letters in these block books were made to look handwritten.

In about 1440, a German goldsmith named Johann Gutenberg developed the idea of movable type. He invented separate letters made of metal for printing. The letters could be joined together to make words and sentences. Ink was applied to the letters to print many copies of the same material. Because they were made of metal, the letters could be used over and over. This wonderful invention made it possible to have more printed material at a lower cost.

Gutenberg had other ideas that were important to printing. He developed a special type of ink that would stick to the new metal letters. Gutenberg's ideas were so successful that the process of printing went almost unchanged for more than 300 years.

1. In what country was the oldest known printed book made?
   China
2. Who made the first printed book?
   Wang Chieh
3. What is "movable type"?
   separate letters made of metal for printing
4. Who developed the idea of movable type?
   Johann Gutenberg
5. What was another important invention of Gutenberg?
   special ink

136

Comprehension: Newspapers

Directions: Read the information about newspapers. Then, answer the questions.

Newspapers keep us informed about what is going on in the world. They entertain, educate, and examine the events of the day. For millions of people worldwide, newspapers are an important part of daily life.

Newspapers are published at various intervals, but they usually come out daily or weekly. Of the nearly 60,000 newspapers published around the world, about 2,600 are published in the United States. More than half—about 1800—of them are dailies.

Some newspapers have many subscribers—people who pay to have each edition delivered to them. *The Wall Street Journal* and *USA Today* each have about two million subscribers. There are many, many newspapers with only a few thousand subscribers. These include small-town weeklies and special-interest papers, like those written for people who enjoy the same hobby.

Newspapers provide a service to the community by providing information at little cost. But newspaper publishing is a business, so like other businesses, newspapers need to make money. They can keep the cost to subscribers low and still stay in business by selling space to businesses and individuals who want to advertise products or services. In most newspapers, between one-third and two-thirds of the paper is taken up by advertising.

1. About how many newspapers are published worldwide?
   nearly 60,000
2. What services do newspapers provide?
   entertain, educate, examine events
3. What are subscribers?
   people who pay to have newspapers delivered to them
4. How often are most newspapers published?
   daily
5. What do newspapers do to keep the cost to the reader low, but still make money?
   They sell space for ads.
6. In most newspapers, about how much of the paper is taken up by advertising?
   between one-third and two-thirds

137

Comprehension: Newspapers

Directions: Read the information about the first newspapers. Then, answer the questions.

Long ago, town criers walked through cities reading important news to the people. The earliest newspapers were probably handwritten notices posted in towns for the public to read.

The first true newspaper was a weekly paper started in Germany in 1609. It was called *The Strassburg Relation*. The Germans were pioneers in newspaper publishing. Johann Gutenberg, the man who developed movable type, was German.

One of the first English-language newspapers, *The London Gazette*, was first printed in England in 1665. *Gazette* is an old English word that means "official publication." Many newspapers today still use the word *gazette* in their names.

In America, several papers began during colonial days. The first successful one, *The Boston News-Letter*, began printing in 1704. It was very small—about the size of a sheet of notebook paper with printing on both sides.

An important date in newspaper publishing was 1833. In that year, *The New York Sun* became the first penny newspaper. The paper actually did cost only a penny. The penny newspapers were similar to today's papers: they printed news while it was still new, they were the first to print advertisements and to sell papers in newsstands, and they were the first to be delivered to homes.

1. How were the earliest newspapers different from today's newspapers?
   They were handwritten notices posted in town.
2. In what year and where was the first true newspaper printed?
   1609 in Germany
3. What was the name of the first successful newspaper in America?
   The Boston News-Letter
4. Why was 1833 important in newspaper publishing?
   The first penny newspaper was published.
5. List four ways penny newspapers were like the newspapers of today.
   printed fresh news
   printed advertisements
   sold at newstands
   delivered to homes

138

Comprehension: Newspaper Jobs

Directions: Read the information about jobs at a newspaper. Then, answer the questions.

It takes an army of people to put out one of the big daily newspapers. Three separate departments are needed to make a newspaper operate smoothly: editorial, mechanical, and business.

The editorial department is the one most people think about first. That is the news-gathering part of the newspaper. The most familiar job in this department is that of the reporter—the person who obtains information for a story and writes it. A photographer takes pictures to go along with the reporter's story.

Editors are the decision-makers. There are many editors at a large newspaper. They assign stories to reporters, read the stories to be certain they are correct, and decide where and if the stories should appear in the paper. The most important stories go on the front page. There are also photo editors who choose which pictures will appear in the paper. Other workers in the editorial department include artists, copy editors, proofreaders, and cartoonists.

The biggest job in the mechanical department is printing the paper. Most large newspapers have their own printing presses. Some small papers send their work to outside printing shops. After an issue, or edition, is printed, it is ready to be sold or "circulated" to the public.

Circulation of the paper is one of the jobs of the business department. This department also sells advertising space. This is very important for newspapers. Many papers make more money selling advertising space than selling newspapers. The business department also takes care of normal business jobs, like paying employees, paying bills, and keeping records.

1. What are the three main departments at a newspaper?
   editorial, mechanical, business
2. Who gets the information for a story and writes it?
   reporter
3. Who are the decision-makers at a newspaper?
   editors
4. What is the biggest job for the mechanical department?
   printing the paper
5. What is the most important job of the business department?
   selling advertising space

139

Comprehension: News Stories

Directions: Read the information about news stories. Then, draw an **X** on the line to show the correct meaning of the bold word.

Here is an example of how a story gets into the newspaper:

Let's imagine that a city bus has turned over in a ditch, injuring some of the passengers. An **eyewitness** calls the newspaper. The editor assigns a reporter to go to the scene. The reporter talks to the passengers, driver, and witnesses who saw the accident. She finds out what they saw and how they feel, writing down their comments or tape recording their answers. At the same time, a photographer is busy taking pictures.

If there isn't time for the reporter to go back to the newsroom, she could call and **dictate** the story to a copytaker who types the story into a computer. Many reporters use portable computers which allow them to write the story on the spot and then send it back to the office over the telephone by modem.

Next, an editor reads the story, checking facts, grammar, and spelling. Meanwhile, the photographer's film is developed and a picture is chosen.

The story is set in print. On most newspapers today, this is done with a computer. The computer makes sets of columns of type, which are pasted onto a sheet of paper exactly the same size as a newspaper page. A **proofreader** checks the story for mistakes. The newspaper is now ready for printing. The presses begin to run.

Miles of paper are turned into thousands of printed, cut, and folded newspapers. They are counted, put into bundles, and placed in waiting trucks. Within a few hours, people can read about the bus accident in their daily newspaper.

1. Based on the other words in the sentence, what is the correct definition of **eyewitness**?
   ____ a reporter
   __X__ a person who saw what happened
   ____ a lawyer
2. Based on the other words in the sentence, what is the correct definition of **dictate**?
   ____ govern without regard for what people want
   ____ use a dictionary
   __X__ read a story word for word for someone else to write
3. Based on the other words in the sentence, what is the correct definition of **proofreader**?
   __X__ person who checks for mistakes
   ____ person who shows proof he has read a book
   ____ a teacher

140

Comprehension: News Services

Directions: Read the information about news services. Then, answer the questions.

When people read daily newspapers, they expect to see current news from all over the world. Some newspapers have offices or reporters in Washington, D.C., and other major cities around the world. Most newspapers rely on news services for international news. News services are organizations that gather and sell news to papers, radio, and television stations. They are sometimes referred to as "wire services," because they originally sent stories over telegraph or Teletype lines, or "wires."

The two largest news services are the Associated Press and United Press International. Stories sent by these services have their initials—AP or UPI—at the beginning of the article. All large American newspapers are members of either the AP or UPI service.

At one time, people had to wait for messengers to arrive by foot, horse, or ship to learn the news. By the time it reached a newspaper, news could be months old.

Gathering news from around the world became much faster after the invention of the telegraph, Teletype, telephone, and transatlantic cable. Today, satellites, computer modems, and fax machines can send stories, pictures, and even videos around the world in seconds.

1. wire services
2. Associated Press (AP) and United Press International (UPI)
3. telegraph, Teletype, telephone, transatlantic cable, satellites, computers, fax machines
4. to obtain news from all over the world
5. by messengers on foot, horse, or ship

141

Comprehension: Samuel Clemens

Directions: Read the information about Samuel Clemens.

Samuel Langhorne Clemens was born in Florida, Missouri, in 1835. In his lifetime, he gained worldwide fame as a writer, lecturer, and humorist.

Clemens first worked for a printer when he was only 12 years old. Soon after that he worked on his brother's newspaper.

Clemens traveled frequently and worked as a printer in New York, Philadelphia, St. Louis, and Cincinnati. On a trip to New Orleans in 1857, he learned the difficult art of steamboat **piloting**. Clemens loved piloting and later used it as a background for some of his books, including *Life on the Mississippi*.

A few years later, Clemens went to Nevada with his brother and tried gold mining. When this proved unsuccessful, he went back to writing for newspapers. At first he signed his humorous pieces with the name "Josh." In 1863, he began signing them Mark Twain. The words "mark twain" were used by riverboat pilots to mean two fathoms (12 feet) deep, water deep enough for steamboats. From then on, Clemens used this now-famous **pseudonym** for all his writing.

As Mark Twain, he received attention from readers all over the world. His best-known works include *Tom Sawyer* and *The Adventures of Huckleberry Finn*. These two books about boyhood adventures remain popular with readers of all ages.

Directions: Check the correct answer.

1. Based on the other words in the sentence, what is the correct definition of **pseudonym**?
   ____ book title
   __X__ a made-up name used by an author
   ____ a humorous article
2. Based on the other words in the sentence, what is the correct definition of **piloting**?
   ____ driving an airplane
   __X__ steering a steamboat on a river
   ____ being a train engineer

Directions: Write the answers.

1. Under what name did Samuel Clemens write his books?
   Mark Twain
2. What do the words "mark twain" mean?
   two fathoms (12 feet)
3. Besides author, list two other jobs held by Mark Twain.
   reporter, pilot, printer, miner
4. List two of the best-known books written by Mark Twain.
   Tom Sawyer and The Adventures of Huckleberry Finn

142

Comprehension: The Arctic Circle

Directions: Read the article about the Arctic Circle. Then, answer the questions.

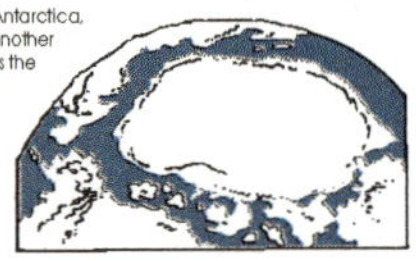

On the other side of the globe from Antarctica, at the northernmost part of the earth, is another icy land. This is the Arctic Circle. It includes the North Pole itself and the northern fringes of three continents—Europe, Asia, and North America, including the state of Alaska—as well as Greenland and other islands.

The seasons are opposite at the two ends of the earth. When it is summer in Antarctica, it is winter in the Arctic Circle. In both places, there are very long periods of sunlight in summer and very long nights in the winter. On the poles themselves, there are six full months of sunlight and six full months of darkness each year.

Compared to Antarctica, the summers are surprisingly mild in some areas of the Arctic Circle. Much of the snow cover may melt, and temperatures often reach 50 degrees in July. Antarctica is covered by water—frozen water, of course—so nothing can grow there. Plant growth is limited in the polar regions not only by the cold, but also by wind, lack of water, and the long winter darkness.

In the far north, willow trees grow but only become a few inches high. The annual rings, the circles within the trunk of a tree that show its age and how fast it grows, are so narrow in those trees that you need a microscope to see them!

A permanently frozen layer of soil, called **permafrost**, keeps roots from growing deep enough into the ground to anchor a plant. Even if a plant could survive the cold temperatures, it could not grow roots deep enough or strong enough to allow the plant to get very big.

1. What three continents have land included in the Arctic Circle?
   Europe   Asia   North America
2. Is the Arctic Circle generally warmer or colder than Antarctica?
   warmer
3. What is **permafrost**? a permanently frozen layer of soil
4. Many tall pine trees grow in the Arctic Circle. True (False) — "False" circled

143

Main Idea: The Polar Trail

Directions: Read the information about explorers to Antarctica.

A recorded sighting of Antarctica, the last continent to be discovered, was not made until the early nineteenth century. Since then, many brave explorers and adventurers have sailed south to conquer the icy land. Their achievements once gained as much world attention as those of the first astronauts.

Long before the continent was first spotted, the ancient Greeks suspected there was a continent at the bottom of the earth. Over the centuries, legends of the undiscovered land spread. Some of the world's greatest seamen tried to find it, including Captain James Cook in 1772.

Cook was the first to sail all the way to the solid field of ice that surrounds Antarctica every winter. In fact, he sailed all the way around the continent but never saw it. Cook went farther south than anyone had ever gone. His record lasted 50 years.

Forty years after Cook, a new kind of seamen sailed the icy waters. They were hunters of seals and whales. Sailing through unknown waters in search of seals and whales, these men became explorers as well as hunters. The first person known to sight Antarctica was an American hunter, 21-year-old Nathaniel Brown Palmer in 1820.

Directions: Draw an **X** on the blank for the correct answer.

1. The main idea is:
   ____ Antarctica was not sighted until the early nineteenth century.
   __X__ Many brave explorers and adventurers have sailed south to conquer the icy land.
2. The first person to sail to the ice field that surrounds Antarctica was
   ____ Nathaniel Brown Palmer.
   __X__ Captain James Cook.
   ____ Neal Armstrong.
3. His record for sailing the farthest south stood for
   ____ 40 years.
   __X__ 50 years.
   ____ 500 years.
4. The first person known to sight Antarctica was
   ____ an unknown ancient Greek.
   ____ Captain James Cook.
   __X__ Nathaniel Brown Palmer.
5. His profession was
   __X__ hunter.
   ____ ship captain.
   ____ explorer.

144

Comprehension: Polar Bears

Directions: Read the information about polar bears. Then, respond to the statements by circling **True** or **False**.

Some animals are able to survive the cold weather and difficult conditions of the snow and ice fields in the Arctic polar regions. One of the best known is the polar bear.

Polar bears live on the land and the sea. They may drift hundreds of miles from land on huge sheets of floating ice. They use their great paws to paddle the ice along. Polar bears are excellent swimmers, too. They can cross great distances of open water. While in the water, they feed mostly on fish and seals.

On land, these huge animals, which measure 10 feet long and weigh about 1,000 pounds, can run 25 miles an hour. Surprisingly, polar bears live as plant-eaters rather than hunters while on land. Unlike many kinds of bears, polar bears do not hibernate. They are active the whole year.

Baby polar bears are born during the winter. At birth, they are pink and almost hairless. These helpless cubs weigh only two pounds—less than one-third the size of most human infants. The mother bears raise their young in dens dug in snowbanks. By the time they are 10 weeks old, polar bear cubs are about the size of puppies and have enough white fur to protect them in the open air. The mothers give their cubs swimming, hunting, and fishing lessons. By the time autumn comes, the cubs are left to survive on their own.

1. Polar bears can live on the land and the sea. (True) False
2. Polar bears are excellent swimmers. (True) False
3. Polar bears hibernate in the winter. True (False)
4. A newborn polar bear weighs more than a newborn human baby. True (False)
5. Mother polar bears raise their babies in caves. True (False)
6. Father polar bears give the cubs swimming lessons. True (False)

145

Comprehension: Walruses

Directions: Read the information about walruses. Then, respond to the statements by circling **True** or **False**.

A walrus is actually a type of seal that lives only in the Arctic Circle. It has two huge upper teeth, or tusks, which it uses to pull itself out of the water or to move over the rocks on land. It also uses its tusks to dig clams, one of its favorite foods, from the bottom of the sea. On an adult male walrus, the tusks may be three and a half feet long!

A walrus has an unusual face. Besides its long tusks, it has a big, bushy mustache made up of hundreds of movable, stiff bristles. These bristles also help the walrus push food into its mouth. Except for small wrinkles in the skin, a walrus has no outer ears.

Like a seal, the walrus uses its flippers to help it swim. Its front flippers serve as paddles, and while swimming, it swings the back of its huge body from side to side. A walrus looks awkward using its flippers to walk on land, but don't be fooled! A walrus can run as fast as a man.

Baby walruses are born in the early spring. They stay with their mothers until they are two years old. There is a good reason for this—they must grow little tusks, at least three or four inches long, before they can catch their own food from the bottom of the sea. Until then, they must stay close to their mothers to eat. A young walrus that is tired from swimming will climb onto its mother's back for a ride, holding onto her with its front flippers.

1. The walrus is a type of seal found only in the Arctic Circle.
2. List two ways the walrus uses its tusks.
   to pull itself out of water — to dig clams
3. A walrus cannot move quickly on land. True (False)
4. A walrus has a large, bushy mustache. (True) False
5. A baby walrus stays very close to its mother until it is two years old. (True) False
6. Baby walruses are born late in fall. True (False)

146

Comprehension: The Desert

Directions: Read the information about the desert. Then, respond to the statements by circling **True** or **False**.

Deserts are found where there is little rainfall or where the rainfall for a whole year falls in only a few weeks' time. Ten inches of rain may be enough for many plants to survive if the rain is spread throughout the year. If the 10 inches of rain falls during one or two months and the rest of the year is dry, those plants may not be able to survive and a desert may form.

When people think of deserts, they may think of long stretches of sand. Sand begins as tiny pieces of rock that get smaller and smaller as wind and weather wear them down. Sand dunes, or hills of drifting sand, are formed as winds move the sand across the desert. Grain by grain, the dunes grow over the years, always shifting with the winds and changing shape. Most dunes are only a few feet tall, but they can grow to be several hundred feet high.

There is, however, much more to a desert than sand. In the deserts of the southwestern United States, cliffs and canyons were formed from thick mud that once lay beneath a sea more than a hundred million years ago. Over the centuries, the water drained away. Wind, sand, rain, heat, and cold all wore away at the remaining rocks. The faces of the desert mountains are always changing—very, very slowly—as these forces of nature continue to work on the rock.

Most deserts have a surprising variety of life. There are plants, animals, and insects that have adapted to life in the desert. During the heat of the day, a visitor may see very few signs of living things, but as the air begins to cool in the evening, the desert comes to life. As the sun begins to rise again in the sky, the desert once again becomes quiet and lonely.

1. Deserts are found where there is little rainfall or where the rainfall for a whole year falls in only a few weeks. (True) False
2. Sand begins as tiny pieces of rock that get smaller and smaller as wind and weather wear them down. (True) False
3. Sand dunes were formed from thick mud that once lay beneath a sea more than a hundred million years ago. True (False)
4. The faces of the desert mountains can never change. True (False)

147

Comprehension: Desert Weather

Directions: Read the information about desert weather. Then, answer the questions.

One definition of a desert is an area that has, on average, less than 10 inches of rain a year. Many deserts have far less than that. Death Valley in California and Nevada, for example, averages fewer than 2 inches of rain each year. The driest of all deserts is the Atacama Desert in Chile, where no rain has been known to fall in 400 years!

Some deserts have a regular rainy season each year, but usually desert rainfall is totally unpredictable. An area may have no rainfall for many years. Sometimes a passing cloud may look like it will send relief to the waiting land, but only a "ghost rain" falls. This means that the hot, dry air dries up the raindrops long before they ever reach the ground.

The temperature in the desert varies greatly. The daytime temperatures in the desert frequently top 120 degrees. In Death Valley, temperatures have been known to reach 190 degrees! In most parts of the world, moisture in the air works like a blanket to hold the heat of the day close to the earth at night. But, because it has so little moisture, the desert has no such blanket. As a result, nighttime temperatures are very chilly. Temperatures have been known to drop 50 or even 100 degrees at night in the desert.

1. On the average, how much rainfall is there in a year in a desert?
   less than 10 inches
2. Where is the driest desert in the world? in Chile
3. What is a "ghost rain"? hot dry air dries up rain before it reaches the ground
4. In other parts of the ... to the earth at night? moisture in the air
5. What happens to the temperature in the desert at night?
   it gets very chilly

148

Context Clues: Desert Plants

Directions: Read the information about desert plants. Use context clues to determine the meaning of the bold words. Then, check the correct answers.

Desert plants have special features, or adaptations, that allow them to **survive** the harsh conditions of the desert. A cactus stores water in its tissues when it rains. It then uses this supply of water during the long dry season. The tiny needles on some kinds of **cacti** may number in the tens of thousands. These sharp thorns protect the cactus. They also form tiny shadows in the sunlight that help keep the plant from getting too hot.

Other plants are able to live by dropping their leaves. This cuts down on the **evaporation** of their water supply in the hot sun. Still other plants survive as seeds, protected from the sun and heat by tough seed coats. When it rains, the seeds **sprout** quickly, bloom, and produce more seeds that can **withstand** long dry spells.

Some plants spread their roots close to the earth's surface to quickly gather water when it does rain. Other plants, such as the mesquite, have roots that grow 50 or 60 feet below the ground to reach underground water supplies.

1. Based on the other words in the sentence, what is the correct definition of **survive**?
   X continue to live
   ___ bloom in the desert
   ___ flower
2. Based on the other words in the sentence, what is the correct definition of **evaporation**?
   X water loss from heat
   ___ much-needed rainfall
   ___ boiling
3. Based on the other words in the sentence, what is the correct definition of **withstand**?
   X put up with
   ___ stand with another
   ___ take from
4. Based on the other words in the sentence, what is the correct definition of **cacti**?
   ___ a type of sand dune
   X more than one cactus
   ___ a caravan of camels
5. Based on the other words in the sentence, what is the correct definition of **sprout**?
   ___ a type of bean that grows only in the desert
   X begin to grow
   ___ a small flower

149

Comprehension: Lizards

Directions: Read the information about lizards. Then, answer the questions.

Lizards are reptiles, related to snakes, turtles, alligators, and crocodiles. Like other reptiles, lizards are cold-blooded. This means their body temperature changes with that of their surroundings. However, by changing their behavior throughout the day, they can keep their temperature fairly constant.

Lizards are among the many animals that live in deserts. They usually come out of their burrows early in the morning. Most lizards lie in the sun to get warm before starting their daily activities. In mid-morning, they hunt for food. If it becomes too hot, lizards can raise their tails and bodies off the ground to help cool off. At mid-day, they return to their burrows or crawl under rocks for several hours. Late in the day, they again lie in the sun to absorb heat before the chilly desert night falls.

Like all animals, lizards have ways of protecting themselves. Some types of lizards have developed a most unusual defense. If a hawk or other animal grabs one of these lizards by its tail, the tail will break off. The tail will continue to wiggle around to distract the attacker while the lizard runs away. A month or two later, the lizard grows a new tail.

There are about 3,000 kinds of lizards, and all of them can bite, but only two types of lizards are poisonous: the Gila monster of the southwestern United States and the Mexican bearded lizard. Both are short-legged, thick-bodied reptiles with fat tails. These lizards do not attack people and will not bite them unless they are attacked.

1. What can a lizard do if it becomes too hot? raise its tail and body off the ground, crawl in burrows or under rocks
2. What is an unusual defense some lizards have developed to protect themselves?
   tails will break off and distract predators
3. What two types of lizards are poisonous? Gila monster and Mexican bearded lizard

150

Main Idea: People in the Desert

Directions: Read the information about people in the desert. Then, answer the questions.

Long before Europeans came to live in America, Native Americans had discovered ways of living in the desert. Some of these Native Americans were hunters or belonged to wandering tribes that stayed in the desert for only short periods of time. Others learned to farm and live in villages. They made their houses of trees, clay, and brush.

The desert met all of their needs for life: food, water, skins for clothing, materials for tools, weapons, and shelter. For meat, the desert offered deer, birds, and rabbits for hunting. When these animals were hard to find, the Native Americans would eat mice and lizards. Many desert plants, such as the prickly pear and mesquite, provided moisture, fruit, and seeds that could be eaten.

The first Europeans in the American deserts were searching for furs and metals, like silver and gold. They explored, but did not settle in the desert. The early pioneers were usually unsuccessful at living in the desert. They found the great heat and long dry periods too difficult. When they moved away, they left behind empty mining camps, houses, and sheds that slowly fell apart in the sun and wind.

1. What is the main idea of this selection?
   - X Before Europeans came to live in America, Native Americans had discovered ways of successfully living in the desert.
   - ___ Some Native Americans were hunters or belonged to wandering tribes who stayed in the desert for only short periods of time.
2. Who were the first people to live in the deserts of North America? Native Americans
3. What did the Native Americans use to make their houses in the desert? trees, clay, and brush
4. What kinds of food did the Native Americans find in the desert? meat, desert plants
5. What were the first Europeans who came to the desert looking for? furs and metals (silver and gold)

151

Main Idea: Camels

Directions: Read the information about camels. Then, answer the questions.

Camels are well suited to desert life. They can cope with infrequent supplies of food and water, blazing heat during the day, low temperatures at night, and sand blown by high winds.

There are two kinds of camels: the two-humped bactrian and the one-humped dromedary. The dromedary is the larger of the two. It has coarse fur on its back that helps protect it from the sun's rays. The hair on its stomach and legs is short to prevent overheating. When camels **molt** in the spring, their wool can be collected in tufts from the bushes and ground.

The legs of the dromedary are much longer than those of the bactrian. Animals that live in very hot countries tend to have longer legs. This gives them a larger area of body surface from which heat can escape. Bactrian camels live in the deserts of central Asia where winters are bitterly cold, so they are not as tall as dromedaries.

Both kinds of camels have pads on their feet that keep them from sinking into the sand as they walk. A camel's long neck allows it to reach the ground to drink water and eat grass without having to bend its legs. It also can reach up to eat leaves from trees.

Camels do not store water in their humps as many people believe. The hump is for fat storage. When there is plenty of food, the camel's hump swells and feels firm. During the dry season when there is little food, the fat is used up and the hump shrinks and becomes soft.

1. What is the main idea of this selection?
   - X Camels are well suited to desert life.
   - ___ There are two kinds of camels.
2. Based on the other words in the sentence, what is the correct definition of **molt**?
   - ___ turns into a butterfly
   - X sheds its hair
   - ___ becomes overheated
3. What are the two kinds of camels? bactrian and dromedary
4. Why don't camels sink into the sand when they walk? They have pads on their feet.
5. What is the purpose of a camel's hump? to store fat

152

Comprehension: Desert Lakes

Directions: Read the information about lakes in the desert. Then, answer the questions.

A few deserts have small permanent lakes. While they may be a welcome sight in the desert, the water in them is not fit for drinking. They are salt lakes. Rain from nearby higher land keeps these lakes supplied with water, but the lakes are blocked in with nowhere to drain. Over the years, mineral salts collect in the water and build up to a high level, making the water undrinkable.

Most desert lakes are only temporary. Occasional rains may fill them to depths of several feet, but in a matter of weeks or months, all the water has been dried up by the heat and sun. The dried lake beds that remain are called **playas**. Some playas are simply areas of sun-baked mud; others are covered with a sparkling layer of salt.

Perhaps the most unusual desert lake is in central Australia. It is called Lake Eyre. It is a huge lake—nearly 3,600 square miles in area—but it is almost totally dry most of the time. Since it was discovered in 1840, it has been filled only two times. Both times, the lake completely dried up again within a few years.

1. Why is the water in a desert lake not fit for drinking? It is salt water.
2. Why are the lakes in the desert salt lakes? Mineral salts collect there.
3. Why are most desert lakes only temporary? The water evaporates.
4. What is a **playa**? a dried lake bed
5. What is the name of the unusual desert lake in central Australia? Lake Eyre
6. How big is this desert lake? nearly 3,600 square miles

153

Reading a Recipe

Directions: Read the recipe. Then, answer the questions.

Graham Cracker Smoothies

Graham crackers

Icing:
- 2 T. peanut butter
- 2 T. butter
- 2 c. powdered sugar
- milk

Break graham crackers in half. Mix peanut butter, butter, and powdered sugar with a spoon. Add enough milk to make creamy icing. Stir vigorously until no lumps remain. Spread on graham cracker half and top with another graham cracker half, sandwich style. Enjoy!

The smoothie icing will keep in the refrigerator for two days.

1. What do these abbreviations stand for?
   - T. tablespoon
   - c. cup
2. Number the steps in the correct order.
   - 4 Spread icing on graham crackers.
   - 3 Add milk and stir until creamy.
   - 1 Break graham crackers in half.
   - 5 Eat and enjoy.
   - 2 Mix the peanut butter, butter, and powdered sugar together.
3. Why is it important to follow the correct sequence when cooking? to be certain it turns out correctly

154

Reading Skills: Labels

Labels provide information about products.

Directions: Read the label on the medicine bottle. Then, answer the questions.

Remember: Children should never take medicines without their parents' knowledge and consent.

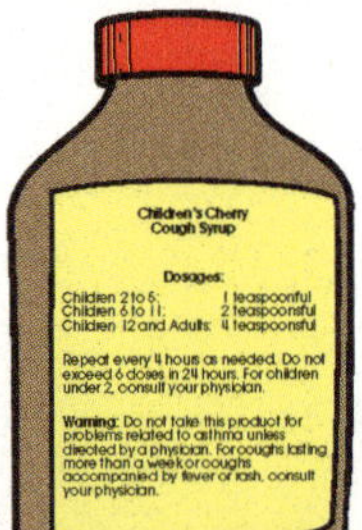

1. What is the dosage, or amount to be taken, for a three-year-old child? 1 teaspoonful
2. How often can you take this medicine if it is needed? every 4 hours
3. How many times a day can you take this medicine? do not exceed 6 times a day
4. What should you do before taking the medicine if you have a rash in addition to your cough? consult your physician
5. Will this medicine help you if you are sneezing? no
6. What is the dosage for an adult? 4 teaspoonsful

155

Reading Skills: Newspapers

Directions: Write the answers to the following questions.

1. What is the name of your daily local newspaper?
2. List the sections included in your local newspaper.
3. What sections of the newspaper do you read on a regular basis?
4. Ask a parent which sections he or sh...
5. Find the editorial se... ...per. An editorial is the opinion of one person. Write the main idea ... editorial.
6. If you could work at a newspaper, which job would you like? Why?

Answers will vary.

Directions: Read a copy of *USA Today*. You can find a copy in most libraries. Compare it to your local paper.

1. How are they alike?
2. How are they different?

156

Reading Skills: A Newspaper Index

An **index** is a listing in a book, magazine, or newspaper that tells where to find items or information.

Newspapers provide many kinds of information. You can read about national events, local news, the weather, and sports. You will also find opinions, feature stories, advice columns, comics, entertainment, recipes, advertisements, and more. A guide that tells you where to find different types of information in a newspaper is called a **newspaper index**. An index of the newspaper usually appears on the front page.

Directions: Use the newspaper index to answer the questions.

Business	8	Local News	5-7
Classified Ads	18-19	National News	1-4
Comics	20	Radio-TV	17
Editorials	9	Sports	11-13
Entertainment	14-16	Weather	10

1. Where would you look for the results of last night's basketball games?
   Section: Sports Page(s) 11-13
2. Where would you find your favorite cartoon strip?
   Section: Comics Page(s) 20
3. Where would you find opinions of upcoming elections?
   Section: Editorials Page(s) 9
4. Where would you find a used bicycle to buy?
   Section: Classified Ads Page(s) 18-19
5. Where would you find out if you need to wear your raincoat tomorrow?
   Section: Weather Page(s) 10
6. Where would you find the listing of tonight's TV shows?
   Section: Radio-TV Page(s) 17
7. Which would be first, a story about the president's trip to Europe or a review of the newest movie?
   the president's trip to Europe

157

Reading Skills: Classified Ads

A **classified ad** is an advertisement in a newspaper or magazine offering a product or service for sale or rent.

Example: For Sale: Used 26" 30-speed bike. $100. Call 555-5555.

Directions: Read these advertisements. Then, answer the questions.

1\.
Yard Work
Breaking Your Back?
Give Mike and Jane a crack!
Mowing, raking, trash hauled.
References provided.
Call 555-9581.

2\.
Pet Sitter
Going on vacation?
Away for the weekend?
I am 14 years old and have experience caring for dogs and cats.
Your home or mine.
Excellent references.
Call Sally Trent.
Phone: 555-8250.

3\.
Singing Lessons for All Ages!
Be popular at parties!
Fulfill your dreams!
20 years coaching experience.
Madame Rinaud . . .
Coach to the Stars.
555-5331.

1. popularity and fulfillment of dreams
2. Is it fact or opinion? opinion
3. What fact is offered in the 20 years coaching experience
4. Example: Yard work breaking your back? Give Mike and Jane a crack!
5. Which ad gives the most facts? #2
6. Which ad is based mostly on opinion? #3

158

Reading Skills: Schedules

A **schedule** lists events or programs by time, date, and place or channel.

Example:

Packer Preseason Games

August 14	7 P.M.	NY Jets at Green Bay
August 23	7 P.M.	Denver Broncos at Madison
August 28	3 P.M.	Saints at New Orleans
September 2	Noon	Miami Dolphins at Green Bay

Directions: Use this newspaper television schedule to answer the questions.

Evening

6:00	3	Let's Talk! Guest: Animal expert, Jim Porter
	5	Cartoons
	8	News
	9	News
7:00	3	Farm Report
	5	Movie. *A Laugh a Minute* (1955) James Rayburn. Comedy about a boy who wants to join the circus.
	8	Spin for Dollars!
	9	Cooking With Cathy. Tonight: Chicken with mushrooms
7:30	3	Double Trouble (comedy). The twins disrupt the high school dance.
	8	Wall Street Today: Stock Market Report
8:00	3	NBA Basketball. Teams to be announced.
	8	News Special. "Saving Our Waterways: Pollution in the Mississippi."
	9	Movie. *At Day's End* (1981). Michael Collier, Julie Romer. Drama set in World War II.

1. What two stations have the news at 6:00? 8 and 9
2. What time would you turn on the television to watch a funny movie? 7:00 P.M.
   What channel? 5
3. What could you watch if you are a sports fan? NBA Basketball
   What time and channel is it on? 8:00 P.M. Channel 3
4. Which show title sounds like it could be a game show? Spin for Dollars!
5. What show might you want to watch if you are interested in the environment?
   "Saving Our Waterways: Pollution in the Mississippi"
   What time and channel is it on? 8:00 P.M. Channel 8

159

Comprehension: Facts About Folk Music

Folk music literally means music "of the folks," and it belongs to everyone. The names of the musicians who composed most folk music have long been forgotten. Even so, folk music has remained popular because it tells about the lives of people. Usually, the tune is simple, and even though folk songs often have many verses, the words are easy to remember. Do you know the words to "She'll Be Comin' 'Round the Mountain"?

Although no one ever says who "she" is, the verses tell you that she will be "riding six white horses" and that "we'll go out to greet her." The song also describes what will be eaten when she comes (chicken and dumplings) and what those singing will be wearing (red pajamas).

"Clementine" is a song that came out of the California gold rush in the mid-1800s. It tells the story of a woman who was "lost and gone forever" when she was killed. ("In a cavern, in a canyon, excavating for a mine/Met a miner '49er and his daughter, Clementine.")

Another famous folk song is "Swing Low, Sweet Chariot." This song was sung by slaves in the United States and today is sung by people of all races. The words "Swing low, sweet chariot, coming for to carry me home . . . ." describe the soul being united with God after death. Like other folk songs that sprang from slaves, "Swing Low, Sweet Chariot" is simple, moving, and powerful.

Directions: Answer these questions about folk music.

1. What is the purpose of folk music? It tells about people's lives.
2. What food is sung about in "She'll Be Comin' 'Round the Mountain"? chicken and dumplings
3. Where did Clementine live?
   ☐ Florida ☐ Mississippi ☒ California
4. Where in the United States do you think "Swing Low, Sweet Chariot" was first sung?
   ☐ the North ☐ the West ☒ the South

160

Recalling Details: Woodwinds

There are four kinds of woodwind instruments in modern bands. They are flutes, oboes, clarinets, and bassoons. They are called "woodwind" instruments for two sensible reasons. In the beginning, they were all made of wood. Also, the musician's breath, or "wind," was required to play them.

Although they are all woodwinds, these instruments look different and are played differently. To play an oboe, the musician blows through a mouthpiece on the front of the instrument. The mouthpiece, called a *reed*, is made of two flat pieces of a kind of wood called *cane*. Clarinet players also blow into a reed mouthpiece. The clarinet has only one reed in its mouthpiece.

To play the flute, the musician blows across a hole near one end of the instrument. The way the breath is aimed helps to make the flute's different sounds. The bassoon is the largest woodwind instrument. Bassoon players blow through a mouthpiece that goes through a short metal pipe before it goes into the body of the bassoon. It makes a very different sound from the clarinet or the oboe.

Woodwind instruments also have keys—but not the kind of keys that open locks. These keys are more like levers that the musician pushes up and down. The levers cover holes. When the musician pushes down on a lever, it closes that hole. When the player lifts his or her finger, it opens the hole. Different sounds are produced by controlling the amount of breath, or "wind," that goes through the holes.

Directions: Answer these questions about woodwind instruments.

1. What instruments are in the oboe, clarinet, flute, bassoon
2. In the beginning, they were all made of wood. They require "breath" to play them.
3. How is a flute different from the It does not have a mouthpiece.
4. What happens when a musician pushes down on a woodwind key? It covers a hole in the instrument.
5. How would a woodwind musician open the holes on his or her instrument? lift his or her finger

161

Comprehension: Harp Happenings

If you have ever heard a harpist play, you know what a lovely sound a harp makes. Music experts say the harp is among the oldest of instruments. It probably was invented several thousand years ago in or near Egypt.

The first harps are believed to have been made by stretching a string tightly between an empty tortoise shell and a curved pole. The empty shell magnified the sound the string made when it was plucked. More strings were added later so that more sounds could be made. Over the centuries, the shape of the harp gradually was changed into that of the large, graceful instruments we recognize today.

Here is how a harpist plays a harp. First, he or she leans the harp against his or her right shoulder. Then, the harpist puts his or her hands on either side of the harp and plucks its strings with both hands.

A harp has seven pedals on the bottom back. The audience usually cannot see these pedals. Most people are surprised to learn about them. The pedals are connected to the strings. Stepping on a particular pedal causes certain strings to tighten. The tightening and loosening of the strings makes different sounds; so does the way the strings are plucked with the hands.

At first glance, harps look like simple instruments. Actually, they are rather complicated and difficult to keep in tune. A harpist often spends as long as half an hour before a performance tuning his or her harp's strings so it produces the correct sounds.

Directions: Answer these questions about harps.

1. When were harps invented? several thousand years ago
2. Where were harps invented? in or near Egypt
3. What is a person who plays the harp called? harpist
4. The harpist leans the harp against his or her
   ☒ right shoulder. ☐ left shoulder. ☐ left knee.
5. How many pedals does a harp have?
   ☐ five ☐ six ☒ seven
6. Harps are easy to play. ☐ true ☒ false

162

Comprehension: Brass Shows Class

If you like band music, you probably love the music made by brass instruments. Bright, loud, moving, and magnificent—all these words describe the sounds made by brass.

Some of the earliest instruments were horns. Made from hollowed-out animal horns, these primitive instruments could not possibly have made the rich sounds of modern horns that are made of brass.

Most modern brass bands have three instruments—tubas, trombones, and trumpets. Combined, these instruments can produce stirring marches, as well as haunting melodies. The most famous composer for brass instruments was John Phillip Sousa. Born in Washington, D.C., in 1854, Sousa was a military band conductor and composer. He died in 1932, but his music is still very popular today. One of Sousa's most famous tunes for military bands is "Stars and Stripes Forever."

Besides composing band music, Sousa also invented a practical band instrument—the sousaphone. The sousaphone is a huge tuba that makes very low noises. Because of the way it curls around the body, a sousaphone is easier to carry than a tuba, especially when the musician must march. This is exactly why John Phillip Sousa invented it!

Directions: Answer these questions about brass instruments.

1. Who invented the sousaphone? John Phillip Sousa
2. What were the first horns made from? hollowed-out animal horns
3. Where was John Phillip Sousa born? Washington, D.C.
4. When did John Phillip Sousa die? 1932
5. Why did Sousa invent the sousaphone? It was easier to carry than a tuba.
6. What types of instruments make up a modern brass band? tubas, trombones, and trumpets

163

Comprehension: Violins

If you know anything about violin music, chances are you have heard the word *Stradivarius* (Strad-uh-vary-us). Stradivarius is the name for the world's most magnificent violins. They are named after their creator, Antonio Stradivari.

Stradivari was born in northern Italy and lived from 1644 to 1737. Cremona, the town he lived in, was a place where violins were manufactured. Stradivari was very young when he learned to play the violin. He grew to love the instrument so much that he began to make them himself.

Violins were new instruments during Stradivari's time. People made them in different sizes and shapes and of different types of wood. Stradivari is said to have been very particular about the wood he selected for his violins. He took long walks alone in the forest to find just the right tree. He is also said to have used a secret and special type of varnish to put on the wood. Whatever the reasons, his violins are the best in the world.

Stradivari put such care and love into his violins that they are still used today. Many of these are in museums. But some wealthy musicians, who can afford the thousands and thousands of dollars they cost, own Stradivarius violins.

Stradivari passed his methods on to his sons. But the secrets of making Stradivarius violins seem to have died out with the family. Their rarity, as well as their mellow sound, make Stradivarius violins among the most prized instruments in the world.

Directions: Answer these questions about Stradivarius violins.

1. Where did Stradivari live? Cremona
2. Why did he begin making because he loved them so much
3. Why are Stradivarius violins special? He used special wood and varnish.
4. Where can Stradivarius violins be found today? museums and some wealthy musicians
5. How did Stradivari select the wood for his violins? He took long walks alone in the forest to find just the right tree
6. Who else knew Stradivari's secrets for making such superior violins? his sons

164

Main Idea: Creating Art

No one knows exactly when the first human created the first painting. Crude drawings and paintings on the walls of caves show that humans have probably always expressed themselves through art. These early cave pictures show animals being hunted, people dancing, and other events of daily life. The simplicity of the paintings reflect the simple lifestyles of these primitive people.

The subjects of early paintings also help to make another important point. Art is not created out of nothing. The subjects an artist chooses to paint reflect the history, politics, and culture of the time and place in which he or she lives. An artist born and raised in New York City, for example, is not likely to paint scenes of the Rocky Mountains. An artist living in the Rockies is not likely to paint pictures of city life.

Of course, not all paintings are realistic. Many artists choose to paint pictures that show their own "inner vision" as opposed to what they see with their eyes. Many religious paintings of earlier centuries look realistic but contain figures of angels. These paintings combine the artist's inner vision of angels with other things, such as church buildings, that can be seen.

Directions: Answer these questions about creating art.

1. Circle the main idea:

   Art was important to primitive people because it showed hunting and dancing scenes, and is still important today.

   (Through the ages, artists have created paintings that reflect the culture, history, and politics of the times, as well as their own inner visions.)

2. Why is an artist living in the Rocky Mountains less likely to paint city scenes? Artists usually portray something that is part of their lives.
3. In addition to what they see with their eyes, what do some artists' paintings also show? their inner feelings or visions

165

Comprehension: Leonardo da Vinci

Many people believe that Leonardo da Vinci, an Italian artist and inventor who lived from 1452 to 1519, was the most brilliant person ever born. He was certainly a man ahead of his time! Records show that da Vinci loved the earth and was curious about everything on it.

To learn about the human body, he dissected corpses to find out what was inside. In the 15th and 16th centuries, dissecting the dead was against the laws of the Catholic church. Leonardo was a brave man!

He was also an inventor. Leonardo invented a parachute and designed a type of helicopter—5 centuries before airplanes were invented! Another of da Vinci's major talents was painting. You have probably seen a print, or copy, of one of his most famous paintings. It is called *The Last Supper*, and shows Jesus eating his final meal with his disciples. It took da Vinci 3 years to paint *The Last Supper*. The man who hired da Vinci to do the painting was upset. He went to da Vinci to ask why it was taking so long. The problem, said da Vinci, was that in the painting, Jesus has just told the disciples that one of them would betray him. He wanted to get their expressions exactly right as each cried out, "Lord, am I the one?"

Another famous painting by da Vinci is called the *Mona Lisa*. Have you seen a print of this painting? Maybe you have been lucky enough to see the original hanging in a Paris art museum called the Louvre (Loov). If so, you know that Mona Lisa has a wistful expression on her face. The painting is of a real woman, the wife of an Italian merchant. Art historians believe she looks wistful because one of her children had recently died.

Directions: Answer these questions about Leonardo da Vinci.

1. How old was da Vinci when he died? 67
2. Name two of da Vinci's inventions. parachute and helicopter
3. Name two famous paintings by da Vinci. *Mona Lisa, The Last Supper*
4. In which Paris museum does *Mona Lisa* hang? ☐ Lourre ☐ Loure ☒ Louvre

166

Comprehension: Michelangelo

Another famous painter of the late 14th and early 15th centuries was Michelangelo Buonarroti. Michelangelo, who lived from 1475 to 1564, was also an Italian. Like da Vinci, his genius was apparent at a young age. When he was 13, the ruler of his hometown of Florence, Lorenzo Medici (Muh-dee-chee), befriended Michelangelo and asked him to live in the palace. There, Michelangelo studied sculpture and met many artists.

By the time he was 18, Michelangelo was a respected sculptor. He created one of his most famous religious sculptures, the *Pieta* (pee-ay-tah), when he was only 21. Then, the Medici family abruptly fell from power and Michelangelo had to leave Florence.

Still, his work was well known and he was able to make a living. In 1503, Pope Julius II called Michelangelo to Rome. He wanted Michelangelo to paint the tomb where he would someday be buried. Michelangelo preferred sculpting to painting, but no one turned down the pope! Before Michelangelo finished his painting, however, the pope ordered Michelangelo to begin painting the ceiling of the Sistine Chapel inside the Vatican. (The Vatican is the palace and surrounding area where the pope lives in Rome.)

Michelangelo was very angry! He did not like to paint. He wanted to create sculptures. But no one turns down the pope. After much complaining, Michelangelo began work on what would be his most famous project.

Directions: Answer these questions about Michelangelo.

1. How old was Michelangelo when he died? 89
2. What was the first project Pope Julius II asked Michelangelo to paint? his tomb
3. What is the palace and grounds where the Pope lives
4. What was the second project the pope asked Michelangelo to do?

   ☐ paint his tomb's ceiling ☒ paint the Sistine Chapel's ceiling

167

Comprehension: Rembrandt

Most art critics agree that Rembrandt (Rem-brant) was one of the greatest painters of all time. This Dutch artist, who lived from 1606 to 1669, painted some of the world's finest portraits.

Rembrandt, whose full name was Rembrandt van Rijn, was born in Holland to a wealthy family. He was sent to a fine university, but he did not like his studies. He only wanted to paint. He sketched the faces of people around him. During his lifetime, Rembrandt painted eleven portraits of his father and nearly as many of his mother. From the beginning, the faces of old people fascinated him.

When he was 25, Rembrandt went to paint in Amsterdam, a large city in Holland where he lived for the rest of his life. There, he married a wealthy woman named Saskia, whom he loved deeply. She died from a disease called tuberculosis (to-bur-ku-lo-sis) after only eight years of marriage, leaving behind a young son named Titus (Ty-tuss).

Rembrandt was heartbroken over his wife's death. He began to spend all his time painting. But instead of painting what his customers wanted, he painted exactly the way he wanted. Unsold pictures filled his house. They were wonderful paintings, but they were not the type of portraits people wanted. Rembrandt could not pay his debts. He and his son were thrown into the streets. The creditors took his home, his possessions, and his paintings. One of the finest painters on earth was treated like a criminal.

Directions: Answer these questions about Rembrandt.

1. How old was Rembrandt when he died? 63
2. In what city did he spend most of his life? Amsterdam
3. How many children did Rembrandt have? one
4. Rembrandt's wife was named

   ☐ Sasha. ☒ Saskia. ☐ Saksia.

5. These filled his house after his wife's death.

   ☐ friends ☐ customers ☒ unsold paintings

168

Nouns

A **noun** is a word that names a person, place, or thing.

Examples:
person — friend
place — home
thing — desk

Nouns are used many ways in sentences. They can be the subjects of sentences.

Example: Noun as subject: Your high-topped **sneakers** look great with that outfit.

Nouns can be direct objects of a sentence. The **direct object** follows the verb and completes its meaning. It answers the question **who** or **what**.

Example: Noun as direct object: Shelly's family bought a new **car**.

Nouns can be indirect objects. An **indirect object** comes between the verb and the direct object and tells **to whom** or **for whom** something was done.

Example: Noun as indirect object: She gave **Tina** a big hug.

Directions: Underline all the nouns. Write **S** above the noun if it is a subject, **DO** if it is a direct object, or **IO** if it is an indirect object. The first one has been done for you.

1. Do alligators (S) eat people (DO)?
2. James (S) hit a home run (DO), and our team (S) won the game (DO).
3. The famous actor (S) gave Susan (IO) his autograph (DO).
4. Eric (S) loaned Keith (IO) his bicycle (DO).
5. The kindergarten children (S) painted cute pictures (DO).
6. Robin (S) sold David (IO) some chocolate chip cookies (DO).
7. The neighbors (S) planned a going-away party (DO) and bought a gift (DO).
8. The party (S) and gift (S) surprised Kurt (DO) and his family (DO).
9. My scout leader (S) told our group (IO) a funny joke (DO).
10. Karen (S) made her little sister (IO) a clown costume (DO).

169

Nouns

Directions: Write 10 nouns for each category. Answers will vary, but may include:

People
1. boy
2. girl
3. child
4. adult
5. person
6. friend
7. neighbor
8. classmate
9. man
10. woman

Places
1. park
2. zoo
3. bridge
4. town
5. city
6. country
7. river
8. desert
9. ocean
10. forest

Things
1. cat
2. dog
3. ball
4. bat
5. cup
6. fork
7. table
8. pen
9. computer
10. ruler

170

Proper and Common Nouns

Proper nouns name specific people, places, or things.

Examples: Washington, D.C., Thomas Jefferson, Red Sea

Common nouns name nonspecific people, places, or things.

Examples: man, fortress, dog

Directions: Underline the proper nouns and circle the common nouns in each sentence.

1. My friend, Josephine, loves to go to the docks to watch the boats sail into the harbor.
2. Josephine is especially interested in the boat named *Maiden Voyage.*
3. This boat is painted red with yellow stripes and has several large masts.
4. Its sails are white and billow in the wind.
5. At Misty Harbor, many boats are always sailing in and out.
6. The crews on the boats rush from bow to stern working diligently to keep the sailboats moving.
7. Josephine has been invited aboard *Maiden Voyage* by its captain.
8. Captain Ferdinand knew of her interest in sailboats so he offered a tour.
9. Josephine was amazed at the gear aboard the boat and the skills of the crew.
10. It is Josephine's dream to sail the Atlantic Ocean on a boat similar to *Maiden Voyage*.
11. Her mother is not sure of this dangerous dream and urges Josephine to consider safer dreams.
12. Josephine thinks of early explorers like Christopher Columbus, Amerigo Vespucci, and Leif Ericson.
13. She thinks these men must have been brave to set out into the unknown waters of the world.
14. Their boats were often small and provided little protection from major ocean storms.
15. Josephine believes that if early explorers could challenge the rough ocean waters, she could, too.

171

Abstract and Concrete Nouns

Concrete nouns name something that can be touched or seen.
Abstract nouns name an idea, a thought, or a feeling which cannot be touched or seen.

Examples:
concrete nouns: house, puppy, chair
abstract nouns: love, happiness, fear

Directions: Write **concrete** or **abstract** in the blank after each noun.

1. loyalty abstract
2. lightbulb concrete
3. quarter concrete
4. hope abstract
5. satellite concrete
6. ability abstract
7. patio concrete
8. door concrete
9. allegiance abstract
10. Cuba concrete
11. Michael Jordan concrete
12. friendship abstract
13. telephone concrete
14. computer concrete

Directions: Write eight nouns for each category. Answers will vary, but may include:

Concrete	Abstract
1. glass	1. love
2. battle	2. faith
3. apple	3. loneliness
4. pig	4. fear
5. ruler	5. anger
6. hand	6. joy
7. page	7. pride
8. paper	8. shyness

172

For Sale

A **possessive noun** shows ownership. To make a singular noun possessive, add an **apostrophe** and an **s**.

To make a plural noun possessive, check the last letter—if the word ends in **s**, add an apostrophe after it to show posession. If it doesn't, add an apostrophe and an **s**.

Examples: my mother's friends   the parents' organization   the women's group

Directions: The Eastborough Youth Center is having its yearly rummage sale. Everyone in town has been asked to donate items to sell to raise money. Rewrite the missing noun from each sentence as a possessive.

1. Carlos's (Carlos) feet had grown, so he brought his used inline skates.
2. Jason's (Jason) chess set was old but had all the pieces.
3. Maddie's (Maddie) toy mouse was broken and no one wanted to buy it.
4. On the other hand, her brother's (brother) teddy bear sold right away.
5. The children's (children) toys were all labeled with price tags.
6. The parents' (parents) job was to take the money.
7. At 2:00, there was an announcement: "someone's (someone) car lights are on."
8. A little girl called out, "Hey, that's my sister's (sisters) car!"
9. We were all surprised when one table's (table) leg gave out and all the donated books fell on the floor.
10. We propped the table back up with the janitor's (janitor) rope and picked up the books.
11. At 3:00, the Director's (Director) husband brought cookies for the volunteers to enjoy.

Directions: Now, fill in the blanks with possessive nouns of your own.

Answers will vary.

1. Belinda was happy when a boy bought ______ toys she had found in her ______ garage.
2. At 5:00, the sale ______ hard work was finished for the day.
3. ______ mother counted the proceeds from the sale; they had earned over $500!

173

A Thunk in the Night

An **interrogative pronoun** asks a question. **Who**, **what**, and **which** are all interrogative pronouns.

An **indefinite pronoun** does not refer to a specific person, place, or thing. **Somebody**, **anyone**, **all**, **everyone**, **something**, **anything**, **both**, **either**, **none**, and **nothing** are all indefinite pronouns.

Directions: Use the code below to fill in the missing interrogative and indefinite pronouns. Once you have finished, go back and circle all the interrogative pronouns.

a	b	c	d	e	f	g	h	i	j	k	l	m	n	o	p	q	r	s	t	u	v	w	x	y	z
z	y	x	w	v	u	t	s	r	q	p	o	n	m	l	k	j	i	h	g	f	e	d	c	b	a

It was midnight when I glanced at the clock. I had been asleep, but something awakened me. THUNK! Didn't anyone hear anything? Apparently not, because everyone was still sleeping soundly.

I decided to wake my sister. I shook her, saying, "There's someone outside. Listen!" She sat up slowly, rubbing her eyes. THUNK! There it was again.

"What is that? Who could it be?" she asked.

Both of us ran to the window.

We saw nothing! THUNK! There it was again.

"That's coming from the bird feeder!" she said.

"What birds come to the feeder at night?"

"None that I know about," I said.

THUNK! We heard it again.

"Let's get the flashlights," my sister said.

"Which do you want?" I asked.

"Either is fine," she answered. Guess what we saw. A raccoon! That's what was making the thunking sound. All I can say is that I'm glad the mystery is solved!

174

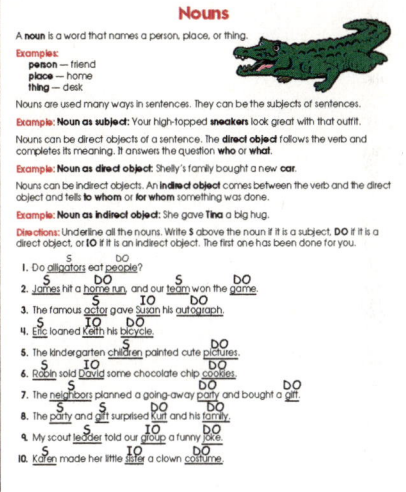

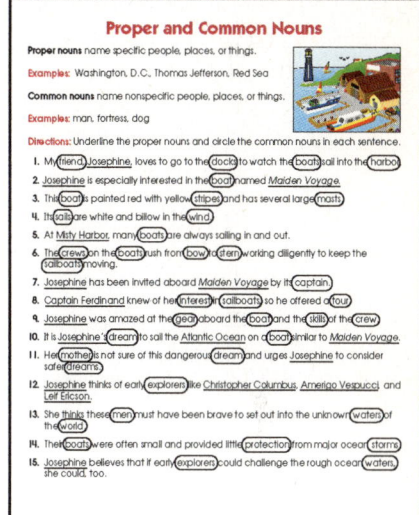

Do You Agree?

A pronoun must agree with its **antecedent**, the word to which it refers. Choosing the correct pronoun can be tricky when your antecedent is an **indefinite pronoun** such as **someone**, **nobody**, **several**, **few**, and **most**. These rules can help:

- Use **his** or **her** if the antecedent is a singular pronoun.
- Use **their** if the antecedent is plural.

Some indefinite pronouns like **most** and **none** can be singular or plural depending on how they are used in the sentence. If it has more than one antecedent joined by **or** or **nor**, the pronoun should agree with the antecedent that is closer to it.

Directions: Underline the pronoun in parentheses that agrees with its antecedent. Give yourself 3 points for each correct item. Then, add up your total points and check the score card at the bottom of the page.

1. ___ Someone left (their, <u>his or her</u>) backpack on the bus.
2. ___ Most of my friends like (<u>their</u>, his or her) classes.
3. ___ She should have had each guest bring (their, <u>his or her</u>) own lunch.
4. ___ Linda and Andy found (<u>their</u>, her or her) notebooks.
5. ___ One of my brothers lost (their, <u>his</u>) baseball mitt.
6. ___ Neither Ann nor Jackie brought (their, <u>her</u>) sneakers.
7. ___ Anyone who wants to go should ask (their, <u>his or her</u>) parents.
8. ___ A few of the parents drove (<u>their</u>, his or her) vans.
9. ___ Each of the boys took (their, <u>his</u>) jacket.
10. ___ Beth or Angie rode (their, <u>her</u>) bike today.
11. ___ Dave and Mark ran into (<u>their</u>, his) friends at the park.
12. ___ None of the girls brought along (<u>their</u>, her) lunch.
13. ___ Does anybody want to read (their, <u>his or her</u>) report?
14. ___ No one has finished (their, <u>his or her</u>) science project yet.
15. ___ Several of the neighbors left (<u>their</u>, his or her) lights on all night.
16. ___ Both of my parents like (<u>their</u>, his or her) job.
17. ___ No one has taken (their, <u>his or her</u>) seat yet.
18. ___ Others are in (<u>their</u>, his or her) room.

_____ = total points

45 - 54	30 - 42	18 - 27	3 - 15
Great job! You know your stuff!	Good going! You're on your way.	Good try! Keep at it.	Reread the rules and try again.

175

Singular or Plural?

A **singular noun** names one person, place, or thing. A **plural noun** names more than one person, place, or thing.

Directions: First, read the rules for making plural nouns. Next, cover the rules with a sheet of paper. Write the plural for each verb listed at the bottom of the page. Finally, compare your answers to the rules. How did you do?

For regular nouns:

- Add **s** to most singular nouns to make them plural: dog/dogs, restaurant/restaurants, crayon/crayons.
- If a word ends in **s**, **sh**, **ch**, or **x**, add **es** to make it plural: class/classes, beach/beaches, fox/foxes.
- If a noun ends in a **consonant** and **y**, change the **y** to **i** and add **es**: party/parties, jelly/jellies, lady/ladies.

For irregular nouns:

- Some nouns have the same singular and plural form: fish/fish, deer/deer.
- Some nouns change spelling completely when they become plural: child/children, goose/geese.
- Some nouns that end in **f** or **fe** can be made plural by replacing the **f** or **fe** with **v** and adding **es**: leaf/leaves, wife/wives.
- Other nouns that end in **f** can be made plural simply by adding **s**: chief/chiefs, oaf/oafs.
- If a noun ends in a consonant followed by **o**, check the dictionary to find out the plural form. Some end in **s** and some end in **es**: cello/cellos, tomato/tomatoes.

1. wolf	wolves	9. jetty	jetties
2. cheese	cheeses	10. galosh	galoshes
3. baby	babies	11. Johnson	Johnsons
4. buffalo	buffaloes	12. bus	buses
5. Walsh	Walshes	13. county	counties
6. idea	ideas	14. sandwich	sandwiches
7. knife	knives	15. sheriff	sheriffs
8. piano	pianos	16. life	lives

176

Perplexing Plurals

calves, echoes, elves, geese, halves, handkerchiefs, heroes, leaves, moose, potatoes, scarves, shelves, thieves, tomatoes, wives, wolves, women, yourselves

Some plurals involve changes in vowels or even consonants. These are called **irregular plurals**. Here are some common rules for spelling plurals.

Most words ending in **f** or **fe** form the plural by changing the **f** or **fe** to **v** and adding **es**. **Example:** wolf-wolves

A few words ending in **f** just add **s**. **Example:** chief-chiefs

Words ending in **o** add **s** or **es**. **Example:** buffalo-buffaloes

Some plurals involve changes within the word.
Examples: foot-feet mouse-mice

Some singular and plural forms have the same spelling.
Examples: deer-deer sheep-sheep

Directions: Write the plural form of each word from the word list in the appropriate category.

f to **v**, add **es**

calves, elves, halves, leaves, scarves, shelves, thieves, wives, wolves, yourselves

same singular and plural: moose

add **s** only: handkerchiefs

vowel change: geese, women

end in **o**, add **es**: echoes, heroes, potatoes, tomatoes

Directions: Complete the following analogies using the words from the word list.

1. **Snow** is to **shovel** as leaves are to **rake**.
2. **Boys** are to **men** as **girls** are to women.
3. Scarves are to **neck** as **belts** are to **waist**.
4. **Lives** are to **life** as calf are to **calf**.
5. **Mouse** is to **mice** as **goose** is to geese.

177

Persistent Plurals

anniversary, beauty, birthday, chimney, decoy, dictionary, highway, holiday, industry, monkey, mortuary, party, quantity, salary, strawberry, survey, turkey, valley

Words ending in **y**, preceded by a vowel, form the plural by adding **s** to the singular. **Example:** boy→boys

Words ending in **y**, preceded by a consonant, form the plural by changing the **y** to **i** and adding **es**.
Example: bunny→bunnies

Directions: Using the rules above, write the **singular** and **plural** forms of each word from the word list in the appropriate category.

vowel **y** = add **s**

1.	birthday	birthdays
2.	chimney	chimneys
3.	decoy	decoys
4.	highway	highways
5.	holiday	holidays
6.	monkey	monkeys
7.	survey	surveys
8.	turkey	turkeys
9.	valley	valleys

consonant **y** = change **y** to **i** + **es**

1.	anniversary	anniversaries
2.	beauty	beauties
3.	dictionary	dictionaries
4.	industry	industries
5.	mortuary	mortuaries
6.	party	parties
7.	quantity	quantities
8.	salary	salaries
9.	strawberry	strawberries

Directions: On the lines below, rewrite the two rules above in your own words.

When a word ends in vowel y, add an s to make a plural. When a word ends in consonant y, change the y to i and add es to make a plural.

178

Transitive Tongue Twisters

A **transitive verb** is an action verb that needs a direct object to complete a sentence's meaning.

Directions: Use the pattern **noun-transitive verb-noun** to write some tongue twisters in alphabetical order. The nouns and verb in each tongue twister must begin with the same letter. **Hint:** Think of your transitive verbs first!

A Apples attract ants.
B Betty bothered the bears.
C Cathy caught a cab.
D ___ E ___ F ___ G ___ H ___ I ___ J ___ K ___ L ___ M ___
N ___ O ___ P ___ Q ___ R ___ U ___ V ___ W ___ X ___ Y ___ Z ___

Answers will vary.

179

The Art Exhibit

A **verb phrase** consists of one **main verb** and one or more **helping verbs**. The main verb is the most important verb in a verb phrase.

Directions: The following is a list of quotes overheard at Lincoln School's Fall Art Exhibit. Find the verb phrase in each quote. Then, circle the main verb and underline the helping verbs. The first one has been done for you.

1. "Who <u>could have</u> (drawn) that picture?"
2. "Bobby <u>must have</u> (been) the artist. He <u>has been</u> (drawing) since the third grade."
3. "My daughter painted that picture. I <u>will be having</u> it (framed) as soon as the exhibit is over."
4. "The art department said that they <u>will be</u> (organizing) another exhibit soon."
5. "I <u>am going</u> to (draw) something for the next exhibit."
6. "Eric <u>will</u> (show) his painting, too. He <u>has been</u> (working) on it for the past few weeks."
7. "Any student <u>can be</u> (considered) for one of the exhibits. But only the best work <u>is</u> (shown.)"
8. "We <u>must not</u> (bring) food or drinks to the room; if someone spilled, the artwork <u>could be</u> (ruined.)"
9. "That's Mr. Franklin, the art teacher. He <u>will be</u> (showing off) the artwork once everyone is here."
10. "The name of the artist <u>must be</u> (written) on each work."
11. "You <u>will</u> (recognize) many of the artists' names."
12. "This is the best exhibit the school <u>has</u> (put on) in two years!"

180

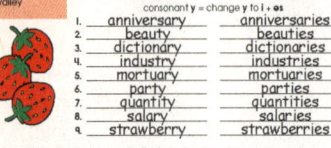

Linking Verbs

Linking verbs link the subject to a word in the predicate. The linking verbs most often used are **am**, **is**, **are**, **was**, and **were**.

Example:
We were **happy** about the outcome.

A linking verb may be followed by a **predicate noun**, which renames the subject, or a **predicate adjective**, which describes the subject.

Examples:
Harry is a **teacher**. (predicate noun)

Answers may include:

Directions: Complete each sentence with a predicate noun.

1. Sarah is a skater.
2. Her best friend is a swimmer.

Directions: Circle each predicate noun. Underline the noun or pronoun in the subject that is renamed.

1. The children were actors.
2. The setting of the play was a garden.
3. Butterflies are main characters in the play.
4. Ralph is the star.

Directions: Complete each sentence with a predicate adjective.

1. Today's weather is sunny.
2. Tom will be funny.

Directions: Circle each predicate adjective. Underline the noun or pronoun in the subject that is described.

1. The trap-door spider is clever.
2. Its building skills are amazing.
3. The webs covering the walls were soft and silky.
4. The trap was invisible.

181

Irregular Verbs

Verbs that do not add **ed** to show the past tense are called **irregular verbs**. Irregular verbs change in spelling in the past tense.

Examples:

Present	Past	Past With Helpers
begin	began	(has, have) begun
see	saw	(has, have) seen
drive	drove	(has, have) driven

Directions: Fill in the blanks on the chart. You may refer to a dictionary.

Present	Past	Past With Helpers
speak	spoke	spoken
take	took	taken
ride	rode	ridden
choose	chose	chosen
ring	rang	rung
go	went	gone
drink	drank	drunk
drive	drove	driven
draw	drew	drawn
know	knew	known
eat	ate	eaten
do	did	done

Directions: Underline the correct verb in each sentence below.

1. Martha has (began, begun) her research project.
2. First, she (chose, chosen) the topic.
3. She (drove, driven) many places to locate information.
4. Martha made a list of the interviews she had (did, done).
5. She (spoke, spoken) to people of many ages.
6. Many (knew, known) a great deal about the subject.
7. While interviewing people, Martha had (took, taken) notes.
8. Diagrams were (drew, drawn) for the project.

182

Forms of Be, Do, and Have

Some forms of the verb **be** can be used as linking or helping verbs. Three forms of **be** cannot be used alone as verbs: **be**, **being**, and **been**. These must always be used with helping verbs.

Examples:
Polar bears **are** carnivores. (**be** as linking verb)
The polar bear **is** hunting the seal. (**be** as helping verb)
A polar bear **has been** seen near here. (**be** with helping verb)
Forms of **be**: am, is, are, was, were, be, being, been

Directions: Complete each sentence below with the correct form of the verb **be** found in parentheses. Add helping verbs where needed.

1. Polar bears are excellent swimmers. (is, are)
2. The polar bear was seen running at a speed of 35 miles per hour. (was, being)
3. I am sure I saw a polar bear swimming in the water. (am, are)
4. Polar bears have been seen swimming many miles from shore. (been, have been)

The verbs **do** and **have** can be used as main verbs or as helping verbs.

Examples:
I **have** traveled to Canada to see polar bears. (helping verb)
I **did** my report on polar bears yesterday. (main verb)
Forms of **do**: do, did, done   Forms of **have**: have, has, had

Directions: Complete the story below using the correct forms of the verbs **do** and **have**.

I do believe polar bears are very beautiful. I have seen them along the coast of Alaska. I did see one come up to our tour bus. By the age of 10 years, a male polar bear has grown to its full size. Countries around the Arctic have done a very good job of trying to save the polar bear from extinction. Polar bears have beautiful coats which have attracted hunters. Now, the bears have protection from hunters by law.

183

Troublesome Verb Pairs

Don't confuse verbs that have similar meanings.

Lay means *put* or *place*.
Lie means *rest* or *recline*.

Set means *put something somewhere*.
Sit means *sit down*.

Let means *allow*.
Leave means *allow to remain*.

Teach means *show how*.
Learn means *find out*.

Lend means *give to someone*.
Borrow means *get from someone*.

Directions: Write the correct verb on each blank below.

"Mark, did you set (set, sit) the saddle on the fence?" David asked.
"Yes, David. I was going to leave (let, leave) it in the barn, but it was heavy."
Did you learn (teach, learn) how to throw the saddle onto your horse's back yet?" Mark asked.
"Yes, and then I needed to lie (lay, lie) down and rest," David answered.
"I was going to lend (lend, borrow) you a hand, but I was too busy trying to learn (teach, learn) how to rope," David remarked.
"Will you let (let, leave) me borrow (lend, borrow) your horse tomorrow morning?" Mark inquired.
"Sure, Mark. I'm going to just sit (set, sit) under a tree and read a book tomorrow morning," David responded.

Directions: Write the correct verb from the parentheses for each sentence.

1. Tell your dog to lie (lay, lie) down in front of the barn.
2. Please, lay (lay, lie) that saddle down in front of the stall and set (set, sit) the bridle on the table.
3. Sit (Set, Sit) on that bale of hay and rest your tired legs.
4. Will you let (let, leave) me wear your boots tomorrow?
5. Don't leave (let, leave) those oats there.
6. I want to learn (teach, learn) how to trim my horse's hooves.
7. We will certainly be happy to teach (teach, learn) you.

184

Review of Verbs

Directions: Underline the complete verb in the following sentences. Be sure to include any helping verbs. Write if the verb is an **action** verb or **being** verb and whether the main verb is **regular** or **irregular**.

action regular **He stepped onto the plane.**

being irregular 1. Black soot and brilliant diamonds are both carbon.
being irregular 2. Diamonds are crystals of carbon.
action regular 3. The carbon must be pressed very hard.
action regular 4. It must be heated to a high temperature at the same time.
action irregular 5. Miners usually find diamonds deep in the ground.
being irregular 6. For centuries, most diamond mines were in India.
action irregular 7. Now the biggest diamond mines are found in Africa.
action irregular 8. One day in 1866, some children saw a pretty pebble in a river near Hopetown, South Africa.
action regular 9. It looked like frosted glass.
action irregular 10. The children brought it home with them.
action regular 11. One day, a neighbor offered money for it.
action irregular 12. The children gave it to him for nothing.
action irregular 13. The children did not know the value of the stone.
being irregular 14. It was a diamond.
action irregular 15. Word about this discovery spread quickly.
action regular 16. Other people hunted for diamonds nearby.
action regular 17. Many of them were disappointed.
action irregular 18. However, some people found diamonds in the area.
action regular 19. They were blessed with good fortune.
action regular 20. Diamonds were discovered in other parts of Africa as well.

185

Where in the World?

A **verb** expresses an action or a state of being. The **tense** of a verb tells whether that action or state of being is taking place in the present, the past, or the future.

present tense = happening now
past tense = already happened
future tense = will happen

Directions: Underline the verb or verbs in each sentence and write whether they are past tense, present tense, or future tense on the line. Then, tell where you think the writer is going.

1. past My best friend, Jake, moved to the East Coast last summer.
2. future This afternoon we will see each other for the first time in a year.
3. past My parents surprised me with a plane ticket for my birthday.
4. present Jake and his parents live in the Empire State now.
5. present His mom has a cool job as a translator at the U.N.
6. past I packed all my stuff last night, except for my Yankees cap Jake sent me.
7. present I am excited about seeing Jake after so long.
8. past I hardly slept at all last night.
9. present My dad says it is time to leave for the airport.
10. future The flight will take about four hours.
11. future I will bring along a book and a couple of games to play.
12. future I will call my parents as soon as the plane lands at La Guardia Airport.
13. past I promised my mom three times already.
14. future On Friday, Jake and I will visit the "Lady With the Lamp" and Ellis Island.
15. present Jake's dad also has tickets for a Yankees game.
16. Where is the writer going?
He is going to New York City.

186

GRADE
5
I. Reading
A. Directions
B. Sequencing
C. Main Idea
II. Writing
A. Capitalization
B. Proofreading

Manuel the Magnificent

The **present tense** tells about something that exists or is happening now. Sometimes you add **s** or **es** to a base verb when the subject is singular.

Manuel Magnifico!

The **past tense** tells about something that has happened or existed in the past. Most regular verbs in the past tense end in **d** or **ed**.

The **future tense** tells about something that will exist or take place in the future. You usually use the helping verbs **will** or **shall** with the main verb.

Directions: Use a verb from the box in the indicated tense to correctly complete each sentence.

place	applaud	perform	borrow	move	observe	plan
volunteer	hope	select	reveal	climb	amaze	attend

1. Manuel the Magnificent __will amaze__ you with his act. **future**
2. He __performs__ some of the coolest tricks I've ever seen. **present**
3. I __will attend__ his matinee and evening performances today. **future**
4. One time, Manuel __borrowed__ a dollar bill from an audience member and __placed__ it at one end of the table. **past**
5. After saying the word "Manuelmagnifico," the dollar bill slowly and mysteriously __moved__ toward his hand! **past**
6. This afternoon I __will observe__ much more carefully to figure out how he does it. **future**
7. A good magician rarely __reveals__ how a trick is done. **present**
8. Last year, I __volunteered__ to let him saw me in half. **past**
9. When I __climbed__ from the box unharmed, everyone __applauded__ enthusiastically. **past**
10. Manuel __plans__ to do my favorite trick tonight—making someone disappear right before your eyes. **present**
11. Perhaps he __will select__ me to be the one who disappears. **future**
12. Someday I __hope__ to become as good a magician as Manuel. **present**

187

As a Matter of Fact . . .

An **adjective** is a word that describes a noun or a pronoun. It answers questions such as which one, how many, or what kind of?

Directions: Read the facts below. Circle each adjective and draw an arrow to the noun it describes. Then, write the adjective where it belongs on the chart.

1. The "red eye" is not a terrible disease but an overnight flight.
2. The human body contains eight pints of blood.
3. A bald eagle is not really bald. It has white feathers on its head.
4. Presidents of the United States have had many unusual pets, including an alligator, a turkey, a parrot, raccoons, and a donkey.
5. The imaginary lines that mark the time zones are called meridians.
6. At night, sea otters wrap themselves in beds of kelp, a type of large seaweed, so the currents do not take them out to sea.
7. Mount McKinley is the highest mountain in the United States and is located in Alaska, the biggest and coldest state.
8. On a ship, the day is divided into five watches of four hours each and two watches of two hours each.
9. Among those astronauts who walked on the Moon, Neil Armstrong was first.
10. The eye of the giant squid is reported to be up to 15 inches across.

How many?
What kind of?
Which one?

How Many?	What Kind Of?		Which One?
eight	red	highest	those
first	terrible	biggest	
many	overnight	coldest	
two	human	imaginary	
five	unusual	time	
four	bald	giant	
fifteen	white	large	
	sea		

188

This and That

A **demonstrative adjective** points out a specific person or thing and answers the question which one or which ones.

This and **these** point out nearby people or things. **That** and **those** point out people or things farther away. Use **these** and **those** with plural nouns. Use **this** and **that** with singular nouns.

Directions: Help Clarence the Cartoonist meet his deadline by writing **this**, **that**, **these**, or **those** to complete the sentence in each speech balloon.

If you give me that magazine, I'll give you this book.
I think these grapes are much sweeter than those over there.
I like this sweater better than all of those other jackets over there.
Try one of these cookies and a piece of that pie.

189

Proper Adjectives

Adjectives are words that describe nouns. **Proper adjectives** are formed from proper nouns, and they must be capitalized. Other adjectives are called **common adjectives**.

Examples:
proper adjectives: French toast, **American** flag
common adjectives: cold toast, **waving** flag

Directions: Circle all the adjectives in the sentences below.

1. Camels have carried loads across desert sands for centuries.
2. They were once the only means of transporting goods across the Sahara Desert and Middle Eastern deserts.
3. The Sahara Desert is in the North African desert region.
4. The Arabian camel has one hump, while the Bactrian camel has two humps.
5. The Bactrian camel got its name long ago from a Central Asian country known as Bactria.
6. Both types of camels are used in some Asian regions.
7. In wars, fighting men have ridden the faithful camel.
8. The camel Napoleon rode during his Egyptian campaign was later put in an exhibit.

Directions: Write each circled adjective under the proper heading.

Proper Adjectives	Common Adjectives
1. Sahara	1. desert
2. Middle Eastern	2. only
3. Sahara	3. desert
4. North African	4. one
5. Arabian	5. two
6. Bactrian	6. some
7. Bactrian	7. fighting
8. Central Asian	8. faithful
9. Asian	
10. Egyptian	

190

Adverbs Modify

You have learned that adverbs modify verbs. An **adverb** can also modify **adjectives** and **other adverbs**. These adverbs usually tell **how much** or **to what degree**.

Examples:
*The eagle's descent was **very** steep.*
(modifies "steep," an adjective)
*The eagle attacked the fish **quite** suddenly.*
(modifies "suddenly," an adverb)

Directions: Underline only the adverbs in the sentences below that modify an adjective or another adverb. Draw an arrow to the word that each modifies. In the blank, write if the modified word is an adjective or an adverb.

1. The eagle spread its wings very wide. *adverb*
2. It had to fly quite far to the lake. adverb
3. The eagle is an extremely graceful bird. adjective
4. It is much larger than most birds. adjective
5. Its hooked beak is rather sharp. adjective
6. The eagle watched the lake very carefully. adverb
7. A large trout is really tasty food for the eagle. adjective
8. A beautiful rainbow trout jumped quite suddenly out of the water. adverb
9. The eagle has extremely sharp eyesight. adverb
10. It swooped almost instantly toward the fish. adverb

Directions: Complete each sentence with an adverb that modifies the adjective or adverb. Answers may include:

1. The eagle flew __extremely__ low over the water's surface.
2. Then, it flew __quite__ high into the blue summer sky.
3. It landed in its nest __very__ gently.
4. The eagle is a __truly__ majestic bird.
5. It has to be __very__ patient as it hunts for food.

191

What's Missing?

Adverbs are words that describe or modify verbs, adjectives, or other adverbs. They answer questions like **when? where? how? how much?**

Directions: Write the correct adverb in each sentence. Use the words in the box. Time yourself. Can you do it in four minutes?

closely	cleverly
little	quite
instantly	carefully
thoroughly	easily
rather	mainly
suddenly	rarely

1. The detectives __thoroughly__ searched the crime scene for clues.
2. Just glancing at my mother's face, I knew __instantly__ that she was upset about something.
3. After working for eight hours we were __rather__ tired.
4. No one knows what to wear because the weather has been __quite__ unpredictable.
5. __Little__ do our parents know about plans for their surprise party.
6. My father has __rarely__ if ever been late to work, even though he commutes over an hour each morning.
7. The children __cleverly__ disguised themselves so that not even their friends recognized them.
8. The storm hit __suddenly__, leaving many unsuspecting residents stranded.
9. My brother is __mainly__ interested in music and spends most of his spare time playing his guitar.
10. I __carefully__ rechecked my calculations to make sure I hadn't made any mistakes.
11. Some people confuse me with my sister because we __closely__ resemble each other.
12. We __easily__ finished the test in no time at all.

192

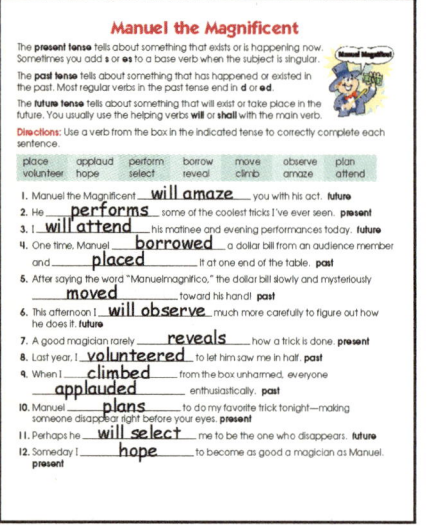

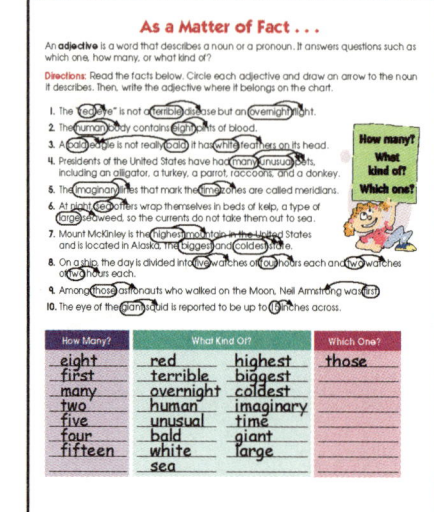

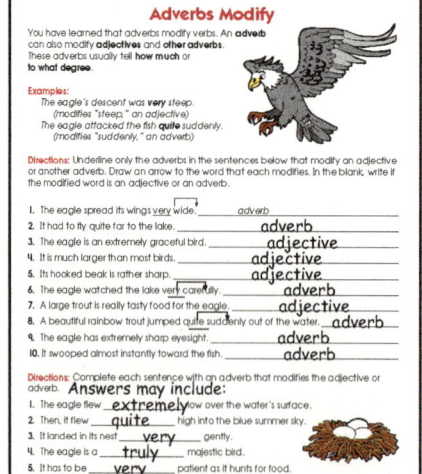

Tongue Twisters

Directions: Theodore Thistle loves tongue twisters. Here are a few of them, but he put the adverbs in the wrong places. Underline the adverbs. Next, rewrite each tongue twister, placing the adverbs where they make the most sense. Then, try to say each sentence five times as fast as you can!

1. Peter Piper picked a pluckily peck of pickled peppers.
Peter Piper pluckily picked a peck of pickled peppers.
2. Six slowly striped snakes slithered southward.
Six striped snakes slowly slithered southward.
3. Betty Botter boasted 'bout her buttery boldly batter.
Betty Botter boasted boldly 'bout her buttery batter.
4. Noisy annoyingly noises annoy Mrs. always Lloyd.
Annoyingly noisy noises always annoy Mrs. Lloyd.
5. Fast always Bo-Peep's sleepy sheep fall asleep.
Bo-Beep's sleepy sheep always fall fast asleep.
6. Bradley Baker burned the brown badly bread.
Bradley Baker badly burned the brown bread.
7. A gaggle of ganders gobbled gobs of goober gloriously peas.
A gaggle of ganders gloriously gobbled gobs of goober peas.
8. Sherry Shiffler's selfish sister seldom Shelly's shellfish sell.
Sherry Shiffler's selfish sister Shelly's shellfish seldom sell.
9. Oodles of noisily poodles nibble oodles of noodles.
Oodles of poodles noisily nibble oodles of noodles.
10. Shy Sam Phipps sips Sally's salty silently soup.
Shy Sam Phipps silently sips Sally's salty soup.

193

Spicy Hot!

A **simple subject** is the main noun or pronoun in the subject of a sentence.
A **complete subject** includes the simple subject and all words that modify it.
A **simple predicate** is the verb in the complete predicate.
A **complete predicate** includes the verb and all the words that modify it.

Directions: Which word is missing from each sentence? Is it the simple subject or the simple predicate? Insert a word from the box into the correct sentence, and use the ^ symbol. Then, draw a vertical line between the complete subject and complete predicate in each sentence. The first one has been done for you.

recipes	causes	spices	spoiled	problem
evaporates	consume	curries	reason	helps

1. People who live in hotter climates | typically ^consume spicy, hot foods.
2. Many Mexican and South American ^recipes | call for hot chili peppers.
3. Hot ^curries | are used in East Indian recipes.
4. The ^reason for this | is really quite simple.
5. Eating foods with hot spices | ^helps a person stay cool.
6. Particularly spicy food | ^causes the body to perspire.
7. Then, the perspiration | ^evaporates and cools off the body.
8. Before the days of refrigeration, food | ^spoiled quickly.
9. The ^problem | was especially bad in hot climates.
10. The hot ^spices | made the food last longer and hid the bad taste of spoiled food.

194

Simon's Silly Sentences

A **simple subject** is the main noun or pronoun in the subject of a sentence.
A **compound subject** consists of two or more simple subjects joined by the conjunctions **and** or **or**.
A **simple predicate** is the verb in the complete predicate.
A **compound predicate** is two or more verbs joined by the conjunctions **and**, **or**, or **but**.

Directions: Simon wants to play a game. In his game, each player has to write four silly sentences using nonsense words. Here's how the game is scored:
1 point for a sentence with a simple subject and a simple predicate
3 points for a sentence with a compound subject or a compound predicate
5 points for a sentence with a compound subject and a compound predicate
Simon has written the following nonsense sentences. Underline each simple subject and predicate. Then, circle the compound subjects and predicates. Determine Simon's score. Finally, see if you can top it by writing four nonsense sentences of your own!

Simon's Sentences **Simon's Score:** 14 points

1. (Slipperty Hibbert, Flapperty Flip, and Hippity Pip) pluckered Flipperty Gip's pretty purple plips. 3
2. (You and Mickety Flickety) (can flipper and flapper) with Dippity Ditz and me on the grippity grop. 5
3. The flippity mip with the frizzy wizzy wuzzles is zippiting zoo dahs today. 1
4. The bibbity mibbity (flapmoddle and tribbled) through the habiet but didn't (briggle) the biblet. 5

Your Sentences **Your Score:** ____ points

Answers will vary.

195

Do the Twist

A **direct object** is a noun or pronoun that receives the action of a verb.

Directions: As you read each sentence, underline the direct object. Then, use a sheet of paper, tape, a pencil, and a pair of scissors to find out what the surprise is.

1. Nikki showed me a really neat trick.
2. She found the directions in her math book.
3. First, she took a sheet of notebook paper.
4. Next, she cut a strip about 1 inch wide and 11 inches long.
5. Then, she started to make a loop.
6. Just before Nikki taped the ends together, she made one twist.
7. Now, she had a model of an endless belt, or Mobius strip.
8. Nikki took a pencil, started to draw a line down the middle of the strip, and ended up where she started!
9. Then, she gave me a pair of scissors, so I could cut along the line.
10. Try the activity yourself to see why I was so surprised.

196

Object-ively Speaking

A **direct object** is a noun or pronoun that receives the action of a verb. An **indirect object** is a word or words that come between a verb and its direct object, telling **to whom** or **for whom** something is done.

Directions: Say each of the following tongue twisters five times as fast as you can, without making a mistake. Then, underline each direct object and circle each indirect object.

1. Betty Blake baked (Blake Baker) a batch of baked beans.
2. Tad told (Todd) two tall tales.
3. Will Willa whittle (Wally) a little wooden whistle?
4. Nate's nice niece Nell knit (Nancy) a fancy cap.
5. Did Dudley Dooley draw (Dewey) a doodle?
6. Lilah loaned (Lola) Layla's lovely lilac leggings.
7. Suki Suzuki saved (Celia) six seats.
8. Simon Shiller sold (Sheila Shiffler) shiny silver slippers.
9. Bart bought (Bertie) a buttery blueberry bagel.
10. Harry handed (Harvey) Harley's heavy hammer.

Challenge: Now, write some tongue twisters of your own! Be sure to include and underline a direct object and an indirect object in each one.

Answers will vary.

197

Conjunctions

A conjunction joins words, groups of words, or entire sentences. The most common conjunctions are **and**, **or**, **but**.

Examples:
Christian Huygens **and** Jean Cassini made discoveries about Saturn. (joins subjects)
The Italian astronomer Galileo first saw Saturn's rings through a telescope, **but** the rings weren't very clear. (joins sentences)
He discovered the rings in the early 1600s **and** thought they were large satellites. (joins predicates)

Directions: Add a conjunction to each sentence below.

1. Did you know that Saturn takes about 29½ Earth-years to orbit the Sun, __or__ are you still looking up that fact?
2. Saturn __and__ Earth have very different day lengths.
3. Earth's day is about 24 hours, __but__ Saturn's is only about 10½ hours.
4. Saturn has 23 satellites that have been discovered, __and__ Earth has only one.
5. Saturn's natural satellites all have different names, __but__ Earth's satellite is just called "the Moon."
6. Saturn has many rings that surround it, __but__ Earth has none.

Directions: Add a conjunction to each phrase below that describes Saturn.

1. beautiful __and__ majestic
2. far away, __but__ gigantic
3. larger than Earth, __but__ lighter in comparison
4. shorter days than Earth __and__ faster rotation
5. atmosphere of mostly hydrogen __and__ helium
6. beautiful rings __but__ not the only planet with them

198

The Conjunction Code

Conjunctions are words that join other words, phrases, and sentences.

Directions: Find the pattern in this conjunction code to discover 18 common conjunctions. Use these conjunctions to complete the sentences below. Each conjunction is used only once.

a i n f d b a u f t t o e r r u w n h t i i l l
e u w n h l e e t s h s e w r h b e e n c n
a o u r s e e i a t l h t e h r o b u e g f h o
f r o e r a w s h s e o n o e n v a e s r

1. While you study for your test, I'm going to finish my math homework.
2. I'll tell Mom if you don't give back my CD right now!
3. Whether you stay or go is completely up to you.
4. We can't go swimming yet, for the surf is too rough.
5. Although it rained all night, the field should be dry by game time.
6. We were just about to eat when the phone rang.
7. My friends will wait for me until I get there.
8. We aren't going unless you can go, too.
9. Neither my brother nor my sister wants to practice right now.
10. We have both math and English homework tonight.
11. As soon as we hear anything, we'll call you immediately.
12. We have to straighten up our room before we can come over.
13. Whenever we plan a picnic, it always rains.
14. I ran as fast as I could because I didn't want to miss the bus.
15. You can go to the dance, but you have to be home by ten o'clock.
16. We will either go to the mall or to a movie tonight.
17. After I return this book to the library, I have to stop at the store.

199

Prepositional Phrases

A **prepositional phrase** is a group of words that begins with a preposition and ends with the object of the preposition.

Example: Water makes up about 65 percent **of the human body**.

Directions: Circle the prepositional phrases in the sentences.

1. An adult skeleton consists (of about 200 bones.)
2. The body (of a 160-pound man) contains about 5 quarts (of blood.)
3. People who live (in high altitudes) may have more blood flowing (in their veins.)
4. Our skin helps protect our inner tissues (from the outside world.)

If a prepositional phrase modifies a noun or pronoun, it acts as an **adjective**.
If a prepositional phrase modifies a verb, it acts as an **adverb**.

Examples: *Fluids* ***in the inner ear*** *help us maintain our balance.* (adjective)
The doctors talked ***in loud voices***. (adverb)

Directions: Circle the prepositional phrase in each sentence. Then, identify it as an **adjective** or **adverb** on the line.

1. The muscles (in the human body) number 600. adjective
2. All adults should brush their 32 teeth (with great care) adverb
3. Our skin might burn (in the hot sun) adverb
4. Every person (on the earth) is warm-blooded. adjective
5. The man went (through the hospital doors) adverb
6. The temperature (inside the body) is about 98.6° F. adjective
7. The dentist looked (inside my mouth) adverb

200

Is That a Fact?

A **preposition** is a word that shows how one word is related to another in a sentence.

A **prepositional phrase** is a group of words that begins with a preposition and ends with a noun or pronoun. This noun or pronoun is called the **object of the preposition**.

Directions: Each fact below is missing a prepositional phrase. Use the code to figure out each one. Write the phrase, underline the preposition, and circle the object of the preposition.

A B C D E F G H I J K L M
N O P Q R S T U V W X Y Z

1. The Iditarod is a 1200-mile dogsled race
over (ice) and (snow).
2. Air rushes through your (nose) at 100 miles per hour when you sneeze.
3. Red is the most commonly found color in national (flags).
4. The Islands of Hawaii evolved as volcanoes erupted under the (Pacific Ocean).
5. French fries are not really from (France) but from (Belguim).
6. Bertrand Piccard and Brian Jones were the first to fly around the (world) nonstop in a (balloon).

201

Kinds of Sentences

There are four kinds of sentences.
A **declarative sentence** makes a statement.
Tuesday was a chilly day.
An **interrogative sentence** asks a question.
Was Tuesday a chilly day?
An **imperative sentence** gives a command or makes a request.
Be at my house at 11 o'clock.
An **exclamatory sentence** expresses excitement or strong feeling.
What a terrible storm!

Directions: Identify each type of sentence.

1. The Hawaiian Islands are really mountaintops. declarative
2. Were those mountains once active volcanoes? interrogative
3. Read the article in the magazine that Sid brought. imperative
4. What beautiful pictures that article has! exclamatory
5. Hawaii is made up of a chain of 132 islands in the Pacific Ocean. declarative
6. Bring your lei to school tomorrow. imperative
7. Which island has the most people living on it? interrogative
8. I just can't believe that the small island of Oahu does! exclamatory
9. I'm astonished that the average temperature is 75° F! exclamatory

Directions: Rewrite each sentence as the type suggested in parentheses.

1. Were the Polynesians the first people on Hawaii? (declarative)
The Polynesians were the first people on Hawaii.
2. An English explorer, Captain Cook, named the islands the "Sandwich Islands." (interrogative) Did the English explorer, Captain Cook, name the "Sandwich Islands"?
3. Will you bring me a present from Hawaii? (imperative)
Bring me a present from Hawaii.

202

Interjections and Direct Address

Strong interjections, which show great feeling, are followed by exclamation points.

Mild interjections, such as **now**, **well**, and **yes**, are set apart by commas.

A comma or commas are used to set apart the name of a person being directly spoken to, or addressed, in a sentence. This is called **direct address**.

Examples:
Ugh! That soup is horrible. (strong interjection)
No, I haven't finished my homework yet. (mild interjection)
Sue, please hand me the pencil. (direct address)
Thank you, **Jean**, for your contribution. (direct address)

Directions: Add commas and exclamation points where they are needed in the following sentences.

1. Yes, we will finish the science project soon.
2. Wow! I forgot that it must be completed by Friday.
3. Oh! I forgot that the materials for the experiment are at home.
4. Jim, bring the microscope to the science lab.
5. Now, Leonard, it's your turn to work on the experiment.
6. Will the research for the project be completed soon, Amy?
7. No, Mrs. Clarke, it will take at least another week.
8. Yikes! That was a scary experiment you did, Mark.

Directions: Add commas and exclamation points where they are needed in the following sentences. In the blank, write the letter of the reason each punctuation mark is used. Some have two answers.

A. Interjection **B.** Direct Address

1. B Lewis, will you attempt this experiment on air pressure?
2. A No! I need to work on my electricity project Sam.
3. B I need some help, Mr. Johnson, with my electrical circuit.
4. B The science lab is too crowded to set up the project, Ms. Chang.
5. A Cool! I would love to use the other lab.
6. A/B Yes, I'll try to set up the project in that room, Sarah.
7. A Well, that solved my problem.

203

Out of Order

To build a good sentence, you must know all the parts of speech and how they function together. For example, adjectives belong before the nouns and pronouns they modify. Adverbs should come as close as possible to the verbs, adjectives, or other adverbs they modify. Interjections usually come at the beginning of a sentence.

Directions: Here are some sentences that Ed wrote. Unfortunately, he misplaced some words or phrases in each one. Rewrite Ed's sentences, correctly placing all the words and phrases where they belong.

1. Would you call kindly me and my brother at your earliest convenience? Would you kindly call my brother and me at your earliest convenience?
2. The woman who across the street lives bakes the chocolate cakes most delicious in the world. The woman who lives across the street bakes the most delicious chocolate cakes in the world.
3. Is the little black dog with spots white, long ears floppy, and stubby tail yours really? Is the little black dog with white spots, long floppy ears, and stubby tail really yours?
4. Hysterically my older sister laughed when she saw my hair how I had fixed for the dance. My older sister laughed hysterically when she saw how I had fixed my hair for the dance.
5. The homemade bread and soup so smelled delicious that hardly we could wait to eat. The homemade bread and soup smelled so delicious that we could hardly wait to eat it.
6. Was that the most terrifying movie ever I've seen. Wow! Wow! That was the most terrifying movie I've ever seen
7. A squirrel our cat chased and was hit by a car almost. Our cat chased after a squirrel and was almost hit by a car.
8. Read first the book and tell then what you think about me the author. First read the book and then tell me what you think about the author.

204

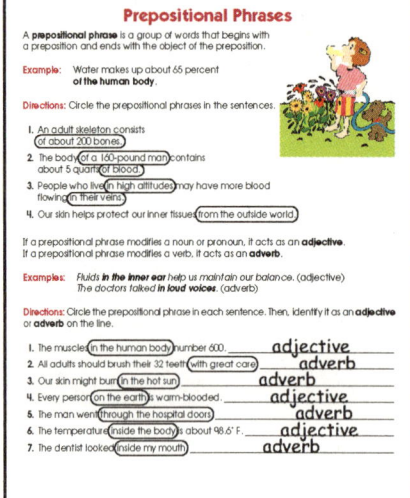

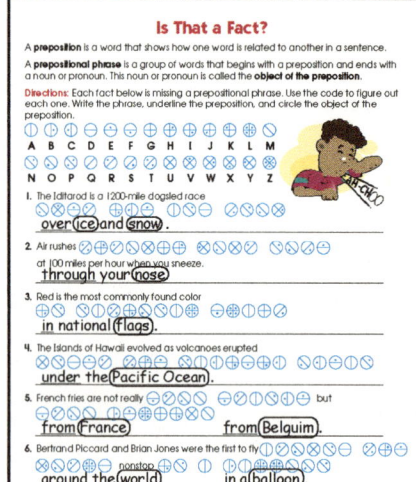

Batter Up!

Remember: a sentence is a group of words that expresses a complete thought.

A **simple sentence** consists of a complete subject and a complete predicate. It can have a simple subject or a compound subject and a simple verb or a compound verb.

A **compound sentence** consists of two or more simple sentences joined by a semicolon or by a comma and a coordinating conjunction.

A **complex sentence** consists of one simple sentence and one or more dependent clauses introduced by a subordinating conjunction.

Directions: Rewrite the following story, changing as many simple sentences as you can into compound or complex sentences. You can add your own words or use the coordinating or subordinating conjunctions in the box. Once you have finished, underline each compound sentence and circle each complex sentence.

and	after	before	because	since	but
if	although	until	whenever	or	while
unless	yet	so	when	just as	even though

It's April. It's also a perfect Saturday afternoon for a game of baseball. It's not too hot or humid. No one is using the old vacant lot at the moment. Jeremy and some of his friends decide to organize a neighborhood game. Luis runs home to get his bat, glove, and a couple of baseballs. Luke is the resourceful one of the group. His job is to come up with something for bases. Yuki gets his brother Yuichi and his glove. Tomas and Ricardo look for Jelani and Devon. Jeremy sees Sammy and Eugene down the street and whistles for them to come.

Most of the neighborhood boys gather at the lot in no time. They begin to choose sides. Jeremy's sisters Lisa and Tina happen to show up. They ask to play too. The boys aren't too crazy about that idea. Lisa convinces them otherwise. They need 18 players for two teams. There are only 16 boys. The boys agree. It's a good thing. Lisa hit a home run in the second inning. Tina drove two runners home in the third inning! It was the perfect Saturday afternoon for a game of baseball.

Answers will vary.

205

Contraction Action

aren't
can't
couldn't
didn't
hasn't
he's
I'd
isn't
let's
shouldn't
they're
they've
wasn't
weren't
we've
wouldn't
you'd
you're

Contractions are a shortened form of two words. Missing letters are replaced by an apostrophe.

Directions: Write the correct contraction for each word pair.

you are	you're	should not	shouldn't
would not	wouldn't	did not	didn't
I had	I'd	could not	couldn't
let us	let's	was not	wasn't
we have	we've	are not	aren't
you had	you'd	is not	isn't
has not	hasn't	they have	they've
he is	he's	can not	can't
they are	they're	were not	weren't

Now, put the contractions into word families.

(n't) not family: wouldn't, hasn't, shouldn't, didn't, couldn't, wasn't, aren't, isn't, can't, weren't

('s) is family: he's

('s) us family: let's

('re) are family: they're, you're

('d) would/had family: I'd, you'd

('ve) have family: we've, they've

206

Shorten the Conversation

Directions: Read the conversation below. Circle all the words that can be shortened into contractions. Then, rewrite the sentences using contractions.

1. I have never had so much fun in a class before.
   I've never had so much fun in a class before.
2. Luckily, the windy day was not a problem.
   Luckily, the windy day wasn't a problem.
3. Our teacher was a great skater. Can you believe how many competitions she has won?
   Can you believe how many competitions she's won?
4. A lot, that is for sure.
   A lot, that's for sure.
5. I wanted to show her I could go fast. She said, "Do not go out so fast."
   She said, "Don't go out so fast."
6. You will do better if you take your time.
   You'll do better if you take your time.
7. I could not skate backwards.
   I couldn't skate backwards.
8. It is hard to do.
   It's hard to do.
9. I know we will improve.
   I know we'll improve.
10. Let us meet here tomorrow to practice.
    Let's meet here tomorrow to practice.

207

More Contraction Action

It's and **its** sound the same, but they have different spellings and meanings. **It's** is a contraction that means *it is*. **Its** means *belonging to*.

Directions: Marla and Darla opened an ice cream parlor. Here's a conversation they had on their first day in business. Write **it's** or **its** to correctly complete each sentence.

1. I hope it's a busy day with lots of customers.
2. The store is on a good street. Its location is perfect.
3. It's going to be a success because of the unusual flavors we offer.
4. Summer is coming. It's going to be a busy time for us.
5. It's the best hot weather treat I know.
6. It's time to unlock the door.
7. I love the bell on the door. Its sound will ring each time someone comes in.
8. Remember to use the newest scoop. Its handle is blue.
9. We can't forget to thank everyone. It's important to be polite.
10. Its cozy feeling will bring everyone back for more.

Directions: Combine each pronoun with verbs from the box to form contractions. See how many contractions you can make.

will · had · have · am · are · is

1. I	I'll	I'd	I've	I'm
2. she	she'll	she'd	she's	
3. he	he'll	he'd	he's	
4. we	we'll	we'd	we've	we're
5. they	they'll	they'd	they've	they're
6. it	it'll	it's		

208

Capitals

Always remember to capitalize the following:

- first word in a sentence
- first word in a direct quotation
- first word in every line of poetry
- pronoun I
- initials
- proper nouns
- proper adjectives

Directions: Underline each word that should begin with a capital letter.

one summer night, seth and tony noticed a bat flying overhead.
"did you know that bats help control insects?" remarked tony.
seth replied, "somehow i always think of dracula when i see a bat."
"long ago, people of slavic countries believed in vampires, but a bat isn't really scary," laughed tony. "a brown bat weighs only about half an ounce." "i haven't seen one up close," admitted seth.
"a good place to see bats is carlsbad caverns in new mexico. a colony of mexican free-tailed bats lives in one of the caves. at dusk, hundreds of thousands of bats fly out to hunt. many american tourists visit there to see this amazing sight."

edwin gould studied the eating habits of bats in cape cod, massachusetts. donald r. griffin photographed bats eating. one tiny bat caught 175 mosquitoes in fifteen minutes of hunting! fredric a. webster discovered that bats catch insects with their tail membranes.

most north american bats hibernate during december, january, and february. when early insects come out in march or april, the bats awaken.

Bats

Bats come out at night,
Catching insects in their flight.
Furry little mammal brown,
Found in country, village, and town.

209

A Comma Conundrum

The **comma** (,) is a punctuation mark that is usually used in a sentence where a pause would be made if you were reading aloud. Commas are always found inside quotation marks.

Directions: There are lots of rules for where to put commas. Connie is making a list of these rules with an example for each one, but she hasn't added the commas yet. Can you help her out? Read the rules. Then, insert commas where they belong.

Always use a comma:

- *before a conjunction when you join an independent clause in a compound sentence.*
  The Sun may be 93 million miles from Earth, but it is more than 200,000 times closer than the next nearest star.
- *after a dependent clause that comes at the beginning of a sentence.*
  Even though there are 30,000 species of plants, 90% of the world's food comes from just 20 species.
- *between a city and a state.*
  We recently moved to San Francisco, California.
- *between the day and year in a date.*
  The Northwest Territories of Canada split in two on April 1, 1999.
- *to separate three or more words or phrases in a series.*
  Dinosaur experts use footprints as clues to tell how fast a dinosaur traveled, if it ate alone or in a pack, and if it was a meat-eater or a plant-eater.
- *after introductory words or phrases and mild interjections.*
  By the way, there are over 250,000 species of beetles.
  Yes, there are more kinds of beetles than any other animal.
- *to set off the person being directly spoken to.*
  Mike, you really ought to check out this book.
  Thanks for the suggestion, Beth.
- *to set off appositives, which stand beside a noun and rename it.*
  San Francisco's Lombard Street, the most crooked street in the world, has ten sharp turns in one block.
- *with words or phrases that interrupt the main idea of a sentence.*
  This symphony, in my opinion, is Beethoven's best.
- *before a direct quotation in the middle of a sentence.*
  Our teacher asked, "How old was Chester Greenwood when he developed his idea for earmuffs?"
- *at the end of a direct quotation that is a statement when it is at the beginning of a sentence.*
  "Chester Greenwood was just 15 years old when he came up with the idea," I answered.

210

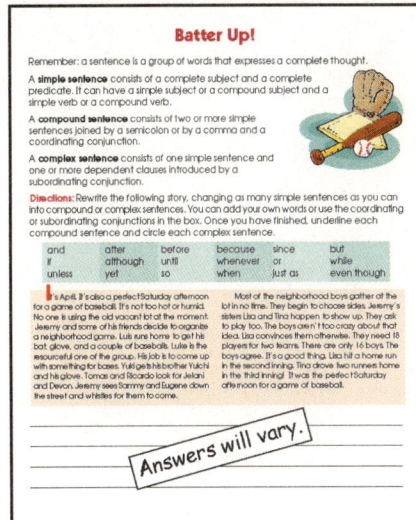

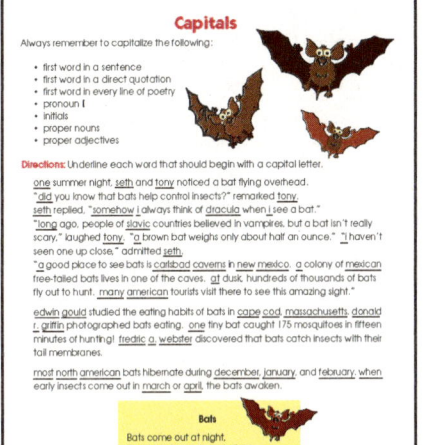

Using Commas

Use commas to set off an **appositive**, a noun or phrase that explains or identifies the noun it follows.
Example: Jack, the janitor, walked down the hall.

Use commas to separate words or phrases in a **series**.
Example: He ate the apple, the peach, and the plum.

Use commas after **introductory** words or phrases.
Examples: Yes, I'm going to the fair.
By the way, did you bring a camera?

Use commas to set off a **noun of address**, the name of the person being addressed or spoken to.
Example: Caroline, will you come with me?

Use commas to set off **interrupting** words or phrases.
Example: He was, as you know, an actor before he was elected.

Directions: Add commas to the sentences where they are needed. On each line, explain why you added the comma by writing **appositive**, **series**, **introductory**, **noun of address**, or **interrupting**.

1. Maryanne, the new girl in school, is a very good cook. appositive
2. My favorite snacks are red apples, pretzels, and popcorn. series
3. My skills, however, do not include cooking. interrupting
4. I know, Sally, that you love to cook. noun of address
5. That was, in my opinion, the best meal ever served. interrupting
6. After they finished the books, Tom and Larry wrote the report. introductory
7. Thomas Edison, an inventor, had failures before each success. appositive
8. Pete, our best soccer player, won't be here for the big game. appositive
9. No, I won't be seeing the movie. introductory
10. The coating on the pecans was sweet, sugary, and crisp. series
11. That is, if I'm not mistaken, my yellow and green pencil. interrupting
12. Sam, would you please pass me my pen? noun of address

211

Proofreading for Punctuation

Anna is running for class president. She has written her last campaign speech before the election but has not done a very good job of punctuating it.

Directions: Read her speech. Write in capital letters where needed and add correct punctuation.

Tomorrow you will choose one of five candidates as your class president. I want to be the one you choose. Why should you vote for me? As class president, I will collect twenty-five cents a month from every class member. The money will be used for a party at the end of the school year. I will listen to your suggestions and try to do something about them. As president of our class, I will go to teachers' meetings. I will try to have homework assignments over weekends reduced. Vote for me. I know I will make the next year the best one for you and our class. It will be a year to remember. Thank you for your support.

Anna did not win the election, but she was a good sport. She wrote a message to Kim, the winner, in the school newspaper. The editor did not proofread Anna's message, and it got published just as she wrote it.

Directions: Correct Anna's work once more.

I want to congratulate Kim. I know she will make a fine class president. I am sorry I did not win, but I want Kim and everyone else to know I support her. Now that the election is over and the class showed their preference, let's all join together and support Kim. Congratulations, Kim!

212

Dolphins

Sometimes the main idea of a paragraph is stated in one sentence. This sentence is called the **topic sentence**. It can be found anywhere in the paragraph, but it usually comes at the beginning or end of the paragraph.

Directions: Underline the topic sentence of each paragraph. Add the missing punctuation.

Dolphins are among the most intelligent animals on Earth. They are playful as well as smart, and are easily trained for zoo and aquarium shows. They jump through hoops and fetch and grab objects from the trainer's hands. Dolphins communicate with each other in a variety of ways using clicking, whistling, and slapping sounds.

Dolphins can locate objects easily under the water through a system called *echolocation*. This is like a built-in sonar system. The dolphin makes a series of clicking sounds, then listens for the sounds as echoes bounce back from the underwater object.

Many dolphins are caught and killed. These friendly mammals are killed by hunters of several nations for their meat and oils and are often caught in fishing nets intended to catch tuna, cod, and other fish. Steps have been taken to try to limit the number of dolphins killed.

213

What's the Problem?

Use a **hyphen** (-) to write two-part numbers from twenty-one to ninety-nine, to write fractions as words, and in some compound nouns and adjectives.

Directions: Willis was in a big hurry to write math word problems for his study group, and he forgot to add hyphens where they belong. Help Willis figure out where the hyphens belong and add them. Then, solve the word problems and write the answers. Use hyphens as needed in your answers.

1. Maxwell bought the latest best-selling kids' book by well-known author Morris Madison. Yesterday, Maxwell read eighty-nine pages, or one-third of the book. It took him an hour and forty-four minutes. How many pages are in the book? How much longer will it take Maxwell to finish the book if he reads nonstop? What time will he finish the book if he begins reading at 7:15 P.M. tonight?

   There are two hundred sixty-seven pages pages in the book.
   It will take Maxwell three hours and twenty-eight minutes finish the book.
   It will be 10:43 P.M. when he finishes the book.

2. Millicent has twenty-one four-by-six inch index cards. Two-thirds of the cards are off-white. The rest of the cards are yellow. Millicent decides to cut the large-sized cards in half to use for a project. How many small sized cards does she have in all, and what are the dimensions? How many cards of each color does she have?

   Millicent has has forty-two four-by-three inch cards
   She has twenty-eight off-white fourteen yellow

3. Marvin has always been a bit of a know-it-all. He felt sure that he had enough gas to drive home last night, even though he had to drive fifteen miles and the gas gauge was almost empty. About three-fourths of the way home, his car sputtered to a stop. How many miles had Marvin driven already? How far was Marvin from home?

   Marvin had already driven eleven and three-fourths miles.
   Marvin was three and one-fourth miles from home.

214

Editing

To **edit** means to revise and correct written work. Learning how to edit your work will help you become a better writer. First, you should write a rough draft of your paper, then edit it to make it better. Remember these things when writing your rough draft:

- **Do not overcrowd your page.** Leave space between every line and at the sides of your pages to make notes and changes.
- **Write so you can read it.** Don't be sloppy just because you're only writing a rough draft.
- **Number your pages.** This will help you keep everything in order.
- **Write on only one side of the page.** This gives you plenty of space if you want to make changes or add information between paragraphs.
- **Use the same size notebook paper for all drafts.** If all pages are the same size, you're less likely to lose any.

Before turning in your report or paper, ask yourself these questions:

- **Have I followed my outline?**
- **Have I told the who, what, when, where, why, and how?**
- **Have I provided too much information?** (Good writers are concise. Don't repeat yourself after you have made a point.)
- **Do I still have unanswered questions?** (If you have questions, you can bet your readers will also. Add the missing information.)

It is always a good idea to let a day or so pass before rereading your paper and making final corrections. That way you will see what you actually wrote, instead of what you **think** you wrote.

When you edit your work, look for:

- **Correct grammar.**
- **Correct spelling.** Use the dictionary if you are not 100 percent sure.
- **Correct punctuation.**
- **Complete sentences.** Each should contain a complete thought.

Directions: Answer these questions about editing by writing **T** for true or **F** for false.

T 1. When you are editing, you should look for correct grammar and spelling.
F 2. Editors do not look for complete sentences.
F 3. Editors do not have to read each word of a story.
F 4. It is best to use both sides of a sheet of paper when writing the rough draft of your report.
T 5. It does not matter how neat your first draft is.
T 6. Editors make sure that sentences are punctuated correctly.

215

Editing

Editors and proofreaders use certain marks to note the changes that need to be made. In addition to circling spelling errors and fixing capitalization mistakes, editors and proofreaders also use the following marks to indicate other mistakes that need to be corrected.

the	Delete.	^	Insert a comma.
a nt	Remove the space.	V	Insert an apostrophe.
Inthis	Insert a space.	V	Insert quotation marks.
is	Insert a word.	⊙	Insert a period.

Directions: Use editing marks to correct the errors in these sentences. Then, write the sentences correctly on the lines.

1. Mr. Ramsey was a man who liked to do nothing
   Mr. Ramsey was a man who liked to do nothing.
2. Lili a young hawaiian girl, liked to swim in the sea.
   Lili, a young Hawaiian girl, liked to swim in the sea.
3. Youngsters who play baseballalways have a favorite player.
   Youngsters who play baseball always have a favorite player.
4. Too many people said, That movie was terrible."
   Too many people said, "That movie was terrible."
5. I didn't wantto go to the movie with sally
   I didn't want to go to the movie with Sally.
6. Prince charles always wants to play polo
   Prince Charles always wants to play polo.
7. The little boy's name was albert leonard longfellow
   The little boy's name was Albert Leonard Longfellow.

216

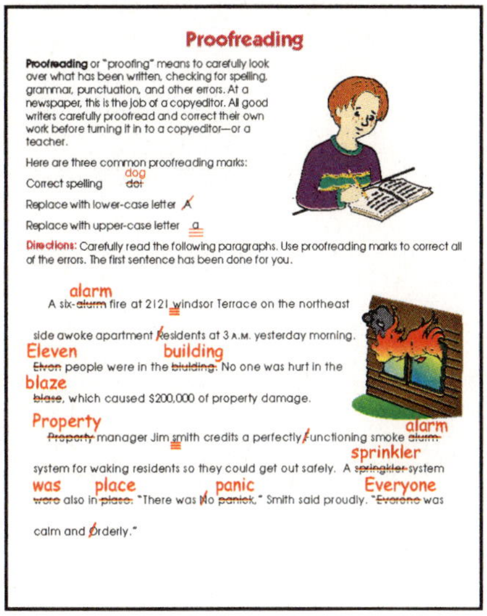

Proofreading

Proofreading or "proofing" means to carefully look over what has been written, checking for spelling, grammar, punctuation, and other errors. At a newspaper, this is the job of a copyeditor. All good writers carefully proofread and correct their own work before turning it in to a copyeditor—or a teacher.

Here are three common proofreading marks:

Correct spelling ~~dot~~ dog

Replace with lower-case letter A

Replace with upper-case letter a

Directions: Carefully read the following paragraphs. Use proofreading marks to correct all of the errors. The first sentence has been done for you.

A six-~~alurm~~ alarm fire at 2121 windsor Terrace on the northeast side awoke apartment Residents at 3 A.M. yesterday morning. ~~Elven~~ Eleven people were in the ~~bluiding.~~ building. No one was hurt in the ~~blase~~ blaze, which caused $200,000 of property damage.

~~Proprety~~ Property manager Jim smith credits a perfectly Functioning smoke ~~alurm~~ alarm system for waking residents so they could get out safely. A ~~springkler~~ sprinkler system ~~were~~ was also in ~~plase.~~ place. "There was No ~~panick.~~ panic," Smith said proudly. "~~Everone~~ Everyone was calm and Orderly."

217

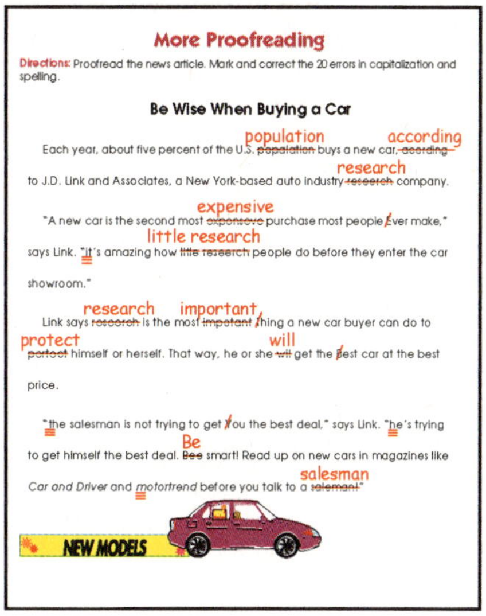

More Proofreading

Directions: Proofread the news article. Mark and correct the 20 errors in capitalization and spelling.

Be Wise When Buying a Car

Each year, about five percent of the U.S. ~~popalation~~ population buys a new car, ~~acording~~ according to J.D. Link and Associates, a New York-based auto industry ~~reseerch~~ research company.

"A new car is the second most ~~expensove~~ expensive purchase most people Ever make," says Link. "it's amazing how ~~litle reserch~~ little research people do before they enter the car showroom."

Link says ~~reseorch~~ research is the most ~~impotant~~ important, Thing a new car buyer can do to ~~portect~~ protect himself or herself. That way, he or she ~~wil~~ will get the Best car at the best price.

"the salesman is not trying to get You the best deal," says Link. "he's trying to get himself the best deal. ~~Bee~~ Be smart! Read up on new cars in magazines like *Car and Driver* and *motortrend* before you talk to a ~~saleman!~~ salesman!"

NEW MODELS

218

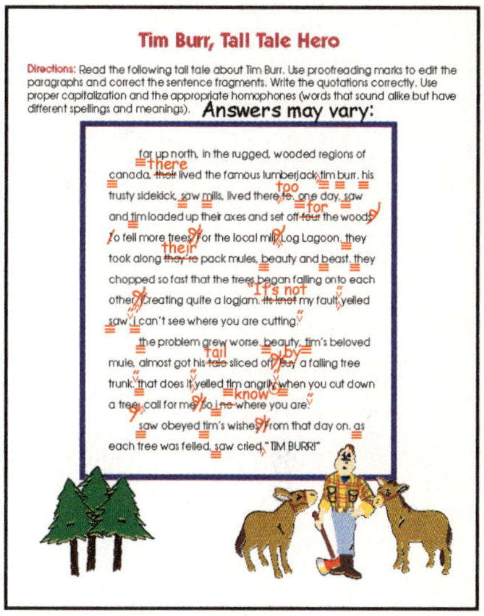

Tim Burr, Tall Tale Hero

Directions: Read the following tall tale about Tim Burr. Use proofreading marks to edit the paragraphs and correct the sentence fragments. Write the quotations correctly. Use proper capitalization and the appropriate homophones (words that sound alike but have different spellings and meanings). Answers may vary:

far up north, in the rugged, wooded regions of canada, ~~their~~ there lived the famous lumberjack tim burr. his trusty sidekick, saw mills, lived there ~~to~~ too. one day, saw and tim loaded up their axes and set off ~~four~~ for the woods To fell more trees For the local mill Log Lagoon. they took along ~~they're~~ their pack mules, beauty and beast. they chopped so fast that the trees began falling onto each other Creating quite a logjam. ~~Its knot~~ "It's not my fault," yelled saw. "I can't see where you are cutting."

the problem grew worse. beauty, tim's beloved mule, almost got his ~~tale~~ tail sliced off ~~buy~~ by a falling tree trunk. "that does it," yelled tim angrily. "when you cut down a tree, call for me so I ~~no~~ know where you are."

saw obeyed tim's wishes From that day on, as each tree was felled, saw cried, "TIM BURR!"

219

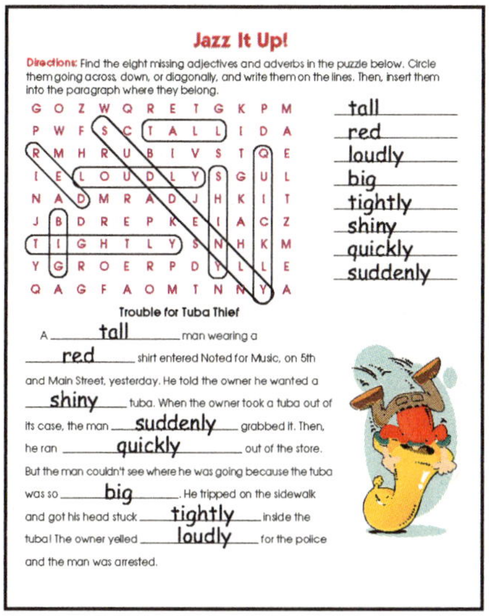

Jazz It Up!

Directions: Find the eight missing adjectives and adverbs in the puzzle below. Circle them going across, down, or diagonally, and write them on the lines. Then, insert them into the paragraph where they belong.

G	O	Z	W	Q	R	E	T	G	K	P	M
P	W	F	S	C	T	A	L	L	I	D	A
R	M	H	R	U	B	I	V	S	T	Q	E
I	E	L	O	U	D	L	Y	S	G	U	L
N	A	D	M	R	A	D	J	H	K	I	T
J	B	D	R	E	P	K	E	I	A	C	Z
T	I	G	H	T	L	Y	S	N	H	K	M
Y	G	R	O	E	R	P	D	Y	L	L	E
Q	A	G	F	A	O	M	T	N	N	Y	A

tall
red
loudly
big
tightly
shiny
quickly
suddenly

Trouble for Tuba Thief

A tall man wearing a red shirt entered Noted for Music, on 5th and Main Street, yesterday. He told the owner he wanted a shiny tuba. When the owner took a tuba out of its case, the man suddenly grabbed it. Then, he ran quickly out of the store. But the man couldn't see where he was going because the tuba was so big. He tripped on the sidewalk and got his head stuck tightly inside the tuba! The owner yelled loudly for the police and the man was arrested.

220

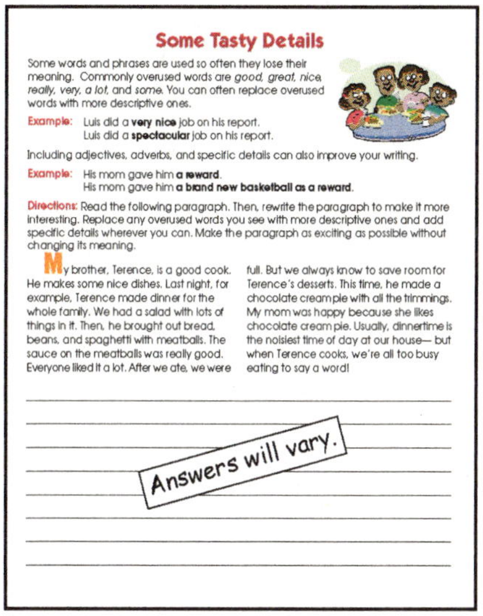

Some Tasty Details

Some words and phrases are used so often they lose their meaning. Commonly overused words are *good, great, nice, really, very, a lot,* and *some*. You can often replace overused words with more descriptive ones.

Example: Luis did a **very nice** job on his report.
Luis did a **spectacular** job on his report.

Including adjectives, adverbs, and specific details can also improve your writing.

Example: His mom gave him **a reward**.
His mom gave him **a brand new basketball as a reward**.

Directions: Read the following paragraph. Then, rewrite the paragraph to make it more interesting. Replace any overused words you see with more descriptive ones and add specific details wherever you can. Make the paragraph as exciting as possible without changing its meaning.

My brother, Terence, is a good cook. He makes some nice dishes. Last night, for example, Terence made dinner for the whole family. We had a salad with lots of things in it. Then, he brought out bread, beans, and spaghetti with meatballs. The sauce on the meatballs was really good. Everyone liked it a lot. After we ate, we were full. But we always know to save room for Terence's desserts. This time, he made a chocolate cream pie with all the trimmings. My mom was happy because she likes chocolate cream pie. Usually, dinnertime is the noisiest time of day at our house— but when Terence cooks, we're all too busy eating to say a word!

Answers will vary.

221

Combining Sentences

Not every pair of sentences can be combined with "who," "which," or "that" clauses. These sentences can be combined in other ways, either with a conjunction or by renaming the subject.

Examples:

Tim couldn't go to sleep. Todd was sleeping soundly.
Tim couldn't go to sleep, **but** Todd was sleeping soundly.

The zoo keeper fed the baby ape. A crowd gathered to watch.
When the zoo keeper fed the baby ape, a crowd gathered to watch.

Directions: Combine each pair of sentences using "who," "which," or "that" clauses, by using a conjunction or by renaming the subject.

1. The box slipped off the truck. The box was filled with bottles.
   The box that was filled with bottles slipped off the truck.
2. Carolyn is our scout leader. Carolyn taught us a new game.
   Carolyn, who is our scout leader, tought us a new game..
3. The girl is 8 years old. The girl called the emergency number when her grandmother fell.
   The girl, who is 8 years old, called the emergency number when her grandmother fell.
4. The meatloaf is ready to eat. The salad isn't made yet.
   The meatloaf is ready to eat, but the salad isn't made yet.
5. The rain poured down. The rain canceled our picnic.
   The rain poured down and canceled our picnic.
6. The sixth grade class went on a field trip. The school was much quieter.
   When the sixth grade class went on a field trip, the school was much quieter.

222

Transformations!

When you combine sentences, make sure to use the correct punctuation. Also, make sure not to change the meaning of the sentences.

Directions: Circle the best combination for each set of sentences below.

1. *I like to use rabbits in my magic show. They are easy to take care of. Everyone likes them.*
   - I like to use rabbits in my magic show but they are easy to take care of; but everyone likes them.
   - I like to use rabbits in my magic show but they are easy to take care of because everyone likes them.
   - I like to use rabbits in my magic show they are easy to take care of everyone likes them.
   - (circled) I like to use rabbits in my magic show because they are easy to take care of and everyone likes them.
2. *Wanda has two sisters. Their names are Abra and Cadabra.*
   - Wanda has Abra and Cadabra; two sisters.
   - Wanda has two sisters; Wanda's two sisters are named Abra and Cadabra.
   - (circled) Wanda has two sisters named Abra and Cadabra.
   - Wanda's sisters are named Abra and Cadabra, and there are two of them.
3. *Abra is black. Oops, I mean, she is white!*
   - (circled) Abra is black—oops, I mean, she is white!
   - Abra is black oops I mean— she is white!
   - Abra is black oops I mean, she is white!
   - Abra is black so oops, I mean she is white!
4. *That means Cadabra is the black one. Probably.*
   - That means Cadabra is the black one and probably.
   - That means; Cadabra is the black one—probably.
   - That means that the one that probably is black is Cadabra.
   - (circled) That means Cadabra is probably the black one.
5. *The problem is keeping the rabbits straight. I always get mixed up!*
   - The problem is keeping the rabbits straight I always get mixed up!
   - The problem is keeping the rabbits straight and mixed up!
   - The problem is keeping mixed up and always get the rabbits straight!
   - (circled) The problem is keeping the rabbits straight; I always get mixed up!
6. *Maybe I should give them name tags. Then my magic tricks might turn out right.*
   - Maybe I should give them name tags, and then—my magic tricks might turn out right.
   - Maybe I should give them name tags but then my magic tricks might turn out right.
   - (circled) Maybe I should give them name tags; then my magic tricks might turn out right.
   - Maybe I should give them name tags after my magic tricks turn out right.

223

Putting It All Together

Directions: Rewrite this report on the lines below. Combine sentences where it makes the most sense. Remember: A sentence must include a noun and a verb and must express a clear thought.

Earthquakes occur. It happens when plates under the Earth's crust move. The plates bump. They bump against each other along fault lines. This causes the ground to shake violently. Some earthquakes can cause damage. They can especially cause damage to buildings. And earthquakes can kill and injure many people.

There is a scale called the Richter scale. This scale measures how strong an earthquake is. The worst earthquake was in the United States. It occurred on March 27, 1964. It occurred in Alaska. That earthquake measured 8.4 on the Richter scale.

Answers will vary slightly, but one possible solution is:

Earthquakes occur when plates under the Earth's crust move. The plates bump against each other along fault lines, causing the ground to shake violently. Some earthquakes can cause damage to buildings and can kill and injure many people.

A scale called the Richter scale measures how strong earthquakes are. The worst earthquake in the United States occurred on March 27, 1964, in Alaska. That earthquake measured 8.4 on the Richter scale.

224

A Little Support

Directions: Read the following article, and fill in the subject and the topic sentence. Then, fill in the supporting details and other details.

Have you ever seen a platypus? Platypuses are unusual creatures. First, they are strange-looking. A playtypus looks like several animals joined together; it has webbed feet like a duck, a flat tail like a beaver, and a long, furry body like an otter. It appears to have no neck. Even more unusual is that the platypus has a snout that looks just like a duck's bill, which it uses to hunt for the worms and bugs that it eats.

The platypus is also one of only two mammals in the world that lays eggs. A mother platypus may lay 2–4 eggs at a time; a group of baby platypuses is called a *clutch*. Platypuses burrow through banks of rivers and streams to make their homes. They are excellent swimmers and divers, and their senses of sight and hearing are unbelievably strong!

Subject of Passage: Platypuses

Topic Sentence: Platypuses are unusual creatures.

Supporting Details: It looks like several creatures joined together; has webbed feet like a duck, flat tail like a beaver, long furry body like an otter, and a snout that looks like a duck's bill. It appears to have no neck.

Other Details: One of two mammals in the world that lays eggs; a group of baby platypuses is called a clutch; burrows through banks of rivers and streams to make homes; excellent swimmers and divers; sense of sight and hearing are strong.

225

It's All a Jumble, Part 2

Directions: Use Troy's outline to answer the following questions.

1. What are the five main sections of Troy's report?
   Introduction, Desert Plants, Desert Animals, Threats to the World's Deserts, and Conclusion
2. What are the three main subsections of Troy's introduction?
   What is a desert?, Where are the world's deserts located? and Deserts are rich ecosystems
3. What is the main idea or argument of Troy's report? What makes you think so?
   Deserts contain a wide variety of life that must be protected is the main argument of Troy's report. We can tell this because this statement will appear in the conclusion, and all the other sections support it.
4. What are two ways in which people threaten the desert habitat?
   mining and farming
5. Troy has organized his notes and is getting ready to write his report. However, he has found that he doesn't have enough information for section IV, Threats to the World's Deserts. Which do you think is a better solution— to reorganize his outline and eliminate section IV, or to do more research? Why?
   Answers will vary, but most students will say that he should do more research. If he gets rid of section IV he may not have enough information in the report to support his argument.

227

Give Me One Reason

Directions: Place each line of information below in the correct spot on the outline. A few are already done for you. Check off the information as you use it.

I would be supervising other children	Program offers tutoring for younger kids
I would be working as a member of a team	Reading
To keep busy after school	Math
To help other children	Science
Program offers activities for younger kids	You wouldn't have to worry about me while you're at work
To gain responsibility	Arts and crafts
Program runs until 5:00	Playground games

Reasons I Should Join the After-School Program

I. To Help Other Children
- A. Program offers tutoring for younger kids
  - 1. Reading
  - 2. Science
  - 3. Math
- B. Program offers activities for younger kids
  - 1. Arts and crafts
  - 2. Playground games

II. To Gain Responsibility
- A. I would be supervising other children
- B. I would be working as a member of a team

III. To keep busy after school
- A. Program runs until 5:00
- B. You wouldn't have to worry about me while you're at work

228

Writing: Topic Sentences

The topic sentence in a paragraph usually comes first. Sometimes, however, the topic sentence can come at the end or even in the middle of a paragraph. When looking for the topic sentence, try to find the one that tells the main idea of a paragraph.

Directions: Read the following paragraphs and underline the topic sentence in each.

The maple tree sheds its leaves every year. The oak and elm trees shed their leaves, too. Every autumn, the leaves on these trees begin changing color. Then, as the leaves gradually begin to die, they fall from the trees. Trees that shed their leaves annually are called deciduous trees.

When our family goes skiing, my brother enjoys the thrill of going down the steepest hill as fast as he can. Mom and Dad like to ski because it gets them out of the house and into the fresh air. I enjoy looking at the trees and birds and the sun shining on the snow. There is something about skiing that appeals to everyone in my family. Even the dog came along on our last skiing trip!

If you are outdoors at night and there is traffic around, you should always wear bright clothing so that cars can see you. White is a good color to wear at night. If you are riding a bicycle, be sure it has plenty of reflectors, and if possible, headlamps as well. Be especially careful when crossing the street, because sometimes drivers cannot see you in the glare of their headlights. Being outdoors at night can be dangerous, and it is best to be prepared!

229

Writing: Supporting Sentences

A **paragraph** is a group of sentences that tell about one topic. The **topic sentence** in a paragraph usually comes first and tells the main idea of the paragraph. **Supporting sentences** follow the topic sentence and provide details about the topic.

Directions: Write at least three supporting sentences for each topic sentence below.

Example: **Topic Sentence:** Carly had an accident on her bike.
Supporting Sentences: She was on her way to the store to buy some bread. A car came weaving down the road and scared her. She rode her bike off the road so the car wouldn't hit her. Now, her knee is scraped, but she's all right.

1. I've been thinking of ways I could make some more money after school.
2. In my opinion, cats (dogs, fish, etc.) make the best pets.
3. My life would be be ... ger sister, younger brother, older sister, older brother).
4. I'd like to live next door to a (swimming pool, video store, movie theater, etc.).

Answers will vary.

230

Writing: Building Paragraphs

Directions: Read the groups of topic sentences and questions below. On another sheet of paper, write supporting sentences that answer the questions. Use your imagination! Write the supporting sentences in order, and copy them on this page after the topic sentence.

1. On her way home from school, Mariko made a difficult decision.

   Questions: What was Mariko's decision? Why did she decide that? Why was the decision hard to make?

2. Suddenly, Conrad thought of a way to clear up ... ion.

   Questions: What was the co... involved in it? What did he do to clear it up...

   Answers will vary.

3. Bethany used to feel awkward at the school social activities.

   Questions: Why did Bethany feel awkward before? How does she feel now? What happened to change the way she feels?

231

Writing: Sequencing

When writing paragraphs, it is important to write events in the correct order. Think about what happens first, next, later, and last.

Directions: The following sentences tell about Chandra's day, but they are all mixed up. Read each sentence and number them in the order in which they happened.

3 She arrived at school and went to her locker to get her books.
7 After dinner, she did the dishes, then read a book for a while.
8 Chandra brushed her teeth and put on her pajamas.
5 She rode the bus home, then she fixed herself a snack.
2 She ate breakfast and went out to wait for the bus.
1 Chandra woke up and picked out her clothes for school.
4 She met her friend Sarah on the way to the cafeteria.
6 She worked on homework and watched TV until her mom called her for dinner.

Directions: Write a short paragraph about what you did today. Use words like **first**, **next**, **then**, **later**, and **finally** to indicate the order in which you did things.

Paragraphs will vary.

232

Descriptive Sentences

Descriptive sentences give readers a vivid image and enable them to imagine a scene clearly.

Example:
Nondescriptive sentence: There were grapes in the bowl.
Descriptive sentence: The plump purple grapes in the bowl looked tantalizing.

Directions: Rewrite these sentences using descriptive language.

1. The dog walked in its pen.
2. The turkey was almost done.
3. I became upset when my comp...
4. Jared and Miche... the ice-cream parlor.
5. The telephone kept ringing.
6. I wrote a story.
7. The movie was excellent.
8. Dominique was upset that her friend was ill.

Sentences will vary.

233

Writing: Descriptive Details

A writer creates pictures in a reader's mind by telling him or her how something looks, sounds, feels, smells, or tastes. For example, compare **A** and **B** below. Notice how the description in **B** makes you imagine how the heavy door and the cobweb would feel and how the broken glass would look and sound as someone walked on it.

A. I walked into the house.
B. I pushed open the heavy wooden door of the old house. A cobweb brushed my face, and broken glass, sparkling like ice, crushed under my feet.

Directions: Write one or two sentences about each topic below. Add details that will help your reader see, hear, feel, smell, or taste what you are describing.

1. Your favorite dinner cooking
2. Old furniture
3. Wind blow...
4. A tired stranger
5. Wearing wet clothes
6. A strange noise somewhere in the house

Sentences will vary.

234

Complete the Story

Directions: Read the beginning of this story. Then, complete the story with your own ideas.

It was a beautiful summer day in June when my family and I set off on vacation. We were headed for Portsmouth, New Hampshire. There we planned to go on a whale-watching ship and perhaps spy a humpback whale or two. However, there were many miles between our home and Portsmouth.

We camped at many lovely parks along the way to New Hampshire. We stayed in the Adirondack Mountains for a few days and then visited the Green Mountains of Vermont before crossing into New Hampshire.

My family enjoys tent camping. My dad says you can't really get a taste of the great outdoors in a pop-up camper or RV. I love sitting by the fire at night, gazing at the stars, and listening to the animal noises.

The trip was going well, and everyone was enjoying our vacation. We made it to Portsmouth and were looking forward to the whale-watching adventure. We arrived at the dock a few minutes early. The ocean looked rough, but we had taken seasickness medication. We thought we were prepared for any kind of weather.

Stories will vary.

235

Writing Fiction

Directions: Use descriptive writing to complete each story. Write at least five sentences.

1. It was a cold, wintry morning in January. Snow had fallen steadily for 4 days. I was staring out my bedroom window when I saw the bedraggled dog staggering through the snow.
2. Mindy was home Saturday stud... ...port cards were due next Friday, and the test o... ...port card. Mindy needed to do well on the test to g... ...phone rang. It was her best friend, Jenny.
3. Martin works every weekend delivering newspapers. He wakes up at 5:30 A.M. and begins his route at 6:00 A.M. He delivers 150 newspapers on his bike. He enjoys his weekend job because he is working toward a goal.

Answers will vary.

236

Writing: Point of View

People often have different opinions about the same thing. This is because each of us has a different "point of view." **Point of view** is the attitude someone has about a particular topic as a result of his or her personal experience or knowledge.

Directions: Read the topic sentence below about the outcome of a basketball game. Then, write two short paragraphs, one from the point of view of a player for the Reds and one from the point of view of a player for the Cowboys. Be sure to give each person's opinion of the outcome of the game.

Topic Sentence: In the last second of the basketball game between the Reds and the Cowboys, the Reds scored and won the game.

Terry, a player for the Reds . . .

Chris, a player for the C...

Paragraphs will vary.

Directions: Here's a different situation. Read the topic sentence, and then write three short paragraphs from the points of view of Katie, her dad, and her brother.

Topic Sentence: Katie's dog had chewed up another one of her father's shoes.

Katie . . .

Katie's father . . .

Katie's brother Mark, w... ...er have a cat . . .

Paragraphs will vary.

237

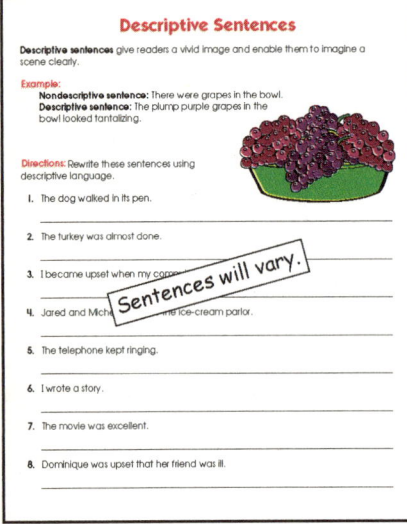

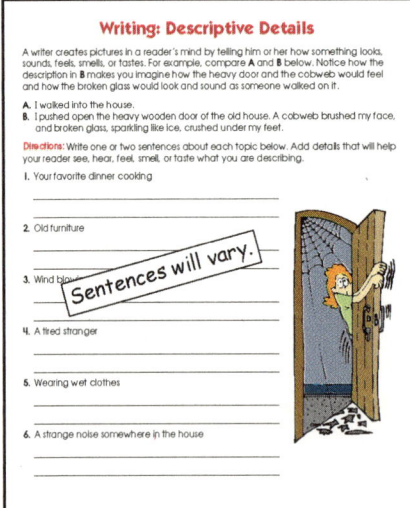

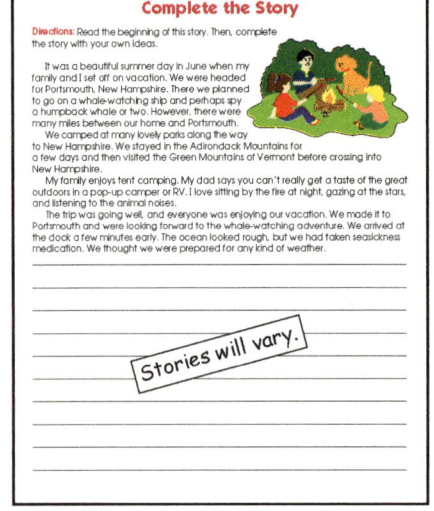

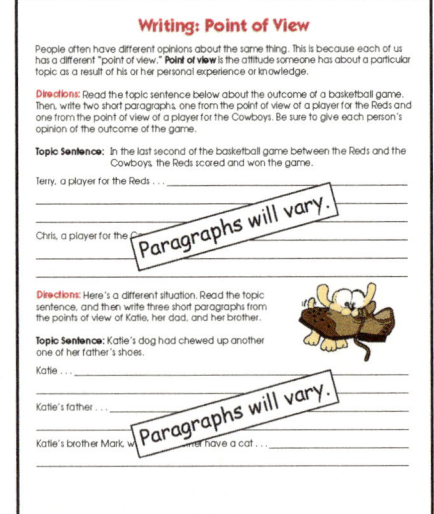

Writing: Personification

Sometimes writers use descriptions like: The fire engine **screamed** as it rushed down the street. The sun **crawled** slowly across the sky. We know that fire engines do not really scream, and the sun does not really crawl. Writers use descriptions like these to make their writing more interesting and vivid. When a writer gives an object or animal human qualities, it is called **personification**.

Directions: For each object below, write a sentence using personification. The first one has been done for you.

1. the barn door
   The old, rusty barn door groaned loudly when I pushed it open.
2. the rain
3. the pickup truck
4. the radiator
5. the leaves
6. the television
7. the kite
8. the river

Sentences will vary.

238

Similes

A **simile** is a comparison of two things that have something in common but are really very different. The words **like** and **as** are used in similes.

Examples:
The baby was **as** happy **as** a lark.
She is **like** a ray of sunshine to my tired eyes.

Directions: Choose a word from the box to complete each comparison. The first one has been done for you.

tack	grass	fish	mule	ox	rail	hornet	monkey

1. as stubborn as a mule
2. as strong as an ox
3. swims like a fish
4. as sharp as a tack
5. as thin as a rail
6. as mad as a hornet
7. climbs like a monkey
8. as green as grass

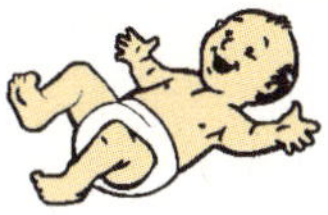

Directions: Use your own words to complete these similes.

1. as ______ as a tack
2. ______ like a bird
3. as hungry as a ______
4. as white as ______
5. as light as a ______
6. as ______ as honey
7. ______ like a snake

Directions: Use your own ... ences.

1. Our new puppy so ______.
2. The clouds were ______.
3. Our new car is ______.
4. The watermelon tasted ______.

Answers will vary.

239

Writing: Common Similes

There are many similes that are used often in the English language. For example, "as frightened as a mouse" is a very common simile. Can you think of others?

Directions: Match the first part of each common simile to the second part. The first one has been done for you.

as slippery as	a mule
as smart as	a statue
as sly as	a rock
as still as	a bee
as quick as	an eel
as slow as	a pancake
as busy as	a whip
as cold as	a turtle
as flat as	a fox
as stubborn as	lightning
as hungry as	ice
as hard as	a bear

Directions: Write sentences using these common similes.

1. eats like a bird
2. fits like a glove
3. sits there like a bump on a log
4. like a bull in a chi...
5. works like a charm

Sentences will vary.

240

Metaphors

A **metaphor** makes a direct comparison between two unlike things. A noun must be used in the comparison. The words **like** and **as** are not used.

Examples:
Correct: The exuberant puppy was a **bundle of energy**.
Incorrect: The dog is **happy**. (**Happy** is an adjective.)

Directions: Circle the two objects being compared.

1. (The old truck) was (a heap of rusty metal.)
2. (The moon) was (a silver dollar in the sky.)
3. (Their vacation) was (a nightmare.)
4. (That wasp) is (a flying menace.)
5. (The prairie) was (a carpet of green.)
6. (The flowers) were (jewels on stems.)
7. This winter (our pond) is (glass.)
8. (The clouds) were (marshmallows.)

Directions: Complete the metaphor in each sentence.

1. The ruby was ______.
2. The hospital is ______.
3. The car was ______.
4. This morning whe... ______.
5. When my brother is grumpy, he is ______.
6. Her fingers on the piano keys were ______.

Answers will vary.

241

Writing: Similes and Metaphors

Using **similes** and **metaphors** makes writing interesting. They are ways of describing things. Similes are comparisons that use **like** or **as**.

Examples: She looked like a frightened mouse.
She looked as frightened as a mouse.

Metaphors are direct comparisons that do not use **like** or **as**.

Example: She was a frightened mouse.

Directions: Rewrite each sentence two different ways to make them more interesting. In the first sentence (a), add at least one adjective and one adverb. In the second sentence (b), compare something in the sentence to something else, using a simile or metaphor.

Example: The baby cried.
a. The sick baby cried softly all night.
b. The baby cried louder and louder, like a storm gaining strength.

1. The stranger arrived.
   a.
   b.
2. The dog barked.
   a.
   b.
3. The children dance...
   a.
   b.
4. The moon rose.
   a.
   b.

Sentences will vary.

242

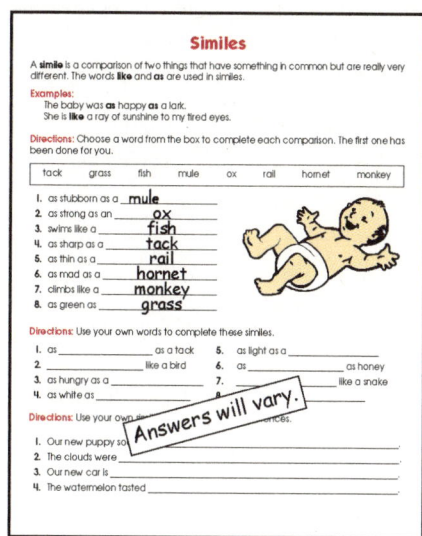

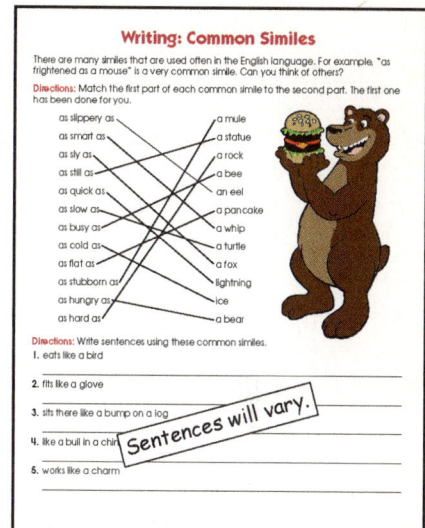

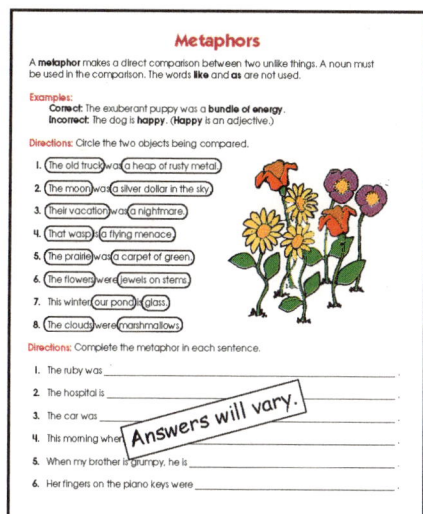

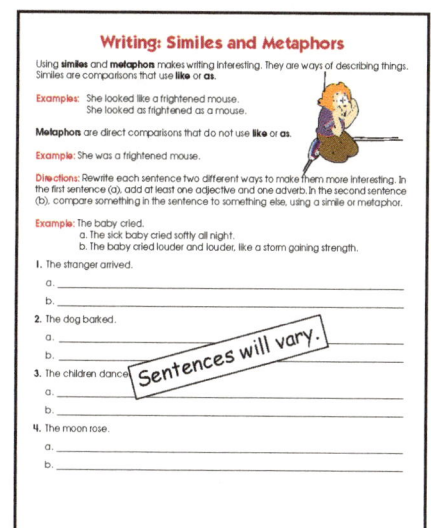

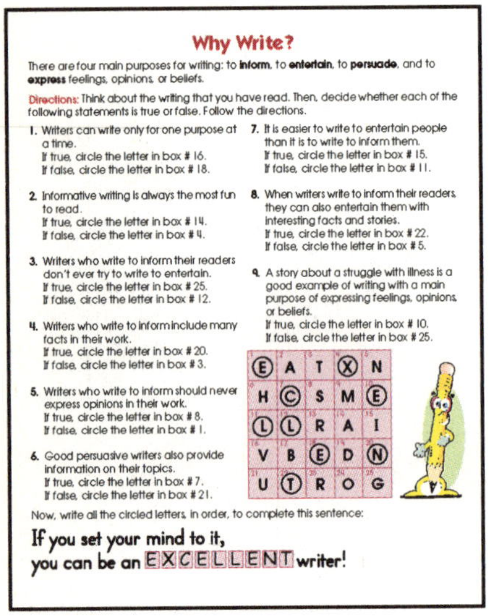

Why Write?

There are four main purposes for writing: to **inform**, to **entertain**, to **persuade**, and to **express** feelings, opinions, or beliefs.

Directions: Think about the writing that you have read. Then, decide whether each of the following statements is true or false. Follow the directions.

1. Writers can write only for one purpose at a time.
   If true, circle the letter in box # 16.
   If false, circle the letter in box # 18.
2. Informative writing is always the most fun to read.
   If true, circle the letter in box # 14.
   If false, circle the letter in box # 4.
3. Writers who write to inform their readers don't ever try to write to entertain.
   If true, circle the letter in box # 25.
   If false, circle the letter in box # 12.
4. Writers who write to inform include many facts in their work.
   If true, circle the letter in box # 20.
   If false, circle the letter in box # 3.
5. Writers who write to inform should never express opinions in their work.
   If true, circle the letter in box # 8.
   If false, circle the letter in box # 1.
6. Good persuasive writers also provide information on their topics.
   If true, circle the letter in box # 7.
   If false, circle the letter in box # 21.
7. It is easier to write to entertain people than it is to write to inform them.
   If true, circle the letter in box # 15.
   If false, circle the letter in box # 11.
8. When writers write to inform their readers, they can also entertain them with interesting facts and stories.
   If true, circle the letter in box # 22.
   If false, circle the letter in box # 5.
9. A story about a struggle with illness is a good example of writing with a main purpose of expressing feelings, opinions, or beliefs.
   If true, circle the letter in box # 10.
   If false, circle the letter in box # 25.

(E)	A	T	(X)	N
H	(C)	S	M	(E)
(L)	(L)	R	A	I
V	B	(E)	D	(N)
U	(T)	R	O	G

Now, write all the circled letters, in order, to complete this sentence:

If you set your mind to it, you can be an EXCELLENT writer!

243

Personal Narratives

A **narrative** is a spoken or written account of an actual event. A **personal narrative** tells about your own experience. It can be written about any event in your life and may be serious or comical.

When writing a personal narrative, remember to use correct sentence structure and punctuation. Include important dates, sights, sounds, smells, tastes, and feelings to give your reader a clear picture of the event.

Directions: Write a personal narrative about an event in your life that was funny.

Narratives will vary.

244

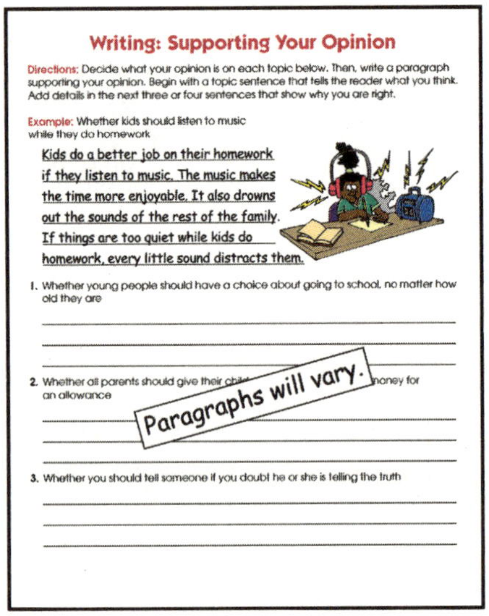

Writing: Supporting Your Opinion

Directions: Decide what your opinion is on each topic below. Then, write a paragraph supporting your opinion. Begin with a topic sentence that tells the reader what you think. Add details in the next three or four sentences that show why you are right.

Example: Whether kids should listen to music while they do homework

Kids do a better job on their homework if they listen to music. The music makes the time more enjoyable. It also drowns out the sounds of the rest of the family. If things are too quiet while kids do homework, every little sound distracts them.

1. Whether young people should have a choice about going to school, no matter how old they are
2. Whether all parents should give their chi... money for an allowance
3. Whether you should tell someone if you doubt he or she is telling the truth

Paragraphs will vary.

245

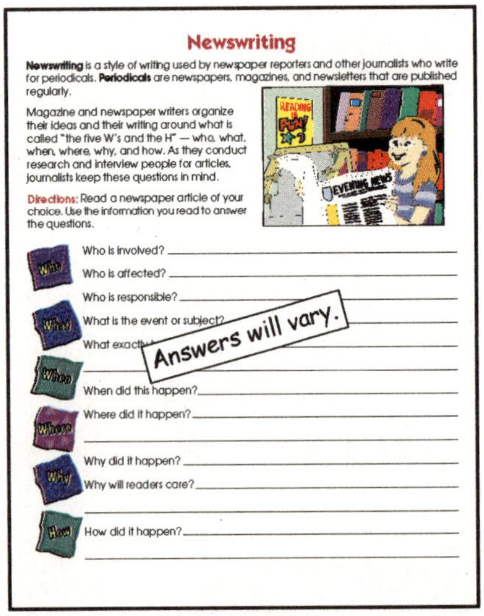

Newswriting

Newswriting is a style of writing used by newspaper reporters and other journalists who write for periodicals. **Periodicals** are newspapers, magazines, and newsletters that are published regularly.

Magazine and newspaper writers organize their ideas and their writing around what is called "the five W's and the H" — who, what, when, where, why, and how. As they conduct research and interview people for articles, journalists keep these questions in mind.

Directions: Read a newspaper article of your choice. Use the information you read to answer the questions.

Who
Who is involved?
Who is affected?
Who is responsible?

What
What is the event or subject?
What exactly...

When
When did this happen?

Where
Where did it happen?

Why
Why did it happen?
Why will readers care?

How
How did it happen?

Answers will vary.

246

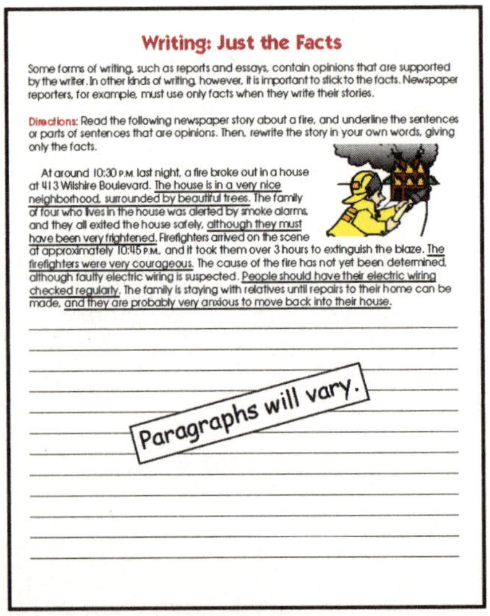

Writing: Just the Facts

Some forms of writing, such as reports and essays, contain opinions that are supported by the writer. In other kinds of writing, however, it is important to stick to the facts. Newspaper reporters, for example, must use only facts when they write their stories.

Directions: Read the following newspaper story about a fire, and underline the sentences or parts of sentences that are opinions. Then, rewrite the story in your own words, giving only the facts.

At around 10:30 P.M. last night, a fire broke out in a house at 413 Wilshire Boulevard. The house is in a very nice neighborhood, surrounded by beautiful trees. The family of four who lives in the house was alerted by smoke alarms, and they all exited the house safely, although they must have been very frightened. Firefighters arrived on the scene at approximately 10:45 P.M., and it took them over 3 hours to extinguish the blaze. The firefighters were very courageous. The cause of the fire has not yet been determined, although faulty electric wiring is suspected. People should have their electric wiring checked regularly. The family is staying with relatives until repairs to their home can be made, and they are probably very anxious to move back into their house.

Paragraphs will vary.

247

Help Me!

Directions: Circle the reference source you would use to answer each question below.

1. Which source would you use to learn how to make pancakes?
   dictionary atlas (cookbook)
2. Which source might show where Treegap is?
   dictionary (atlas) thesaurus
3. Which source would describe the peacock?
   book on insects (encyclopedia) newspaper
4. Which source would describe the sounds a cricket makes?
   (book on insects) thesaurus atlas
5. Which source would give the meaning of "constable"?
   newspaper (dictionary) atlas
6. Which source would describe the most recent world events?
   (newspaper) encyclopedia thesaurus
7. Which source would tell how to divide "accommodations" into syllables?
   thesaurus book on insects (dictionary)
8. Which source could give a synonym for "push"?
   (thesaurus) cookbook encyclopedia
9. Which source might best forecast tomorrow's weather?
   encyclopedia atlas (newspaper)

Use references to answer the following questions:

Which countries border Nepal?
Answer: ____
Source: ____
Page #: ____

What are the headlines in today's pa[per?]
Answer: ____
Source: ____
Page #: ____

Sources will vary.

248

Writing: Just the Facts

Directions: Unscramble the words in the box below. Each one is the name for one of the sections of your local library. Then, look at the list of books. Next to each one, write the section of the library where it would be located.

nitofniocn — nonfiction
freerceen — reference
noticif — fiction
ciolasredip — periodicals

Book Titles:

Encyclopedia of Dogs	reference
Hound Dog Journal	periodicals
Private Eye Pooch—A Novel	fiction
The Old Dog's New Almanac	reference
Marvelous Mutts—Doggie Olympic Heroes	nonfiction
Tough Mutts, a Doggie Romance	fiction
Sit! Stay! Dog Training for Dodos	nonfiction
Grr! Bark! Woof! A Doggie Thesaurus	reference
The Hooperville Daily Hound	periodicals
Wonderful Working Dogs	nonfiction
The Complete List of Dog Names	reference or nonfiction
The Mongrel Monthly	periodical
Raising Happy Puppies	nonfiction
The Poodles Play Ping-Pong	fiction

249

Magazine Material

Magazines can be useful sources of information for research reports. When you use a magazine, you need to know how to write it correctly in your bibliography. The following information is important to include in your citation: author, article title, magazine title, magazine date, and pages the article is located on.

Directions: Mary Magazine is a very careful student. She is writing a report about aliens, and she has found a magazine article to use as a source. Use Mary's source to answer the questions below. Circle the letter of your answer.

Nokidding, Joe. "Famous People Who Are Actually Space Aliens." Unreal Truth June 2000: 36–54.

1. The title of the article is
   (a) Joe Nokidding
   ((b)) Famous People Who Are Actually Space Aliens
   (c) Unreal Truth
2. The name of the magazine is
   (a) Joe Nokidding
   (b) Famous People Who Are Actually Space Aliens
   ((c)) Unreal Truth
3. The author of the article is
   ((a)) Joe Nokidding
   (b) Famous People Who Are Actually Space Aliens
   (c) Real Truth
4. The article is on pages
   (a) 2000
   ((b)) 36–54
   (c) 2
5. The date of the magazine is
   (a) 2000
   ((b)) June 2000
   (c) June
6. What punctuation mark follows the date?
   (a) comma
   (b) period
   ((c)) colon

250

Online Odyssey

When using the Internet, it is important to be able to tell which sites are reliable and contain accurate information.

Directions: Connie Confused is looking for information about the early frontiersman, Daniel Boone, on the Internet. Help Connie by underlining the Web sites you think might contain relevant and reliable information.

1. <u>the Daniel Boone page of the University of Kentucky Library Web site</u>
2. home page for Daniel Boone High School
3. Danny Loone's own Daniel Boone-themed Web site
4. <u>an article on Daniel Boone from the American Heritage Articles on Frontiersman Web site</u>
5. the home page of the Daniel Boone Coin Club
6. <u>the Daniel Boone page of the Kentucky Historical Society Web site</u>
7. a Web site containing Mrs. Bea Quiet's 5th grade class reports on Daniel Boone
8. the Realsmart family home page containing Timmy Realsmart's research report on Daniel Boone for Mrs. Bea Quiet's 5th grade class

Directions: The Internet makes doing research convenient, but sometimes you must use other resource materials to find your information. Name at least two other sources, besides the Internet, where you might find reliable informatio[n for a repo]rt on Daniel Boone.

Answers will vary.

251

Library Research

Directions: Read about doing research in a library. Then, answer the questions.

Step 1: Look in a general encyclopedia, such as *Encyclopedia Americana* or *World Book*, for background information on your topic. Use the index volume to locate the main article and all related articles. Look at the suggested cross-references that direct you to other sources. Also, check for a bibliography at the end of the article for clues to other sources. A **bibliography** lists all the books and magazines used to write the article.

Step 2: Use a special encyclopedia for more specific information or for definitions of special terms. The *Encyclopedia of Education*, *International Encyclopedia of the Social Sciences*, and the *Encyclopedia of Bioethics* are examples of special encyclopedias.

Step 3: Look for a general book on your topic using the subject headings in the library catalog. Be sure to note the copyright date (date published) on all books you select. For current topics such as medical research or computers, you will want to use only the most recently published and up-to-date sources.

Step 4: Use *Facts on File* to pinpoint specific facts or statistics related to your topic. *Facts on File* is a weekly summary of national and international news.

Step 5: An index helps you locate magazine articles on your topic. To find the most current information, try the *Reader's Guide to Periodical Literature*. The *Guide* lists articles by subject published during a particular month, the magazines containing the articles, and the date and page numbers of the articles.

1. Name two general encyclopedias. *Encyclopedia Americana, World Book*
2. Name three special encyclopedias. *Encyclopedia of Education, International Encyclopedia of the Special Sciences, Encyclopedia of Bioethics*
3. Which reference book contains a weekly summary of national and international news? *Facts on File*

252

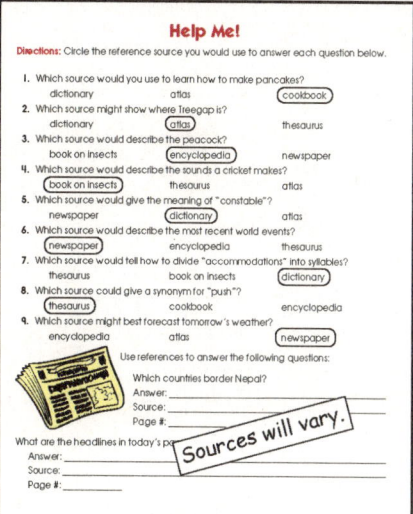

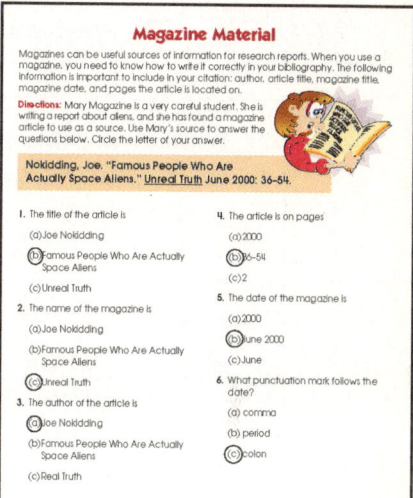

Answers to puzzles printed on cardboard in the back of this workbook:

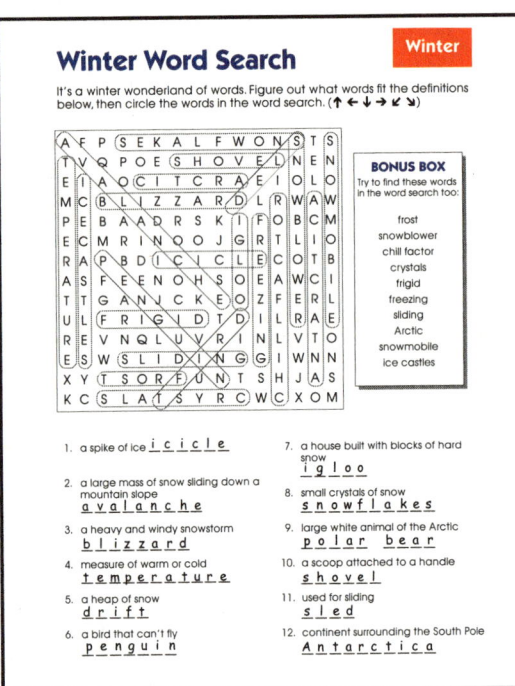

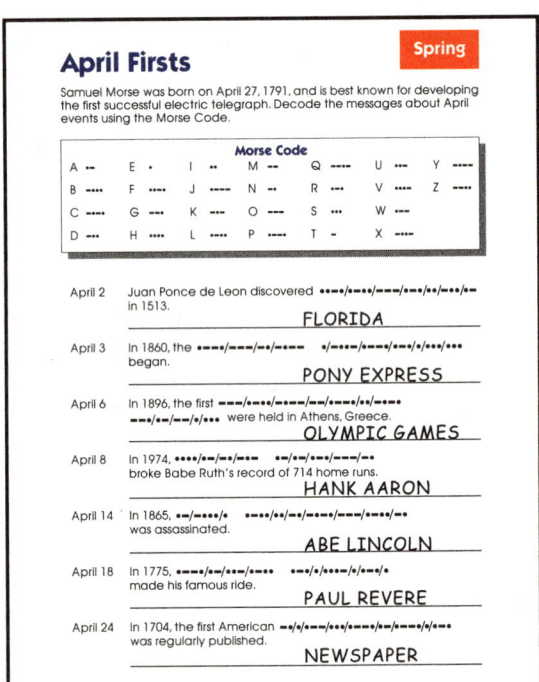

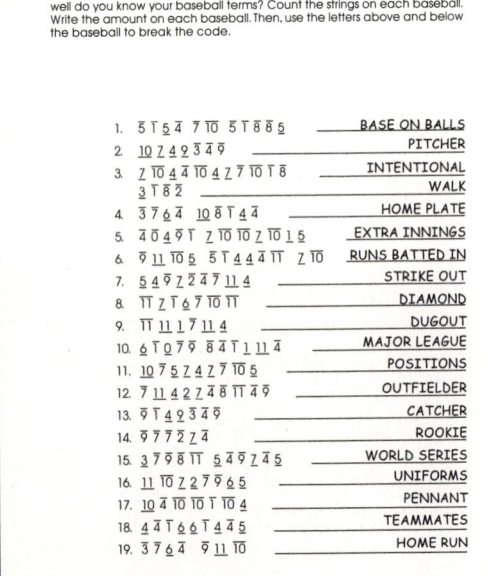

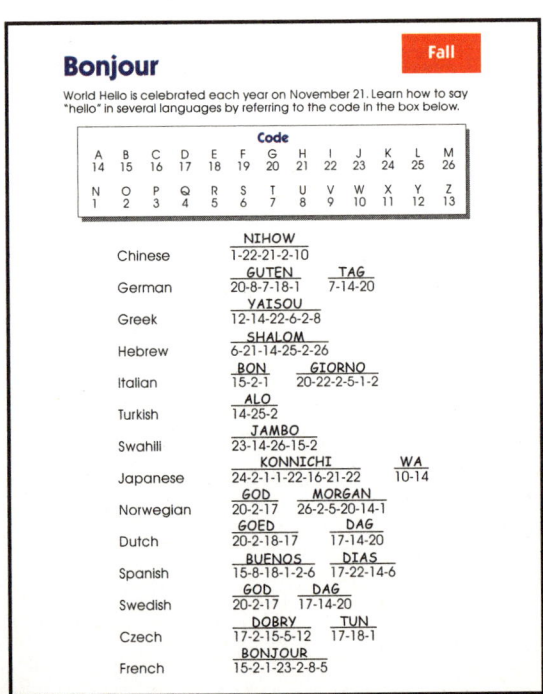

Winter Word Search

Winter

It's a winter wonderland of words. Figure out what words fit the definitions below, then circle the words in the word search. (↑ ← ↓ → ↙ ↘)

A	F	P	S	E	K	A	L	F	W	O	N	S	T	S
T	V	Q	P	O	E	S	H	O	V	E	L	N	E	N
E	I	A	O	C	I	T	C	R	A	E	I	O	L	O
M	C	B	L	I	Z	Z	A	R	D	L	R	W	A	W
P	E	B	A	A	D	R	S	K	I	F	O	B	C	M
E	C	M	R	I	N	O	O	J	G	R	T	L	I	O
R	A	P	B	D	I	C	I	C	L	E	C	O	T	B
A	S	F	E	E	N	O	H	S	O	E	A	W	C	I
T	T	G	A	N	J	C	K	E	O	Z	F	E	R	L
U	L	F	R	I	G	I	D	T	D	I	L	R	A	E
R	E	V	N	Q	L	U	V	R	I	N	L	V	T	O
E	S	W	S	L	I	D	I	N	G	G	I	W	N	N
X	Y	T	S	O	R	F	U	N	T	S	H	J	A	S
K	C	S	L	A	T	S	Y	R	C	W	C	X	O	M

BONUS BOX

Try to find these words in the word search too:

frost
snowblower
chill factor
crystals
frigid
freezing
sliding
Arctic
snowmobile
ice castles

1. a spike of ice i c i c l e
2. a large mass of snow sliding down a mountain slope a v a l a n c h e
3. a heavy and windy snowstorm b l i z z a r d
4. measure of warm or cold t e m p e r a t u r e
5. a heap of snow d r i f t
6. a bird that can't fly p e n g u i n
7. a house built with blocks of hard snow i g l o o
8. small crystals of snow s n o w f l a k e s
9. large white animal of the Arctic p o l a r b e a r
10. a scoop attached to a handle s h o v e l
11. used for sliding s l e d
12. continent surrounding the South Pole A n t a r c t i c a

April Firsts

Spring

Samuel Morse was born on April 27, 1791, and is best known for developing the first successful electric telegraph. Decode the messages about April events using the Morse Code.

Morse Code

A •–	E •	I ••	M ––	Q ––•–	U ••–	Y –•––
B –•••	F ••–•	J •–––	N –•	R •–•	V •••–	Z ––••
C –•–•	G ––•	K –•–	O –––	S •••	W •––	
D –••	H ••••	L •–••	P •––•	T –	X –••–	

April 2 — Juan Ponce de Leon discovered ••–•/•–••/–––/•–•/••/–••/•– in 1513.
FLORIDA

April 3 — In 1860, the •––•/–––/–•/–•–– •/–••–/•––•/•–•/•/•••/••• began.
PONY EXPRESS

April 6 — In 1896, the first –––/•–••/–•––/––/•––•/••/–•–• ––•/•–/––/•/••• were held in Athens, Greece.
OLYMPIC GAMES

April 8 — In 1974, ••••/•–/–•/–•– •–/•–/•–•/–––/–• broke Babe Ruth's record of 714 home runs.
HANK AARON

April 14 — In 1865, •–/–•••/• •–••/••/–•/–•–•/–––/•–••/–• was assassinated.
ABE LINCOLN

April 18 — In 1775, •––•/•–/••–/•–•• •–•/•/•••–/•/•–•/• made his famous ride.
PAUL REVERE

April 24 — In 1704, the first American –•/•/•––/•••/•––•/•–/•––•/•/•–• was regularly published.
NEWSPAPER

Have a Ball!

Summer

There's nothing better than a game of baseball on a summer day. How well do you know your baseball terms? Count the strings on each baseball. Write the amount on each baseball. Then, use the letters above and below the baseball to break the code.

1. $\overline{5}\ \overline{1}\ \underline{5}\ \overline{4}\quad \overline{7}\ \overline{10}\quad \overline{5}\ \overline{1}\ \overline{8}\ \overline{8}\ \underline{5}$ BASE ON BALLS
2. $\underline{10}\ \underline{7}\ \underline{4}\ \underline{9}\ \overline{3}\ \overline{4}\ \overline{9}$ PITCHER
3. $\underline{7}\ \overline{10}\ \underline{4}\ \overline{4}\ \overline{10}\ \underline{4}\ \underline{7}\ \overline{7}\ \overline{10}\ \overline{1}\ \overline{8}$ INTENTIONAL
   $\underline{3}\ \overline{1}\ \overline{8}\ \overline{2}$ WALK
4. $\overline{3}\ \overline{7}\ \underline{6}\ \overline{4}\quad \underline{10}\ \overline{8}\ \overline{1}\ \underline{4}\ \overline{4}$ HOME PLATE
5. $\overline{4}\ \overline{0}\ \underline{4}\ \overline{9}\ \overline{1}\quad \underline{7}\ \overline{10}\ \overline{10}\ \underline{7}\ \overline{10}\ \underline{1}\ \underline{5}$ EXTRA INNINGS
6. $\overline{9}\ \underline{11}\ \overline{10}\ \underline{5}\quad \overline{5}\ \overline{1}\ \underline{4}\ \underline{4}\ \overline{4}\ \overline{11}\quad \underline{7}\ \overline{10}$ RUNS BATTED IN
7. $\underline{5}\ \underline{4}\ \overline{9}\ \underline{7}\ \overline{2}\ \overline{4}\ \overline{7}\ \underline{11}\ \underline{4}$ STRIKE OUT
8. $\overline{11}\ \underline{7}\ \overline{1}\ \underline{6}\ \overline{7}\ \overline{10}\ \overline{11}$ DIAMOND
9. $\overline{11}\ \underline{11}\ \underline{1}\ \overline{7}\ \underline{11}\ \underline{4}$ DUGOUT
10. $\underline{6}\ \overline{1}\ \underline{0}\ \overline{7}\ \overline{9}\quad \overline{8}\ \overline{4}\ \overline{1}\ \underline{1}\ \underline{11}\ \overline{4}$ MAJOR LEAGUE
11. $\underline{10}\ \overline{7}\ \underline{5}\ \underline{7}\ \underline{4}\ \underline{7}\ \overline{7}\ \overline{10}\ \underline{5}$ POSITIONS
12. $\overline{7}\ \underline{11}\ \underline{4}\ \underline{2}\ \underline{7}\ \overline{4}\ \overline{8}\ \overline{11}\ \overline{4}\ \overline{9}$ OUTFIELDER
13. $\overline{9}\ \overline{1}\ \underline{4}\ \underline{9}\ \overline{3}\ \overline{4}\ \overline{9}$ CATCHER
14. $\overline{9}\ \overline{7}\ \overline{7}\ \overline{2}\ \underline{7}\ \overline{4}$ ROOKIE
15. $\underline{3}\ \overline{7}\ \overline{9}\ \overline{8}\ \overline{11}\quad \underline{5}\ \overline{4}\ \overline{9}\ \underline{7}\ \overline{4}\ \underline{5}$ WORLD SERIES
16. $\underline{11}\ \overline{10}\ \underline{7}\ \underline{2}\ \overline{7}\ \overline{9}\ \underline{6}\ \underline{5}$ UNIFORMS
17. $\underline{10}\ \overline{4}\ \overline{10}\ \overline{10}\ \overline{1}\ \overline{10}\ \underline{4}$ PENNANT
18. $\underline{4}\ \overline{4}\ \overline{1}\ \underline{6}\ \underline{6}\ \overline{1}\ \underline{4}\ \overline{4}\ \underline{5}$ TEAMMATES
19. $\overline{3}\ \overline{7}\ \underline{6}\ \overline{4}\quad \overline{9}\ \underline{11}\ \overline{10}$ HOME RUN

Bonjour

Fall

World Hello is celebrated each year on November 21. Learn how to say "hello" in several languages by referring to the code in the box below.

Code

A	B	C	D	E	F	G	H	I	J	K	L	M
14	15	16	17	18	19	20	21	22	23	24	25	26
N	**O**	**P**	**Q**	**R**	**S**	**T**	**U**	**V**	**W**	**X**	**Y**	**Z**
1	2	3	4	5	6	7	8	9	10	11	12	13

Language	Answer	Code
Chinese	NIHOW	1-22-21-2-10
German	GUTEN TAG	20-8-7-18-1 7-14-20
Greek	YAISOU	12-14-22-6-2-8
Hebrew	SHALOM	6-21-14-25-2-26
Italian	BON GIORNO	15-2-1 20-22-2-5-1-2
Turkish	ALO	14-25-2
Swahili	JAMBO	23-14-26-15-2
Japanese	KONNICHI WA	24-2-1-1-22-16-21-22 10-14
Norwegian	GOD MORGAN	20-2-17 26-2-5-20-14-1
Dutch	GOED DAG	20-2-18-17 17-14-20
Spanish	BUENOS DIAS	15-8-18-1-2-6 17-22-14-6
Swedish	GOD DAG	20-2-17 17-14-20
Czech	DOBRY TUN	17-2-15-5-12 17-18-1
French	BONJOUR	15-2-1-23-2-8-5

Winter Word Search

It's a winter wonderland of words. Figure out what words fit the definitions below, then circle the words in the word search. (↑ ← ↓ → ↙ ↘)

A	F	P	S	E	K	A	L	F	W	O	N	S	T	S
T	V	Q	P	O	E	S	H	O	V	E	L	N	E	N
E	I	A	O	C	I	T	C	R	A	E	I	O	L	O
M	C	B	L	I	Z	Z	A	R	D	L	R	W	A	W
P	E	B	A	A	D	R	S	K	I	F	O	B	C	M
E	C	M	R	I	N	O	O	J	G	R	T	L	I	O
R	A	P	B	D	I	C	I	C	L	E	C	O	T	B
A	S	F	E	E	N	O	H	S	O	E	A	W	C	I
T	T	G	A	N	J	C	K	E	O	Z	F	E	R	L
U	L	F	R	I	G	I	D	T	D	I	L	R	A	E
R	E	V	N	Q	L	U	V	R	I	N	L	V	T	O
E	S	W	S	L	I	D	I	N	G	G	I	W	N	N
X	Y	T	S	O	R	F	U	N	T	S	H	J	A	S
K	C	S	L	A	T	S	Y	R	C	W	C	X	O	M

BONUS BOX

Try to find these words in the word search too:

frost
snowblower
chill factor
crystals
frigid
freezing
sliding
Arctic
snowmobile
ice castles

1. a spike of ice _______
2. a large mass of snow sliding down a mountain slope

   ____
3. a heavy and windy snowstorm

   ____
4. measure of warm or cold

   ____
5. a heap of snow

   ______
6. a bird that can't fly

   ____
7. a house built with blocks of hard snow

   ______
8. small crystals of snow

   ____
9. large white animal of the Arctic

   ______ _____
10. a scoop attached to a handle

    ____
11. used for sliding

    ____
12. continent surrounding the South Pole

    ____

April Firsts

Spring

Samuel Morse was born on April 27, 1791, and is best known for developing the first successful electric telegraph. Decode the messages about April events using the Morse Code.

Morse Code

A •−	E •	I ••	M −−	Q −−•−	U ••−	Y −•−−
B −•••	F ••−•	J •−−−	N −•	R •−•	V •••−	Z −−••
C −•−•	G −−•	K −•−	O −−−	S •••	W •−−	
D −••	H ••••	L •−••	P •−−•	T −	X −••−	

April 2 Juan Ponce de Leon discovered ••−•/•−••/−−−/•−•/••/−••/•− in 1513.

____

April 3 In 1860, the •−−•/−−−/−•/−•−− •/−••−/•−−•/•−•/•/•••/••• began.

____

April 6 In 1896, the first −−−/•−••/−•−−/−−/•−−•/••/−•−• −−•/•−/−−/•/••• were held in Athens, Greece.

____

April 8 In 1974, ••••/•−/−•/−•− •−/•−/•−•/−−−/−• broke Babe Ruth's record of 714 home runs.

____

April 14 In 1865, •−/−•••/• •−••/••/−•/−•−•/−−−/•−••/−• was assassinated.

____

April 18 In 1775, •−−•/•−/••−/•−•• •−•/•/•••−/•/•−•/• made his famous ride.

____

April 24 In 1704, the first American −•/•/•−−/•••/•−−•/•−/•−−•/•/•−• was regularly published.

____

Have a Ball!

There's nothing better than a game of baseball on a summer day. How well do you know your baseball terms? Count the strings on each baseball. Write the amount on each baseball. Then, use the letters above and below the baseball to break the code.

H

W

E

T

O

I

K

F

B

S

L

y

A

G

n

P

V

M

D

U

X

J

R

C

1. $\overline{5}$ $\overline{1}$ $\underline{5}$ $\overline{4}$ $\overline{7}$ $\overline{10}$ $\overline{5}$ $\overline{1}$ $\overline{8}$ $\overline{8}$ $\underline{5}$ ________________
2. $\underline{10}$ $\underline{7}$ $\underline{4}$ $\underline{9}$ $\overline{3}$ $\overline{4}$ $\overline{9}$ ________________
3. $\underline{7}$ $\overline{10}$ $\underline{4}$ $\overline{4}$ $\overline{10}$ $\underline{4}$ $\underline{7}$ $\overline{7}$ $\overline{10}$ $\overline{1}$ $\overline{8}$ ________________
   $\underline{3}$ $\overline{1}$ $\overline{8}$ $\overline{2}$ ________________
4. $\overline{3}$ $\overline{7}$ $\underline{6}$ $\overline{4}$ $\underline{10}$ $\overline{8}$ $\overline{1}$ $\underline{4}$ $\overline{4}$ ________________
5. $\overline{4}$ $\overline{0}$ $\underline{4}$ $\overline{9}$ $\overline{1}$ $\underline{7}$ $\overline{10}$ $\overline{10}$ $\underline{7}$ $\overline{10}$ $\underline{1}$ $\underline{5}$ ________________
6. $\overline{9}$ $\underline{11}$ $\overline{10}$ $\underline{5}$ $\overline{5}$ $\overline{1}$ $\underline{4}$ $\underline{4}$ $\overline{4}$ $\overline{11}$ $\underline{7}$ $\overline{10}$ ________________
7. $\underline{5}$ $\underline{4}$ $\overline{9}$ $\underline{7}$ $\overline{2}$ $\overline{4}$ $\overline{7}$ $\underline{11}$ $\underline{4}$ ________________
8. $\overline{11}$ $\underline{7}$ $\overline{1}$ $\underline{6}$ $\overline{7}$ $\overline{10}$ $\overline{11}$ ________________
9. $\overline{11}$ $\underline{11}$ $\underline{1}$ $\overline{7}$ $\underline{11}$ $\underline{4}$ ________________
10. $\underline{6}$ $\overline{1}$ $\underline{0}$ $\overline{7}$ $\overline{9}$ $\overline{8}$ $\overline{4}$ $\overline{1}$ $\underline{1}$ $\underline{11}$ $\overline{4}$ ________________
11. $\underline{10}$ $\overline{7}$ $\underline{5}$ $\underline{7}$ $\underline{4}$ $\underline{7}$ $\overline{7}$ $\overline{10}$ $\underline{5}$ ________________
12. $\overline{7}$ $\underline{11}$ $\underline{4}$ $\underline{2}$ $\underline{7}$ $\overline{4}$ $\overline{8}$ $\overline{11}$ $\overline{4}$ $\overline{9}$ ________________
13. $\overline{9}$ $\overline{1}$ $\underline{4}$ $\underline{9}$ $\overline{3}$ $\overline{4}$ $\overline{9}$ ________________
14. $\overline{9}$ $\overline{7}$ $\overline{7}$ $\overline{2}$ $\underline{7}$ $\overline{4}$ ________________
15. $\underline{3}$ $\overline{7}$ $\overline{9}$ $\overline{8}$ $\overline{11}$ $\underline{5}$ $\overline{4}$ $\overline{9}$ $\underline{7}$ $\overline{4}$ $\underline{5}$ ________________
16. $\underline{11}$ $\overline{10}$ $\underline{7}$ $\underline{2}$ $\overline{7}$ $\overline{9}$ $\underline{6}$ $\underline{5}$ ________________
17. $\underline{10}$ $\overline{4}$ $\overline{10}$ $\overline{10}$ $\overline{1}$ $\overline{10}$ $\underline{4}$ ________________
18. $\underline{4}$ $\overline{4}$ $\overline{1}$ $\underline{6}$ $\underline{6}$ $\overline{1}$ $\underline{4}$ $\overline{4}$ $\underline{5}$ ________________
19. $\overline{3}$ $\overline{7}$ $\underline{6}$ $\overline{4}$ $\overline{9}$ $\underline{11}$ $\overline{10}$ ________________

Bonjour

Fall

World Hello is celebrated each year on November 21. Learn how to say "hello" in several languages by referring to the code in the box below.

Code

A	B	C	D	E	F	G	H	I	J	K	L	M
14	15	16	17	18	19	20	21	22	23	24	25	26
N	O	P	Q	R	S	T	U	V	W	X	Y	Z
1	2	3	4	5	6	7	8	9	10	11	12	13

Chinese	1-22-21-2-10	
German	20-8-7-18-1	7-14-20
Greek	12-14-22-6-2-8	
Hebrew	6-21-14-25-2-26	
Italian	15-2-1	20-22-2-5-1-2
Turkish	14-25-2	
Swahili	23-14-26-15-2	
Japanese	24-2-1-1-22-16-21-22	10-14
Norwegian	20-2-17	26-2-5-20-14-1
Dutch	20-2-18-17	17-14-20
Spanish	15-8-18-1-2-6	17-22-14-6
Swedish	20-2-17	17-14-20
Czech	17-2-15-5-12	17-18-1
French	15-2-1-23-2-8-5	